# A Practical Guide to
# Commercial
# Real Estate
# Transactions

## From Contract to Closing
### Second Edition

Gregory M. Stein
Morton P. Fisher, Jr.
Marjorie P. Fisher

247 - 286
319 - 337

SECTION OF **REAL** | **TRUST &**
**PROPERTY** | **ESTATE LAW**

Defending Liberty
Pursuing Justice

Cover design by ABA Publishing.

Printed in the United States of America

12 11 10 09 08   5 4 3 2 1

**Library of Congress Cataloging-in-Publication Data**

Stein, Gregory M.,
 A practical guide to commercial real estate transactions / by Gregory M. Stein, Morton P. Fisher, Jr., Marjorie P. Fisher.—2nd ed.
     p. cm.
 Includes index.
 ISBN 978-1-60442-079-1
 1. Vendors and purchasers—United States. 2. Commercial real estate—United States. I. Fisher, Morton P. II. Fisher, Marjorie P. III. Title.

 KF665.S73 2008
 346.7304'37—dc22

                                                        2008028306

# Contents

CHAPTER 5
**Post-Loan Commitment Due Diligence   227**

CHAPTER 6
**Loan Documents   247**

CHAPTER 9

**Post-Closing Matters 331**

**Appendices   337**

**About the Authors   495**

# Preface and Acknowledgments

Our aim in this second edition continues to be to introduce the lawyer who is unfamiliar with transactional real estate law to this area of practice. Whether you are a newly admitted lawyer, a lawyer who specializes in another type of law but handles the occasional real estate matter, or a lawyer who is beginning to refocus on real estate law, we hope this book will help you break into this fascinating practice area. We have taken our first edition, updated and revised it, revamped the appendices, and added several new documents. Throughout the revision process, we were attentive to comments we received from readers of the first edition, and we thank you for your advice.

We have written this book at an intermediate to advanced level. Our assumption is that most people who use it will be working on challenging transactions that require a high degree of skill and therefore will want a detailed and careful treatment of commercial real estate law. Nonetheless, the lawyer who is looking for a less comprehensive approach also can benefit from this book by using selected sections to obtain more of an overview.

No matter how recently you graduated from law school, we have assumed that you have a reasonably strong understanding of real property and real estate finance law but less of an idea of how to undertake the day-to-day tasks that commercial real estate lawyers must perform in a practice setting. We hope this book will aid you in closing the gap between your basic law school knowledge and your current law practice by helping you take that basic legal knowledge and use it productively on behalf of your clients.

For this reason, we have tried throughout to combine the practical and the academic. Toward that end, the book offers detailed textual explanations of different aspects of commercial real estate practice followed, as appropriate, by forms, checklists, comments, cautions, and suggested techniques. This approach reflects our own backgrounds: One of us is a law professor who previously practiced at a large firm in New York, and the other two of us are lawyers at large firms in Baltimore and Washington who frequently lecture and write on topics of interest to real estate lawyers.

We are grateful to a number of people and organizations who have supported us in different ways as we revised this book. We would particularly like to thank the University of Tennessee College of Law; Ballard Spahr Andrews & Ingersoll, LLP; Jeanette Kelleher; Michelle McGeogh; and Sheila Becker. We also wish to thank all the wonderful people we have worked with at ABA Publishing.

We continue to welcome any comments you have, any corrections you want to point out to us, and any suggestions for ways to improve this book. Please e-mail your comments to us at <gstein@ utk.edu>.

# Part I
# Introduction

# CHAPTER 1

# Introduction

*§ 1.01 Bridging the Gap between Law School and Real Estate Practice*

You have filled out your employment forms and your W-4 and received a quick tour of the office. You know where the copier, the coffee machine, and the restrooms are. The office manager has just introduced you to your assistant and walked you into your nearly empty office. A thick document, sitting alone in the middle of the desk, has a cover memo from one of the partners in the firm: "Draft the representations and warranties for this contract of sale. I need to send the contract to opposing counsel tomorrow evening."

After four years of college, three years of law school, eight weeks of the bar review course, two or three days of the bar exam, and tens of thousands of dollars of debt, you feel like you have learned something about the law. But your heart is thumping a bit too heavily, and your hands have just gone cold. You have no idea what representations and warranties are, and you need to learn quickly. Your first impulse is to write back, "Don't ask me, ask a lawyer."

Who put you in this situation? Is it the fault of your law school? Perhaps it is, but law schools are not well structured for providing this kind of experience, and even if they were, that is not their primary function. Law school survey classes are large, and your real estate transactions professor may not have practiced law since Richard Nixon was president. The Socratic method is hardly designed

3

to prepare students for a transactional law practice involving much drafting and negotiation of documents. There are few clinical or case-study opportunities in the real estate field, student–teacher ratios often are too high for individualized training, and your professor cannot tailor a class to your particular future when the sixty students in the class have sixty different futures ahead of them. It is difficult for law schools to provide the intensive and individualized type of training that would have helped.

Is it the fault of your law firm? Again, perhaps, but the economics of modern law practice make it difficult for firms to provide the type of practical training you need. Some clients have informed their law firms that they will not pay the high hourly rates for junior lawyers that rising salaries now compel firms to charge. These clients argue that it is not their job to educate their law firm's associates. Your firm either must absorb the cost of your training or forego it altogether. The partner who sent you the memo may be running sixteen different deals at once, supervising four other associates, renegotiating the firm's health plan, and chairing a committee of the state bar association. She does not have the time. The seventh-year associate in the office next to yours looks like he has not slept in three nights. He will be considered for partner in eight weeks, and he cannot spare a minute either. The third-year associate in the office next to his has been in Detroit reading leases for the past three weeks. They are not being uncharitable, but they will not provide you with the same mentoring and advice that experienced lawyers gave to their junior colleagues twenty or thirty years ago.

That is why we wrote this book. It is designed to help you navigate your way through your first real estate deals. Whether you are that brand new lawyer with the unfinished document on your desk, a skilled criminal defense lawyer managing your first real estate transaction, or an in-house or municipal lawyer who only occasionally handles real estate matters, you need some assistance breaking into this new legal world. You have the intelligence, you have the training, but you lack the experience, and we want this book to help you compensate for that shortage of prior experience. We have structured it to help you take the basic knowledge you acquired in law school or in your prior practice and use it the way real estate lawyers do. A few years from now, all of this may seem like second nature, but not yet.

---

*Comment:* Some law firms with larger real estate departments offer in-house training courses. Firms that do not provide such instruction often will be happy to send you to some of the excellent real estate programs sponsored by the American Bar Association Section of Real Property, Trust and Estate Law, ALI-ABA (American Law Institute–American Bar Association), the Practising Law Institute, state and local bar associations, and law schools. Other non-profit and for-profit organizations also offer fine continuing legal education programs.

## § 1.02 *Format of the Book*

This book will guide you through the types of work that real estate lawyers do. It will focus on the documents you may have to draft, review, or revise; the due diligence you may have to undertake; the issues that may arise; and the ways in which you may have to resolve those issues. While it will touch upon structural and planning matters such as entity selection and tax issues, it will assume that your primary concerns are with the practical aspects of closing a deal. It will walk you through the steps you are likely to have to follow in the order in which they are likely to arise.

You may find it worth your time to skim through this book quickly to get a sense of the patterns of real estate practice. Later, you may find it productive to use the index to locate specific sections that are relevant to the particular matters you are working on. The table of contents should function as a useful checklist of issues.

## § 1.03 *The Mechanics of a Transaction: Drafting, Negotiation, and Revision*

A commercial real estate practice revolves around transactional documents. You may never draft a pleading or an interrogatory and may never even set foot in a courtroom (if you do your job well), but you will draft contracts, mortgages, notes, deeds, leases, opinion letters, and dozens of other documents that help your clients acquire, transfer, finance, develop, lease, and otherwise use real property.

For example, in a loan transaction, lender's counsel will draft a loan commitment. Borrower's counsel will review it, discuss it with her client, mark it up, send it back to lender's counsel, and then speak with lender's counsel to discuss areas in which the document may need to be modified. The lawyers will agree on some changes but not on others, and will confer with their clients about any remaining differences. Lender's counsel then will revise the loan commitment and send it out again. Borrower's counsel is certain to be dissatisfied with at least some of these revisions. After several rounds of drafting, negotiation, and revision, the document may be ready for the clients to sign. Then, the pattern repeats itself with the mortgage and the other financing documents.

## § 1.04 Gathering Information and Allocating Risk

There is more to real estate practice than just the documents. If you represent a buyer or a lender, you also will be helping your client learn about the property. Does the person who is selling it really own it? Does the parcel have access to the main road or only to a side street? Has the clothing store tenant been paying its rent on time? What is that oily brown liquid in those rusting fifty-five-gallon drums? As you and your client learn more about the property, you are likely to discover a wide variety of problems, many of which you can assist in solving. But you have to learn how to identify the problems and how to solve them.

The documents, if prepared well, will educate the buyer or the lender about the real estate. For example, in those representations and warranties, a party that is selling property or borrowing money is likely to reveal an enormous amount of information about the property. If the party makes a misstatement, it may be breaching a contract or defaulting on a mortgage. Real estate documents provide the parties with a tremendous amount of knowledge.

These same documents allocate various risks among the parties. That brown liquid may be dry-cleaning fluid from the store that stood there from 1955 to 1964. The fluid may have leaked, it may have to be cleaned up, and it could be quite expensive to fix this problem. If they can, the parties will figure out what the problem is and decide how to remedy it. If they cannot accomplish these tasks, the buyer may be faced with a huge risk. Will the buyer accept this risk, or will it insist on an indemnity from the seller? Can the buyer convince a third party, such as a liability insurer or a title insurer, to accept various risks, and how much will this cost? Real estate documents serve to apportion a wide variety of perils among the parties. This book will emphasize the ways in which real estate documents help the parties acquire information and allocate risk.

# Part II
# Conveyancing Transactions

# CHAPTER 2

# The Contract of Sale

## §2.01 The Need for a Contract

The operative document for transferring real estate is a deed, not a contract. Deeds are usually short—generally no more than a page or two—and simple, with language mandated by state law or established by local custom. Any property owner can convey real estate in the time it takes to sign a deed before a notary public, but most purchasers of real estate, and commercial investors in particular, are not impulse buyers. These investors need time to confirm that the seller really owns the property, to locate financing on favorable terms, to investigate the physical condition of the property, to verify that the tenants have signed leases at certain rental rates, and to perform an array of other investigations. Buyers do not wish to spend time and money on these tasks only to have the owner sell the property to someone else. They need to ensure that, for a period of time, they can perform all of this due diligence work with certainty that the property is theirs if they choose to proceed. Similarly, the owner does not want to commit the property to the buyer only to have the buyer back out months later because it gets cold feet or finds a better deal elsewhere.

In short, each party wants the other party to be committed to proceed as long as things turn out to be the way they appear to be. The parties typically accomplish this result through the use of an executory contract, in which each party promises to perform in the future if certain conditions precedent are met. The buyer promises to pay an agreed price for the land, as long as it receives certain information about the property and finds the property and the information to be acceptable. The seller promises to deliver title to the buyer in return for payment of the purchase price. Each party desires as much flexibility as possible for itself, while simultaneously wanting the other party to be as irrevocably committed as possible.

---

*Comment*: On occasion, this book will use terms such as "demand," "insist," "require," and "should" when describing the positions a party might take on various issues. The practitioner should understand these terms in the context of each transaction, tempering his or her positions with a practical view as to what is important to the client; how to reduce risk without losing the transaction for the client; and—most significantly of all—what the relative negotiating leverage of the parties is. Generally speaking, the party who wants or needs the transaction the most has the least negotiating leverage. Only a party with the strongest negotiating leverage can "demand," "insist," or "require." All others can "request."

---

*Comment*: Certain "hot-button" issues are deal breakers for certain parties. If someone in your firm or at another firm knows what these key issues are, it can be very useful to obtain this information. This knowledge may save your client the time and money it otherwise might spend on futile negotiations.

---

In nearly every commercial transaction, the parties will sign a contract of sale weeks or months before the seller is scheduled to deliver title to the buyer. This executory period may even last for years if the buyer needs to obtain a permit to develop the property or needs a rezoning. The contract will disclose certain information to the parties and allow them the opportunity to gather other information on their own. It will list exactly what conditions each party must meet before the other party is obligated to perform. It will allocate a variety of risks between the parties. It will serve as a road map for the next several weeks, months, or years by spelling out the obligations of each party. Finally, it will provide remedies that each party may exercise if the other breaches.

---

*Comment*: On occasion, the parties may decide to enter into an option agreement instead of a contract of sale. Under an option agreement, the buyer may choose whether to perform, but the seller is bound if the buyer so elects. For obvious reasons, some sellers may be reluctant to enter into option agreements. While there are important legal differences between an option and a contract, there may end up being little practical distinction between an option agreement and a contract containing numerous broad closing conditions that the seller must meet.

## § 2.02 Buyer's Perspective

The contract is not always as reciprocal and evenly balanced as the preceding section may have made it sound. In most cases, the seller knows a great deal more about the condition of the property than the buyer does. For this reason, the buyer will use the contract as a way of unearthing as much information about the property as it can. In particular, the buyer will seek to persuade the seller to represent certain facts about the property in the contract.

The traditional rule of *caveat emptor* (buyer beware) survives about as strongly in the law of commercial real estate as it does anywhere in the law. Sellers, especially sellers of commercial property, usually have few disclosure obligations.[1] This rule does not, however, allow the seller to misrepresent the condition of the property. The more disclosure the buyer seeks, the more it will learn about the property. If the seller is unwilling to represent certain facts about the property in writing, then the buyer will wonder why and will undertake its own investigation or will refuse to sign the contract. If the seller makes a representation that turns out to be untrue, then the buyer will be able to enforce its rights under the contract, which may include the right not to close and the right to seek contract damages. Thus, the buyer uses the contract and the negotiation process leading up to it as investigative tools.

The buyer will also use the contract as a means of obtaining information on its own. For example, the buyer must determine whether it can borrow enough money at an acceptable interest rate to be able to purchase the property. The buyer needs to obtain this loan commitment before it can close, and it is unlikely to be able to obtain a loan commitment before entering into a contract in which the seller promises to convey certain land at a certain time for a certain price. The buyer ordinarily will not receive financing from the seller (although it occasionally will), but it can use its contract with the seller as a way to obtain a loan commitment from a third-party lender.

The buyer will also employ the contract as a way of allocating risks to others and away from itself. Suppose the buyer is acquiring an entity that owns a shopping center, and a patron slipped and fell in the shopping center two months ago but has not yet commenced a claim. The buyer surely will not know about this potential liability, and the seller may not know either. But until the statute of limitations expires, a stranger may show up unexpectedly with a viable claim against the entity for damages. The buyer will want the seller to remain responsible for all tort liability and other liability that accrued prior to the closing date.[2]

## §2.03 Seller's Perspective

The seller's perspective is quite different. Its goal is to convey the property, receive its money, and retain little or no liability. Therefore, a simple contract with few disclosures ordinarily will be in its interest. At the same time, the seller recognizes that the buyer has good reasons for wanting to learn about the property and also recognizes that some of this information is available only from the seller. Therefore, the seller should realize that it may have to disclose certain facts about the property and about itself.

If the seller is uncertain about a factual matter, it may limit its representations to its own knowledge rather than make absolute representations. Instead of representing that there are no occupants at the property, for example, the seller might state that it has no knowledge of any occupants at the property. The seller's goal is to avoid making any contractual representations that may later lead to liability for misrepresentation. Sellers, then, tend to prefer short contracts with few disclosures, while buyers prefer lengthier documents in which the seller provides more information.

> *Comment:* It is common for experienced sellers of real estate to include a provision, often in bold type, expressly disclaiming any representations and warranties not specifically set forth in the contract. Under this provision, the buyer agrees that it is accepting the property in "as is" condition.

## §2.04 Statute of Frauds

The statute of frauds applies to contracts for the sale of real estate. Although the contours of the statute of frauds vary somewhat from state to state, the statute generally requires that certain essential terms of the contract be committed to a writing that is signed by both parties. Most real estate sales contracts contain far more than this central core of relevant information, but it is important to ensure that this core appears in the contract.

At minimum, the contract should identify the parties, identify the property, state that the buyer is agreeing to buy this property and that the seller is agreeing to sell it, state the price or the manner in which the price will be calculated, and contain the signatures of the buyer and the seller. The contract also should contain an outside closing date, to forestall any argument that it violates the rule against perpetuities. Each of these terms will be examined in more detail below; the point here is to remember to include all of them.

### § 2.05—Caution: Letter of Intent

Frequently, before the parties begin to prepare or negotiate a contract, they will enter into a letter of intent that contains the essential business terms of the transaction. A letter of intent often is designed to be nonbinding. However, unless it is very carefully drafted, either the letter of intent itself may be binding or it may obligate the parties to negotiate the contract under an obligation of good faith and fair dealing. If the parties choose to enter into a letter of intent, the document should clarify whether or not the parties intend to be bound. Buyers and sellers often want their lawyers to draft letters of intent that bind the other party but not themselves. Poorly drafted documents that seek to achieve this result have been the subject of much litigation.

At the same time, if the parties enter into a contract with a lengthy list of conditions precedent, a court may view the document as nothing more than an option. If the parties truly intend to be bound, the conditions must be drawn narrowly enough that the buyer cannot easily walk away.

### § 2.06—Form: Letter of Intent

See Appendix A for a Form of Letter of Intent.

### § 2.07 Parties

The names of the parties should appear at the beginning of the contract. If a party is a business entity, its name should be followed by a statement of the type of entity and the state under whose law it is formed. Each party's name should be followed by its current mailing address. Finally, the parties should be identified as the "Seller" and the "Buyer," or by similar capitalized names, for ease of reference throughout the document. For example, the contract might identify the seller as "XYZ, Inc., a Delaware corporation, having an address at 345 Main Street, Wilmington, Delaware 19899 (the 'Seller')." By defining the term "Seller" at the outset, the contract incorporates all of this information by reference each time this capitalized term subsequently appears.

---

*Comment:* Once the drafter defines a party by name in the document, he should be careful to use this name, and all relevant pronouns, in a way that minimizes confusion to the reader.

---

In the case of the seller, the name of the party that appears in the contract nearly always will be the same as the name of the current title holder. If the buyer seeks to acquire a fee simple, then all parties with interests in the property will have to convey their interests to the buyer. A lawyer who is representing the buyer and who knows that the party identified as the seller is not the current title holder needs to determine why. In some cases, the party identified as the seller in the contract may itself have a separate contract to acquire the property from the current owner, and may be purchasing the property and then immediately reselling it to the buyer. If the person who signs this contract as the seller does not own the property and cannot obtain title before it has agreed to deliver title to the buyer, then it will be in breach of this contract at the closing, if not sooner. While this breach will allow the buyer to exercise its contractual remedies, it is always better to avoid a lawsuit than to win one. Of course, until the buyer's counsel reviews the state of the seller's title, she may not yet know the identity of the current title holder, and in many cases she will not investigate the state of title until after the contract is executed.

In the case of the buyer, several twists may arise. Sometimes the intended buyer will be a business entity that has not yet been formally created. A principal of the buyer, such as a general partner of a to-be-formed limited partnership, may serve as nominee, and then will assign its rights under the contract to the partnership once it is formed. Buyers that are attempting to assemble a larger parcel from several contiguous smaller parcels often will use different nominees for each component as a way of maintaining secrecy during the assembly process and keeping the price down.

In addition, the buyer may choose to "flip" a real estate sales contract. It can accomplish this goal by locking up the rights to the property at a favorable price and then immediately assigning its contract rights to a third party without ever taking title to the property. In essence, this party is selling the property at a profit without ever acquiring title to it.

If the contract vendee plans to proceed in any of these ways, it needs to ensure that the contract is fully assignable without the seller's consent.[3] It also would prefer to be released from all contract liability once it assigns the contract. In the majority of cases, however, the party that signs the contract as the buyer is the party that plans to acquire the property itself.

> Comment: A seller who is negotiating with a buyer entity must be cautious if it seeks to restrict the buyer's right to assign the contract. A holder of a beneficial interest in the buyer entity, such as a general partner of a partnership or a corporate shareholder, can assign its interest without technically violating a restriction on transfers by the buyer. Following such an action, the same entity would still be the buyer, even after the beneficial owner has succeeded in transferring its interest to another party.

### § 2.08—Caution: Entities Still to Be Formed

It is quite dangerous for a party to execute a contract in the name of an entity that has not yet been formed. The party that signs the contract may incur personal liability. It is essential that the entity be formed before the contract is executed.

### § 2.09—Form: Contract of Sale

See Appendix B for a Form of Contract of Sale.

## § 2.10 Recitals

Many contracts contain lengthy recitals immediately below the paragraph that identifies the contract parties. In their most archaic form, these recitals will be prefaced by the underlined term

"Witnesseth," although many drafters simply call them "Recitals" or "Background and Purposes," or do not label them at all. The recitals set forth a general statement of the purpose of the contract and often summarize the contract in a few sentences. They also may provide useful background information, such as how the parties came to this agreement and why they are entering into the contract.

Recitals can cause problems, however. Sometimes they address matters that appear nowhere else in the contract, and courts are not always certain whether to treat the recitals as legally binding contract terms or merely as useful but nonbinding background material. Worse still, the recitals sometimes contradict language that appears later in the contract. It is easy to see how this can happen, with the lawyers revising draft after draft and forgetting to conform the recitals to the evolving agreement. It is a good idea to keep the recitals short and to be sure that substantive matters are handled in the body of the contract rather than in the recitals.

## §2.11 Definitions

The decision whether to include a definitions section is a matter of personal preference, although in longer contracts it probably is a good idea. Even if the drafter uses clear, precise language, some terms will have special meaning within the document. For example, suppose the parties have agreed that the seller will deliver title to the property subject to three encumbrances: a prior mortgage, a right-of-way, and a disputed mechanics' lien. Rather than listing these three matters every time there is a reference to the acceptable quality of title and taking the chance of listing them in different ways in different parts of the document, the drafter might choose instead to define these three encumbrances as the "Permitted Exceptions." This shorter term is easier to use, and to use consistently. The fact that it is capitalized will remind any reader that it is a defined term that is being used in a specialized way. Some drafters even choose to underline defined terms or to use bold or italic type.

---

Comment: Whenever possible, a definition should correspond to a word's natural meaning. In other words, define a dog as a "Dog" and not as a "Cat." Defining a term in a way that does not correspond to its ordinary meaning can lead to confusion. It is important for the drafter to define terms with this in mind.

---

Once the lawyer defines a term, she ought to make it easy for the reader to find the definition. Remember that these documents may be reviewed months or years later by people who did not participate in the drafting process. For this reason, it may be useful to place all of the defined terms and their definitions at the beginning of the document or to include an index of defined terms at the end. As the document grows more complex and the list of defined terms expands, the drafters can simply expand the definitions section or the index.[4]

## §2.12 *Identity of Property*

While it seems evident that the contract of sale must identify the property, it may not be quite so evident how to accomplish this goal. The most obvious answer—use of the street address—often is not the best approach. While the address can help identify the property, it ordinarily does not describe the boundaries of the land. References to tax lot numbers are equally dangerous.

The parties typically will prefer to use the legal description of the property.[5] This description often will take the form of a metes and bounds boundary description and may be quite lengthy; for this reason, it may be attached at the end of the contract as an exhibit rather than included in the body of the contract itself. The lawyer who chooses to attach the legal description as an exhibit should be careful to incorporate that exhibit into the contract by reference. Remember to include the less obvious elements of the property that may not be encompassed by the legal description of the boundary, such as beds of public roads, rights-of-way, subsurface rights (including mineral rights), air rights, and development rights.

In some locations, a street address or block and lot number will suffice. Parties are increasingly using references to numbered subdivided lots that are shown on recorded subdivision plats. These devices are particularly useful in newer developments that have been platted, such as residential subdivisions or industrial parks; in heavily urbanized areas, where addresses or block and lot numbers may have been issued in a predictable way and where lots may be of a uniform size and shape; and in condominium properties, where the units typically will be described in a recorded condominium plan. The use of U.S. Government Survey information is standard in many western and some midwestern and southeastern states, particularly when referring to agricultural property. In all of these examples, the drafter's use of the "shorthand" information serves to refer the reader to a more precise method of determining the boundaries of the property.

---

*Comment*: Occasionally properties are identified either by imprecisely drawn plats or by tax plats that are prepared by the local jurisdiction. Tax plats tend to be extremely inaccurate and should not be relied on as the basis for a property description. Properties more frequently are described by reference to recorded subdivision plats and numbered recorded lots. This information is more reliable and should be easy to ascertain.

---

The seller must be careful that the description of the property it provides is accurate. If the seller inadvertently contracts to deliver more property than it owns, it either has to acquire and deliver the additional property or breach the contract. Similarly, the buyer must be sure that the contract description covers all that the buyer believes it is getting. If the buyer is acquiring an entire business, but the legal description does not include the parking lot or the loading dock, then the buyer may have to close, even though it is receiving less than it expected and needs.

The lawyer can find the legal description most readily in the deed that the seller received when it acquired the property, which should be in the seller's possession and also should be available from the county recording office. Other documents, such as the seller's mortgage and title insurance policy, also will include the legal description. Even these documents will not be sufficient if the property that the seller is selling differs from the property it originally acquired. For example, if the seller originally acquired a large lot and is now selling only a part of it, the boundary description contained in the deed by which the seller acquired title will describe too much land, and the parties probably will need to retain a surveyor to describe the smaller piece that the seller plans to sell to the buyer.

If the parties are in a hurry at the time they prepare the contract and cannot ascertain the precise legal description of the property, they may have to use the street address of the property out of necessity. They should attempt to amend the contract with the more precise legal description as soon as possible.

## §2.13 *Agreement to Buy and Sell the Property*

The central clause of the contract of sale is the sentence that states, "Buyer agrees to buy and Seller agrees to sell the property." The reason this executory contract exists is to bind each party to perform in the future, and this clause states directly what that performance entails. This required performance is subject to numerous qualifications and conditions precedent that are detailed in the sections of the contract that follow, but the drafters should be sure to include this fundamental provision. Without this language, the parties may sign a lengthy document that does not actually obligate them to do anything.

> *Comment*: Remember that the agreement to buy and the agreement to sell must be supported by a recital of consideration, as the next section discusses.

## §2.14 *Purchase Price*

The contract must state the sale price for the property. In most cases this price is expressed in dollars and cents.[6] Occasionally, the parties may agree on a method for fixing the price at some time in the future, perhaps by relying on a specified appraisal method or adjusting based on actual acreage. Make sure that the method of calculation is sufficiently precise, because if a court later finds that the parties merely agreed to agree on a price, the contract may be unenforceable under the statute of frauds.

> *Comment*: In some jurisdictions, the parties may not have a binding contract unless the price can be determined with some degree of precision. For this reason, contractual agreement on the method of determining the price, such as by appraisal, may not be sufficient unless there are ceilings or floors stated in the contract.

The balance of the purchase price, net of the down payment, usually will be paid at the closing. The "Purchase Price" section of the contract should state which portion of the price will be paid before the closing,[7] which portion will be paid by the buyer at the closing from its own funds, which portion will be paid by the buyer at the closing with funds borrowed from the seller[8] or from a third party,[9] and which portion will be paid at the closing by the buyer's assumption of existing debt.[10] This section of the contract also should state whether the buyer is purchasing the property subject to any existing debt.[11]

The "Purchase Price" section of the contract should specify acceptable methods of paying that portion of the price that will be delivered at the closing. For example, if the seller wishes to be paid only by wire transfer or certified check, the contract should state these limitations. The typical seller will not wish to be paid in cash, by a check that is not certified, or by an endorsed check from a third party.

The parties also need to be attentive to concerns that the buyer may be violating the USA Patriot Act or attempting to engage in money laundering—issues that have deservedly received heightened attention from lawyers during the past several years. This evolving area of law is beyond the scope of this book, but the parties must be sure to comply with all applicable laws and should consider addressing this issue in the "Purchase Price" section of the contract or elsewhere in the document.[12]

### §2.15—Purchases Subject to Existing Financing

In some cases, the parties will agree that the buyer will accept title subject to existing financing. Perhaps there is a substantial penalty for prepaying this financing, or perhaps the interest rate on the existing debt is lower than the rate that now prevails. If the parties have agreed to these terms, they should clarify this point here.[13]

It is important to understand exactly what the parties are doing when the buyer purchases "subject to." If the property is worth $100,000 and the parties agree to leave a $25,000 mortgage in place, then the buyer is not paying $100,000 for $100,000 worth of property. Rather, the buyer is paying $75,000 for the seller's $75,000 worth of encumbered property, and the contract should be clear on this point. In addition, the buyer presumably expects to remove the $25,000 encumbrance by paying it off according to its terms, thereby clearing the title. When the debt is paid off, the buyer then will have paid a total of $100,000 for the property, but will not have paid all of it directly to the seller.

Recall that in a "subject to" transaction, the buyer is not making any promises to anyone that it actually will pay the debt. If it chooses not to pay this debt, then it may lose the property to the existing lender, but it bears no personal responsibility for the debt and cannot be held liable on the note if there is a deficiency. If property values were to drop precipitously, the buyer could walk away from the property with no liability for this amount, while the seller would remain personally liable for repayment of this debt.[14] The buyer would lose its previous investment in the property but nothing more, while the lender could recover only from the original borrower.

The existing mortgage may prohibit sales "subject to" or may require the lender's consent. If this is the case, or if the parties plan to execute the contract before they can determine whether this is the case, then the contract should state what will happen if the lender refuses to consent.

---

*Comment:* Almost all commercial loans contain a due-on-transfer clause, which provides that the loan will be due at the lender's option in the event of a sale or other transfer.

---

### §2.16—Portion to Be Paid by Assumption of Existing Debt

The buyer may agree to pay part of the purchase price by assuming existing debt. For the same reasons as those described in the previous section, the buyer and the seller may find it advantageous to leave existing financing in place, but this time with the buyer taking responsibility for paying it. Once again, this point should be spelled out precisely in the "Purchase Price" section of the sales contract.[15] Do not forget that the lender may be able to prevent the buyer from assuming the debt. Be sure that the contract is clear about what the parties will do if the lender denies its consent.

Even though the buyer will deliver the same amount of cash to the seller in either case, there is an enormous legal difference between a purchase with an assumption and a purchase subject to, and the lawyer must be sure to clarify what the parties have agreed to. Imagine again that the property is worth $100,000, but now the buyer has agreed to assume $25,000 in existing financing. In this instance, the buyer is paying $100,000 for $100,000 worth of property, but is paying $25,000 of this amount by assuming personal responsibility for the seller's preexisting debt. If the buyer fails to meet its responsibilities to the original lender, not only may the lender foreclose on the property, it also may seek satisfaction from the buyer personally.[16]

### §2.17—Caution: Assumptions and Purchases "Subject To"

In almost every instance, the seller and the lender both will want to be certain that the buyer is assuming any existing financing and is not merely taking "subject to." The buyer's promise to pay binds the buyer and protects the seller and the lender. Note, though, that if the buyer is a thinly capitalized entity, the buyer's assumption may be of little practical value to the seller or the lender.

### §2.18—Portion to Be Paid by Amount Borrowed from a Third-Party Lender

The buyer probably will borrow a portion of the funds it needs from a third-party lender. The seller does not care what the source of the buyer's funds is and will deliver the deed as long as the buyer delivers good funds at the closing. The parties may, however, want to clarify that a portion of the purchase price will be provided by someone other than the buyer.

More important from the buyer's perspective is the fact that it may not yet have secured a commitment for its financing at the time it executes the contract of sale. It is essential to the buyer that it have the right to withdraw from the contract without penalty if it is unable to obtain the financing it needs. While this matter is discussed in more detail below in connection with the closing conditions contained in the contract,[17] it would be wise to reference that provision here, if only to remind the seller that some of the funds must come from a third-party lender that has not yet committed to provide those funds.

### §2.19—Portion to Be Paid by Seller Financing

In some cases, the seller will provide a portion of the buyer's funds. Unlike the third-party financing just discussed, seller financing does not actually involve an advance of funds to the buyer. Rather, the seller accepts payment of less than all of the purchase price in cash, with the buyer's note and mortgage making up the difference. Seller financing is particularly useful in cases in which the buyer does not expect to be able to qualify for a third-party loan of all the funds that it needs: the buyer obtains a loan from the seller to fill the gap left after the buyer borrows all that it can from outside sources.

If the parties have agreed to seller financing,[18] they should indicate in the "Purchase Price" section the portion of the purchase price that the seller is to provide. This provision not only should state the amount of the loan from the seller to the buyer, but also should specify the repayment terms, including the interest rate, the duration of the loan, and the default provisions. If these provisions are fairly lengthy—and if the parties are careful, these provisions often will be lengthy—then it might make more sense to include all of the terms of the seller's loan in a separate section of the contract or to attach agreed versions of the note and mortgage as exhibits to the contract. Even if the contract treats this matter in detail elsewhere, the "Purchase Price" section still should indicate the portion of the purchase price that the seller will provide in the form of a loan.

### § 2.20—Caution: Seller Financing

In many cases of seller financing, the property will be encumbered by two or more mortgages after the transaction closes. If the portion of the financing that the seller is providing will be secured by a second mortgage, the parties must ascertain whether the first mortgage permits junior financing. This issue can arise if the buyer is borrowing funds from both the seller and a third-party lender, because the third-party lender almost certainly will insist on senior status. It also comes up if the seller plans to lend funds to the buyer while also leaving existing financing in place, because the existing financing already will be senior to the new mortgage. The buyer, seller, and lender may need to execute a subordination agreement to clarify the relative priorities of the mortgages.[19]

### § 2.21 Down Payment

The buyer ordinarily will pay a portion of the purchase price at the time that it executes the contract of sale. This payment, often referred to as a "down payment," "deposit," or "earnest money deposit," serves several purposes. It indicates that the buyer is serious (or "earnest") enough about the sale to put its own funds on the line. The down payment also gives the seller some confidence that the buyer actually has some cash available to complete the purchase. Obviously, the extent to which the down payment serves either of these functions depends on its size and the conditions under which it will be returned to the buyer, both of which are highly negotiable.

---

*Comment:* In many cases involving land that is to be developed for commercial use, the initial down payment will be inconsequential. A further down payment may be required when the review period ends or when certain contingencies have been satisfied.

---

The down payment will often serve as liquidated damages in the event that the buyer breaches the contract. If the parties intend for the down payment to serve this function, they need to be quite clear in their drafting. Different jurisdictions apply different standards as to when parties may make use of liquidated damages[20] and also have different rules about the mechanics of accomplishing this result.[21]

If the down payment is to serve as liquidated damages, then the parties must be particularly careful when they agree to the size of the down payment. At minimum, the seller will want to be sure that the amount is sufficient to cover its net carrying costs for the duration of the contract period plus some of the subsequent time during which the property is back on the market. These carrying costs of the seller include interest on its own mortgage, real property taxes, and insurance and maintenance costs, minus anticipated income from tenant rents and other sources. After all, if the buyer breaches the contract two months after executing it, then the seller is right back where it started and has incurred the extra costs of carrying the property for at least these two months. If the seller fears that the property will depreciate, it must also consider the extent to which the liquidated damages need to make it whole if the seller later must sell the property for a price below the contract price. Conversely, the buyer will want to keep the down payment as small as possible so that its losses after a breach will be minimized.

The seller may end up suffering no financial loss at all if the buyer breaches. The property may be economically productive, with income exceeding expenses, and it may appreciate, allowing the seller to find another buyer who is willing to pay an even higher price for the property. These matters may be difficult to estimate in advance, which helps explain why the parties may wish to use a liquidated damages provision in the contract rather than trying to reconstruct these figures in court later on. Use of a liquidated damages provision allows each of the parties to know the precise consequences of a breach by the buyer.

The parties should be sure they are clear about their understanding of the term "liquidated damages." If they intend for retention of the down payment to be the seller's sole remedy, they should state this unequivocally. If they fail to do so, then a court might later award the seller additional damages. Recall also that some states will specifically enforce contracts for the sale of land even if it is the buyer that breaches, which means that the buyer needs to be sure that the liquidated damages remedy supersedes the specific performance remedy.

Even if the parties do not formally agree to treat the down payment as liquidated damages, that may turn out to be the practical effect of the down payment. If the buyer breaches, the seller may decide to retain this amount rather than seek actual damages.[22] This is particularly true if the buyer is a thinly capitalized entity that might prove to be judgment-proof even if a lawsuit succeeds. The buyer, meanwhile, may decide that there is little reason to seek to recover the down payment if it faces a certain counterclaim from the seller for the seller's actual damages. Thus, the down payment may function as liquidated damages even if the parties have not technically agreed to use these funds in this way. The likelihood of this outcome increases the closer the size of the down payment is to the seller's actual losses, because neither party will have much to gain by suing the other.

### § 2.22—Caution: Interest on Down Payment

In some states, the down payment must be placed in an interest-bearing account, although this is not true everywhere. In these states, the parties should be certain to state when and how the deposit is to be invested and to specify which party is to receive the benefit of the interest on the deposit.

### § 2.23—Caution: Brokerage Commissions

Note that in the event of a default on the contract, the brokerage agreement between the seller and the seller's broker may provide that the broker is entitled to a portion of its commission, often as much as one-half of the total. If the seller has such an agreement with its broker, it may not receive the entire benefit of the deposit, and the broker may share in the forfeited deposit.

## §2.24 Escrow for Down Payment

While the buyer and the seller may trust each other, the buyer may be uncomfortable with the thought of the seller holding a large sum of the buyer's money. If the deal proceeds to closing, then the buyer needs only to pay the balance, but if the seller breaches or if the buyer fails to close for an excusable reason, the buyer may worry that the seller will not return the down payment. For this reason, the parties often will agree that the down payment will be held in escrow by a third party.

The parties and the escrow agent need to be clear as to the escrow agent's responsibilities and liabilities, either in the contract or in a separate agreement. For example, suppose the seller claims that the buyer has breached but the buyer denies it. Each party may demand the down payment from the escrow agent, and the escrow agent may find itself defending a lawsuit even if it acts properly. For this reason, all parties, and especially the escrow agent, should insist on a clear escrow agreement. This agreement should state explicitly when the escrow agent may and must turn the escrowed funds over to one of the parties and also should specify procedures for the escrow agent to follow if it is unsure which party is entitled to the funds.

The escrow agreement should state whether the escrowed funds bear interest, which party will receive that interest, and how the funds are to be invested. This issue obviously is more critical if the down payment is large or if the contract will not be performed for many months after its execution.

## §2.25—Caution: Lawyers Serving as Escrow Agents

The parties may prefer to have one of the lawyers serve as the escrow agent. In many instances, lawyers are prohibited by their firms' policies, or by good judgment, from serving as escrow agent, because the lawyer represents one party while the escrow agent must treat two or more parties impartially.[23] This inherent conflict might disqualify the lawyer in the event of a subsequent dispute between the party that it represented in connection with the contract and the opposing party. It may be wiser from the lawyer's point of view to select a title company or another third party to act as escrow agent. Nonetheless, it still is customary in some states for lawyers to serve in this capacity.

## §2.26 Sale or Removal of Personal Property

Contracts of sale often address personal property issues and not just real property matters. In some cases, the personal property may be a critical aspect of the deal, and the value of the personal property may equal or exceed the value of the land and improvements. A partnership that is purchasing a hotel with the idea of running it as an ongoing business will have little interest in outfitting an empty building. In other cases, such as the sale of agricultural property that is to be subdivided for residential use, personal property will not be a factor in the transaction or will be undesirable to the buyer. Even if personal property is not a major component of the transaction, inclusion of a personal property provision in the basic contract will remind each party to think about this issue.

The contract needs to address the fate of all personal property located at the site, and should clarify which party will own this personal property after the deal closes. It should provide a mechanism for transferring title to this property, which does not pass by deed.[24] The parties also need to investigate the extent to which a sale of personal property subjects the transaction to sales taxes. To the extent there is or may be sales tax liability, the contract obviously needs to allocate responsibility for paying it.

> *Comment:* Defining the intellectual property to be sold or retained is an increasingly important task. Careful attention should be given to computer programs associated with the operation of the property, billing and collection software programs, trademarks, copyrights, and agreements with providers of cable and information services.

If the buyer does not wish to acquire some or all of the personal property at the site, then the contract should state whether the seller is responsible for removing this property and repairing any damage that results from this removal. If the personal property has no value to the buyer and is expensive to remove, then this property is a liability rather than an asset. In the hypothetical hotel, for instance, if the buyer intends to gut and rehabilitate the property immediately after the purchase, it can save a substantial amount of money if it convinces the seller to remove all of the personal property at its own expense.

### §2.27—Caution: Liquor Licenses

One of the most important elements of the personal property to be conveyed in connection with a sale of commercial real estate such as a restaurant or hotel may be a liquor license. If the liquor license can legally be transferred, it is essential that the contract of sale spell out whether or not the license is a part of the personal property that the buyer is acquiring; whether the buyer must pay additional compensation for the license; and who is responsible for applying for and prosecuting the transfer of the liquor license.

### §2.28—Caution: Sales Tax

In some states, the rate of the sales tax on the personal property may far exceed the rate of the transfer tax and recording charges incurred upon transfer of the real property. Therefore, the contract of sale should allocate the purchase price carefully between real and personal property and should specify which party bears the responsibility for payment of sales taxes. This is particularly important in cases such as industrial facilities, which may contain expensive manufacturing and other equipment.

## §2.29  Seller's Representations, Warranties, Covenants, and Indemnities

Two of the primary purposes of the contract of sale are the obtaining of information and the allocation of risk.[25] Each party needs to ascertain information about the other, and the buyer needs to learn as much as it can about the real estate before the closing. The parties can use the contract as a method of unearthing this critical data. One way of accomplishing this result is by asking the other party to state in the contract exactly what it knows, with contractual remedies available for breach. The representations, warranties, covenants, and indemnities contained in the contract are designed to achieve this outcome.

Be aware that representations, warranties, covenants, and indemnities differ from one another and sometimes appear in different parts of the contract. They are treated together here, because there is significant overlap among these four types of provisions. Whether the drafter chooses to group these provisions together in the contract or to treat them separately is largely a matter of personal drafting style.

In brief, a *representation* is a statement of current fact, such as, "The Seller represents that there are no tenants currently occupying any portion of the property." A *warranty* is a statement or promise of future fact, such as, "The Seller warrants that there will be no tenants occupying any portion of the property on the closing date," although the terms "representation" and "warranty" often are used interchangeably. A *covenant* is a promise of future action, such as, "The Seller covenants that it will remove all tenants currently occupying any portion of the property by the closing date." An *indemnity* is a promise to make the other party whole in the event that a representation or warranty proves to be untrue or a covenant is not performed. For example, the contract might state, "The Seller agrees to indemnify the Buyer and hold the Buyer harmless against any expenses that it incurs, including reasonable attorneys' fees and costs, if any of the Seller's representations or warranties is untrue."

For ease of drafting, the parties might not include all of these statements in full. For example, the representations section of the contract might include a long list of representations, including the representation that there are no tenants, and a subsequent warranty section simply might state, "The Seller warrants that all of its representations will remain true through the closing date." The legal effect is the same as in the prior paragraph. Although the indemnity then might seem superfluous, it provides the basis for recovery of attorneys' fees and costs.

To understand better the distinctions among these different provisions, assume that a buyer is purchasing an office building that the seller had managed as rental property but that the buyer wishes to use as its own offices. This buyer does not want any preexisting tenants to be leasing space when it acquires title and wishes to address this concern in the representations, warranties, covenants, and indemnities of the contract. It should be apparent that this buyer's concern can give rise to all four of these provisions. If the seller has told the buyer that the property currently is vacant, then the buyer should request the stated representation and warranty.[26] If, however, the seller has informed the buyer that two holdover tenants remain in occupancy, then the seller cannot give that blanket representation, and the buyer will be more concerned about receiving the warranty, the covenant, and the indemnity.[27] The buyer that wishes to acquire a vacant building will want all four of these provisions included in the document, but its emphasis will differ depending on whether the property currently contains tenants or not.

> *Comment:* In many cases, the practical differences among representations, warranties, and covenants may be somewhat illusory, and a prudent buyer will often demand all three. The specific importance of the indemnity provision is that it gives the benefited party the right to attorneys' fees, legal expenses, and other associated costs. It would be best to spell out the entitlement to these fees and costs in the indemnity.

The buyer uses these portions of the contract to gather information and confirm its understandings about the property. If the buyer does not yet know whether there are any tenants in occupancy or does not wish to rely on what the seller has stated orally, then the buyer can seek relevant representations, warranties, covenants, and indemnities. If the seller provides these assurances, then it has made a written commitment and the buyer can look to its contractual remedies if the statements turn out to be inaccurate. If the seller refuses to offer these assurances, then the buyer is alerted to possible problems before it signs the contract and can investigate on its own or withdraw from the transaction at an early stage.

The party asked to provide a representation must decide the extent to which it feels comfortable making this statement in the contract. If this party knows the statement to be untrue, then it will breach the contract as soon as it signs it and will leave itself open to a claim for damages. If this party believes that the statement is generally true but is subject to certain exceptions, it should be sure to modify the representation to list these exceptions, either in the body of the document or in an exhibit to the contract. In some cases, the party asked to make an absolute statement may believe the representation to be true but may lack certainty. This party may respond by modifying the representation and limiting it to the best of the representing party's knowledge. Lawyers for buyers and sellers spend many hours negotiating which representations will be made absolutely and which will be limited to the best of the representing party's knowledge.

*Comment:* Terms such as "to a party's knowledge" and "to the best of a party's knowledge" may have different connotations in different jurisdictions. In some jurisdictions, a party is under a good-faith obligation to have made inquiry, and a representation made "to the best of a party's knowledge" means that this party will be deemed to have made a study or analysis in order to form the basis for its representation.

*Comment:* Very frequently, a party that is a business entity may give a representation that is limited to the knowledge of named individuals within the entity. This limitation may be very important to a company that has a large number of employees, that has experienced significant turnover in personnel, or that may have voluminous files in storage or otherwise not readily available.

Note that many of the matters that are addressed in representations, warranties, covenants, and indemnities will also be the subject of closing conditions and that the accuracy of these representations and warranties and the performance of these covenants may also be conditions precedent to the other party's obligation to close. Closing conditions are discussed in more detail in subsequent sections of this chapter.[28]

Contracts of sale for commercial property often include detailed lists of representations, warranties, covenants, and indemnities, especially those provided by the seller. Sometimes, however, the seller may be perfectly willing to allow the buyer to inspect the premises for itself as a means of determining whether the property is acceptable but may not wish to provide any information directly to the buyer. In some cases, this may be an entirely reasonable position for the seller to take. The seller may recently have acquired the property itself and may not know much more about the property than the buyer does. In other cases, the seller simply may be attempting to negotiate a favorable contract with little risk of personal liability. The trend in recent years has been for sellers to provide fewer representations and for buyers to rely more heavily on their own due diligence investigations, particularly if the issue in question is one that the buyer can investigate on its own.

Whatever the seller's reasoning, the buyer must decide the extent to which it is willing to rely entirely on its own investigation, without the inclusion of any of these provisions in the contract. The buyer also must be sure that the contract provides it with the time and the access to the property it will need to undertake its own investigation. The buyer needs to retain the right to terminate the contract without penalty if its due diligence discloses unacceptable problems, because it will have no other contractual recourse. The lawyer's task in this setting is to advise the buyer of these risks and to assist the buyer in deciding whether these risks are acceptable.

The sections that follow describe the seller's representations, warranties, covenants, and indemnities that often appear in a contract of sale. The buyer may want to include variations of all of these provisions, while the seller is likely to be far less accommodating. Even if the seller insists that the buyer take the property "as is," these sections of this book will remind the buyer what the relevant issues are and alert the buyer to the risks it will face if it agrees to a contract that lacks these protections. They help the buyer prepare a checklist of the issues that it must investigate on its own. They may help the buyer negotiate a more favorable list of closing conditions—a seller that will not provide representations, warranties, covenants, and indemnities probably recognizes the buyer's heightened need to address these matters in closing conditions. Later sections will address the buyer's representations, warranties, covenants, and indemnities.[29]

To avoid continually restating the awkward phrase "representations, warranties, covenants, and indemnities," this book sometimes will refer to these provisions collectively as "representations," but will not do so in situations in which the distinction matters. Remember, however, that most of the issues discussed in the sections that follow may also be addressed in contractual warranties, covenants, and indemnities, and not just in representations.

## §2.30—Caution: Continuing Representations

It is very dangerous for a party to give a "continuing representation" as to a factual matter, in which the party states that its representation was true on the date it was made and also will be true as of the date of the closing. If something changes, the party will be liable for a misrepresentation. The better course of action in this situation is to require the party to disclose any relevant change and to make the nonoccurrence of any change that would adversely affect the other party a condition precedent to the other party's obligation to close. This protects the representing party from liability for damages for misrepresentation if a change occurs after the contract is signed.

### §2.31—Caution: "As Is" Representations

As will be detailed later, the use of "as is" language does not always insulate the seller.[30] A seller that is aware of a dangerous condition, a serious environmental problem, or another condition that would prevent the buyer from using the property for its obviously intended purpose would be required under the laws of many jurisdictions to reveal the problem to the buyer or to the broker, who in turn would be required under applicable brokerage standards to reveal the condition to the buyer.

### §2.32—Due Organization of Seller

If the party executing the contract as the seller is an entity rather than an individual, the buyer must confirm that this entity actually has a legal existence. The buyer should insist that the party signing the document as seller include a representation to this effect in the contract, and should also verify this fact for itself. It would be an expensive and embarrassing error to sign a contract with a nonexistent entity, pay the earnest money to that entity or to an escrow agent, and begin the costly due diligence process, only to discover later that the seller does not exist under state law.

This due organization representation should state that the entity—whether a corporation, a partnership, or a limited liability entity—is legally formed in accordance with the laws of the state in which the property is located, assuming that this is the case.[31] If the entity that is selling exists under the laws of another state or of a foreign jurisdiction, the representation should so specify and also should confirm that the out-of-state entity is authorized to do business in the state in which the property is located.

If the purported seller makes a misrepresentation in this portion of the contract and the buyer relies on this statement, then the buyer may not be any better off. The buyer may be left with only a contractual remedy against a nonexistent entity and perhaps a fraud claim against the person purporting to sign on that entity's behalf. If the buyer is truly concerned at this stage but still wishes to proceed, it can easily confirm the seller's legal existence on its own, thereby avoiding any problems before they arise. The prudent buyer should also guard against this problem by insisting that any down payment be held in escrow. The buyer will have time during the due diligence phase of the transaction to confirm that the seller's legal existence continues through the closing date, a point that should be addressed in a closing condition.[32]

### §2.33—Caution: Seller's Good Standing

It is essential to both parties that the seller be in good standing at the time of the closing.[33] Ideally, the seller will already be in good standing at the time it executes the contract, but the buyer may discover that the seller is not in good standing at that time, perhaps because of its failure to comply with annual reporting requirements or to pay franchise, personal property, or other similar taxes under state law. A telephone call or e-mail inquiry to the state agency that is responsible for the formation of business entities and the issuance of certificates of good standing should resolve whether or not the seller is in good standing. The buyer also should request that a good standing certificate be delivered at the closing.[34] For similar reasons, lenders almost always require good standing certificates from the state in which the seller entity is formed and the state in which the property is located.

### §2.34—Authority of Seller; No Approvals Required; No Violations of Other Agreements

Not only must the seller be validly formed under state law, it also must have taken the proper state law steps to authorize the sale of the property. If the seller is a corporation, for example, its board of directors must approve the seller's decision to execute a sales contract, must approve the consummation of the sale in accordance with the terms of the contract, and must authorize one of its officers to sign the necessary documents. Before the buyer closes and delivers the balance of the purchase price, it will have adequate time to confirm that the seller has taken all internal steps required to authorize the sale, including any actions necessary if the seller's own organizational documents are more restrictive than is normally the case. The buyer probably will not have undertaken this investigation before it signs the contract, however, and should ask the seller to represent that the contract has been properly authorized and to covenant that all steps necessary to closing the transaction will be taken before the closing date.[35]

*Comment:* It may be difficult for the buyer to ascertain for itself whether the seller has undertaken the internal steps necessary to authorize the sale. If the buyer wishes to confirm these matters, it should review copies of articles of incorporation, bylaws, certificates of incumbency, corporate resolutions, and other documents. Title companies often undertake a similar review.

*Comment:* In some states, if the property constitutes all or substantially all of the assets of the seller entity, further approvals may be required from the seller's shareholders or partners, and the transfer documentation may differ.

The seller's ability to convey the property may be limited in other ways, and other approvals may be necessary before the seller can follow through with the sale. Depending on the type of property and the type of business, approvals from the government or from other third parties may be required. Uses ranging from nuclear power production to the serving of alcohol are subject to government regulation, and the buyer should begin to determine whether regulatory approval is necessary and available.[36] The property may be subject to a right of first refusal, an option,[37] a restrictive covenant, a noncompetition agreement, or a consent decree, and another party to that document may have the power to prevent the sale from proceeding. Because the seller will not necessarily know yet about the existence of some of these agreements and requirements, it should seek a representation stating that no third-party approvals are required and that the consummation of the sale will not conflict with any other agreement to which the seller is a party.

In many cases in which consents from third parties are necessary, the parties will agree to defer the obtaining of these consents until after the contract is signed. The seller may not wish to go to the trouble of determining which approvals are necessary and obtaining these approvals until the buyer has committed itself to the purchase in writing. If this is so, then the parties may be better off handling these matters through the use of closing conditions and covenants rather than representations.[38] In these cases, the seller may represent in the contract that it has taken all steps required under state law and its organizational documents to authorize the contract of sale, may covenant to obtain all regulatory and other third-party approvals that are necessary for the sale, and may agree that its receipt of these consents will be a condition precedent to the buyer's obligation to close.

> Comment: The seller may agree to use "reasonable efforts" or "commercially reasonable efforts" to obtain the third-party approvals it needs. A seller should avoid covenanting to use "best efforts," as this standard may, under state law, require the seller to spend substantial sums of money.

### §2.35—Entire Premises — Prof says he wouldn't make this rep.; but buyer will rarely request this rep.

The seller should represent that the property described in the contract consists of the entire premises necessary for the operation of the structure or business that is being conveyed. At this early stage in the conveyancing process, the buyer has no way of knowing whether a metes and bounds description in an exhibit to the contract defines the boundaries of all the property it thinks it is buying.

This "entire premises" language must go beyond a simple statement that the buyer is receiving the entire building and the usual appurtenances. The clause also needs to address critical ancillary needs of the property such as parking, easements for access, and easements for utility connections. If the seller is transferring a resort hotel, for example, the buyer needs to know that the legal description covers all buildings, parking lots, and rights-of-way for utilities and beach access.

> Comment: In the "entire premises" clause, the lawyer should be certain to include typical appurtenances such as alleys and the beds of adjoining streets. This clause also must address other property interests that are necessary to the operation of the property, including access to rail service, piers, boat slips, and public roads. If the buyer does not receive "entire premises" language addressing all of these interests, it may find itself bound to acquire part of a building or part of a business. The imaginary hotel buyer may find that it is contractually required to purchase the structure even though the contract addresses neither the easement that the seller has been using for the most convenient access to the beach nor the rear parking lot needed to comply with the local zoning ordinance. The buyer then will own less desirable—perhaps unusable—property and may have to spend additional money to acquire the rights to use this easement and parking lot.

The buyer should always obtain a survey of the property, which will reveal problems of this type. Surveyors need time to work, however, and the buyer will want to avoid this delay and expense until after the seller signs the contract binding itself to close.[39] The buyer has no other practical way of discovering at the time of contract execution whether it is getting the entire package it thinks it is getting.

> *Comment:* The buyer should ask the seller to provide it with copies of prior surveys. Surveyors can update existing surveys more quickly and cheaply than they can prepare new ones.

### § 2.36—No Options

The buyer should ask the seller to represent that no party holds an option to purchase the property or a right of first refusal or first offer on the property. Once the parties sign the contract, the buyer will incur substantial due diligence expenses and will be most unhappy to learn that some other party has the prior right to obtain the land. If the property is subject to a prior right of this type, then the buyer needs to hear this bad news early in the process. It can learn exactly what these previously granted rights are and can decide whether it wishes to proceed and how to handle the rights of the prior party. A representation from the seller will either disclose any options at the earliest possible time or provide the buyer with a remedy for the seller's breach of a representation.

The buyer also can determine if there are any outstanding options by conducting a title search. However, the buyer probably would rather not incur the expense and consume the time necessary to search title until it knows that the seller has made a written commitment to sell the property. Moreover, a title search alone probably will be insufficient, because unrecorded leases of which the buyer has constructive notice also may contain prior rights. The buyer needs to be sure that it is aware of all tenants at the property and that it obtains copies of all occupancy agreements, including those that are not recorded, and reads them thoroughly.[40]

> *Comment:* The buyer will also need to inspect the property. There are cases holding that a buyer is on constructive notice of the rights of a tenant or other occupant, because a close inspection of the property would

have revealed the presence of the tenant, thereby placing the buyer on constructive notice of all rights contained in that tenant's lease.

*Comment:* In addition to revealing whether a tenant has any rights against the buyer, the buyer's review of written leases and site plans may also disclose whether any tenant has rights against any other tenant. For example, one tenant may have the right to approve an expansion or a change in use by another tenant.

## §2.37—Caution: Inquiring about Options

The buyer may be able to identify outstanding options through a title search. However, as just noted, the buyer is also under a duty to make inquiry of parties who are in possession as to whether there are any unrecorded options of this type. In one reported case, a tenant alleged that the buyer failed to make proper inquiry of that tenant as to its rights under an unrecorded master lease. The court ultimately vacated its opinion favoring the tenant, but the issue remains an important one for both parties.[41]

## §2.38—Condition of Property and Improvements

*— prof says the seller would never make this warranty*

The buyer may have made a preliminary inspection of the property before committing to buy it but probably has not had the time to examine the premises as thoroughly as it needs to. If the property is improved, the buyer will want to inspect it carefully. This inspection will entail retaining someone with sufficient expertise in architecture and engineering to confirm that the building is structurally sound and to alert the buyer to any looming problems. Even if the property is unimproved, the buyer will want to confirm that the land can physically be used in the way that the buyer intends to use it.

If the buyer undertakes this expense before the contract is signed, it runs the risk that the seller will receive a better offer and contract with someone else. The seller might even take advantage of the buyer's inspection, using it to learn of any problems with the property without having to pay for an inspection itself. The buyer probably will want to postpone its inspection until after the contract is signed.

By signing a contract unconditionally, however, the buyer commits itself to buying the property, and by signing this contract before having the property inspected, the buyer commits to buying the building in its current condition. To avoid this risk, the buyer must learn as much as it can about the building from the seller and must leave itself with the right to terminate the contract if it discovers problems during its own due diligence investigation. The buyer accomplishes the first of these goals by asking the seller to include a representation in the contract of sale addressing the condition of the property and improvements, and it accomplishes the second goal by using a closing condition.[42] If the contract covers significant personal property, the representation and closing condition should extend to that personal property.

*Comment:* Sellers of income-producing property are unlikely to agree to provide representations that address the condition of the property. When they do, their representations typically are limited to certain conditions, such as hazardous wastes, mold, and latent defects, that an inspector would be unlikely to discover.

If the contract covers land that is already improved, then the buyer will be most concerned with representations addressing the physical condition of the structure. If the contract covers unimproved land that the buyer plans to develop, then the buyer may request representations addressing the land, its zoning, and its suitability for the buyer's purposes. The buyer also should ask the seller to represent that the property is free of hazardous wastes.[43]

*Seller wouldn't agree to make this rep.*

*Comment:* Several years ago, it appeared that mold was going to become a significant and enduring issue in real estate transactions. Because of the difficulty of proving causation when mold is present, the number of lawsuits addressing this issue, including class-action lawsuits, has been smaller than expected, particularly in commercial real estate settings. As a result, the mold issue has turned out to be less significant than many real estate professionals anticipated. Nonetheless, the buyer should ask the seller to represent that it has no knowledge of any mold conditions at the property and should also be sure to inspect for mold on its own. Insurance protection may be available, but it tends to be expensive and difficult to obtain.

While it is reasonable for the buyer to ask the seller to disclose existing conditions and to back up those disclosures with contract liability and indemnities, it is less reasonable for the buyer to ask the seller to speculate as to the fitness of the property for the buyer's planned use. The seller's response will be that the buyer is free to inspect the property and to be released from the contract if the property fails to meet some objective standard, but that the seller will not represent that the property is fit for the buyer's purpose. If this is how the parties resolve the issue, they are likely to address it in a closing condition rather than in a representation.

### § 2.39—Caution: Condition of Property and Caveat Emptor

Although the doctrine of *caveat emptor* ("buyer beware") may survive, it clearly is under attack. There may be significant perils for the seller that does not disclose essential information concerning the property, even if the property is sold on an "as is" basis. In one reported case, a seller did not reveal the presence of asbestos to the buyer. The buyer was awarded a huge verdict even though there was no representation or warranty or other provision that required the seller to reveal this information. Although this decision was reversed on appeal, the trend probably does not favor sellers who fail to disclose this type of information.[44] At the same time, while the buyer may ask the seller to include representations about the condition of the property and improvements in the contract of sale, the seller often will do its best to give extremely limited representations.

*→ should also contain negative covenants (seller will not...)*

### § 2.40—Maintenance and Operation of Property until Closing

*needs to be a covenant not rep & warranty*

Once the seller demonstrates its resolve to sell the property by entering into a binding contract, it is likely to lose some of its interest in maintaining the property. The soon-to-be-former owner may no longer be as motivated as it once was to sweep sidewalks, polish brass, and replace flickering light bulbs. This illustration of the "moral hazard" problem may cause the seller to treat its property in the same way that many automobile renters treat their rental cars, and the buyer should be concerned about this normal human tendency. The buyer can address these concerns through the careful use of warranties, covenants, and closing conditions in the contract.

The buyer should request that the seller agree to operate and maintain the property during the contract period in a manner similar to its operation and maintenance of the property before it signed the contract. If the buyer is particularly worried about the seller's future dedication to the property, it can include more specific and detailed management standards. The parties should be sure to address the extent to which the seller must undertake major capital expenses, as opposed to normal maintenance. Separate provisions of the contract should address responsibility for restoration following a casualty loss or a condemnation.[45]

> *Comment:* The seller must be sure that the contract does not require it to replace major building systems, such as mechanical, electrical, and heating and air conditioning systems, rather than merely maintaining them. Replacing these systems is extremely costly, and only the buyer will benefit.

### § 2.41—Seller's Title and Permitted Encumbrances

Most buyers will ask the seller to represent that it owns unencumbered fee simple title to the property or fee simple title that is subject only to certain enumerated encumbrances.[46] If the seller will not provide this representation—perhaps because it is uncertain as to the quality of its title—the buyer may obtain a title report even before it signs the contract.

The seller may be unwilling to make a title representation of this broad scope or may want to limit this representation to the best of its knowledge. This is particularly true if the seller has owned the property for only a short time or if the seller acquired the property by devise, by purchase at a foreclosure sale, or in some other manner that causes it to have its own doubts about the quality of its title. The seller may suggest that the parties omit this representation and that the buyer rely entirely on a closing condition that will excuse its nonperformance if the title fails to meet some agreed standard. The seller will argue that it is not a title insurer and that the buyer should address its title concerns with an entity that is more experienced in examining and insuring title.

This option may be acceptable to the buyer, but there are some pitfalls of which the buyer should be aware. The buyer will discover problems earlier if the seller reveals them in its representations. If the buyer relies on its own due diligence, however, it may not learn of the same problems for weeks, during which time the buyer is incurring other transaction costs. In addition, the seller's breach of a representation will allow the buyer to bring a contract claim against the seller for damages, while the seller's failure to meet a closing condition merely excuses the buyer's nonperformance at the closing and entitles the buyer to the return of its down payment.

---

*Comment:* A sophisticated seller will often be willing to deliver a copy of its own title policy to the buyer before the parties execute the contract or immediately afterward. This practice greatly simplifies the process of determining good title.

---

If the parties have agreed that the buyer will accept title subject to certain encumbrances, such as existing mortgages, tenant leases, and restrictive covenants, then any title representation must be modified to list these exceptions to the more general blanket representation. The parties may prefer to attach a list of permitted exceptions as an exhibit to the contract, particularly if the list is long. This allows the lawyers to negotiate and agree to the final language of the more general contract representation early in the drafting process. The parties and their lawyers will still need to agree on the list of permitted exceptions and can attach this list to the contract shortly before the parties execute it.

The fact that the seller reveals title encumbrances in its representation need not imply that the buyer is agreeing to accept them, and examination of these exceptions is an important part of the buyer's due diligence responsibility. To the extent that the buyer will undertake this examination after the contract is executed, it needs to be sure that it has the right to address problems or terminate the contract without penalty if the encumbrances prove to be troublesome. For example, the seller may disclose that a neighboring property owner has a right-of-way across the subject property, but the parties may be unable to determine at this early stage whether this easement passes along the edge of the property or through the middle of the buyer's planned structure. The buyer will need to reserve the right to cancel the contract without penalty if the easement holder's rights will frustrate the buyer's plans, a matter that is best addressed in the closing conditions. Meanwhile, a representation from the seller helps the buyer begin the process of gathering information.

*buyer should ask for a rent roll*

## §2.42—Schedule of Tenant Leases; Status of Tenant Leases

*important to get this rep & warranty*

Commercial property is often occupied by rent-paying tenants.[47] The presence of these tenants and the tenants' ongoing rental payment obligations are often major inducements to the buyer: a fully occupied shopping center is worth far more than an empty one, and the price the buyer offers to the seller is a function of the stream of rents paid by tenants. The buyer will want to be absolutely sure that these tenants are required to remain in possession and pay rent. At the same time, the buyer will want to ensure that there are no tenants of which it is unaware. The buyer does not wish to discover later that it owes expensive obligations to and receives limited benefits from these unexpected occupants.

It is premature for the buyer to commence its own thorough analysis of the rental status of the property, so the buyer will need to rely for the time being on the seller's representations as to the tenants' current and future occupancy rights and monetary obligations. The buyer should require the seller to represent that the schedule of tenant leases included in the contract accurately sets forth the current and future occupancy status of all space in the building. This schedule of tenant leases, which typically will appear in an exhibit to the contract, should state for each lease the name of the tenant; the space that the lease covers; the duration of the lease; the amount of rent that the tenant must pay, including any increases, adjustments, and expense pass-throughs; any landlord obligations for tenant improvements; any rights that the tenant has to renew or terminate its lease; any rights that the tenant has to expand or reduce its space; and whether the tenant has an option to purchase the property or a right of first refusal.[48] Short of examining the leases itself, which it will do after the contract is signed,[49] this is the buyer's best way to determine who has the right to occupy space in the building and what the terms of those possessory rights are.

The seller should have no objection to disclosing this information. The value of the property reflects the value of these leases, and the seller probably has been touting the strengths of the building's tenant roster throughout the negotiation process. Now is the time when the seller must back up those claims in writing by providing this representation.

The buyer should also ask the seller to represent that all of these leases remain in full force and effect, that there are no defaults, that there are no known events that will ripen into defaults with the passage of time, and that there are no other relevant agreements not listed in the schedule. The buyer will have adequate opportunities after the contract is signed to communicate with the tenants and investigate the status of the leases. Until that happens, however, a representation from the seller may be the buyer's only way of learning whether trouble is brewing with any of the building's tenants. The representation also should state that no tenant has prepaid more than one month's rent to the seller. In this way, the buyer ensures that it will not be inheriting any occupants that possess many rights without corresponding responsibilities.

### § 2.43—Caution: Accuracy of Tenant Lease Schedules

The seller should be very careful when it prepares rent rolls and similar schedules. Mathematical errors are common, and erroneous documentation is often used as the basis for a claim by the buyer. In addition, the buyer will presume that the rent is being collected on a monthly basis and that the tenants are not in arrears.

### § 2.44—No Brokerage Commissions on Leases

Brokerage commission obligations arising from tenant leases may be contained in contractual arrangements between the seller and real estate brokers. The seller, in its capacity as landlord, may have retained one or more agents to assist in leasing the building. These agents may be entitled to leasing commissions that are to be paid in the future. If the lease is a long-term lease, as often will be the case with commercial property, the brokerage contract may have been structured so that commissions are payable as the landlord receives rent from the tenant over time, or when the tenant exercises renewal or expansion options.

The buyer cannot determine the extent to which it might become personally responsible for these obligations without reviewing all brokerage agreements and without examining relevant state law, but there is a possibility that the buyer will become liable for some of these payment obligations. The buyer needs to be sure that the seller represents that there are no obligations of this type or, if there are, how much they will amount to, who will be paying them, and when they will come due.

### § 2.45—Access to the Property

The buyer needs to be absolutely certain that there is access to the property from a public road or from a private right-of-way that the seller has the legal right to use and convey. This access must be adequate for the buyer's intended use. In the most typical case, the property will abut a public roadway, and it may appear to the buyer that access will not be a problem. Even in these cases, the buyer should confirm that the curb cut allowing access to the property is a legal one. If the only legal access to the property is inconveniently situated, the buyer's investment may suffer. This point is particularly important to location-specific businesses, such as gas stations and hotels at interstate exits. The casual customer with no allegiance to any one of these establishments may pass several competitors on its way to the buyer's less convenient entrance and may never reach the buyer's property. If the property fronts on a divided roadway, the buyer also should verify that traffic from the far side of the road has ready access to the property, or else the property may lose half its traffic to competitors located across the street.

In some cases, there may not be any direct access to a public thoroughfare, and the only ingress to the seller's property may be across private property owned by a third party. If this is the case, then the buyer must be certain that the seller owns and can convey these access rights. The seller may hold an appurtenant easement across neighboring property that connects its property to a public road. The seller may own a landlocked store in a large regional shopping center in which all owners have executed a reciprocal easement agreement. The property may be a unit in a commercial condominium, and the condominium plan may dictate the means of access. In any of these cases, the buyer needs to confirm that this access exists, that it is not limited or restricted in any material way, that it can be transferred, and that the seller will convey it along with the fee simple estate in the property.

The seller may claim that it has access rights pursuant to an easement implied by prior use, an easement implied by necessity, or a prescriptive easement. The seller may be correct, but the buyer should not rely on an undocumented easement of this type. The servient estate holder may challenge the buyer's right to continue to use this easement, and even if the buyer prevails, it will waste resources in doing so. Instead, the buyer should insist that the seller enter into a written agreement with the servient estate holder before the closing that resolves any possible disputes. Even if the buyer is willing to take this type of risk, its lender will not be.

Once again, there will be adequate time for the buyer to explore these matters between contract execution and closing. For now, the buyer should insist that the seller represent that there is access to the property. This representation should clarify the precise locations of these points of entry and should also indicate the legal basis that the seller has for using these means of ingress and egress. If necessary, the buyer should confirm that these means of access are included in the legal description of the property that the seller will convey.

### § 2.46—Caution: Scope of Easements

Even though the seller may hold an appropriate easement across neighboring property that the buyer can use for access, a change in use by the buyer or an increase in the number of users may place an unreasonable burden on the easement and thus may violate its terms. The buyer may not be entitled to employ the easement for the upgraded use of the property.

### § 2.47—Utilities

Just as the buyer needs to be sure invitees can reach the property, it also needs to confirm that the property is connected to all necessary utilities and that the buyer will have the legal right to continue to use all of these connections. Electricity, water, natural gas, telephone lines, cable television lines, and high-speed Internet lines all must run from the providers of these services onto the property, and storm water and sewage must move in the other direction. In some cases, the buyer needs to verify only that the main line runs down the abutting street and that the seller received permission to hook up to it. In other cases, the seller may have had to construct a lengthy connection at its own expense, and that connection may run across land owned by others. The buyer must be sure that it can trace that connection along a series of rights-of-way until it joins the utility's main line and that the buyer will have the continuing legal right to use that connection and the underlying land at an acceptable cost.

Sometimes a commercial parcel can provide these needs for itself. A rural bed-and-breakfast may be able to function quite comfortably with a generator, a well, a satellite dish, and a septic system. Even in these settings, the buyer must confirm that the seller has addressed these matters legally. Local and even federal law may place limits on wells, septic systems, and other similar operations at the property, and the buyer must verify that all of these uses are legal and can continue. In most commercial settings, however, the property probably will need to connect to outside providers of these services, for both practical and legal reasons.

*Comment:* Note that in many jurisdictions, the local fire code may require more than one water line. The buyer's lawyer should carefully review all code requirements of this type. At this early point in the transaction, the buyer needs only to ask that the seller represent that it has access to all of these necessary utilities (which should be specifically enumerated in the representation), that this access can continue, and that the seller will transfer these access rights to the buyer. Later on, the buyer can confirm these representations directly.

### §2.48—Certificates of Occupancy and Other Permits

Local governments regulate the use and occupancy of property in a variety of different ways. Many jurisdictions require that owners obtain certificates of occupancy that confirm that the building has passed all necessary inspections and may be used for those purposes that are set forth in the certificate. The buyer needs to verify that the seller possesses a valid certificate of occupancy and that this document permits the buyer's planned uses of the property, including new uses. For example, the seller of a five-story urban property may possess a certificate that permits parking in an underground garage, retail uses on the ground floor, professional offices or residences on the second and third floors, and residences only on the fourth and fifth floors. If the current uses comply with these limitations, then the buyer has nothing to worry about unless it plans to convert the entire property into medical offices, in which case it will need to begin the process of obtaining a new certificate.

The property may require other permits. In addition to permits for access[50] and utility connections,[51] the property may connect to a parking garage, train station, or other public amenity. That connection may have required official authorization, and this authorization may not be easy to transfer. If the business operating at the property is heavily regulated, such as a tavern or a casino, similar issues may arise, and permits for these sorts of activities may be difficult or impossible to transfer.

At this point, the buyer needs to request that the seller give a representation that sets forth a list of all required permits. The buyer will also ask the seller to represent that it possesses all of these authorizations, that they are transferable, and that it will transfer them at the closing. To the extent that the seller cannot offer any of these representations, the buyer will seek a precise exception to this more general representation, along with a covenant that the seller will cooperate with the buyer to have these permits issued, reissued, or assigned. The exceptions to the blanket representation will alert the buyer to any possible permit problems and will allow the buyer to begin to address these problems. The seller may be unwilling to provide a representation of this type and instead may advise the buyer to review these matters for itself during the due diligence period.

> *Comment:* The parties must focus particular attention on liquor licenses, which frequently are nontransferable. Any transfer or reissuance will almost certainly require that the relevant licensing authorities examine and approve the transferee.

### § 2.49—Compliance with Law

Regardless of whether the property or the businesses operating at the property require permits from the government, the owner of the property must operate in compliance with all applicable laws. If the property is a residential apartment building, the jurisdiction may have a detailed housing code that addresses a wide range of health and safety issues. The owner will need to comply with applicable building and fire codes. The building may need to contain a self-locking entry door with an intercom system. The county may mandate minimum room sizes and maximum occupancy limits and may require childproof safety screens on all upper-story windows. The owner may have to file periodic reports addressing the rental status of the building and, in a small number of jurisdictions, will need to comply with rent-control laws. Older buildings may need to be brought into compliance with laws that protect the rights of the disabled and with laws addressing the presence of lead paint. Zoning ordinances may dictate minimum parking requirements.

Even if the building owner possesses all necessary permits, it nonetheless may be operating the building in violation of one or more of these laws. The buyer may purchase the building only to discover that it must spend additional funds to bring the building into compliance; in fact, the new owner may find itself liable for violations predating the transfer of title.[52] The buyer needs to ensure that the seller is operating the real estate in compliance with any applicable laws. If the buyer plans to change the use of the property, it also must remember that the new use may be subject to stricter controls for parking, fire safety, and other matters.

The buyer should ask the seller to represent that it is operating the property in compliance with all applicable laws. This representation should be broad enough to cover statutes, ordinances, regulations, and rules of all federal, state, and local authorities that have jurisdiction over the property. After the parties sign the contract, the buyer will have an adequate opportunity to determine what these laws are, to confirm that the seller is obeying them, and to investigate any exceptions that the seller made to its blanket representation.

### § 2.50—Zoning

Zoning matters merit special attention. While the previous section's discussion of the seller's compliance with applicable laws includes compliance with zoning laws, zoning issues are so common and so troublesome in real estate transactions that the parties may want to address zoning specifically in the contract of sale.

The buyer will frequently request that the seller represent that the structure and the present use of the property comply with all zoning laws and all other applicable laws governing use and occupancy, including rules governing setbacks and density. This representation either provides the buyer with the comfort that it seeks or alerts it to any potential zoning problems early on. If the use of the property is grandfathered but does not comply with existing zoning, for instance, then the buyer learns of a potential problem and can investigate whether the current use may be expanded and whether the present structure may be renovated or rebuilt following a casualty. The seller is likely to respond that the buyer is capable of investigating these zoning matters on its own.

*Comment:* At a minimum, the seller should represent that it has received no notice of any zoning violations and no notice that the property may be rezoned.

*Comment:* Buyers who seek assurances that the property is in compliance with existing zoning laws can request a zoning compliance letter from the local zoning authorities. Many local authorities will provide such a letter. Be aware, however, that a request for a zoning compliance letter can trigger an inquiry that might reveal noncompliance.

Buyers may go further than this and may seek assurances that their planned future uses for the property comply with existing zoning laws. Sellers should be extremely reluctant to provide warranties as to future uses and will respond that concerns about future zoning compliance are better addressed with closing conditions. A closing condition will allow the buyer to pursue its own investigation but will not lead to seller liability if a use planned for the future proves to be impermissible.

If the buyer plans to change the use of the property, the seller may be willing to agree to cooperate with the buyer in seeking any permits or variances during the contract period, at the buyer's expense. Contract vendees may lack standing to submit applications in their own names, and the contract should require the seller to expedite the process by initiating the permit or variance application before the transaction closes.

### §2.51—Claims and Litigation

Owners of commercial property, like other business owners, often find themselves defending against lawsuits. Suppliers, employees, or patrons may bring claims alleging that the owner has failed to comply with the terms of a binding contract or has committed a tort. Tenants may claim that the landlord is in default under their leases, and neighboring property owners may bring nuisance claims or suits over boundary disputes. A governmental authority may have filed a claim or a notice of violation stating that the property is not in compliance with law.

In any of these cases, the buyer will want to learn now of any pending litigation, threatened litigation, or potential claims that it may be inheriting. The buyer's initial request should be that the seller disclose all pending litigation, threatened litigation, and potential claims that have not yet ripened into litigation. As for pending litigation, the seller should be willing to represent either that there is none or that there is none except for the matters enumerated by the seller in the contract or in an exhibit to it. Threatened litigation poses a trickier problem for the seller, which may not yet know that a potential plaintiff is out there. Thus, the representation as to threatened litigation should be limited to the seller's knowledge of threatened claims. The same knowledge standard should apply to matters that may lead to litigation in the future. If the seller knows that a patron broke his leg in the parking lot but has not yet threatened to sue, the seller should disclose this matter. The buyer may ask that the seller indemnify it against losses the buyer suffers as a result of any of these matters, to the extent that they arose during the seller's ownership of the property.

### § 2.52—Environmental Matters

Environmental matters should receive particular attention from the buyer. Because federal environmental laws and the environmental laws of some states create strict liability for certain environmental cleanup costs, the buyer should ask that the seller disclose any environmental matters in the contract. The buyer will start by requesting a blanket representation that there are no violations of environmental laws and no materials used or stored at the property that might lead the buyer to incur any costs of this type. The seller that refuses to give this broad representation should respond by listing any exceptions to it and explaining them to the buyer's satisfaction. For example, a seller may be uncomfortable offering a representation as to actions undertaken at the property by its tenants or by former owners or users and may insist on limiting this portion of the representation to the best of its own knowledge.

> *Comment:* It is common for the seller to turn over to the buyer any environmental reports that the seller may already have in its possession, and the typical contract will simply state that the seller has no environmental reports or analyses other than those that have been disclosed in the contract and delivered to the buyer. It then would be up to the buyer to perform any further testing that might be required. Even if the seller provides earlier reports to the buyer, the buyer usually may not rely on them. The buyer should always obtain its own reports or direct certification of these earlier reports from their issuer.

"Owners and operators" of property are potentially responsible for the costs of remediating certain environmental problems described in the Comprehensive Environmental Response, Compensation and Liability Act of 1980 (CERCLA)[53] and other federal environmental laws. Once the buyer accepts the deed, it becomes an "owner" for CERCLA purposes. Prior responsible owners may have to contribute to these cleanup costs, but these contribution obligations may be of little practical use to the buyer after the closing.[54] Many states have laws or regulations that address these same issues.[55]

The only way the buyer can avoid the risk of environmental liability entirely is by refusing to accept title at the closing, and the only way the buyer can decide whether to take this drastic step is by including appropriate closing conditions in the contract and then learning as much as possible about the property before the closing. The buyer will undertake a thorough environmental investigation of the property but will not want to incur such a significant expense before the parties have signed the contract. Until it investigates the property, the buyer's principal means of discovering any environmental problems is by obtaining a seller representation in the contract.

*Comment:* A buyer will begin its due diligence by obtaining a so-called Phase I environmental report. If the Phase I report reveals conditions suggesting that further investigation is warranted, such as the presence of underground storage tanks, then the buyer will order a Phase II report.

In some cases, both parties will be well aware of environmental problems even before they begin to negotiate the contract. The buyer of a lead-recycling facility can hardly claim surprise if the property is environmentally tainted. In these cases, the buyer knows that a problem exists but still needs to learn its extent, and the contract is one of the first steps in the buyer's environmental due diligence.

*Comment:* Many states now have Brownfields legislation that permits the buyer to work with state and local government authorities to ascertain what steps must be undertaken for remediation of certain environmental problems. Under this legislation, if the buyer complies with a remediation plan approved by the state and local governments, then the state and local agencies will release the buyer from liability.

### § 2.53—*Employment Matters; Service Contracts*

Owners of property are likely to retain a wide variety of employees on the premises, ranging from building managers to rental agents to custodial staff to security guards. Not all of these workers will be direct employees of the owner, but many owners will have some direct employees working at the property on a full-time or part-time basis. The buyer needs to learn the status of these workers and needs to determine whether it will incur any liabilities to any of these workers as a result of its acquisition of the property. The buyer also may wish to continue to employ some or all of these persons.

These concerns are particularly acute if the buyer will be purchasing the entity that owns the property rather than the property itself. The corporation or partnership may be liable to its workers in a wide variety of ways. The entity may have entered into long-term employment contracts with some of its employees. It may face enormous liabilities for health and retirement benefits. Some or all of the entity's employees may be subject to collective bargaining agreements that establish the terms of employment. The buyer cannot decide whether it is willing to accept these liabilities until it knows what they are.

The buyer needs to learn as much as possible about these employment matters and once again should seek a seller representation as a means of eliciting this information. Once it learns this information, the buyer can accept these liabilities, attempt to modify the terms of the property transfer, ask the seller to renegotiate the terms of these employment agreements, or choose not to move forward with the acquisition.

The buyer also needs to determine the extent to which the property is subject to service contracts. Rather than hiring its own employees, the seller may have contracted with third parties that provide building services such as maintenance, custodial services, lawn care, and pest control. The buyer can use a representation to discover the existence of these contractual relationships.

### §2.54—Covenants, Servitudes, Easements, and Reciprocal Easements

Real property often is benefited and burdened by covenants, servitudes, and easements, including reciprocal easements. This chapter already has discussed easements for access and utilities,[56] but easements can exist for a variety of other reasons.

The large regional shopping center provides a perfect example of the kinds of covenants and easements that might affect commercial property. Even though the typical regional center appears to operate as a single unified project, the legal ownership of the property may be far more complex than that. The developer may have assembled the large lot from parcels owned by a dozen or more prior owners. Some of these owners may have sold their land outright, while others may have ground leased it to the developer. One of the anchor tenants may have insisted on leasing land from the shopping center developer while owning its own building; a second anchor may have a real estate subsidiary that owns all of its land and leases it to the retail arm of the business; and a third anchor may have insisted on owning its own building and parking. Large tenants in the mall and fast-food restaurants operating on outparcels may have options to purchase their space. Satellite parking may be located in a municipally owned structure. The shopping center patron may never imagine the complexities of the legal ownership of the center, but the buyer's lawyer must understand them thoroughly.

The buyer thus may not actually be buying the entire shopping center but, instead, may be buying those portions of the center that the seller owns, along with access and parking rights to those portions of the center that are owned by others. Typically, these access rights will be governed by recorded covenants, servitudes, easements, reciprocal easements, or even condominium plans. These documents should address a wide variety of matters, including reciprocal access and parking; responsibility for maintenance, security, and insurance; apportionment of all costs and expenses associated with the property; and various indemnity issues. They should dictate how and when these rights can be modified or terminated. They may address such matters as hours of operation and permissible uses of the property. They should clarify that these agreements benefit the buyer's tenants and the business patrons of those tenants and not just the buyer itself.

The buyer's title search will reveal these documents, and the buyer will have ample time to determine whether its portion of the center can function in concert with other owners' portions as a cohesive unit. At the contract phase, however, the buyer needs to learn of these documents and their essential terms. It accomplishes this result by requesting that the seller represent that there are no documents of this type necessary to the operation of the project as a whole or, if there are such documents, that the seller provide the buyer with copies of them and represent that there are no others.

### § 2.55—Licenses and Franchises

The seller may be operating the property in accordance with a wide range of contractual relationships that the buyer will want to continue after acquiring it. If the seller is a licensee or franchisee of a national hotel chain, the buyer will need to ensure that it can continue to use the widely recognized name. It will need uninterrupted access to the chain's computerized reservations system and will want to benefit from company-wide advertising initiatives. It will need to know that suppliers will continue to provide food, linens, and office materials to the business at a predictable and reasonable price. It will want to benefit from any discounted prices that the national chain has been able to negotiate because of the large volume of its purchases. It will need to determine the duration of the license or franchise agreement and the terms on which it can be extended.

At this point, the buyer should ask that the seller represent that it is a party to all agreements necessary to the continued operation of the business in its current form, each of which should be listed in the contract. The buyer also needs a representation from the seller that these agreements are transferable and a listing of the steps that the parties must take to effect this transfer. Most likely, the parties already will have contacted the licensor or franchisor and begun negotiations with that party, but the buyer also needs the seller's representations in the contract.

### § 2.56—Caution: Franchisor's Approval

If the buyer is purchasing a franchise such as a fast-food restaurant or hotel, it is absolutely essential that the buyer also include a closing condition that the franchisor's approval be obtained.

### § 2.57—Trademarks; Copyrights; Visual Artists' Rights

The buyer often needs or wants to acquire personal property that is protected by federal or state intellectual property laws. The building may be known and commonly recognized by a name that is a registered trademark of the owner, one of its tenants, or a former owner. The structure may display an unusual architectural feature that has been copyrighted by its designer.[57] An artist who created a mural or sculpture at the premises may enjoy protection for her work under the Visual Artists' Rights Act.[58] The buyer may want to continue to use the building's current name, modify its architectural features in the future, and relocate or remove art that is attached to the building. There is an obvious potential for conflict between the buyer and the holders of intellectual property rights.

The new owner of a building already bearing a name that is also a trademark probably can continue using the name as a non-confusing nominative fair use.[59] Many of the other problems can be avoided by the prudent seller long before it ever contemplates a sale of the property. The architect and owner typically allocate their intellectual property rights when the architect signs a design services contract at the time the building is developed, and federal copyright law allows building owners to modify or destroy architectural works without the consent of the copyright owner.[60] Artists and owners should consider artists' rights at the time the owner commissions any work at the property, and the owner should consider asking the artist to waive its visual rights.[61] Once these parties divide up their rights, the owner will then be in a position to transfer the rights it controls to its successor or to tell its successor that it is not in a position to transfer those rights.

The buyer needs to learn early on if any third parties hold any of these intellectual property rights. It can initially make this determination by asking the seller to represent that it owns or controls all of these intellectual property rights, which should be specifically listed in the representation, subject to any enumerated exceptions. The seller should also represent that it has the legal right to transfer these intellectual property rights to the buyer and should covenant that it will do so at the closing. If the seller is unable to make any of these statements, the buyer needs to learn of this problem at the outset so that it can contact the holders of these rights and decide how to proceed.

### § 2.58—Insurance

Once the parties execute the contract, certain attributes of title may be said to pass from the seller to the buyer even before the execution and delivery of the deed. While state law varies on this point, some states have adopted the principle of *equitable conversion*, by which title is deemed to pass to the buyer in all but the legal sense when the parties execute the contract. Under this equitable principle, the buyer enjoys many of the rights of a legal owner. States that have not adopted this principle in full nonetheless may conclude that the buyer possesses some of the rights of ownership as soon as it signs the contract.

With these rights come responsibilities. The buyer that enjoys equitable title may also bear the risk of loss should any structures on the property be damaged or destroyed by fire or other casualty. In the event of an uninsured casualty, the buyer may be required to close, pay the contract price, and accept the damaged or destroyed structure. Therefore, it is essential that the buyer secure casualty insurance on the property or require the seller to do so on its behalf.

---

*Comment:* In many instances, the buyer will not secure its own casualty insurance but will depend on the seller to have its existing policy endorsed to name the buyer as a loss payee. If this is the case, the buyer should insist on receiving an insurance certificate that evidences the buyer's loss payee rights.

---

The principle of equitable conversion varies greatly from state to state. However, equitable conversion is only a default rule. Whatever state law is on this point, the seller and the buyer can reach their own contractual agreements as to who bears the risk of loss, who must insure the property between the date of the contract and the date of the closing, and who will receive any insurance proceeds. In the typical case, the seller will bear this risk and will insure the property for the benefit of the buyer, notwithstanding the equitable conversion default rule. This convention makes sense, because the seller is already insuring the property and the buyer may not have had time to investigate insurance matters.

If the parties decide that the seller will bear the risk of loss, or if they decide that the buyer will bear this risk but that the seller will continue to insure the property until the closing for the benefit of the buyer, then the buyer should insist on a representation and a covenant that address this issue. If the property is located in an area that is particularly prone to unusual casualties, such as floods or earthquakes, or if the structure is an iconic one that is disproportionately likely to be a target of terrorism, the buyer should be sure that the representation addresses these risks specifically.

### § 2.59—Casualty

The buyer should request that the seller represent that there have been no unrepaired casualty losses at the property as of the contract date. If there have been any casualty losses, the seller will need to list these as exceptions to this representation. Once the buyer is aware of these specific problems, the parties then can address the questions of who is responsible for correcting these problems and who must pay. The parties may agree that the seller must make these repairs before the closing, or they may decide that the buyer will accept the property in its damaged state and will receive a corresponding price reduction (perhaps taking the form of a direct payment of insurance proceeds from the seller's insurer). If the buyer planned all along to renovate or demolish the improvements at the property, the parties may even agree that no one needs to make the repairs. Whatever they decide, the parties should address this issue in the contract, and the buyer can begin to gather the information it needs by asking for a representation. Casualty losses between the date of the contract and the date of the closing can be addressed by a covenant or a closing condition.[62]

If there is an insurance claim pending that will not be resolved before the closing, the parties need to factor the value of this claim into the purchase price or resolve this uncertainty in some other way. The buyer should insist that the seller cooperate in any post-closing settlement of the claim, as the seller probably possesses factual information that the buyer and insurer will need later on.

### § 2.60—Condemnation

The possibility that a government body will condemn some or all of the property raises many of the same issues discussed in the preceding sections in connection with casualty losses. Just as the seller may lose part of its building to a fire and may need insurance proceeds to rebuild, the seller also may lose part of its parking lot to a road-widening project and may need the condemnation award to expand its lot on the other side. Condemnation issues, like casualty issues, need to be addressed in the contract, including in the seller's representations. If there are no imminent condemnations, the seller's representations should state that there are no pending or, to the best of the seller's knowledge, threatened condemnation actions. If there are condemnations pending or threatened, the seller's representations should provide a listing and description of these actions.

There are some significant differences between casualty losses and condemnation losses. First, casualties occur with little or no warning, while the condemnation process is much slower and allows owners a greater opportunity to plan and adapt. Thus, the condemnation representation should address pending or threatened acts and not just completed events. The seller cannot represent that there are no pending fires (one hopes!) but should be able to inform the buyer whether there are pending condemnation actions.

Condemnations are also more likely to render the property useless than casualties are. If the property is destroyed by fire, it can usually be rebuilt. It may be inconvenient or more expensive than the parties anticipated, but, typically, it will not be impossible.[63]

In contrast, if the government takes the entire property or a large portion of it, reconstruction may not be a possibility. Even the condemnation of a smaller portion of the property may render reconstruction impracticable by forcing the building out of compliance with parking, open space, or other land use regulations. In some ways, the seller's condemnation representation may be even more important to the buyer than the seller's casualty representation.

### § 2.61—Real Property Taxes and Assessments

As part of its calculation of the value of the real estate, the buyer needs to know the amount and frequency of all real property tax and assessment payments. The buyer is trying to determine whether the property will be profitable to operate, and it needs information about these large monetary obligations to make this judgment. The buyer also needs to verify that all payments are current. These matters are easy for the buyer to investigate during the course of its normal title search, but until the buyer undertakes that search, it must rely on the seller's representations as to these matters.

The seller may be willing to provide a representation that states the amounts of all real property taxes and assessments, that lists the amounts of these payments for the last several years, and that confirms that all payments that are currently due have been made. The seller also should represent that there are no pending changes, such as reassessment proceedings or new assessments, or, if there are any such changes pending, the status of those changes, because these matters may be difficult for the buyer to discover on its own. This last matter is of particular concern if any of the improvements at the property are new or have been renovated recently, or if the property has just been subdivided, because these actions typically trigger reassessments.

The buyer should determine what the tax year is and whether payments are made in advance or in arrears. To the extent that there are any ongoing tax disputes, such as contested reassessments or disagreements as to amounts due, the seller should provide information about them. If the possibility exists that the buyer may become liable after the closing for amounts that the seller should have paid already, including arrearages that might result from the outcome of any of these disputes, then the parties will need to arrange to have the seller place the approximate amounts of these arrearages in escrow until all disputes are resolved.

### § 2.62—No Prior Mortgages

For many of the reasons just noted in connection with real property taxes and assessments, the buyer needs some assurance that there are no mortgages encumbering the property. Often, there will be mortgages encumbering the property at the time the contract is signed, and the seller will be unable to give a representation to this effect without including exceptions. In these situations, the seller should represent that there are no mortgages on the property other than those specifically listed and should covenant to satisfy those outstanding mortgages on or before the closing. The reason that the parties usually agree to this structure is simple: the seller will not have the funds to satisfy existing mortgages until it receives the sale proceeds from the buyer at the closing, and it will concurrently transmit some of those funds to its lenders in satisfaction of these mortgages.[64]

The seller also needs to verify that satisfaction of these mortgages will not lead to the imposition of any prepayment fees. If a lender may impose such a fee, the contract should specify which party is responsible for paying it. The seller most commonly pays prepayment fees.[65]

If the parties have agreed that the buyer will assume existing financing,[66] will purchase the property subject to existing financing,[67] or will receive financing from the seller,[68] then this representation will need to be modified accordingly. The seller will list all existing mortgages as exceptions to its "no mortgages" representation. It will also list any of these mortgages that are to remain on the property as exceptions to its covenant to deliver marketable title. These exceptions should be reflected in the section of the contract that states the method of paying the sale price and in the closing conditions.[69]

### § 2.63—No Other Liens

Just as the buyer does not wish to acquire the property subject to a lien for unpaid taxes or, in most cases, subject to existing mortgage financing, the buyer also probably does not wish to purchase the property subject to other liens. The buyer wants the seller to deliver marketable title free and clear of any liens and encumbrances and thus should ask that the seller represent that there are no other liens on the property.

There could be qualifications to this statement, and the parties may agree on a list of "Permitted Exceptions." For example, covenants, easements, and servitudes all constitute clouds on title that are sufficient to render it unmarketable, but the buyer may be willing to purchase the property subject to these matters—in fact, the buyer may insist on them.[70] As long as the buyer is aware of any liens and agrees to accept them, it cannot object to the seller listing these liens as exceptions to its blanket representation that there are no liens on the property. There should be no exceptions other than those the parties have agreed to, however, and this is the buyer's chance to avoid due diligence surprises.

The buyer may be aware of a lien but may lack sufficient information to decide whether the lien is acceptable. If this is the case, then the seller should include the lien as an exception to its blanket representation, and the buyer should make sure that satisfactory resolution of the matter is addressed in the closing conditions.

Mechanics' liens pose a particular problem. Mechanics may file liens against the property for a fixed amount of time after they complete their work, and these liens often relate back to an earlier date for purposes of determining their priority under state recording statutes. Thus, a seller could accurately state as of the contract date that there are no prior liens, and the buyer later might discover that a lien filed after the execution of the contract or even after the closing relates back to a date before the contract. While mechanics' liens will be addressed in more detail later,[71] the buyer should be careful that the representation discussed here is broad enough to address this problem. To accomplish this, the representation should state that there are no mechanics' liens filed and no unpaid mechanics who have an unexpired right to file a mechanics' lien in the future. The possibility of mechanics' liens is of particular concern to the party that is buying a newly constructed or recently renovated building.

## §2.64 Buyer's Representations, Warranties, and Covenants

The sections devoted to representations, warranties, covenants, and indemnities have focused so far on statements that the seller makes in the contract. These statements provide information to the buyer and allow the buyer to determine whether it wants to execute the contract. Once the parties sign the contract, the buyer will continue its due diligence so that it can determine whether it wishes to close and whether any nonperformance by the buyer is excused by the seller's failure to satisfy a closing condition.

In similar fashion, the buyer also makes representations in the contract, as a way of disclosing essential information to the seller. Just as the buyer uses the contract to learn about the seller, the seller also will use this document to gather important information about the buyer.

The contract is not always as reciprocal as the preceding paragraphs may make it seem, however, because the buyer and the seller are in different positions. The buyer is acquiring a complex asset—land that often is improved with physical structures—and uses the contract to learn as much as it can about this complicated asset. The seller almost certainly knows a great deal more about the property than the buyer does, and the buyer employs this document as a way of forcing the seller to disclose some of what it knows. In contrast, the buyer's contractual performance is much simpler. In the typical transaction, the buyer's only significant obligation is to show up at the closing with good funds, and there is little for the seller to investigate. Accordingly, the representations that the seller seeks from the buyer are far fewer and far less extensive, focusing primarily on the buyer's legal existence and its ability to perform its one principal obligation: the payment of the purchase price.[72]

### §2.65—Due Organization of Buyer

If the party that signs the contract as buyer purports to be a business entity such as a corporation, partnership, or limited liability entity, then the seller should confirm that this is the case. The language of the buyer's "due organization" representation should track the format of the corresponding representation provided by the seller.[73]

If the entity signing as the buyer represents that it has legal existence when in fact it does not, the seller could have difficulty enforcing the contract. However, the seller probably has the right to retain the earnest money that it (or an escrow agent) is holding. Even though the buyer does not validly exist, if it placed funds in escrow, then the seller may be entitled to keep those funds as liquidated damages.[74]

As noted earlier, the buyer entity may not have been formed yet at the time the contract is executed.[75] If this is the case, then an individual or an existing entity may sign the contract as the buyer's nominee, with the intention of assigning the buyer's interest to the new entity once that entity has been formed. The seller will want this information spelled out in the contract. The party that signs the contract as buyer will want to be sure that this assignment from itself to the new entity is permitted without restriction under the contract. The party that signs as buyer also is likely to want a provision that releases itself from all liabilities under the document once it has assigned its contractual rights and obligations to this new entity. After the assignment, this nominee does not wish to be any more liable to the seller than it would have been had the intended buyer existed from the outset and signed the contract in its own name.

### § 2.66—Caution: Forming Buyer Entity before Executing Contract

As noted previously, it is far wiser for the principals of the buyer to be sure that the buyer entity is formed at the time the buyer enters into the contract of sale. If the buyer entity does not yet exist, then any individual or entity that signs the contract on behalf of the entity that is to be formed risks personal liability.

### § 2.67—Authority of Buyer; No Approvals Required; No Violations of Other Agreements

The seller should ask the buyer to represent that the buyer has authorized the transaction, that no third-party approvals are required for the buyer to perform, and that performance of the agreement will not violate any other agreements to which the buyer is a party. This representation should mirror the comparable representation that the seller gives.[76] The seller's most practical remedy following a breach by the buyer may turn out to be retention of the buyer's down payment as liquidated damages.

## § 2.68 Survival of Representations, Warranties, Covenants, and Indemnities; Relationship to Due Diligence

What are the benefits of representations, warranties, covenants, and indemnities to the parties, particularly the buyer? A breach of one of these statements by the seller allows the buyer to pursue one of its contractual remedies. This section will review the doctrine of merger and will remind the drafter that he must consider the survival of any promises he manages to extract from the opposing party in the contract.

The doctrine of merger, a common law concept, has undergone some modification in recent years. In its most traditional form, the merger doctrine holds that contractual promises survive only until the seller delivers its deed to the buyer. After the closing, all contractual provisions are said to merge into the deed and be superseded by it. In other words, once the buyer accepts the deed, it has only those rights that the deed specifies.

Modern courts have a tendency to apply the merger doctrine most strictly in cases arising from title matters. For example, if the seller represents that its title is unencumbered when in fact there is a large outstanding mortgage on the property, the buyer's right to recover for breach of this representation would last only until the closing. After the closing, any right to seek recovery for losses due to any title encumbrances would arise from the deed warranties, if any, and not from the now-merged contract. The buyer already has had an adequate opportunity to investigate the state of title; to raise any objections; to sue for breach of contract; and, if the closing conditions allow, to withdraw from the transaction.[77] By accepting the deed, the buyer is implicitly agreeing to give up the benefits of any contractual representations as to the quality of title and to rely exclusively on any deed warranties for recourse against the seller.

Courts seem more willing to allow contract representations to survive the closing if those representations address matters other than title defects. For example, a court might allow a buyer's suit against the seller to proceed after the closing if that suit arises from the seller's breach of its "no litigation" representation. If the seller has stated in writing that there is no pending litigation when, in fact, there is, the court might overlook the merger doctrine and allow the buyer's suit to proceed even after the closing.

What does all this mean to the buyer? It is clearly in the buyer's interest to obtain the widest possible array of representations in the contract. Each of these representations provides the buyer with information about the seller or the property and the ability to exercise its remedies if that statement is inaccurate. After the closing, however, some of these representations will merge into the deed. Worse still, the law may be unclear as to which representations merge and which do not. The buyer faced with this uncertainty is well advised to investigate the accuracy of each of these representations before the closing. In the title example just offered, the buyer is perfectly capable of discovering the undisclosed mortgage between contract and closing and should immediately inform the seller that it is in breach of its representation. The parties then can address this problem, and if they are unable to agree, the buyer can pursue its contract remedies if it wishes. If the buyer waits until after the closing, it may be too late.

The doctrine of merger thus forces the buyer to undertake an enormous amount of due diligence between the contract and the closing. The buyer may wisely decide not to investigate these matters before the contract is signed, because it does not wish to undertake the effort and expense until the buyer is sure that the seller has committed to deliver title at an agreed price. Once the contract is executed, however, the buyer must begin its due diligence and pursue these matters vigorously, because the door may slam shut on closing day.[78]

There is another way for the parties to address these matters. They can agree that certain enumerated representations will survive the closing, thereby providing the buyer with the ongoing right to sue for a set period of time after it accepts the deed. This is particularly appropriate for those matters that are difficult to investigate and resolve during the relatively short period between contract and closing. Any survival clause of this type should specifically list the representations that survive and should clarify the period of time for which they survive.[79] By raising these issues before it signs the contract, the buyer emphasizes to the seller the importance of specific representations and extends the period during which it can investigate these matters and pursue a remedy. This solution may allow the parties to close under conditions of uncertainty rather than waiting for the buyer to complete all of its investigations. The seller also may benefit, by requesting a reciprocal statement confirming that the remaining representations do not survive beyond the closing.

More likely, the seller will resist the buyer's demands for a survival clause. Its position may be, "Do all the investigating you want between the contract and the closing, but after the closing, I never want to hear from you again." The seller may even seek a clause confirming that all representations merge into the deed at the closing.[80] From these opposing positions, one hopes that the parties can reach some resolution of their differences. If the contract is silent, then both parties will have to wonder about the extent to which the court will apply the unsettled merger doctrine to the promises in question.

*Comment*: If a buyer is aware before closing that a representation is untrue, closes anyway, and then seeks to enforce the provision under the survivorship clause, a court may hold that the buyer has waived its claim under the representation.

### § 2.69—Caution: Survival Clause

A survival clause is only as valuable to the buyer as the credit of the seller. If the seller plans to distribute the sale proceeds to its equity holders and dissolve, then a survival clause has no practical benefit to the buyer. In these circumstances, the buyer may ask the seller to leave some portion of the sales proceeds in escrow or to provide some other type of security for payment of any claims arising from the surviving representations and warranties.

The survival issue may be most important with regard to representations and warranties addressing environmental matters, because the buyer may inherit responsibility for remediating environmental problems upon closing.

### § 2.70—Technique: Survival Clause

Even if the seller agrees that certain representations will survive the closing, the seller should provide that any suit against it must be brought within a prescribed period of time, such as six months or one year after the closing.

## § 2.71 Conditions Precedent to Buyer's Obligation to Close

The preceding discussions of representations, warranties, covenants, and indemnities, and of due diligence, merger, and contract survival, lead directly to an examination of conditions precedent to closing. The buyer quite likely will use these earlier sections of the contract to obtain information about the property and to give itself the right to damages in the event of breach. At least as important, however, is the buyer's concern that it not be forced to acquire property that does not live up to its contractual billing or that cannot be developed or used for its intended purpose. In many cases, the buyer would rather terminate the contract than seek damages for breach of a representation. For this reason, the buyer should seek an appropriate array of closing conditions that must be met before the buyer is obligated to deliver the purchase price and accept the deed. If these conditions are not met, then the buyer will have the contractual right to terminate the contract and receive a refund of its down payment. A given closing condition may last until the closing, but, in many cases, the parties will agree that the buyer must exercise its right to terminate the contract during a study period that ends on a specified date before the closing, as discussed later.

As a starting point, these conditions precedent should track the seller's representations, warranties, covenants, and indemnities. If the seller has represented that it owns fee simple title to the property without encumbrances, then it also should be a condition precedent to the buyer's obligation to close that the seller meet this title standard. In many cases, however, the conditions precedent will extend beyond the seller's representations. The seller may be reluctant to make a representation that would give the buyer the right to damages if it proves to be inaccurate, but may be more willing to allow the buyer to terminate the contract without penalty if the statement is untrue. For example, if the seller is uncertain about the quality of its own title or the zoning of the property, it may refuse to provide any representations as to title or zoning and instead may suggest that the buyer undertake its own investigation and decide for itself. This seller may not be in a position to offer title or zoning representations and should not do so, but it is willing to offer closing conditions that address these matters.

> *Comment:* Sellers are reluctant to provide representations, warranties, or covenants addressing matters over which they have little or no control, such as rezonings, subdivision approval, approval of entrances and exits, and provision of traffic signals. These are appropriate subjects for closing conditions.

The list of closing conditions in the contract also helps the buyer begin to construct its closing checklist.[81] The buyer's counsel will want to prepare a detailed checklist of matters to be addressed after the execution of the contract and before the closing, and each of the closing conditions set forth in the contract should appear on that list. Before closing, the buyer will want to confirm that all of these conditions have been met. While the buyer may be willing to waive some of these conditions at the closing if they have not been met, it surely does not wish to do so unknowingly.

*Comment:* What happens if the parties do not agree whether a condition has been met? Who finally decides whether the condition has been satisfied, and by what standard? The ultimate answer, if the parties cannot agree, is that a court may have to decide. If the contract does not state what standard applies, the court likely will employ the familiar tort law standard of what is "reasonable" or "commercially reasonable." Unless the contract specifically allows the benefited party to decide, in its subjective discretion, whether a condition has been met, a benefited party that arbitrarily refuses to perform and that argues—perhaps pretextually—that a condition precedent has not been met risks being found liable for breach of contract. Parties usually do not agree to a subjective standard of this type because of the obvious potential for abuse.

## §2.72—Review Period

In many cases, one or more of the closing conditions in a contract of sale will not remain open until the closing date, because the seller does not want to take its property off the market for a substantial period of time without knowing that the buyer is committed to close. A contract of sale will often provide for some closing conditions to be satisfied or waived within a defined shorter period of time running from the date of the contract, commonly referred to as the "review period," "study period," or "due diligence period." By the end of this period, the buyer must notify the seller whether the pertinent conditions have been satisfied. The contract of sale should clarify what happens if the buyer fails to notify the seller either way, typically by deeming the conditions to have been satisfied if the buyer does not give the seller notice to the contrary within the specified time. The seller's representations and any remaining closing conditions continue to apply from the end of the review period to the closing date. The buyer should also ensure that the contract contains language protecting the buyer against any adverse changes that occur after the review period expires.

## §2.73—Continuing Accuracy of Seller's Representations and Warranties; Performance of Covenants

The first closing condition that the buyer should request is one that confirms that all representations and warranties are accurate as of the closing date and not just as of the contract date. The fact that a statement was true when the seller signed the contract does not necessarily mean that it will remain true as of the closing date weeks or months later, and the buyer will want the continuing accuracy of the representations and warranties to be a condition precedent to its obligation to perform at the closing. The seller may have represented accurately that certain enumerated tenants occupy space under leases and pay monthly rents that are listed in the contract. If an anchor tenant later were to close its doors unexpectedly, the seller would not be in breach of its representation, which was accurate when made. The buyer, however, needs the right not to close under the contract or, perhaps, to renegotiate the sale price to reflect this devaluation of the property. It obtains this leverage by ensuring that the continued accuracy of this major representation is a condition precedent to its own obligation to close.

---

*Comment*: If any representation becomes untrue before the closing, the seller should be required to specify what has changed.

---

The seller is likely to respond that the buyer needs the ability to terminate the contract only with respect to some of the seller's representations. The buyer may agree and might acknowledge that some of the representations are more critical to its investment than others. The parties may decide to make the continued accuracy of only the more important representations into closing conditions. Of course, if they agree to a division of this type, the closing condition section needs to identify precisely which representations must be accurate as of the closing date. The parties also are likely to agree that only material adverse changes give the buyer the right to terminate the contract. The buyer should not be permitted to withdraw from the purchase of a multimillion-dollar shopping center solely because of an inconsequential change after the contract was signed.

The same reasoning applies to the seller's performance of its warranties and covenants. Perhaps the shopping center was mostly vacant when the parties began negotiating the contract, but the seller was well along in negotiations with several high-quality tenants. The buyer may be less concerned with the occupancy of the center as of the contract date and more concerned that these negotiations lead to signed leases by the closing. This concern may have led the buyer to ask the seller to covenant that the structure will be at least 80 percent occupied by rent-paying tenants on the day of the closing. This covenant may be fairly specific. For example, it might state that these tenants must have committed to remain in place for at least five years at a specified minimum monthly rental. In this instance, the buyer is not relying on the seller's representation as to the state of the property on the contract date and is depending instead on the seller's promise to deliver the property in a certain state on the closing date. The buyer must be sure to request a closing condition that mirrors this covenant and that allows it to terminate the contract if the seller fails to meet this contractual obligation.

Even if the buyer receives a long list of closing conditions that parallel the seller's representations, warranties, covenants, and indemnities, the buyer remains free to waive any of these conditions at the closing. If the seller has met all of the major closing conditions and most of the minor ones, the buyer may feel comfortable that it is receiving what it bargained for and may be content accepting property in a condition that does not conform exactly to that described in the contract. That is up to the buyer, but the buyer's counsel must remind the client that once the buyer waives these conditions, it cannot resurrect them. An unmet closing condition gives the buyer the right not to close, but after the closing, that right is worthless. To the extent that this closing condition reflects one of the seller's representations, the buyer may retain a contract claim on this representation, but claims on representations may merge into the contract at the time of the closing.[82] If the seller has not met one of its closing conditions on the closing date, the buyer may have to choose between rejecting the property or accepting it and forever waiving any objection. Even if a representation does survive, the buyer's only recourse after the closing is to bring a contract claim.

One possible compromise if a condition has not been met is for the parties to agree to a contract amendment that addresses the corresponding representation, warranty, or covenant. This amendment might specify that the seller's corresponding obligation will survive for a fixed period of time after the closing and enumerate remedies that the buyer may pursue. If the seller covenanted to deliver a shopping center that is 80 percent occupied but can deliver a center that is only 78 percent occupied, the parties may agree that the parties will place a portion of the sales proceeds in escrow and that the buyer may retain this amount if it is unable to execute leases that bring the center into conformity with the covenant in the next sixty days. This compromise allows the closing to occur on schedule, provides the seller with its full consideration if the buyer can bring the property into conformity with the covenant shortly after the closing, and provides the buyer with a price discount if it accepts property that fails to meet the contractual standard within the agreed time.

Note that this "continuing accuracy" closing condition is only as valuable to the buyer as the representation it mirrors. If the seller represents broadly that the property is in excellent physical condition and is suitable for the buyer's intended purpose, then a closing condition to this effect is of great value to the buyer, and the buyer can back out of the sale if its own investigation proves that the representation is inaccurate. If the seller merely agrees to allow the buyer access to the property to undertake its own physical inspection, then a parallel closing condition does not provide the buyer with much benefit at all. The seller meets the closing condition by providing the buyer with access, and the buyer has no choice but to close no matter what the inspection reveals. In this second case, the buyer does not just need access to the property, it also needs the right to withdraw from the contract if the inspection discloses problems. The less the seller's representation divulges about the property, the more important it is for the buyer to include a detailed closing condition that will allow it the flexibility to terminate the contract if the property does not meet the buyer's expectations. Many of the sections that follow will describe how the buyer can accomplish this goal.

### §2.74—Caution: Continuing Accuracy of Seller's Representations and Warranties

As stated previously, a seller should be reluctant to give a representation as to the continuing accuracy of other representations.[83] A representation of this type requires the seller to predict the future accurately. For example, a seller may safely represent that no condemnation proceeding has been filed as of the date of the contract. The seller should not, however, offer a representation that this statement will continue to remain accurate through the closing, because if a condemnation proceeding commences after the contract and before the closing, the seller will be in breach. If the seller provides the first of these two representations, it can agree that the continuing accuracy of this representation is a condition precedent to the buyer's obligation to close. This approach should protect the seller from contract damages while allowing the buyer to withdraw from the transaction without penalty if there is a material change.

### § 2.75—Buyer's Access to the Property during Due Diligence Period

If the buyer is to meet its due diligence responsibilities, it will need access to the property during the contract period for itself and its employees and agents. The buyer must examine the property to verify physical and financial information that the seller has provided and may want to speak with individual tenants. Agents such as surveyors, engineers, and appraisers will need to undertake their own investigations on the site. Lenders, real estate agents, and potential future tenants all may wish to visit the property. The seller should agree to provide these parties with access to the property, and the buyer should be permitted to terminate the contract if the seller fails to do so.

The buyer must recognize that the seller probably will continue to operate the property as a going concern during the contract period and may want to restrict this access, limiting the buyer to certain hours and reasonable amounts of time, with some advance notice required. The parties are free to negotiate the contours of this access in a mutually acceptable way. For example, it might be perfectly reasonable for the seller to limit access to its office and books to its regular business hours but equally unreasonable to limit access by surveyors and contractors to these same hours. The parties should specify what they mean by "reasonable access" but should clarify that the buyer and its representatives are entitled to this access. The buyer should also agree to repair any damage it causes to the property, to indemnify the seller against any losses arising from the acts of the buyer or its representatives while on the property, and to carry insurance against these risks.

### § 2.76—Financing

Most buyers will need third-party financing to close the sale. Even those buyers that do have sufficient funds available are unlikely to want to use those funds to pay cash for the property because of the significant tax and leverage benefits of borrowing. The buyer should insist that the availability of these funds is a condition precedent to its obligation to close. If it fails to include this closing condition in the contract and then is unable to borrow the funds in time, it will forfeit its down payment or be liable for contract damages.[84] Note, however, that some sellers may be reluctant to agree to financing conditions. In these cases, the buyer must determine before it signs the contract whether financing will be available.

The financing condition must be drafted with great specificity. The buyer should avoid including a financing condition that simply says that the buyer must close if it can obtain a loan after reasonable application. Virtually anyone can "obtain a loan" at an exorbitant interest rate, and the buyer does not want to be in the position of having to close if it receives a loan on disadvantageous terms. The buyer does not just need a loan, it needs an acceptable loan, and would prefer a condition that allows it to reject any financing that it finds unacceptable in its sole discretion. The seller will object to a provision that is this flexible, however, because it allows the buyer to back out of the deal too easily. What the buyer needs, and what the seller may be willing to agree to, is a closing condition that states that the buyer is not obligated to close unless it obtains a loan from an institutional lender of at least a minimum stated amount, amortized over no less than a specified minimum term, at an interest rate not in excess of an agreed amount. By detailing the parameters of the minimum acceptable loan, the buyer allows itself the right to terminate the contract unless it is able to secure funds on satisfactory terms. The seller may have little theoretical objection to a detailed provision of this type but will want to negotiate exactly what the minimum acceptable terms are.

> *Comment:* In some jurisdictions, the law requires that the terms of the required financing be set forth in the contract. A clause that simply permits the buyer to obtain financing on terms acceptable to the buyer in its sole discretion may not be specific enough to bind the parties.

The seller may be concerned that the buyer can use the failure to meet the financing condition as an excuse to back out of the contract later on if it changes its mind or decides that it can get a better deal on the property. For this reason, the seller needs to ensure that the buyer takes all steps necessary to pursue a loan. The buyer should be allowed to terminate the contract if the loan is denied on its merits but not if the loan is denied because the buyer failed to complete its application or furnish the lender with the documents the lender needed to make its decision. The contract often includes language that requires the buyer to apply to a minimum number of lenders set forth in the contract, to supply those lenders with all the information they need to make their decisions, and to keep the seller informed of the progress of the loan applications.

In most cases, lenders that are willing to lend will issue loan commitments based on these applications. These commitments may issue several weeks before the closing and are likely to contain numerous closing conditions of their own. These loan commitment conditions typically mirror the contract conditions discussed here, because the lender is as concerned as the buyer with issues of incorporation, authority, title, access, utilities, and tenant occupancy.[85] The fact that the lender issues a conditional commitment presents problems for both the buyer and the seller. The buyer will worry that despite making a commitment, the lender later will refuse to fund, either because it breaches its commitment or because it claims that the buyer has failed to meet one of the closing conditions in the loan commitment. The seller will worry that the buyer might intentionally fail to meet one of these loan closing conditions so that it then can claim the right to terminate the contract of sale without penalty because of its inability to meet the financing condition.

The buyer is right to be concerned that the lender's commitment is not sufficiently binding. Lenders often draft their commitments with lengthy lists of contingencies that give them the right to refuse to fund the loan without penalty. The buyer may worry that after it receives a commitment and informs the seller of this fact, the lender then will refuse to fund on the closing date, leaving the buyer in breach of the contract. For this reason, the buyer would be wise to insist that the actual receipt of the borrowed funds, and not just the receipt of a commitment from the lender, is necessary before this closing condition has been met.

The seller is likely to object to structuring the financing condition in this way. It will argue that the condition should be deemed met once a lender commits to providing a loan that conforms to the contractual criteria and that any subsequent failure of the lender to deliver these funds is due either to the lender's breach (for which the buyer should have remedies under the loan commitment) or to the buyer's failure to meet one of the conditions in the loan commitment. The seller will also want to know as early as possible whether the deal is going to fall through and would prefer advance notice that funds are unavailable to a cancellation on the closing date. It will argue that the closing condition should include an outside date by which the buyer must cancel because of the unavailability of funds. After this date, the condition is deemed to have been met whether or not a lender actually funds the loan.

The buyer's ability to attain its goal here may depend in large part on the strength of its overall bargaining position. If the buyer cannot convince the seller to agree to the language the buyer wants, then it must pursue its loan application vigorously, attempt to receive a commitment that is as unqualified as possible, and be sure to cancel by the deadline if it decides that the condition will not be met. If the buyer does receive the language it wants, then the seller must be sure that the buyer does not use this closing condition as an escape hatch if the buyer decides to back out of its contractual obligations for other reasons. There is no right or wrong answer to this question, but the parties should be sure to address these issues in their contract.

*Comment:* Depending on market conditions, funds might be readily available at reasonable rates. If this is the case, the seller may be more inclined to reject the buyer's request for a financing condition, and the buyer may be more inclined to accept the contract anyway. The buyer may even offer a contract without this language in the hope that the offer will be more attractive to the seller.

### § 2.77—Caution: Financing Condition

One of the problems with financing conditions, as just described, is that the condition is often deemed to be satisfied on the basis of the buyer's receipt of a loan commitment during the due diligence period and not by receipt of the actual funds at the closing. If the closing does not occur, it is most commonly because of some improper action or inaction by the borrower. During the savings and loan crisis, however, many loans failed to close because of the inability of the lender to fund the loan. In these cases, the buyer often found itself in default: the commitment satisfied the contractual condition, the lender then breached its commitment, and the buyer's only recourse was against an insolvent lender. As the subprime mortgage crisis develops, this situation may recur, and it may be exacerbated by the inability of lenders to sell their loans in the secondary market.

### § 2.78—Authority of Seller

This chapter already has discussed the buyer's need for representations that the seller is properly organized under state law, that the seller has the authority to enter into the transaction, that the transaction does not require any third-party approvals, and that the transaction does not violate any other agreements to which the seller is a party.[86] If these statements by the seller are not accurate as of the contract date, then the seller breaches the contract when it signs it, and the buyer may pursue its contractual remedies.[87]

The buyer should confirm that the seller has taken all necessary entity action and should make the seller's delivery of certain corroborating documents a condition precedent to the buyer's closing obligations. More specifically, the buyer should insist that the seller provide it with a good standing certificate from the secretary of state of the jurisdiction in which the seller entity is formed; proof that the seller may legally transact business in the state in which the property is located; a corporate or partnership authorization from the seller entity; an incumbency certificate from this entity, listing the parties who are authorized to sign on its behalf; and confirmation that the seller's performance does not require any third-party approvals and does not violate any other agreements to which the seller is a party. The buyer also may seek an opinion from the seller's counsel that confirms these matters. Chapter 3 discusses these deliveries in more detail as part of its discussion of the buyer's due diligence responsibilities.[88] It is important at the contract stage for the buyer to remember to include a closing condition that will allow the buyer to withdraw from the transaction if the seller fails to deliver these documents before the closing.

### § 2.79—Condition of Property and Improvements

The prudent buyer will seek a representation from the seller that addresses the condition of the property as of the contract date[89] and also a closing condition that all representations remain true and accurate as of the closing date.[90] This representation should apply to significant personal property as well as to the real property and improvements. If the seller's representation provides detailed information about the physical condition of the property and sets forth the minimum acceptable quality of the property, then these two provisions may be sufficient to give the buyer what it needs: the right to back out, sue the seller, or both, if the property fails to meet the stated standard.

The seller may be reluctant to provide the buyer with a detailed representation concerning the condition of the property, particularly if the buyer wants this representation to satisfy its concerns about the suitability of the property for a specific purpose. Even if the seller is unwilling to tell the buyer that the property is perfect for the buyer's needs, it may be entirely comfortable allowing the buyer to make that judgment for itself. The seller can achieve this outcome by covenanting that it will provide the buyer with reasonable access to the property during the contract period or during a shorter study period so that the buyer can undertake its own investigation of the property and its suitability.

The buyer may prefer this resolution, because it allows the buyer to rely on its own examination of the property and not just on the seller's contractual statements. This solution is valuable to the buyer, however, only if it provides the buyer with the right to terminate the contract without penalty if the property does not meet some standard established in the contract.

Each party should have concerns about this contractual standard. The seller fears that if the standard is expressed in loose terms, then the buyer will use it as a free pass to escape from the contract later on. The seller may reject the inclusion of a closing condition that allows the buyer to opt out of the closing if the buyer finds the property unacceptable in its own judgment. Conversely, the buyer may be reluctant to agree to a more objective contractual standard because of its concern that it cannot know what the problems with the property are until it sees for itself. Any attempt by the seller to draft a specific listing of reasons for which the buyer may choose not to close is likely to meet with resistance from the buyer.

If the buyer is concerned about physical problems with the property, there are several ways in which the parties might draft contractual provisions that can help resolve these worries. The parties may agree that the buyer will have a specified number of days to examine the property and then will provide the seller with a detailed list of repairs that the seller must make before the closing. The parties may decide that the buyer will receive a credit against the purchase price so that it can make these repairs on its own after the closing. The seller may demand that the buyer accept any nonconformities up to a stated dollar limit, with the seller agreeing to make the repairs, to reduce the purchase price, or to terminate the contract if the cost of the repairs exceeds this limit.

It is more difficult for the contract to address questions about the suitability of the property for the buyer's purpose, because those questions are inherently more subjective. If the buyer is purchasing unimproved land on which it plans to construct an office building, it may not know for sure whether the construction is feasible until it hires geologists to assess subsurface conditions. The seller, fearing that the buyer is looking for a contract that binds the seller but not the buyer, may demand that the buyer undertake its investigation before signing the contract or during a short post-contract study period, or it may insist that the buyer purchase an option on the property for a fixed time period. If the parties can agree to a specific closing condition in objective terms, then they have resolved this problem. The seller will covenant to allow the buyer to inspect the property, and the buyer will have the ability to withdraw from the contract if the property fails to meet this objective standard. If the parties cannot agree on a reasonably specific closing condition, then either one party will have to assume this risk, or the parties should consider using the alternatives just described.

### §2.80—Delivery of Deed

One of the most obvious conditions precedent to the buyer's obligation to perform is the seller's delivery of a deed to the property. This closing condition should clarify the type of deed that the seller must deliver—general warranty, special warranty, or quitclaim—so that there is no dispute at the closing as to the post-closing liability that the seller will retain under the deed.[91] The parties often will resolve this issue by following local custom.

> Comment: Broadly speaking, the seller that delivers a *general warranty deed* warrants that that there are no title encumbrances, whether or not those encumbrances predate the seller's acquisition of the property. Thus, by delivering a general warranty deed, the seller may become liable for the actions of prior owners. By contrast, the seller that delivers a *special warranty deed* warrants only that it has not encumbered the property. *Quitclaim deeds* contain no warranties at all.

The buyer should recognize that parties other than itself will care about the quality of title that it receives from the seller. Even if it is willing to take a risk on a quitclaim deed, third parties ranging from title insurers to mortgage loan participants may be less comfortable with this risk. The buyer needs to consider the interests of these other parties before it agrees to accept a deed of a lesser quality.

Even if the seller agrees to deliver a general warranty deed or special warranty deed, the parties may agree that this deed will be delivered subject to specifically enumerated exceptions. If existing financing will remain in place, the seller should not deliver a warranty deed without exceptions, and the buyer must recognize that the prior mortgage will constitute an exception to the more general deed warranties. That exception should be stated in both the contract and the deed. Documents such as covenants, servitudes, easements, and tenant leases also constitute encumbrances on title, and they need to be listed as exceptions to the deed warranties. While the buyer's actual or constructive knowledge of these matters may be sufficient to undercut any argument it later may make that these encumbrances violate the deed warranties, it is wiser for the seller to list the specific exceptions to the more comprehensive warranties in both the contract and the deed. Once again, the lawyer should be aware of local law and custom with respect to these matters.

*Comment:* From the seller's perspective, it is important for the deed to contain language that expressly excludes "matters of record" from the scope of the warranties. In the absence of this language, the existence of any recorded instrument that encumbers title, such as an easement or a memorandum of lease, will be a technical breach of the warranty.

### § 2.81—Caution: Types of Deed Warranties

Note that the statutory and common law meanings of the terms "general warranty" and "special warranty" vary from state to state and that some states use deeds with different names altogether. In some states, a general warranty deed warrants title from the beginning of time, while in other states the term may provide a less expansive warranty. The lawyer must be familiar with the law of the jurisdiction in which the property is located in order to interpret these designations.

### § 2.82—Title Insurance Policy

While deed warranties provide the buyer with some confidence in the quality of the seller's title and some recourse if there are title problems, most buyers want more protection than just this. Litigation costs may be substantial if title problems arise later on, and the seller may no longer exist or may be unable to pay a judgment. Most buyers want the additional comfort provided by an owner's policy of title insurance and are wise to obtain one. The buyer should insist that its receipt of a title policy be a condition precedent to its obligation to close.

From the buyer's perspective, a requirement that it receive a title policy is necessary but not sufficient to provide it with the level of assurance that it needs. The buyer does not just need a policy of title insurance, it needs a policy that provides it with a certain level of protection. Just as the contract's financing condition should specify the minimum acceptable terms of the loan that the buyer must be able to obtain,[92] the title insurance condition should describe the attributes of the minimum acceptable title policy.

The closing condition should state the amount of title insurance that must be available to the buyer (typically the amount of the purchase price) and also should clarify which party will be paying for this insurance (ordinarily the buyer). The buyer may want to specify that the policy must be issued by a specific company with which it has a good relationship or by a company selected from a list of acceptable insurers. The buyer also may want to state that title must be insurable at regular rates, to avoid the problem of title that is technically insurable but sufficiently risky that the insurer is charging an unusually high premium.

This closing condition also should specify the form of policy that the buyer is to receive. Ordinarily, the parties will agree that the buyer must receive the American Land Title Association (ALTA) Owner's Form, 2006 edition, although other forms still may be used in certain states during the transition period following the introduction of the new forms. Lawyers who represent buyers should become familiar with this standard form, which is several pages long and contains a lengthy list of matters that are excepted from coverage. Buyers willing to accept this form will often insist that the title insurance company remove certain of these standard exceptions upon receipt of assurances that the problems described in these exceptions do not exist or have been addressed in a satisfactory manner.[93]

Schedule B of the ALTA form, which is where the insurer lists each of the title encumbrances that it discovers during its title search, will be discussed in greater detail in the context of the buyer's due diligence.[94] It is important to note here, however, that the items listed in Schedule B are exceptions to coverage, which means that the insurer is disclosing them to the parties before the closing and will not pay any claims that arise from them. In most cases, the buyer will insist on a closing condition in the contract stating that there are no objectionable matters excepted from coverage in Schedule B. If the insurer's title commitment discloses any worrisome matters, then the buyer can demand that the seller take the steps necessary to have these items removed from Schedule B before the closing.

In some cases, the parties will agree from the outset that there will be exceptions to title insurance coverage. The most obvious example is the buyer that is assuming existing financing.[95] The title searcher will discover the seller's mortgage, which is recorded and predates the buyer's contract, and will list it as an exception to coverage on Schedule B of the title commitment. The buyer should not be permitted to object when the title policy excepts a matter that both parties agreed would remain as an encumbrance, and the closing condition needs to specify that coverage will be subject to this prior mortgage. Other matters, such as restrictive covenants and utility easements, will also appear as exceptions. The drafter should begin to see how this closing condition must dovetail with some of the representations and conditions discussed earlier.[96] At the same time, the buyer's counsel should not accept title that is subject to exceptions that she has not yet had the opportunity to scrutinize.[97]

Sometimes the buyer may desire coverage that goes beyond the matters set forth in the ALTA form. Title companies often are willing to issue this additional coverage in the form of endorsements to the policy. Both the availability and cost of endorsements vary widely from state to state, and state insurance regulations may limit the insurer's ability to issue endorsements.

Title companies usually issue two policies of insurance at a real estate closing: one for the buyer and one for its lender. This second policy is discussed in greater detail in connection with the loan transaction.[98]

---

*Comment:* Unsophisticated buyers, particularly in the residential setting, may believe that the lender's policy of title insurance provides them with coverage. This belief may arise from the fact that the buyer usually pays for the lender's policy. In fact, the buyer must obtain an owner's policy of title insurance in order to be insured, and the buyer's lawyer should so advise the buyer.

---

### § 2.83—*Affidavit to Title Company*

Some of the standard exceptions to the title insurance policy involve matters that the insurer has little or no way of verifying. One example that arises in many sales transactions is mechanics' liens. Unpaid contractors and suppliers of materials may place a lien on the property, which has benefited from their labor or materials. Typically, the unpaid mechanic can file its lien for a period of weeks or months after payment is due, and in most states, the priority of the lien will relate back to an earlier date, such as the date on which construction commenced. Mechanics' liens can pose an enormous problem for the buyer, which may purchase property with a clean title report only to learn that a subsequently filed mechanics' lien relates back to a date before the closing. Title companies are acutely aware of this problem, which is why the ALTA form contains a standard exception to coverage for mechanics' liens.

The title insurer may be amenable to omitting this exception if it receives some form of assurance that all mechanics have been paid in full. The only party in a position to provide this assurance is the seller,[99] and if the seller provides the insurer with an affidavit to this effect, the insurer ordinarily will omit the mechanics' lien exception from the buyer's title insurance policy. If the affidavit turns out to be inaccurate, the buyer will recover from its insurer, which then must proceed against the seller that gave it a false affidavit. In this way, the buyer transfers the risk of the seller's unavailability or insolvency to the title company.[100]

The title affidavit may address other matters as well. The title company has no foolproof way of identifying occupants of the property other than those whose occupancy is disclosed by recorded leases or memoranda of leases, so the title policy includes an exception for those parties who are in possession other than by virtue of a recorded instrument. If the seller's affidavit states that there are no such parties in possession, then the insurer will usually remove this exception. If the seller's affidavit discloses that there are parties in possession and provides a detailed list of who those parties are, then the insurer should remove the standard exception and replace it with a Schedule B exception that lists each of the parties that the seller disclosed in its affidavit.[101]

The insurer's amenability to removing these standard exceptions will depend largely on the seller's willingness to issue a title affidavit and the content of the affidavit. For this reason, the buyer should request that the seller's delivery of an affidavit addressing these specifically enumerated title matters be a condition precedent to the buyer's obligation to close. This condition, which may be coupled with the more general title policy condition discussed in the previous section, ensures the buyer that it will receive a title policy of an enhanced quality and not just a bare-bones ALTA policy. Note, however, that some sellers will not be willing to provide title affidavits.

### § 2.84—Caution: The Title Insurance Policy, the Title Affidavit, and Mechanics' Liens

Mechanics' lien laws vary so widely from state to state that it is extremely important that the lawyer be familiar with the mechanics' lien law in the state in which the property is located in order to deal with this common issue. The lawyer who is unfamiliar with the relevant law should not render advice concerning mechanics' liens and the title affidavit that addresses them.

### § 2.85—Technique: The Seller's Title Affidavit

Many standard contracts of sale do not set forth the obligation of the seller to provide an affidavit to the title company. Under those circumstances, the seller may refuse to give any affidavit whatsoever, with the result that the standard exceptions may not be removed from the title policy. For this reason, the buyer's lawyer must remember to include this closing condition in the contract. Some title companies, however, will remove the standard exceptions even if they do not receive an affidavit from the seller.

### § 2.86—Survey

Even though the seller may represent that it owns the property and covenant to deliver a deed to the property at the closing, the buyer and the seller may not have a clear idea of exactly what "the property" is. The sole characterization of the property in the contract may be an attached metes and bounds legal description that is unintelligible to the parties and their lawyers.[102] The only way to convert this written description of the property into a more useful depiction of the land is to have the property surveyed. For this reason, the buyer will want its receipt of an acceptable survey to be a condition precedent to its obligation to close. The buyer will need to review the survey it receives as part of its due diligence work.[103] The buyer must also remember that its lender will need to approve the survey.

It would be prudent for the buyer to insist that the survey be prepared by a licensed surveyor; that it meet the "Minimum Standard Detail Requirements for ALTA/ACSM Land Title Surveys" as currently adopted by the American Land Title Association (ALTA) and the National Society of Professional Surveyors (a member organization of the American Congress on Surveying and Mapping [ACSM]);[104] and that it be certified to the seller, the buyer, the buyer's lender, the title company, and the title company's agent. In this way, any of these parties will have recourse against the surveyor if they rely to their detriment on a negligently prepared survey.

### §2.87—Caution: Inconsistent Legal Descriptions

Modern surveying techniques differ considerably from the methods used earlier, so it is very common for a newer survey to be inconsistent with an older one. The buyer's surveyor may determine that the description contained in the old deed does not accurately describe the property and may provide a new description that, in its view, describes the boundaries of the property more accurately. The seller may be willing to warrant title to the property only as it is described by the older description but should be willing to quitclaim title to the remaining property.

### §2.88—Appraisal

The buyer may want an independent appraiser to determine that the property is worth the agreed price. The buyer may harbor fears that it has offered too much for the property and may want its offer to be confirmed by an expert. To address this concern, the buyer will seek a closing condition that allows it to terminate the contract if the contract price exceeds the appraised value. At first blush, one might think that this is an absurd request and that the buyer should investigate this matter on its own before signing the contract. The seller will also fear that the buyer may attempt to use a low appraisal as a means of obtaining a price reduction after the parties have signed the contract.

Unfortunately for the seller, the lender will nearly always include an appraisal condition in its loan commitment to the buyer as a way of confirming that it is not lending more than a certain percentage of the actual value of the property.[105] If this is the case, then an appraisal condition in the contract is largely redundant: if the contract contains a financing condition,[106] the buyer's ability to obtain a loan commitment will depend on the lender's receipt of an acceptable appraisal. Nonetheless, the buyer would be wise to seek an appraisal condition in the contract as well.

### § 2.89—Assignment of Seller's Interest in Leases

The buyer will want to receive a formal assignment from the seller of the seller's interest in existing tenant leases at the property, and the seller will want the buyer to assume responsibility for the seller's obligations under these leases. While it is probably the case that a deed to the property automatically effects this transfer, the parties can use this assignment to clarify the two parties' rights and responsibilities under these leases. To illustrate, this document can specifically assign all tenant security deposits from the seller to the buyer[107] and can clarify the rights and responsibilities of the parties as to overdue obligations of the landlord and the tenants. Thus, if the seller has breached its promise to pay for construction within a tenant's space or if a tenant is overdue in paying its rent, this assignment can spell out whether the seller or the buyer will meet this responsibility and enjoy this benefit.

> *Comment:* A separate assignment is always desirable from the seller's perspective. This assignment should require the buyer to assume the obligations of the seller under the leases and should address indemnification issues between the buyer and the seller.

### § 2.90—Tenant Estoppels

When the contract is executed, most or all of the buyer's information about tenants comes from the seller. The seller probably has provided the buyer with a rent roll and summaries of the leases, and the representations and warranties may include a more detailed description of these agreements. Between the contract and the closing, the buyer may want to have the tenants verify this information as one way of confirming its accuracy and learning more detail. The buyer can accomplish this by demanding that the seller obtain estoppel letters from those tenants whose leases require them to provide these letters.

A tenant estoppel letter, which also can take the form of an estoppel certificate, is a letter signed by the tenant in which it confirms the accuracy of certain factual information set forth in the letter. For example, the letter may state that an attached copy of the lease is true and complete, that the parties have not amended the lease, that neither party to the lease has breached it, that the tenant has paid all rent due through the date of the letter, and that the tenant has not prepaid any rent beyond the current month. By signing this letter with knowledge that the buyer will rely on its accuracy, the tenant is equitably estopped from later denying the accuracy of any of the statements contained in it.

Buyers would often like to receive tenant estoppels, particularly from the more important tenants at the property. For this reason, they will want receipt of acceptable estoppel letters from these tenants to be a condition precedent to the buyer's obligation to close. If the buyer does not receive an estoppel, or if a tenant discloses worrisome information in its estoppel, the buyer will learn of any problems with this tenant before it closes on the property.

### § 2.91—Technique: Tenant Estoppels and Landlord Affidavits

Tenants have become increasingly reluctant to provide estoppel letters, because issuing them can be an administrative headache. When issuing an estoppel, the tenant must check its records carefully to be sure that it is not waiving any valuable rights. Unless the lease specifically requires the tenant to provide an estoppel, the tenant may not be willing to do so. If this is the case, then an affidavit from the landlord may have to suffice.

### § 2.92—Form: Tenant Estoppel Certificate

See Appendix C for a Form of Tenant Estoppel Certificate.

### § 2.93—Notices to Tenants

Once the deal closes, the buyer will be the new landlord of the property and will be entitled to receive and use all tenant rents. The tenants may not be aware of this change of ownership immediately after the closing occurs. Even if the new owner sends notices to the tenants on the date of the closing, the tenants may have no way of verifying that the new owner's letter is genuine and may continue to pay rent to the former owner of the property.

To avoid this problem, the buyer should insist that the seller prepare notices to the tenants advising them of the sale of the property and instructing them to begin paying their rent to their new landlord. If these letters are signed by the seller (or by both parties) and are in conformance with the notice requirements contained in the leases, then the tenants will be legally obligated to send their rent to the new landlord. The seller will not want these letters sent before the closing, in case something goes awry, but should not object if the letters are sent once title passes.

The buyer should insist that the seller's preparation and execution of these letters be a condition precedent to the buyer's obligation to close. The seller should prepare and sign these letters and turn them over to the buyer at the closing. The buyer probably will prefer to handle delivery of the letters itself so it will know they were sent in a timely fashion.

### §2.94—Delivery of Security Deposits

Many tenant leases require the tenant to deposit funds with the landlord as security for the tenant's performance of all its leasehold obligations. The landlord retains these deposits and can draw against them if the tenant fails to pay its rent or meet any of its other obligations. Depending on the terms of the lease and state law, these deposits may have to be held in trust or in escrow, may have to be segregated from other funds held by the landlord, and may earn interest for the tenant.

When the lease relationship ends, the nonbreaching tenant will be entitled to a refund of this deposit, and the current owner will usually be responsible for returning this money to its tenant. The buyer must ensure that the seller turns all of these deposits over to the buyer at the closing. This matter should be raised in the closing conditions section of the contract, with the seller agreeing that the buyer's obligation to close is conditioned on its receipt of all tenant security deposits from the seller.

The buyer can verify the amount of any security deposit by examining the lease under which it was established[108] and by including a statement corroborating this amount in the estoppel letter that the tenant will sign.[109] The buyer should also be aware that the landlord's security sometimes takes a form other than a cash deposit. For example, the tenant may have arranged to have a letter of credit issued to its landlord. In cases such as this, transfer of the security from the seller to the buyer may require the participation of a third party, and the parties must remember to attend to this matter before the day of the closing.

### §2.95—Opinion of Seller's Counsel

While the buyer is probably most concerned with issues such as the physical condition of the structure, the status of tenant leases, and the availability of acquisition financing, many of the representations, warranties, covenants, indemnities, and closing conditions address legal matters of great importance. The buyer needs to confirm that the seller exists legally and has taken all entity actions necessary to authorize the sale of the property.[110] In the representations, warranties, covenants, and indemnities, the buyer asks the seller to make these statements. In the closing conditions section, the buyer reserves the right to terminate the contract without penalty if any of these assertions proves to be untrue.

Verification of these statements can be a demanding task. The seller's operative documents may be lengthy and complex, and the seller entity may exist under the laws of a state or country with which the buyer and its lawyers have little familiarity. The seller may be reluctant to turn some of these documents over to the buyer for confidentiality reasons. Even if the buyer receives and examines an enormous stack of documents, it may fear that the seller has withheld the one critical piece of information that the buyer would need to assess the desirability of the transaction accurately.

The buyer may want some additional confirmation that the seller's legal house is in order and may also ask for a written opinion from the seller's counsel that confirms these entity matters, especially in larger or more complex transactions. This request should appear in the closing conditions section so that the buyer will have the right to back out of the sale if the opinion letter is unacceptable. By issuing this letter, the seller's lawyer puts his own credibility (and the credit of his malpractice insurer) on the line and provides the buyer with additional assurance that the seller has taken all of the legal steps it needs to take to convey the property to the buyer.

Given that the buyer will be relying on the good name and reputation of the seller's law firm, the closing condition often will state the name of that law firm or will allow the buyer to veto any law firm that it does not find satisfactory.

*Comment*: It is relatively uncommon for the buyer to request an opinion from the seller's counsel. However, the buyer's lender will frequently request an opinion confirming the valid existence and authority of the seller.

The legal opinion letter may be extremely detailed, and the language of the closing condition should be quite specific as to the matters that the legal opinion must cover. Typical opinion letters will confirm that the seller entity exists and is in good standing under the laws of the jurisdiction in which it was created; that it is authorized to do business in the state in which the property is located; that the seller's conveyance of the property does not violate any of the seller's operative documents, does not require the approval of any third parties, and does not violate any other agreements to which the seller is a party; and that the seller entity has taken all action required under state law and its operative documents to convey the property to the buyer. Buyers may seek far more extensive letters, while sellers and their lawyers will seek to restrict the legal opinion to purely factual legal matters about which the lawyer has firsthand knowledge.

The preparation of any legal opinion can place the lawyer asked to prepare the opinion in an awkward position. Most likely, the seller is anxious to close the deal and may encourage its lawyer to provide a letter that meets all the buyer's demands, while the lawyer will want to pen an opinion that is brief and general and creates little potential liability for the lawyer's firm. Legal opinions may also require a significant amount of lead time, because the lawyer needs to investigate each matter that the letter will address. Some law firms insist that all legal opinion letters receive the approval of a firm committee because of the liability that the firm might face if the letter proves to be inaccurate. Negotiation of legal opinion letters can be stressful and difficult, especially if the letter contains terms that are not standard.

In an effort to limit their own liability while meeting the demands of their client and the buyer, lawyers preparing opinions for a seller will often list the documents on which they relied. The letter will state that the lawyer's opinion is based exclusively on a review of these documents, that the seller provided these documents, and that the lawyer is assuming the documents to be genuine. This is particularly true in cases in which the lawyer preparing the opinion letter is not the seller's regular in-house or outside counsel, because the lawyer may have little personal knowledge of the seller's business and may have no idea whether the documents provided are authentic and are the only pertinent documents.

> *Comment*: Some lawyers are unwilling to verify in writing that certain statements are true. If this is the case, the party seeking assurances must rely instead on an affidavit from the other party rather than an opinion letter from the other party's lawyer.

Sometimes the lawyer providing the opinion may have to rely on an opinion of another lawyer. For example, if the property is located in New York, the seller will probably use New York counsel for the transaction. If the seller corporation is formed under Texas law, the New York lawyer may be legally prohibited from opining that the entity is properly created under Texas law and has taken all steps necessary to authorize the sale.[111] The seller may need to retain Texas counsel to opine as to these matters, and the New York firm's opinion will state that, as to matters of Texas law, it has relied exclusively on the opinion of the Texas law firm. Because the New York firm will be shifting some of its potential liability to the Texas firm, the buyer must be sure that it is satisfied with the identity of this Texas firm.

> *Comment*: Note that in many areas of the country, the so-called Opinion Accord, which was developed by the American Bar Association and the American College of Real Estate Lawyers, may be incorporated into the opinion by reference.[112] Some lenders, however, will not agree to accept the provisions of the Accord.[113]

### §2.96—Caution: Risks to Seller's Counsel in Preparing Opinions

Occasionally a lawyer is asked to provide an opinion stating that no further approvals are required and that there have been no violations of other agreements. This is an opinion that would be virtually impossible for any lawyer to sign without being fully familiar with the seller's corporate documentation and bylaws and with every other document to which the seller is a party. Matters such as this should be handled by an affidavit of the seller or a representation and warranty, and not by a lawyer's opinion. If the lawyer does provide an opinion, that opinion should state that its scope is limited to matters within the lawyer's actual knowledge.

### § 2.97—Assignment of Seller's Interest in All Other Property and Agreements

The contract of sale memorializes the seller's obligation to convey the real estate to the buyer in return for the buyer's payment of the purchase price, but real estate transactions often include property other than real estate. The buyer may be acquiring a considerable amount of personal property and may be succeeding to the seller's rights under a variety of different contracts. The buyer must ensure that the seller conveys this property and assigns these rights to the buyer. The buyer should also confirm that the seller is current in meeting all of its obligations under any third-party contracts. To accomplish these goals, the buyer should make sure that the contract conditions the buyer's obligation to perform on the seller's transfer of this property and these rights. The seller also should be required to continue to perform under these third-party contracts between the time the real estate contract is signed and the time the seller conveys title to the buyer.

The sale of a hotel provides a clear illustration of the importance of this closing condition. The buyer most likely plans to continue operating the hotel after the closing and wants to smooth the owner- ship transition as much as possible. It does not want to acquire an empty building, which it then will have to equip and furnish. It also does not want to renegotiate contracts with food suppliers, linen ser- vice companies, and the national chain whose name and trademark it uses. What the buyer wants is to acquire everything the seller had, including all of this personal property and all of these contractual rights. The buyer must be sure that its obligation to close is condi- tioned not just on the seller's conveyance of the real property, but also on the seller's transfer of all these other valuable rights. To the extent that any third parties must consent to any of these transfers, receipt of these consents should be addressed in a closing condition. The buyer should also condition its own closing obligation on the absence of any breach of these contracts by the seller before the closing.

### § 2.98—FIRPTA Affidavit

Were it not for the Foreign Investment in Real Property Tax Act (FIRPTA),[114] it would be easy for foreign owners to sell real property in the United States and avoid paying taxes on any gains they might have enjoyed. After the sale, these sellers may no longer be subject to the jurisdiction of U.S. courts and may have no other domestic property that can be seized. FIRPTA addresses this problem by requiring that a portion of the sale proceeds be withheld if the seller is a foreign entity or if any of its principals are foreign nationals.

The buyer can avoid this withholding obligation and any liability for failing to meet it if the buyer receives an affidavit from the seller in which the seller confirms that it is not a foreign entity subject to withholding. To ensure that the seller furnishes a satisfactory affidavit at the closing, the buyer should ask for a closing condition requiring the seller to deliver an affidavit that complies with the regulations promulgated under FIRPTA. This provision should state that if the seller fails to deliver its FIRPTA affidavit, the buyer may withhold a portion of the purchase price to meet any potential liabilities under federal tax laws.

### § 2.99—Form: FIRPTA Affidavit

See Appendix D for a Form of FIRPTA Affidavit.

### § 2.100—Permits, Certificates, Plans, Warranties, and Keys

Most of the documents delivered at closing are legal documents needed to effect the proper transfer of real and personal property. There are several other items that the seller should physically hand over to the buyer at the closing or shortly beforehand. If the buyer does not receive these items at closing, it may find that it has little remaining leverage to wrest them from the seller later. Therefore, the buyer should request that the seller's delivery of these items be a condition precedent to the buyer's closing obligations.

The buyer should make sure that the seller must deliver any permits and certificates that the buyer will need to operate the property. These will include any building permits, certificates of occupancy, and business licenses. The seller should also deliver the plans and specifications for the premises so that the buyer will have complete knowledge of the structure. In some jurisdictions, these plans may already be filed with a public official and thus a matter of public record, but the buyer should still ask for a set for its own office use. Along with these plans, the seller should deliver any warranties that remain in effect, including contractors' warranties for recent construction. Although it seems painfully obvious, the contract should also require the seller to turn over all keys to the premises at the closing.

## § 2.101 Conditions Precedent to Seller's Obligation to Close

The previous sections have emphasized how important it is to the buyer that the seller meet certain conditions before the buyer must close. For similar reasons, the seller should require the buyer to meet certain conditions before the seller must close. The seller should request a list of closing conditions that the buyer must meet, and the buyer will usually have few objections to meeting these conditions.

Because of the differing nature of the two parties' obligations, the two closing conditions sections will not directly parallel each other. The seller is conveying property to the buyer, and the buyer needs to learn as much as it can about the property before acquiring it. The buyer uses representations, warranties, covenants, and its own investigation as due diligence tools and uses closing conditions as escape routes. The buyer cannot determine whether it should proceed to close until it has gathered much critical information from the seller or on its own.

The buyer, on the other hand, is required to deliver only the purchase price. The seller, therefore, does not have to undertake a significant amount of due diligence and is concerned primarily with receiving the right number of dollars on the right day. The closing conditions in the contract will reflect this asymmetry of obligation.

The following sections detail the few closing conditions that sellers typically seek. As these sections show, the conditions precedent to the seller's obligation to close address two principal matters: the ability of the buyer to pay the purchase price and the buyer's legal authority to enter into the transaction.

### § 2.102—Payment of Purchase Price

The seller cares about one closing condition more than any other: it must leave the closing either in possession of the purchase price or with the knowledge that the buyer has transferred these funds to the title company or escrow company. If the buyer pays for the land, it has met its primary obligation, and the seller should be willing to deliver the deed. If the buyer does not pay for the land, it has breached its primary obligation, and the seller will retain title and pursue its remedies under the contract. The closing conditions section should state clearly that the seller's obligation to convey title to the buyer is conditioned on the buyer's payment of the purchase price in the manner set forth in the contract.

The seller does not want to wait for a check to clear and needs to be satisfied that the buyer has transferred good funds. This concern is easy to address. The parties may agree that cash is acceptable. Most sellers probably do not want to receive enormous quantities of cash, and many may harbor suspicions about buyers who insist on paying for real estate with suitcases full of hundred-dollar bills. Nothing, however, prevents the parties from agreeing to a sale for currency.

Most commonly, the buyer will transfer the funds by wire or will deliver a certified check. In the former case, the seller should await confirmation from its own bank or from the title company or escrow company that the funds have arrived before delivering the deed to the buyer. The parties should address the mechanics of this wire transfer in the closing conditions section and should contact their respective banks in advance. In the latter case, the seller must confirm that the check is satisfactory before delivering the deed to the buyer.[115]

### §2.103—Caution: Confirmation That Wired Funds Have Been Received

Note that wired funds are not good funds until the wire instructions actually have been executed by the wiring bank. It is possible for the buyer to revoke its wire transfer at any time until the funds have been wired. The closing condition should state that the seller is not required to deliver the deed until it receives a confirmed wire number.[116]

### §2.104—Continuing Accuracy of Buyer's Representations and Warranties; Performance of Covenants

The seller needs to be sure that all of the buyer's representations and warranties are as true and accurate on the closing date as they were on the contract date. The fact that the buyer could provide an accurate representation when it signed the contract provides little assurance to the seller that this representation remains true weeks or months later. The seller needs to have the ability to withdraw from the contract if the accuracy of an essential representation has changed, and it accomplishes this result by seeking a closing condition that all of the buyer's representations remain true and accurate as of the date of the closing. The parties may decide that this closing condition will apply only to the buyer's more important representations and may limit the closing condition to material adverse changes. The same closing condition should allow the seller to withdraw if the buyer has failed to meet any of its contractual covenants.

While this condition precedent to the seller's obligation to close appears to mirror a similar condition precedent to the buyer's obligation,[117] this appearance is somewhat of an illusion. Remember that the seller may have provided a lengthy list of representations, warranties, covenants, and indemnities. When the seller offers a "continuing accuracy" closing condition, it is giving the buyer the right to terminate the contract if any of these representations has become untrue in any materially adverse way. Because there is so much that can change, the buyer may find that it has the right not to close or the ability to renegotiate the deal so that it receives more favorable terms. Stated differently, this closing condition may place a significant burden on the seller during the contract period, with the seller making every effort to ensure that all its representations remain true.

The buyer, in contrast, generally provides few representations to the seller. When the buyer allows the seller the right to back out of the deal if any of the buyer's representations become inaccurate, it is providing very little to the seller. The buyer's representations probably deal with its own legal existence and authority, and the seller ought to confirm that the buyer entity exists legally on the closing date and has properly authorized the transaction. Other than that, the seller's only significant concern is that the buyer deliver the acquisition funds. The asymmetry of the parties' contractual representations, which arises from the huge difference in their due diligence burdens, is reflected in the "continuing accuracy" closing conditions.

### § 2.105—Authority of Buyer

The seller needs to confirm that the buyer is properly organized and may transact business under state law, that the buyer is internally authorized to contract to acquire the property, and that the transaction does not violate any other agreements to which the buyer is a party or require the approval of any third parties. In other words, the seller has the same concerns as the buyer that the other party is acting properly and within its authority.[118] The closing conditions section of the contract should state that the seller is not obligated to deliver title unless the buyer has met these requirements.

### §2.106—Opinion of Buyer's Counsel

The seller will occasionally request an opinion from the buyer's lawyer confirming the accuracy of certain legal representations that the buyer has made, particularly with regard to entity formation, existence, and authorization. This opinion letter will echo many of the statements contained in the opinion that the buyer will seek from the seller's lawyer. The seller's concerns here are far less acute than those of the buyer. The seller is fully satisfied as soon as it receives payment and can experience few post-closing surprises, so it has considerably less to worry about if the buyer has breached one of its representations. However, the seller may want to confirm the accuracy of the legal representations made by the buyer and can do so by requesting that the buyer's lawyer verify in writing that these statements are true.[119]

> *Comment:* As previously noted, some lawyers will not verify in writing that statements of this type are true. In these cases, the seller instead must rely on an affidavit from the buyer. The buyer's title insurance company will probably require the same assurances and may also request supporting documentation such as articles of incorporation, bylaws, and corporate resolutions.

## §2.107 Waiver of Closing Conditions

Previous sections in this chapter have stressed the importance of closing conditions, particularly to the buyer, and have recommended and explained the need for including a wide variety of different conditions in the contract. Not all of these conditions are equally important to every buyer and seller, and the extent to which some conditions are more important than others will depend on the property itself and the reasons the parties are selling and buying it.

When the closing date arrives, it may turn out that the seller has met nineteen of twenty required closing conditions and probably will be unable to meet the twentieth. The buyer then has a choice to make. Although the buyer would be contractually protected if it elected not to close because of the seller's failure to meet a material condition precedent, the buyer may determine that it is comfortable closing anyway and that it will take its chances with this last condition. For example, a buyer may be willing to close even though the fourth-largest tenant at the shopping center has refused to execute an estoppel certificate, because the buyer believes that the center will be a good investment even if this tenant is disputing some of its leasehold obligations. The buyer thus may waive this closing condition and close anyway.

If the contract does not address waivers of closing conditions, it will probably be the case that either party can waive conditions that run to its benefit at the closing. The sole contractual purpose of a condition precedent is to clarify that Party B is not required to perform until Party A has met a specified obligation. This implies that Party B may choose to perform even if the obligation is not met and that Party A could not itself refuse to perform simply because Party B had waived the condition. Nonetheless, it is a good idea to state directly in the contract that each party retains the right to waive any conditions precedent that run to its benefit and may choose to close anyway.

The parties may also address related matters in this contractual provision. They might agree that the seller can delay the closing to resolve certain problems. They might decide that the buyer may withdraw from the contract only if the monetary value of these unmet conditions exceeds a certain minimum. They might address the extent to which unmet closing conditions will turn into post-closing obligations of the seller.[120] They even might agree that a portion of the purchase price will be held in escrow pending the post-closing resolution of disputed matters. As is true in so many other situations, the parties may be able to avoid a dispute at the closing by considering the matter in advance and addressing it in the contract.[121]

### § 2.108—Technique: Waiver of Closing Conditions and Drafting the Conditions Section

When providing for a waiver of closing conditions, it is essential that the drafter clarify which of the parties is entitled to waive each condition. For example, if financing is a closing condition, the buyer should have the opportunity to waive the closing condition, but the seller ordinarily should not. It is a good drafting technique to put the conditions precedent to the buyer's and the seller's obligations to close in different sections of the contract or in different subparagraphs of the conditions section for this purpose.

## §2.109 Casualty or Condemnation before Closing

The parties should decide in advance what their respective rights and responsibilities will be if the property is damaged or destroyed before the closing. The most likely way in which this could occur is if the property were to suffer a casualty, such as a fire, after the contract is signed. Government condemnation might also lead to the same result, although condemnations take longer, and the parties usually have some advance notice that they are pending. In either case, the damage to improvements may be total or partial, and some or all of the land will be gone after a condemnation.

The buyer may argue that it contracted to purchase certain property in a certain state and that it has lost the benefit of its bargain. It may rely on the contractual doctrines of impossibility or frustration of purpose to absolve itself from the obligation to proceed with the acquisition of the property. The seller may respond that it contracted to sell certain land and that it is prepared to perform. Any risk that the improvements would be damaged was a risk of the buyer's, and the buyer may not terminate the contract.

State law is likely to provide a default rule that answers this question, although the answer will vary from state to state. If a state has adopted all or much of the doctrine of equitable conversion,[122] then this may mean that most of the rights and responsibilities of ownership pass to the buyer on the date of the contract and that the buyer already "owns" the property in all but the legal sense. In this setting, that would mean that the buyer must close even though it is receiving less than it bargained for, because the risk of loss passed to the buyer as soon as it executed the contract. Other states will reach the opposite conclusion, under the principle that the seller retains this risk until it conveys legal title to the property to the buyer.

Neither of these default rules matters if the parties address this issue in their contract, and that is what they should do. By addressing this question directly, the parties remove themselves from the uncertainties of the state's common law, reduce the likelihood of subsequent litigation, and establish the risk allocation they both want.

This issue does not usually prove to be as significant as it may initially sound, because the property is likely to be insured. If the parties agree that the seller bears the risk of loss until the closing, what they really are saying is that the seller must continue to insure the property until that date. This expense should not be excessive, and both parties will factor it into their calculation of an appropriate sale price. If there is an insured casualty or a condemnation, the damaged or lost property should be replaced by cash of roughly equivalent value. One or both parties may be disappointed, but neither party will suffer any significant economic loss.

> *Comment:* If there is an insured loss, the buyer will often want to have the option either to terminate the contract or to close and receive the insurance proceeds. The buyer may want to have the seller's insurance policy endorsed to reflect its interest.

In some cases, improvements to the property may detract from its value. If the buyer intends to clear away some rotting agricultural structures and replace them with a new office building, a casualty loss would actually be beneficial to both parties. In these cases, the issue of risk of loss becomes insignificant, because there is nothing of value for either party to lose.[123]

## § 2.110 Closing Date, Time, Location, and Mechanics

The contract should specify the manner in which the closing will be conducted and the date, time, and location of the closing. There are two principal closing formats: escrow closings and so-called New York–style closings. While the differences between these two types of closings will be addressed in a later chapter,[124] the contract should specify which type of closing the parties will use. If the buyer and the seller are operating under different conceptions of how the closing will proceed, they need to become aware of those differences and resolve them before they sign the contract.

The contract should also address the when and where of the closing. Parties tend to think of contractual provisions as firmly established, but the time, date, and location of the closing may change even after the parties sign the contract. For example, the buyer's lender may insist that the closing occur at its office or at the office of the title insurance company that it selects, and the seller ordinarily will not object. Even the date and time established in the document are not as firm as one might think. Parties that are laboring to meet their conditions precedent and other contractual obligations may request additional time, and their counterparts will often agree to reasonable extensions, perhaps in exchange for additional consideration. Many courts are unwilling to find a party in breach if it is unable to close on the date set forth in the contract, particularly when it is obvious that the party could meet an unmet condition with a reasonable extension, unless the contract states that time is of the essence.[125] While the parties need not put up with indefinite stalling, they should anticipate that the closing date may be pushed back somewhat. At the same time, the parties can avoid any potential problems under the rule against perpetuities by remembering to include an outside closing date.

### §2.111—Caution: Outside Closing Date

It is absolutely essential that every contract contain an outside closing date, particularly if there is no fixed closing date in the contract. In some states, a contract that lacks a fixed closing date may violate the rule against perpetuities unless it contains an outside date. Consequently, stating that the closing will occur at some indefinite future time, such as "when building permits are issued," may be very dangerous unless an outside date is specified.

## §2.112 Defaults and Remedies

The buyer and the seller, like parties to any contract, each must recognize the possibility that the other party will default in the performance of its contractual obligations. The contract must state clearly what acts and omissions constitute defaults and what the remedies for those defaults are.

Many defaults occur because a party violates representations, warranties, covenants, or indemnities. If the seller represents that it owns fee simple title to the property and covenants that it will remove all liens on or before the closing date, it will be in default if it attempts to deliver title subject to a parking easement held by an abutting landowner. The buyer then must look to the remedies section to determine what its options are.

Bear in mind that closing conditions differ from representations. The failure to meet a closing condition excuses nonperformance by the other party but will not constitute a breach of the contract unless the matter that the closing condition addresses also is covered by one of the representations. To illustrate, imagine that the buyer wants the seller to deliver the premises in broom-clean condition, cleared of all furnishings and trash. The buyer may receive the benefit of a closing condition to this effect but may decide not to ask the seller to covenant that it will deliver the space in clean condition. If the seller attempts to deliver dirty, cluttered space and if the buyer is confident that a court would find this attempt to be a material breach of a closing condition, the buyer may refuse to close. The buyer will be acting entirely within its rights if it rejects the seller's delivery of the deed, because it is a condition precedent to the buyer's obligation to close that the seller turn over premises that are empty and clean. However, this is the only recourse that the buyer has under the document; the buyer's failure to address this matter in a covenant means that the seller technically has not breached the contract.

The parties may opt to include grace periods and notice requirements for some of their contractual obligations. If the seller has covenanted that it will allow the buyer to inspect its books and records, the seller may insist that the buyer provide three days' written notice before it can view these documents. The seller will not be in default unless it fails to provide access three days after receiving this notice from the buyer. Similarly, the parties may include deductibles or caps on some of their obligations. They may agree that the seller is responsible for repairing physical damage to the property that will cost more than $1,000 and less than $20,000 to remedy. Smaller repairs will be viewed as immaterial, while larger ones will allow the seller to cancel the contract without penalty. This approach allows each party to estimate more precisely the cost of its contractual responsibilities. The seller will be in default only if it fails to remedy a problem that falls within this dollar range.

The remedies portion of the contract should state what remedies are available to each party and should clarify whether these remedies are exclusive or alternative. The parties may want the seller's sole remedy for breach by the buyer to be retention of the down payment as liquidated damages. If this is the case, then the seller must ensure that the contract sets forth this remedy, while the buyer must confirm that the contract allows the seller no other recourse. By contrast, if the seller is the party to breach, the buyer may prefer to have the option of seeking damages, specific performance, or both, and needs to verify that the contract lists these remedies and states that the choice of remedy rests with the buyer. An asymmetry of this type is not unusual, as it reflects the differing natures of the parties' obligations: the seller is conveying unique land, while the buyer is paying for it with fungible cash.

> *Comment*: The seller will wish to limit the time within which a suit for specific performance may be brought, so that the contract will not remain as a cloud on the seller's title indefinitely. Customarily, the time is ninety days to six months.

> *Comment*: Note that the availability of specific performance need not be limited to the buyer. In certain states, such as Maryland, the seller is also entitled to the remedy of specific performance unless the contract provides otherwise. The parties need to be clear in the contract as to which remedies each party may pursue.

## §2.113 Nonrecourse

Either party may ask that the other party's remedies be limited in amount or confined to certain specified property. This is particularly important for a party that is an individual, a cotenancy, a partnership, or a trust, because, in those situations, specific people may worry about potentially limitless liability. If the concerned party is insistent and the other party agrees, they can contractually limit the liability of the concerned party.

In the case of the seller, the parties may decide to limit liability to the seller's interest in the property. In this way, the seller ensures that it can lose no more than its equity in the property. In the case of the buyer, the parties may agree that liability is limited to the down payment, a specified larger amount of money, or an alternative asset of sufficient value. If either party is an entity, it may seek to limit its liability to the assets of the entity, thereby shielding the assets of the entity's principals. Thus, if the buyer is a partnership, it may seek a provision that allows the seller to recover from the partnership but not from its partners.[126]

In either case, the party that is giving up part of its ability to recover must be sure that it is satisfied with the recourse that will remain. If the seller agrees that only the buyer partnership will be liable, it needs to be sure that this partnership has and will continue to have assets that are adequate to satisfy the likely amount of a judgment. If the buyer agrees to look only to the property, it must be sure that the seller has and will continue to have sufficient equity in the property to satisfy a judgment against the seller. The parties should also be aware that exculpation from contractual liability does not release a party from liability in tort.

## §2.114 Transfer Taxes, Gains Taxes, Sales Taxes

The occurrence of a real estate transfer may lead to the imposition of a variety of different state and local taxes. The contract needs to specify which party is responsible for paying each of these taxes. Because the types of taxes that may be triggered and the industry customs regarding payment of those taxes vary from jurisdiction to jurisdiction, the discussion here is a general one. However, this section should serve to remind the drafter to determine the types of taxes that are due, to investigate who ordinarily pays those taxes, to consider whether the parties should depart from this typical pattern, and to document the agreement the parties reach.

Some jurisdictions impose taxes that arise directly from the transfer of property. These taxes typically are calculated as a percentage of the purchase price and are collected when the buyer records its deed. The buyer is the party that is most likely to pay these taxes, but the parties are free to negotiate on this point and to factor the magnitude of this imposition into the purchase price they are willing to offer and accept.

*Comment:* Although the buyer may be the party that is most likely to pay transfer taxes and recording charges, law and practice differ from state to state. For example, in Maryland, by statute, transfer taxes and recording charges are split unless the contract provides otherwise.

*Comment:* Some states impose transfer and recordation taxes on transfers of entity interests, such as corporate shares and partnership interests. Even if the buyer is acquiring an entity that owns real estate rather than acquiring the real estate directly, it still may find that it owes these taxes.

If the seller is selling the property at a price that exceeds the seller's basis, the jurisdiction may impose a tax on the seller's gain on the property. Because this is a tax on the seller's profit, payment of it should be the seller's responsibility. Once again, the parties may reach a different agreement and also may attempt to structure the sale in a way that minimizes or defers the impact of this tax.

Many jurisdictions impose sales taxes, and the range of items subject to these taxes varies widely. Generally speaking, real property is not subject to sales tax but personal property may be. The parties need to consider the extent to which their contract will lead to the conveyance of personal property and not just real property. A hotel buyer may end up owing enormous sales taxes not on the hotel itself, but on the beds, furnishings, linens, and towels that it is buying at the same time. Similar concerns can arise in the sale of manufacturing and other industrial property. Fixtures and building materials present an additional puzzle. A heating system may be subject to sales tax when a developer purchases it from a supplier but may be exempt when the building into which it has been incorporated is sold.

In some cases, the parties may be uncertain whether certain items are subject to sales tax, and each may fear that it later will be pursued by the taxing authorities. In cases such as this, it is appropriate for one party, typically the buyer, to indemnify the other against any costs and expenses that this other party incurs arising from a subsequent sales tax levy, including the amount of the tax itself, interest, penalties, and attorneys' fees. This issue should be addressed in a contractual provision that survives the closing or in a separate agreement executed at the closing.

## §2.115 Apportionments and Adjustments

When the property changes hands, the buyer and the seller will need to apportion any charges and income that are attributable to the property during the month or year in which the closing occurs.

The contract should specify which charges will be apportioned and should clarify the methods that the parties will use to apportion these amounts.

Real estate taxes provide the clearest example of the need for apportionment. In many jurisdictions, real property taxes will appear as a lien on the property at the beginning of the taxing year (which may not correspond to the calendar year) but will not be due and payable until later in the year. If this is the case, the seller will own the property for part of the tax year but will not have paid any real estate taxes as of the closing date. The buyer will ultimately pay these taxes and should be sure that the seller reimburses the buyer for the portion of these taxes attributable to the time during which the seller still owned the property. Conversely, if the taxes are paid in advance rather than in arrears, the seller will have already paid the taxes for the current tax year and should demand that the buyer reimburse it for the fraction of the taxes attributable to the post-closing portion of the tax year.

Real estate assessments may be handled differently. Suppose the local utility installed underground sewers and passed the cost back to the benefited landowners by imposing an assessment that is being paid over a thirty-year period. The buyer may argue that the seller is responsible for paying this entire cost, because the buyer has factored the value of the completed sewer into its offer price. The assessment is paying for an improvement that already has been completed, while taxes pay for regular and ongoing municipal expenses.

*Comment:* Real estate taxes and special assessments may be apportioned in different ways. The lawyers must determine what assessments exist and the period over which they are payable. They then will be in a better position to address the question of how to apportion these assessments. If these charges are payable over an extended period of time, the parties may agree to adjust the purchase price. Frequently, though, the buyer simply takes on the responsibility for paying these charges after the closing.

Other expenses associated with the property need to be apportioned in a similar manner. If the property is ground-leased and the rent is paid in advance, the buyer should reimburse the seller for that portion of the last payment attributable to the post-closing period. Similar treatment is appropriate for fees imposed by a condominium, cooperative, or property owners' association.

With respect to utilities such as electricity, gas, water, sewer, local and long-distance telephone, cable television, and Internet, the seller typically closes its accounts and the buyer opens new ones of its own, and both these events should occur on or just before the closing date. If the parties decide instead that the buyer will continue an existing account, then these bills need to be apportioned as well.[127] For those services where the amount of the bill varies from month to month, such as electricity, the parties should have the meter read just before the closing so that they can apportion the last bill accurately. In cases in which the service provider is holding a security deposit, the seller should remember to make sure that it is reimbursed by the buyer or the service provider. The parties may also decide to continue and apportion long-term service contracts, such as those for landscaping care, custodial services, pest control, and snow removal. If the property is heated with oil, the seller should check the amount of oil in the tank on closing day and should receive reimbursement for that amount.

Apportionments work both ways. If the property produces income, such as tenant rentals and parking fees, the buyer should be sure that it receives payment for the portion of the rental period after the closing. The tenants probably paid their rent to the seller on the first of the month, but the seller is entitled to retain only a prorated share of that rent.

Generally, the parties will agree that these amounts will be off-set against one another, with the net apportionment amount added to or deducted from the purchase price. Sometimes, however, the mechanics of delivering the sale proceeds will make this impossible. If the buyer needs to obtain a certified check, it may have to fill in the amount before these costs can be accurately apportioned. The parties will need to agree on, and the contract should clarify, the manner in which these apportionments will be paid or credited.

Note that there are different methods of apportioning these amounts and that different methods can lead to slightly different results. One party may wish to calculate per diem amounts by dividing annual charges by 365. The other party may prefer to divide annual charges into twelve equal monthly installments and then to divide each monthly amount into thirty equal daily amounts. The contract should be clear as to which method the parties will use. Remember also that different charges are billed on different schedules: condominium fees may be paid quarterly, the cable bill may be due on the seventeenth of each month, and tenant rents may be received on the first of each month.

## §2.116 Brokerage Commissions

One or both parties may have used the services of a real estate broker in bringing about the sale of the property. Each party should state in the contract the name of the broker or brokers it retained and should covenant that it will pay all commissions and fees that it owes to its own broker. While a broker's right to collect these amounts should be governed by its brokerage agreement and not by the contract of sale, the buyer and the seller should clarify in the contract that each will meet its obligations under any independent brokerage agreements.

> *Comment:* Buyers have become more likely to retain so-called buyers' brokers. In these circumstances, either the seller's broker pays a portion of its commission to the buyer's broker or the buyer pays its own broker's commission directly. In addition, brokers are increasingly acting as dual agents for both of the parties. In this instance, many states require that each party sign a dual-agency disclosure statement. Brokerage relationships are generally governed by statute, and these statutes can vary widely from state to state.

The buyer may fear that an unexpected party will appear after the closing and claim that the seller owed a brokerage commission to it. This party may seek to recover from the buyer or may attempt to place a lien on the property. For this reason, the buyer should request that the seller indemnify it against any costs or expenses that it incurs, including court costs and legal fees, arising from the seller's failure to pay any amounts due to any brokers. This is a particular concern in states that do not apply the statute of frauds to brokerage agreements, because, in those states, a broker who had a more casual relationship with the seller may be entitled to a commission because of the broker's actions in procuring a buyer for the property.

The seller should receive a similar indemnity from the buyer. While the post-closing risk of having to pay a commission that someone else should have paid is lower for the seller than it is for the buyer, the buyer should have no objection to promising that it will pay any commissions that it owes to any real estate brokers.

If the parties agree to an indemnity of this type, they should be sure that their agreement will survive the closing. The most common way of accomplishing this result is to include the indemnity in the contract of sale and to specify that it will survive. The parties also can reach this result by agreeing in the contract that they will execute a separate indemnity agreement at the closing.

> *Comment:* The buyer and the seller also should consider and address the possibility that a broker may claim a commission arising from a tenant lease at the building and not just from the sale of the building to the buyer.

### § 2.117—Caution: Brokerage Indemnities

An agreement by a party to indemnify the other party for the payment of a specified brokerage commission may, unless the language is carefully drafted, imply that the broker actually is entitled to a commission, even though the parties believe that no such commission is due and payable. The parties should take care to draft a provision that creates no new rights in any broker.

### § 2.118 Recording of Contract

In some cases, the buyer may wish to record the contract of sale. This is particularly true in cases in which there will be a lengthy period of time between the execution of the contract and the closing, such as installment land contracts or sales contracts with lengthy due diligence periods arising from permitting uncertainties. The buyer is concerned that the seller will convey the property to a second buyer or create a new lien on the property during this period. While the first buyer will have a contract claim against the seller, the second buyer will be able to retain its property interest if it had no notice of the prior contract. Recordation would provide that notice, and the buyer may seek to have the contract recorded.

The seller may wish to resist the buyer's request to record the contract. If the closing does not occur, the contract will continue to cloud the seller's title and the buyer may be uncooperative in executing a recordable document that releases the contract of record. In addition, the buyer may have requested a lengthy executory period precisely because it expects to have difficulty in procuring financing or permits, which suggests that this is a contract that may not close.

If the parties do agree that the contract will be recorded, they should be sure that they execute it in recordable fashion. Both parties will need to sign before a notary public and comply with any other local recording requirements. If state law allows, the parties may prefer to record a memorandum of the contract. This shorter form will allow the parties to maintain some confidentiality as to the essential terms of the transaction while still providing record notice to those who later search title.

### §2.119—Caution: Releasing Recorded Contracts

If the contract is recorded, some sellers will insist that a release of the contract be placed in escrow. This release will automatically be recorded in the event that the buyer defaults. The buyer may not be willing to execute a release later on, and title could otherwise remain clouded by the recordation of the contract or a memorandum of the contract.

## §2.120 Payment of Expenses

Each party ordinarily pays its own expenses. For the seller, this obligation includes paying its brokers, lawyers, advisers, and consultants; maintaining existing insurance on the property; making any repairs to the property that it agrees to make in the contract; clearing any title problems; procuring tenant estoppel letters; and paying any gains taxes that result from the sale.

The buyer may have a longer list of expenses, reflecting its greater due diligence burden. The buyer typically must pay its own brokers, lawyers, advisers, and consultants; any expenses incurred in connection with its loan application and its loan; the costs of a survey, an appraisal, an investigation of title, and policies of title insurance for itself and its lender; and transfer taxes, sales taxes, and recording costs. Each party is normally responsible for the cost of preparing or obtaining its own internal documents, such as corporate resolutions and certificates of good standing.

Customs vary on some of these matters. For example, different conventions may apply in different places as to responsibility for preparing the closing documents, including the deed. No matter what the local custom is and what expenses each party pays in the typical transaction, the parties generally are free to allocate these expenses in a different way. An anxious seller may sweeten the deal by agreeing to pay some costs that the buyer usually pays, and the contract should reflect this agreement.

---

*Comment:* With regard to the payment of expenses, custom varies from jurisdiction to jurisdiction. In certain areas, it is customary for the seller to pay for the buyer's title insurance policy. In many other areas, the buyer pays the cost of its own title insurance policy, survey, and other similar items. With regard to transfer taxes and recording costs, the custom also varies from jurisdiction to jurisdiction. Many states have statutes that determine who must pay sales taxes on personal property in the absence of an agreement to the contrary.

---

For unusual or expensive items, the parties may negotiate as to who will bear the expense. For example, if the property is likely to pose environmental risks, the buyer may argue that the seller should pay for any investigations, since the seller is attempting to transfer tainted property. The seller may respond that the buyer must investigate the property at its own expense as part of its ordinary due diligence burden. This disagreement should not be confused with the related question of who must pay to remediate any problems that the investigation discloses.

The parties may decide to sign a less formal agreement before they execute a contract, addressing the payment of various costs in the event they never reach a contractual agreement. Each party may be attempting to force the other to pay both parties' expenses if the deal falls through because of some act or omission of the other party. The parties should be careful when executing a precontractual document of this type, because they do not want a court to determine that it constitutes a contract of sale.

## § 2.121 Time Is of the Essence

As noted earlier, parties to a real estate sales contract will often agree to postponements of the closing.[128] Even if one party is unwilling to extend the sale date, courts often will favor the party seeking a delay. Their reasoning is that the closing date is not an essential term of the contract and that the parties can substantially perform even if the contract occurs a few days or weeks late. This argument makes sense in the real estate setting, because the parties have incomplete information when they sign the contract and are agreeing to a wide variety of closing conditions. It may take somewhat longer than anticipated for the buyer to procure its loan and for the seller to obtain the one missing satisfaction of an old mortgage.

Sometimes, however, one party is facing a strict deadline and will suffer greatly if the closing is postponed. The seller may need to close before the end of its tax year in order to lock in a gain or a loss. The transfer may be part of an exchange or a liquidation with inflexible deadlines. One of the parties may be ailing and may wish to close before his health fails. In these cases, the concerned party should rebut the presumption that the closing date is not a material term by including a "time is of the essence" clause. This clause tells the other party (and, if need be, a judge) that the closing date is an essential term of the contract and cannot be changed without causing substantial damage to the concerned party.

It might be wise for the concerned party to specify the reasons time is of the essence. This will allow the other party to estimate the damages it might incur if it does not close on the stated date. Another approach is for the concerned party to seek liquidated damages that will make it roughly whole in the event that performance of the contract is postponed.

### § 2.122—Caution: Time Is of the Essence

Time is of the essence clauses are more common in some jurisdictions than in others. In some states, such as New York, these clauses are not customary.

### § 2.123 Assignment of Contract

Sometimes, the party that signs the contract as buyer does not plan to acquire the property itself but instead anticipates assigning its rights to a third party. There are at least two situations in which an assignment of contract is common. In some cases, a party may execute a contract to acquire property with the idea that it will immediately assign the contract at a profit. If the purchase price is favorable or if property values are appreciating rapidly, the contract vendee may be able to "flip" the contract and turn a profit on land it never legally owns.[129]

The other situation in which contract assignments are common is when the buyer entity has not been formed yet on the contract date and another entity, or one of the principals of the to-be-formed entity, executes the contract as the buyer.[130] Both parties will recognize that the contract is going to be assigned to an entity that, for legal and practical reasons, does not yet have the power to sign the contract for itself.

The contract should state whether or not it is assignable. The buyer's argument will be that the seller should not care whether the buyer assigns the contract as long as the seller receives the agreed sales price. The seller may fear that the assignee will not be able to perform and that the assignor will have little interest in the contract and little ability to pay a judgment.[131] The seller also may worry that the buyer who plans to assign the contract possesses some critical market information that the seller does not.

In cases in which the buyer entity has not yet been formed, the seller should have fewer objections to an assignment. The principals of the buyer are seeking to save time and money by not forming the entity until they know the property is locked up, and the seller will be no worse off after the assignment than it would have been had the new entity signed the contract in the first place. The seller would be wise to limit these assignment rights so that the party who executes the contract initially may assign it only to a specifically listed assignee with contractually stated characteristics.

In this last setting, the party that signs as buyer may ask the seller to release it from contractual liability as soon as the assignment to the new entity is effective. The seller should have little objection, because it will end up in the same position as it would have been in had the new entity been the original party to the contract. In other settings, however, the seller will be more reluctant to release the original party unless the successor entity is at least as financially capable as its predecessor.

---

*Comment*: In most circumstances, the seller will not object to an assignment to an entity that is related to the assignor if the principal with whom the seller has been dealing is also a principal of the assignee.

---

> *Comment:* Assignment clauses frequently permit assignments to entities related to the buyer or its principals even though they may prohibit assignments to unrelated third parties. For example, the party that executes the contract as buyer may wish to retain the flexibility to assign the contract to a single-purpose entity, and the contract should be drafted specifically to allow this.

### §2.124—Caution: Assignability by Buyer

If the party that executes the contract as buyer intends to assign the contract at or prior to the closing, it is essential in some states that the contract so provide. Although free assignability when there is no express prohibition is the law in many jurisdictions, in other states, a state law prohibition on assignments may undercut the buyer's plans. An outright prohibition in the contract, of course, will lead to the same result. Note also that a prohibition on assignment may impair the ability of the named buyer to merge, consolidate, or sell substantially all of its assets until after the closing.

### §2.125—Caution: Signing on Behalf of Entities to Be Formed

A previous section noted the potential dangers of entering into a contract in the name of an entity that has not yet been formed.[132] It is far wiser to form the entity first and to make sure that it has been properly organized and has duly authorized the transaction. If this is not done, then the party that signs the contract as buyer is personally liable unless the contract provides otherwise.

## §2.126 Miscellaneous Contract Sections

The final portion of the contract ordinarily contains a variety of unrelated provisions addressing miscellaneous matters. While it is common to refer disparagingly to this part of the contract as "boilerplate," each one of these provisions creates important substantive rights. The matters these contractual provisions address may not be as significant as the purchase price, the representations, and the closing conditions, but these paragraphs still need to be considered carefully by the parties and their lawyers. In other words, these provisions of the contract may not require as much thought and negotiation as the ones discussed earlier, but they still should be reviewed with care. The sections that follow discuss these miscellaneous matters.

### §2.127—Further Assurances

Real estate documents typically include a further assurances clause or further documentation clause. This clause obligates each party to execute and deliver any other documents necessary to the proper effectuation of the transaction. For example, if the deed does not meet the jurisdiction's technical requirements for recordation, the further assurances clause would force the seller to execute an amended deed after the closing. This clause should survive the closing.

Lawyers unaccustomed to working with real estate often are amazed at the scope of this clause, but it is commonly employed in real estate transactions.[133] Note that warranty deeds typically include a further assurances clause as well.

### §2.128—Integration, Merger, and Waiver

It is common for a contract of sale to include clauses addressing integration, merger, and waiver. An integration clause states that the contract incorporates and supersedes all of the parties' prior discussions. The clause thus integrates all previous discussions, negotiations, correspondence, and other documentation into the contract. If one of the parties raised an issue and discussed it but did not insist that it be addressed in the contract, the contract will control and the prior discussions will have no legal effect. All past discussions are said to be integrated (or merged) into the written contract.

If the buyer has relied on the seller's verbal statements about the condition of the property, it needs to make sure that these statements appear in the representations section of the contract. By failing to include these provisions in a contract with an integration clause, the buyer effectively agrees to accept the property "as is" with respect to these matters. While the seller that commits fraud—a tort—probably cannot use an integration clause to exculpate itself from the effects of its own intentional misstatements, an effective integration clause should serve to absolve it of any contractual liability for most of its prior verbal statements. Stated bluntly, the buyer must be sure that the seller is willing to back up any puffery in writing.

The function of a merger clause is to merge contractual matters into the deed as of the closing date. A merger clause expressly rebuts any presumption that certain contract provisions survive the closing. If either party, and especially the buyer, wants any representations, warranties, covenants, or indemnities to survive after the closing, it should be sure either that the contract contains a clause specifying that these provisions survive or that the deed warranties cover these matters. While the question of survival already has been addressed at length,[134] the drafter should note how the merger clause and the survival clause interact. Note also that an integration clause occasionally may be referred to as a merger clause, because all prior statements are deemed to be merged into the contract.

> Comment: In some jurisdictions, it is not possible for the buyer to settle and to retain its right to damages for a misrepresentation that it knew about or should have known about as of the time of the closing. Thus, if the buyer discovers a misrepresentation at or prior to the closing, the buyer should notify the seller promptly and should wait for the seller's response before closing.

A waiver clause states that a party's failure to insist on strict performance of an obligation at one point does not impair its ability to insist on strict performance of that same obligation later. This clause also commonly states that a party's decision to rely on one remedy for breach does not preclude it from later seeking to employ another remedy for that same breach.

### §2.129—*Choice of Law; Choice of Forum*

The contract should specify the state whose law will apply to the resolution of any disputes and also might clarify where a party may bring any lawsuit. The deed will be interpreted and enforced under the law of the state in which the property is located, but the same is not necessarily true of the contract of sale. If a New York seller contracts to sell California property to a New York buyer, the parties may agree that New York law shall apply to the contract of sale even though it will not apply to the deed. The parties and their lawyers may be more accustomed to New York law and may prefer to operate in this more familiar legal environment.

> Comment: When drafting a contract of sale, be certain that the chosen forum has some nexus to the property. For example, it would be rather odd to provide that New York law applies if the property is not located

in New York and neither of the parties is headquartered in New York. Practically speaking, the parties are likely to choose the law of the jurisdiction in which the property is located. Note that this is not necessarily the case, however, with respect to the buyer's loan documents.

The parties may also decide that any legal action arising from the contract must be brought in the state courts of New York. Once again, they may be more familiar with these courts and their local rules and procedures. It will be more convenient and less expensive for the parties to resolve their disputes locally; in fact, they may have no tie to California other than the fact that the seller planned to convey California property to the buyer. Note also that the state whose law will apply will not always be the state in which claims must be brought.

### § 2.130—Notices

The buyer and the seller will probably need to send notices to one another during the executory period, and the notices section of the contract provides a mechanism for initiating and memorializing those notices. Although the parties will often ignore this provision and will interact more casually, it is important to have this mechanism in place for the parties to use for their more important correspondence or if their relationship takes a turn for the worse.

The notices section should specify that all notices must be in writing and should state the address to which notices should be sent. This official address should include a street address for deliveries by hand or by carriers that require a signed receipt; a post office box, if applicable, for mailed notices; a telecopier number for notices by fax; a telephone number; and an e-mail address. This section also should note whether the sender is required to send a copy to any other party, such as the recipient's lawyer.

---

*Comment*: Overnight delivery services usually will not deliver to post office boxes.

---

The notices section should list acceptable methods for delivering notices and the dates on which notices are deemed sent when each of these methods is used. For example, this provision may state that for certain enumerated purposes, notice is acceptable only if delivered in person, by overnight carrier, or by U.S. mail. Notices delivered in person might be deemed delivered on the date sent, notices sent by overnight carrier might be deemed delivered on the day after they are sent, and notices sent by U.S. mail might be deemed delivered on the date that is three days after they are sent. These "deemed effective" dates are important if the contract specifies deadlines or grace periods. If the buyer is required to cancel the contract by October 17 if it is unable to obtain financing, it had better be sure that any cancellation notices to be delivered by mail are sent by October 14. This section should also clarify that Saturdays, Sundays, and national holidays do not count as "days" for this purpose.

### § 2.131—Other Miscellaneous Provisions

It is customary to include several other miscellaneous clauses, and these may vary from jurisdiction to jurisdiction. One such clause is a severability clause, which provides that if any provision is in violation of law or is not enforceable for any other reason, its invalidity will not affect the enforceability of the other provisions of the contract. Another clause often included is a clause stating that section headings or captions are for convenience only and shall not affect the meaning of the contract. A third common clause that the parties may choose to include is a waiver of jury trial. Under this clause, each party agrees to be tried by a judge without a jury.

## § 2.132 Counterparts and Multiple Originals

The parties will often sign multiple originals of the contract. Each party should receive an original, and the lawyers are likely to want originals for their files. There is no reason the parties cannot execute multiple originals, but the contract should provide that each of these is deemed to be an original document and may be enforced as such even if the other originals are not produced.

For reasons of convenience, the buyer and the seller will sometimes sign different copies of the same document. There might be eight copies in existence, four signed only by the seller and the other four signed only by the buyer. Technically, each party needs only one original that has been signed by the other party. However, if the parties recognize that they will be signing different duplicates of the same document, they should clarify that each party may enforce the document against the signing party even though its own signature does not appear on the same piece of paper.

If one party will be relying on a faxed copy of an original document or a document that has been signed electronically, this section should confirm the validity and enforceability of a document that does not contain an original handwritten signature. If the parties lack confidence that the courts of the relevant jurisdiction will enforce a document "signed" in one of these ways, it probably would be wise to follow up by obtaining a handwritten original as soon as possible.[135]

## § 2.133 Signature Lines; Date

The contract must be executed by each party against whom it may be enforced, which means that the buyer and the seller both must sign. These signatures belong at the end of the document, although exhibits that are incorporated by reference into the main body of the document are usually attached after the signature page. These signatures need not be affixed before a notary public unless the contract is to be recorded; in fact, the seller would probably prefer that the signatures not be acknowledged before a notary public as a means of ensuring that the contract cannot be recorded.[136] Note that some states require that certain internal provisions of a contract, such as liquidated damages provisions, be separately initialed or signed.

If an individual is a party to the contract, the signature block should contain a blank line on which that party will sign. The person's name should be typed below the line. If a business entity is a party, the name of that entity should be typed. Underneath the name of the entity, the word "By" should appear, followed by a colon and a blank signature line. Below this line should be typed the name and title of the person authorized to sign the document on behalf of the entity. While this sounds simple and straightforward, signature blocks can become rather complicated if, for example, a partnership with a corporate general partner is signing:

ABCXYZ General Partnership
    By: XYZ, Inc., General Partner
        By:_____
            Mary Xyz, President

*Comment:* State laws differ as to whether signatures need to be witnessed or accepted and whether corporate signatures require a seal. Although these formalities have been relaxed in many states, it is prudent practice to have the signatures of the parties witnessed to prove their authenticity, and it also is a good idea to print the name of each executing party under his or her signature.

Some contracts may require the signatures of multiple parties, and the signature portion of the contract may prove to be more than one page long. Depending on the terms of the contract and the provisions of state law, others, such as escrow agents and real estate brokers, may also need to sign.

The date of the contract may be important for several reasons. It is the date on which the accuracy of representations must be tested. It is the date from which any time periods will run: if the contract states that the buyer must cancel within thirty days if it cannot obtain financing, that is the date from which this time span is measured. It is the date by which the party signing as the buyer must exist and the date by which all its entity authorizations of the contract must have become effective. For certain purposes, the statute of limitations may run from that date.

The date of the contract often appears in the very first sentence of the contract, on page one, which may begin, "This Contract, entered into on _____, 20__, . . . ." If so, the signatories do not need to date their signatures and the contract will be effective as of the date stated in the first sentence. In fact, dates on the signature page may create ambiguities. These dates may not correspond to the date on page one and may not even correspond with one another if the parties do not sign contemporaneously. To avoid creating inconsistencies, the signature block should not state the date, and the final sentence of the contract might note that the parties that are signing below intend for the contract to be effective as of the date stated in the first sentence of the contract.

*Comment:* It is important that the effective date of the contract be set forth without ambiguity. The contract may define the closing date, the length of the review period, and other important deadlines by reference to the contract date.

## §2.134 Legal Description and Other Exhibits

As noted throughout this chapter, the parties may wish to attach exhibits to the contract. In many cases, important factual terms of the contract, while essential, may be quite lengthy. The parties may prefer to group this indispensable clutter at the end so that the rest of the contract is easier to read. For example, a fifteen-page legal description of the property must be included but ought to be attached as an exhibit rather than incorporated into the beginning of the contract.[137]

These exhibits often will be prepared by the parties themselves and not by their lawyers. If a representation requires the seller to provide a list of all tenants and the recent rental payment histories for their space, the seller and not the seller's lawyer will possess the information necessary to prepare this exhibit. By including this information in an exhibit rather than in the body of the document, the lawyers can draft the text of the contract without any gaps and can incorporate the exhibit by reference. The exhibit then can be attached to the back of the document when the seller prepares it.

Exhibits should be numbered carefully so that a reader can move easily from the contractual provision to the exhibit and back again. The lawyers must also be sure that the information these exhibits contain is reviewed carefully before the parties execute the contract. It is not unusual for the parties to leave exhibit preparation until the last minute, and a party that receives an exhibit shortly before the contract is signed must be careful to review this exhibit before signing.

Note that much of the information contained in exhibits must be reviewed by someone other than a lawyer. Legal descriptions must be passed along to the surveyor and the title company, rental histories must be sent to the buyer, and environmental reports must be transmitted to the buyer and to the appropriate consultant. The lawyer needs to be sure that this information is received, reviewed by the appropriate person, and attached to the contract.

---

*Comment:* The lawyer and the client must be sure that they both agree as to which party is responsible for reviewing each of the exhibits.

---

## Notes

1. The doctrine of *caveat emptor* has come under attack of late, even in the area of commercial real estate law. *See infra* §2.39.

2. Note that the last example assumes that the buyer is acquiring an entity that owns real estate rather than acquiring the real estate asset directly. A buyer may prefer to acquire the entity if that approach will reduce the transfer costs associated with the transaction. If, instead, the buyer were to acquire the real estate itself, it is unlikely that a liability such as a pending tort suit would encumber the buyer's title.

3. *See also infra* §§ 2.123–2.125.

4. The use of an index is slightly more cumbersome to the reader, who must look in two places to locate a definition (the index and the section to which the index points) instead of one (the definitions section). In addition, if the drafter defines a term at the point in the document where she first uses it and later decides to use that term at an earlier point in the document, she will have to move the definition to this earlier point. Thus the use of an initial definitions section may reduce the amount of cutting and pasting the drafter later must undertake.

5. In some states, use of a correct legal description is essential. *See, e.g.*, Key Design Inc. v. Moser, 983 P.2d 653 (Wash.), *amended by* Key Design, Inc. v. Moser, 993 P.2d 900 (Wash. 1999) (holding that failure to include a legal description violates Washington's statute of frauds).

6. Avoid denominating the price in a foreign currency. This practice may confuse those unaccustomed to it, such as some loan officers, recording officers, or tax officials. Currency fluctuation risks usually can be better handled in other ways.

7. *See infra* §§ 2.21–2.27.

8. *See infra* §§ 2.19–2.20.

9. *See infra* § 2.18.

10. *See infra* §§ 2.16–2.17.

11. *See infra* §§ 2.15, 2.19.

12. For useful examinations of relevant laws and their impact on real estate practice, see Timothy J. Boyce & Thomas C. Bogle, *Are You Doing Business with Osama: Terrorism-Related Provisions in Real Estate Documentation (With Forms)*, Prac. Real Est. Law., Sept. 2004, at 24; Kevin L. Shepherd, *The USA PATRIOT Act: The Complexities of Imposing Anti-Money Laundering Obligations on the Real Estate Industry*, 39 REAL PROP. PROB. & TR. J. 403 (2004).

13. The parties also should make sure that the section of the contract that lists permitted title exceptions notes this arrangement. If they simply agree in the contract to a marketable title standard without any qualifications, then that section and this one will be inconsistent with each other. *See infra* § 2.41. While the specific exception for existing financing that is discussed here will probably override the general marketability language in the title section, it is easy to avoid ambiguities by noting this exception in the section that addresses title matters.

14. The buyer that acquires title subject to existing financing will be liable to the lender for its torts. If the buyer were to commit waste at the property, the lender could not recover from this nonassuming grantee on the note, but could recover in tort. *Cf. infra* §§ 4.18, 6.18.

15. Again, this matter should be noted in the list of permitted title exceptions.

16. The seller also remains liable on the debt unless the lender specifically releases the seller. The seller is not released from its obligations merely by selling the property to an assuming buyer. In the event of a default on the debt, the lender can recover from either the seller or the assuming buyer. If the seller is called upon to pay the lender, the seller can seek reimbursement from the assuming buyer or from the property itself.

17. *See infra* §§ 2.76–2.77.

18. Seller financing sometimes is referred to as "purchase money financing." Use of this term is somewhat inaccurate, because purchase money financing actually means any financing used to provide part of the purchase price, including financing from someone other than the seller. Thus, the use of the term "purchase money financing" to refer to seller financing, while common, is misleadingly narrow.

19. *See infra* §§ 4.13, 5.16–5.17, 6.11, 6.36.

20. For example, a state may hold that liquidated damages are appropriate only if actual damages would be difficult to calculate both at the time of the contract and at the later time of the breach. Moreover, liquidated damages are intended to function as damages and not as a penalty, so they cannot be excessive in amount.

21. A state may require that the parties specifically initial the liquidated damages clause or that the provision be set forth in bold type or in a certain size typeface.

22. The seller may not be holding the down payment itself and next may have to enforce the terms of an escrow agreement. *See infra* §§ 2.24–2.25.

23. *Cf.* Splash Design, Inc. v. Lee, 103 Wash. App. 1036 (2000) (finding that law firm acted negligently in its role as escrow agent).

24. *See infra* §§ 2.97, 7.09–7.10. The parties also must consider the fate of fixtures located at the property, particularly if these fixtures are leased or if they remain subject to existing financing. *Cf. infra* §§ 6.27–6.28.

25. *See supra* § 1.04.

26. It ought to demand the covenant and the indemnity as well but will not need them if the representation is true.

27. In this situation, the buyer also should demand a qualified representation that states, "The Seller represents that there are no tenants currently occupying any portion of the property other than X and Y." In this way, the buyer forces the seller to represent that these two holdovers are the *only* tenants.

28. *See infra* §§ 2.71–2.108.
29. *See infra* §§ 2.64–2.67.
30. *See infra* § 2.39.

31. Similar concerns arise and can be similarly addressed if the seller is an estate, a trust, or the guardian of a minor. If the sellers are tenants in common and the buyer wishes to acquire a 100 percent interest in the property, the signatures of all cotenants will be necessary unless an agreement among the cotenants specifies otherwise. If the sellers are spouses, the signatures of both spouses will typically be required; remember, however, that states differ as to the forms of ownership available to married couples and the legal effects of these forms of ownership. *See generally* WILLIAM B. STOEBUCK & DALE A. WHITMAN, THE LAW OF PROPERTY 175–240 (3d ed. 2000) (discussing tenancy in common, joint tenancy, tenancy by the entirety, and community property).

These concerns do not arise if the seller is an individual, although even in this case the buyer may never know for certain whether the person who signs the document is the person he or she purports to be. The ultimate lesson here may turn out to be that a reputable escrow agent should retain any earnest money payment at least until the buyer has time to complete its due diligence investigation of the seller.

32. *See infra* §§ 2.78, 3.61–3.62.
33. *Cf. supra* §§ 2.07–2.08.

34. A lawyer generally should not issue an opinion as to good standing except in reliance on a good standing certificate from the applicable jurisdiction. *See infra* §§ 2.78, 2.95.

35. The buyer may question the value of including this representation in the contract because of its concern whether the person signing the document on behalf of the seller has been authorized to do so. If the document states that the corporation has authorized the sale but in fact the corporation has not, then the buyer may find itself trying to enforce the contract on an apparent authority theory. The purported seller entity likely will respond that the person who signed the document had no more authority to bind the entity to this representation than to any other statement in the document.

Even so, inclusion of this representation is useful. It may serve to remind the individual that he needs to obtain entity authority before signing the document and that his failure to obtain this authority could lead to personal liability for his ultra vires actions.

This problem differs slightly from the due organization issue discussed in the previous sections. There, the buyer's fear was that the seller did not exist and that the contract thus was a nullity. Here, the buyer's concern is that the seller exists but that it will disclaim any obligations, because the party that signed on its behalf did not have authority to bind the entity.

36. *See infra* § 3.57.

37. *See infra* §§ 2.36–2.37, 3.42.

38. *See infra* §§ 2.78, 2.100, 3.57, 3.61–3.64.

39. *See infra* §§ 2.86–2.87.

40. *See infra* §§ 2.37, 2.43–2.44, 3.15, 3.38–3.42.

41. *See* Washington Post Co. v. Clay Properties, Inc., 580 A.2d 1042 (D.C.) (en banc) (per curiam), *vacating* 573 A.2d 1227 (D.C. 1990).

42. Even if the seller is willing to provide the buyer with a fairly extensive representation as to the condition of the property, the buyer should not rely exclusively on this representation and also should include a closing condition that addresses this matter. The seller probably wants the right to withdraw from the transaction, and not just the right to recover damages. *See infra* § 2.79.

43. *See infra* § 2.52.

44. *See* Prudential Ins. Co. of America v. Jefferson Assocs., 896 S.W.2d 156 (Tex. 1995), *rev'g* 839 S.W.2d 866 (Tex. Ct. App. 1993).

45. *See infra* § 2.109.

46. This blanket statement needs to be modified if the property is subject to a ground lease.

47. This is not always true. The property may be undeveloped or under construction; it may have been occupied entirely by the seller; or it may be subject to shorter-term occupancy agreements, as with a hotel (although hotels often contain tenants such as restaurants, gift shops, and newsstands). In those settings, this section and the next two may be inapplicable.

48. A large tenant may have the right to acquire the entire building or to match any outside offers to do so. This matter already has been discussed earlier, *see supra* §§ 2.36–2.37, but it should also be addressed or referenced here.

49. *See infra* §§ 3.31–3.52.

50. *See supra* §§ 2.45–2.46.

51. *See supra* § 2.47.

52. This last concern is particularly worrisome for the buyer that is acquiring the entity that owns the real estate rather than acquiring the real estate itself. If the buyer is purchasing all of the shares of a corporate owner, then the corporation that owned the real estate before the transfer will continue to own it afterward, even though a different party owns the corporation's shares. The corporate owner of the property will remain liable for violations that occurred before the previous shareholders transferred their shares.

53. 42 U.S.C. §§ 9601–9675 (2000 & Supp. IV 2004).

54. *See id.* §§ 9607(a), 9613(f)(1). Even if a prior responsible owner is liable under CERCLA, it may dissolve or otherwise be judgment-proof by the time the buyer seeks contribution from it.

55. *See, e.g.,* N.J. Admin. Code tit. 7, ch. 1E (addressing discharges of petroleum and other hazardous substances).

56. *See supra* §§ 2.45–2.47.

57. *See* 17 U.S.C. § 102(a)(8) (2000) (extending copyright protection to architectural works); *id.* § 101 (defining "architectural work" to include "the design of a building as embodied in any tangible medium of expression, including a building, architectural plans, or drawings").

58. 17 U.S.C. § 106A (2000).

59. J. THOMAS MCCARTHY, MCCARTHY ON TRADEMARKS AND UNFAIR COMPETITION § 23:11 (2006) ("Non-confusing nominative fair use").

60. 17 U.S.C. § 120(b) (2000).

61. 17 U.S.C. § 106A(e) (2000) (permitting express waivers; statute is not clear whether waivers bind successor owners).

62. *See supra* § 2.58; *infra* § 2.109. The parties also need to consider the possibility that replacement will be impossible or impracticable.

63. There are exceptions, of course. The cost of rebuilding may be prohibitively expensive. A grandfathered use or structure may no longer be permissible, and the municipality may refuse to authorize its replacement. The building may have been significant for historical reasons, and mere physical replacement may not provide the parties with the benefit of their original bargain.

64. *See infra* §§ 7.12, 8.09.

65. *See infra* § 3.14. The issue of existing mortgages, like so many of the other matters addressed in representations, warranties, and covenants, also needs to be addressed in a closing condition in the contract of sale.

66. *See supra* §§ 2.16–2.17.

67. *See supra* §§ 2.15, 2.17.

68. *See supra* §§ 2.19–2.20. Technically, a mortgage from the buyer to the seller should be executed, delivered, and recorded immediately after the seller's deed to the buyer and is not a prior mortgage. To avoid any ambiguity, however, the parties might clarify that this lien will affect the buyer's title from the time of the closing forward.

69. *See supra* §§ 2.14–2.20, 2.41; *infra* §§ 2.71, 2.82.

70. *See supra* §§ 2.41, 2.54.

71. The mechanics' lien problem arises in other contexts during the course of the typical transaction. *See infra* §§ 2.83–2.84, 3.16, 5.05.

72. The seller will have greater concerns if it is providing purchase money financing. In that setting, the contract of sale also is functioning as a loan commitment. *See infra* chapter 4 (addressing loan commitments).

73. *See supra* § 2.32.

74. The buyer's due organization representation thus may provide the seller with a remedy that has more practical value than the remedy provided to the buyer by the seller's due organization representation. *Cf. supra* § 2.32.

75. *See supra* §§ 2.07–2.08.

76. *See supra* § 2.34.

77. Note how the merger doctrine ties in with the use of contract conditions. The buyer that demands a marketable title representation should also insist on a condition precedent that title be marketable. *See infra* § 2.71 (discussing closing conditions). If the seller does not meet this condition, then the buyer's nonperformance would be excused, and the nonperforming buyer would not be in breach and would be entitled to a return of its deposit. If the buyer decides to close even though the seller has not met this closing condition, then the buyer is waiving this condition: the buyer cannot refuse to close after the closing. Thus, the closing condition effectively survives only until the closing and becomes worthless (and linguistically nonsensical) after the buyer accepts the deed.

78. Again, note how the buyer's due diligence obligations are related to the closing conditions specified in the contract. Closing conditions ordinarily track seller representations and provide the buyer with excusable reasons for failing to perform at the closing. *See infra* § 2.71 (discussing closing conditions). Once the buyer closes, however, the closing conditions evaporate. The buyer loses the leverage that the legal right to back out provides and is left with only the right to seek contractual recourse under any documents that still apply.

79. In the absence of a clause specifying duration of survival, the enumerated representations presumably would survive for the limitations period applicable to contracts in the particular jurisdiction.

80. *See infra* § 2.128.

81. *See infra* §§ 7.02–7.03.

82. *See supra* §§ 2.68–2.70.

83. *See supra* § 2.30.

84. Depending on the remedies provided in the contract, the buyer instead may be liable for actual damages, which may be greater or less than liquidated damages. The contract and state law may also permit the seller to seek specific performance—a remedy that may have little practical benefit if the buyer does not have the funds it needs to complete the closing.

85. These loan commitment provisions are addressed in a separate chapter. *See infra* chapter 4.

86. *See supra* §§ 2.32–2.34.

87. Some of these statements may take the form of covenants that, while not true as of the contract date, must become true by the closing date.

88. *See infra* §§ 3.61–3.64.

89. *See supra* §§ 2.38–2.39.

90. *See supra* §§ 2.73–2.74.

91. Note how this issue dovetails with the seller's representation as to the quality of title. *See supra* § 2.41. If the seller is willing to deliver only a

quitclaim deed, the buyer must be attentive to the possibility that there are title problems lurking and must worry about the availability of title insurance. Note also how deed warranties can address some of the buyer's concerns about the seller's post-closing liability: even if the contract merges into the deed, the deed may provide remedies to the buyer. *See supra* §§ 2.68–2.70. Finally, be aware that these three types of deeds may go by different names in different states.

92. *See supra* §§ 2.76–2.78.

93. Among the alternative forms of assurance that the title company may demand is an owner's title affidavit. *See infra* §§ 2.83–2.85. If the seller is to be required to deliver an affidavit, the contract should state this fact in the closing conditions section and should specify the matters that this affidavit will address. *See infra* §§ 2.83–2.85.

94. *See infra* §§ 3.07–3.08.

95. *See supra* §§ 2.16–2.17.

96. For example, if the shopping center purchaser described in Section 2.54, *supra*, is purchasing a center with a reciprocal parking easement, that recorded document will appear as an exception to title. The presence of this easement may be an important element of the deal from the buyer's perspective, but this encumbrance will show up on Schedule B of the title insurance commitment. The buyer should not complain when Schedule B is not "clean," and the seller should be careful that the buyer is not permitted to terminate the contract on the basis of this title exception.

97. This same reciprocal easement may be highly unfavorable to the buyer, and buyer's counsel may not discover this problem until it examines the document and a survey of the property after the contract is signed.

98. *See infra* §§ 5.03–5.05.

99. The mechanics themselves also could provide this information, but in some states the only way to determine the identity of all mechanics is to ask the seller. Even the seller may not know the identity of all mechanics, because lien laws often give subcontractors the right to file liens, and the owner of the property may not know the identity of all subcontractors.

100. In the absence of title insurance coverage, the buyer would have to pursue the seller directly under the deed warranties. The title coverage allows the buyer to recover from the insurer, an entity that is more likely to be present in the jurisdiction and solvent. The insurer then may pursue the seller.

101. In many cases, these parties will be desirable occupants, such as the tenants of smaller stores in a shopping center.

102. *See supra* § 2.12 (discussing reasons for using legal description to describe property).

103. *See infra* § 3.27.

104. These requirements can be found at *http://www.acsm.net/alta.html* (last visited Feb. 25, 2008). The standards include both minimum standards for a survey and form certification language.

105. *See infra* § 4.14. Lenders may have internal policies or may be subject to laws or regulations that place limits on loan-to-value ratios for commercial loans. They will need independent appraisals in their files to prove that they confirmed the value of the property before lending.

106. *See supra* §§ 2.76–2.78.

107. *See infra* § 2.94. The buyer also should be sure to address security deposits specifically in the contract.

108. *See infra* § 3.44.

109. *See supra* §§ 2.90–2.92; *infra* §§ 3.49–3.50.

110. *See supra* §§ 2.32–2.34.

111. Opining as to the law of a state in which the lawyer is not licensed can create many problems for the lawyer. Such an opinion may constitute the unauthorized practice of law in that state and may violate ethical rules in that state or in the lawyer's home state. If the lawyer's opinion is inaccurate and she is sued, her malpractice insurer may deny coverage.

112. *See* American College of Real Estate Lawyers Attorneys' Opinion Committee and American Bar Association Section of Real Property Probate and Trust Law Committee on Legal Opinions in Real Estate Transactions, *Real Estate Opinion Letter Guidelines*, January 15, 2003, *available at http://www .abanet.org/rppt/cmtes/rp/i5/final-opinion-2003.pdf* (last visited Feb. 25, 2008); Section of Business Law of the American Bar Association, Committee on Legal Opinions, *Guidelines for the Preparation of Closing Opinions*, 57 Bus. Law. 875 (2002); Section of Business Law of the American Bar Association, Committee on Legal Opinions, *Legal Opinion Principles*, 53 Bus. Law. 831 (1998).

113. For a discussion of legal opinions given to lenders, see *infra* § 4.17.

114. I.R.C. § 1445 (2000 & Supp. V 2005).

115. In theory, the exchange of money for property occurs simultaneously. In an actual closing, however, the transfer of funds may take longer than the delivery of a deed and can take hours or even days if the buyer wires the funds. The mechanics of this exchange will vary, depending on the type of closing that the parties employ. *See infra* chapter 8.

116. *See infra* § 8.10.

117. *See supra* §§ 2.73–2.74.

118. *See supra* § 2.78.

119. The buyer's efforts here are not wasted, because it will need to provide its lender with an extensive opinion letter. *See infra* § 4.17.

120. If the parties agree that the seller will have obligations after the closing, they should be sure that these obligations are specifically enumerated in the survival clause. *See supra* §§ 2.68–2.70; *see also infra* § 7.23.

121. Even so, the party with the gripe still may be able to wrest additional concessions at the closing from the party that failed to meet the condition. If there is uncertainty as to a title matter, the buyer may decide that it will not close without a reduction in the price, and the seller will have to choose

between reducing the price and losing the sale. The fact that the buyer may waive a condition does not imply that it must do so.

122. *See supra* § 2.58.

123. In fact, the parties may have argued over which of them will bear the cost of removing these structures.

124. *See infra* chapter 8.

125. *See infra* § 2.121.

126. *See generally infra* §§ 4.18, 6.18 (discussing nonrecourse provisions in the lending context).

127. The parties may act in this way if the buyer is purchasing the entity that owns the real estate rather than the real estate asset itself. If, for example, the buyer is buying all of the shares of a corporate seller rather than buying the real estate directly, then the owner entity is not changing, and the buyer may prefer to keep its existing accounts open.

Even if the property itself is conveyed, the parties may elect to continue existing arrangements. If this is the case, the seller should insist that the buyer change the name of the responsible party on the account so that the service provider does not seek recourse from the seller if the buyer fails to pay its bills.

128. *See supra* §§ 2.110–2.111.

129. This technique is particularly popular among investors seeking to obtain contractual rights to property that they believe others are seeking to acquire as part of the assemblage of a larger parcel. If one investor can lock up the rights to a small portion of a larger lot, it can probably flip the contract at a substantial profit to another investor that already has spent its funds on acquiring neighboring lots.

130. *See supra* §§ 2.07–2.08.

131. In this instance, the seller has a strong argument that the down payment should be sizable and should serve as liquidated damages for breach.

132. *See supra* § 2.08.

133. Lawyers for the parties should be pleased to include a further assurances clause in a contract of sale. If one of the lawyers has forgotten to insist on the delivery of an important document, the presence and operation of the further assurances clause may be sufficient to avert a malpractice claim.

134. *See supra* §§ 2.68–2.70.

135. Forty-six states and the District of Columbia have adopted the Uniform Electronic Transactions Act. Uniform Electronic Transactions Act (1999). The Act itself notes, however, that electronic signatures are problematic when affixed to documents that must be recorded. *Id.* § 3, Legislative Note 3. More recently, fourteen states and the District of Columbia have adopted the Uniform Real Property Electronic Recording Act, with several other states considering adoption. Uniform Real Property

ELECTRONIC RECORDING ACT (2004). *See also* ELECTRONIC SIGNATURES IN GLOBAL AND ELECTRONIC COMMERCE ACT (E-SIGN), 15 U.S.C. §§ 7001–31 (2000).

136. *See supra* § 2.118. Note that the notarial form must meet the requirements of the jurisdiction in which the document will be recorded. *Cf. infra* § 8.07 (discussing acknowledgment of other documents).

137. This approach also allows the parties to attach photocopies more easily, rather than retyping or scanning lengthy provisions into the body of the document. In the case of a long and complex legal description in which a typographical or scanning error can be devastating, the parties may be better off avoiding this risk.

# CHAPTER 3

# Post-Contract Due Diligence

### §3.01 What Is Due Diligence? Gathering Information, Reviewing Information, and Addressing Problems

The buyer needs to obtain as much information as it can about the property before the closing. If the buyer discovers problems after it signs the contract but before it closes, the buyer may have contract remedies against the seller, and it may retain the right to terminate the contract without losing its deposit. If the buyer does not discover these same problems until after the closing, it may be left with remedies that have little practical value or with no remedies at all. The prudent buyer will undertake a thorough investigation of the property—often referred to as the buyer's "due diligence"—before the closing so that it can take advantage of these preclosing options if it needs to.

Chapter 2 emphasized the ways in which the buyer can use the contract as a discovery device. The buyer obtains representations, warranties, covenants, indemnities, and closing conditions from the seller, thus causing the seller to disclose facts about the property, including some facts that the seller might not have volunteered without this prompting. The buyer's first tool in its due diligence arsenal is a contract drafted in a way that forces seller disclosures.

The buyer's due diligence does not stop with the contract, and the buyer will use the period between the contract and the closing, known as the "inspection period," the "executory period," or the "due diligence period," to undertake further due diligence investigation of the property. In addition to reviewing the seller's contractual statements and exhibits and confirming their accuracy and acceptability, the buyer should undertake its own independent investigation of the property. This is the time when the buyer continues and completes the process of gathering and reviewing information. From this information, the buyer determines if there are any problems with the property and, if there are, how to address them.

This chapter discusses the buyer's due diligence obligations and how the buyer meets them. It lists the major issues that the buyer must consider, describes how the buyer can investigate these issues, gives examples of problems that commonly arise, and illustrates ways of resolving these problems.

## §3.02 Due Diligence and the Contract of Sale

This chapter's discussion of the buyer's due diligence obligations will, in many ways, mirror the previous chapter's coverage of the contract of sale. This is not surprising, because the contract plays a significant part in the buyer's due diligence investigation. The contract of sale takes a prospective approach: the buyer asks the seller to reveal information about the property, and the parties agree ahead of time what will happen if this information proves to be inaccurate. Once the parties sign the contract of sale, their emphasis shifts from planning for problems that may be discovered in the future to investigating and addressing them now.

The typical buyer knows much less about the property than the seller does and must learn everything it can before it closes. As a result of this asymmetry, the buyer bears most of the due diligence burden during the executory period. For this reason, the first part of this chapter will examine most due diligence matters from the buyer's perspective, focusing on the responsibilities of the buyer, the buyer's lawyer, and the other professionals working for the buyer. If the buyer discovers problems during the course of its investigation, the parties must next attempt to address them in a mutually satisfactory way, and this chapter will also discuss the resolution of due diligence issues.

Note that the sequencing of this chapter differs from that of the previous one. Chapter 2 discussed contractual matters in the order in which they appear in a typical contract. It began with preliminary matters specific to each sale before shifting to representations, closing conditions, and miscellaneous other matters. This chapter, in contrast, groups due diligence matters by topic, on the assumption that most lawyers will find it more useful to prepare their own checklists on a topic-by-topic basis. The chapter begins by discussing title and survey matters and then turns to lease review and estoppels, the physical condition of the property, corporate matters, and loan issues.

## §3.03 Contract Remedies for Problems Unearthed during Due Diligence

The executory period is the time during which the buyer is given the opportunity to uncover due diligence problems. If the buyer negotiated a fair contract, it will provide the buyer with an array of possible responses, and the buyer will have to choose the one that is most appropriate to any problem that arises. The buyer's lawyer should already be thinking about the legal responses the buyer can make upon discovery of specific due diligence concerns. The buyer's legal position will be strongest if it negotiated for an expansive list of seller obligations in the contract and if the buyer enjoys a wide range of options if it discovers problems about which it was previously unaware.

> *Comment:* What are the buyer's options if it discovers problems during the due diligence period? The seller may have agreed to resolve the problems the buyer discovers, to resolve them up to a set dollar limit, to reduce the purchase price, to compensate the buyer in another way, or to allow the buyer to terminate the contract and receive a refund of its down payment.

In some cases, the seller will have offered the buyer a representation, a warranty, or a covenant. This statement will have told the buyer something about the current condition of the property or will have promised the buyer that the seller will take some action before the closing. The buyer must independently verify the accuracy or confirm the performance of the seller's representations, warranties, and covenants. If the seller breaches one of these statements, the buyer may pursue the remedies available for breach, including any remedies provided in an indemnity. The seller's breach of a representation may allow the buyer to obtain damages, compel specific performance, or seek other remedies provided in the contract.

In other cases, the seller will have provided the buyer with a closing condition that will allow the buyer to terminate the contract without penalty. If the buyer determines that the seller has failed to meet a closing condition, it may withdraw from the contract and receive a refund of its down payment.

Most of the buyer's leverage disappears after the closing, so it must complete its due diligence research during the executory period. If the buyer has not insisted on a survival clause, its rights under some or all of the seller's representations will merge into the contract at the closing, and its ability to exercise its contractual remedies may vanish. Even if some of the buyer's contractual remedies survive the closing, the practical benefit of these remedies is far greater before the buyer hands over the acquisition funds to the seller. Closing conditions, which allow the buyer to back out of the deal without penalty, are useless if the buyer has already closed. It is imperative that the buyer undertake its entire due diligence investigation before the closing, while the seller's representations and conditions still allow the buyer to react in a useful way.[1]

### §3.04—Checklist: Due Diligence and Closing Checklist

See Appendix E for a Form of Due Diligence and Closing Checklist.

### §3.05—Technique: Allocating Responsibility for Due Diligence Matters

The buyer often expects its lawyer to arrange for various due diligence investigations. While it is customary for the lawyer to order certain items (such as the title commitment and the survey), other items (such as appraisals, physical inspections, or environmental reports) are the responsibility of the client. With respect to these last matters, the lawyer's role is to advise the client as to what types of due diligence review might or should be undertaken, while making it clear that it is not the lawyer's duty to arrange for examination of these matters. Even if the lawyer is not responsible for initiating these portions of the due diligence review, the lawyer should monitor the due diligence checklist and make sure the client undertakes these tasks.

## §3.06 Title and Survey Matters

One of the buyer's most important obligations during the executory period is to investigate the seller's title to the property. The buyer must ensure that the seller actually owns the property and wants to avoid paying the purchase price to someone who lacks the legal power to convey title. Beyond mere ownership, the buyer also must determine the quality of the buyer's title. The buyer must learn of any liens or encumbrances and, if they cannot be removed, must determine whether they are acceptable.

A title investigation will not always provide the buyer with all the information it needs to make these important decisions. If the buyer learns that there is a utility easement across the property, its next question is likely to be, "Where?" The buyer will need an accurate survey of the property to be able to answer questions of this type, and the survey is a major component of the buyer's investigation of title. The following sections discuss these important title and survey issues.[2]

The title and survey due diligence process can be broken down into three segments for analytical purposes. First, the buyer's lawyer must identify title problems. The lawyer will order a commitment to insure title from a title company or title agency and a survey from a licensed surveyor and will review these documents upon receipt.[3] Second, the lawyer must decide if there are any title problems that are important enough that they need to be resolved before closing and must initiate the process of resolving these problems. Third, at the closing, the lawyer must determine whether any of these title problems remain unresolved, must advise the client whether and how to proceed, and must ensure that the title insurance policy and survey are in acceptable final form. Throughout this process, the lawyer will confer with her client, with opposing counsel, and with the title insurance company representative and the surveyor.

The next two sections of this chapter examine the first of these three segments of the title due diligence process. These two sections discuss the title commitment and the form title insurance policy and show how the buyer's lawyer identifies title problems from these two documents. These sections also address some standard title insurance issues. Following this introductory discussion, the chapter turns to the second segment of the process, by describing specific title problems that commonly arise in commercial real estate transactions and ways to address these issues. Each of these sections selects a particular problem and suggests ways to resolve it before the closing. One of these sections focuses on the survey, the problems it might disclose, and different ways of addressing these problems. Sections in later chapters address the real estate closing, which is the third segment of the title due diligence process.[4]

> *Comment:* The buyer should determine the title and survey requirements of its lender as soon as possible to avoid duplicating effort. If the buyer selects a title company or surveyor that is not acceptable to the lender, the lender may insist on using a different service provider. This is likely to increase the cost to the buyer.

## § 3.07—The Title Commitment

The buyer wants someone to examine title before the closing and to provide it with a report disclosing what the examination reveals. This title search may contain mistakes or may omit an important matter, however, so the buyer wants more than a mere report: the buyer wants a policy of insurance issued by a licensed, reputable, and creditworthy title insurance company that states the condition of title and insures the new owner that this statement is accurate. Even if the buyer is willing to take a risk on title to save the insurance premium, its lender will require a policy of title insurance.

The title insurance company should issue the policy of title insurance at the closing. The lawyer for the buyer does not want to review title matters at the last minute, however. The lawyer needs time to examine the report and decide if any matters need further attention and also needs comfort beforehand that the title company actually will issue the policy at the closing. For these reasons, the buyer will demand a commitment to insure from the title insurance company. This commitment will disclose all information that the title searcher has discovered, will track the format of the policy, and will advise the buyer of the steps that must occur before the insurer is obligated to issue the final policy. The lawyer for the buyer must review this title commitment with great care, must determine whether there are any problems with title, must help the parties figure out how to address these problems, and must ensure that all of the conditions precedent contained in the title commitment are met by the closing date.

> *Comment:* In some cases, the buyer's lawyer will ask a title company to search title and issue a commitment. In other cases, the buyer's law firm will search title and issue the commitment itself, acting as an agent for a title insurance company. Local practice varies greatly.

> *Comment:* Practice also varies as to whether the buyer or the seller will provide the title commitment and pay for the title insurance policy. The

buyer that retains its own title insurer obviously will be in a better position to negotiate changes to the policy.

The title commitment should be exactly that—a written commitment on the part of the insurer that it will provide title insurance to the buyer on stated terms. These stated terms are important, and the buyer's lawyer must review the commitment with great care. The remainder of this section discusses the title commitment and the issues to which the buyer's lawyer should be attentive. The next section turns from the title commitment to a discussion of the owner's insurance policy itself. The American Land Title Association (ALTA) adopted a new set of title forms in 2006, including a form of title commitment and new owner's and lender's insurance policies. These forms are widely used in real estate transactions and are readily available to lawyers.[5] The discussion here focuses on the ALTA forms.

The insurer's title commitment will list the conditions that must be met before the insurer is required to issue its policy. For example, it will state that the company is not obligated to insure title to the property until the premium is paid. The commitment also includes an expiration date so that the company's commitment does not last indefinitely.

Schedule A of the commitment should specify the effective date of the commitment and the name of the current title holder. The current title holder usually will be the seller, although in some cases the buyer will know that the seller has contracted to convey property that it does not yet own. If the name of the current title holder does not match the buyer's expectations, then the buyer needs an explanation from the seller. This section of the commitment also should state the name of the party that will be insured at the closing, typically the buyer or the buyer's designee, and the amount of insurance to be issued.

The insured property should be identified in Schedule A. The buyer's lawyer must confirm that the legal description set forth in the title commitment exactly matches the one contained in the contract. The title searcher has examined the property described in the title commitment, and if this description does not match the one in the contract, the buyer may insure the wrong property or less than all of the correct property. The legal description should include any easements or other property interests that the buyer will be acquiring from the seller.

*Comment:* In many instances, easements are not included in the description of the property to be insured. It is a good idea for the buyer to obtain affirmative title insurance for any easements that benefit the property. This affirmative coverage insures the buyer that it will have the benefit of the easements that are included in the description. Title insurance covering these easements also should be addressed in a closing condition.

Schedule A will also state the type of ownership interest that the title company is committing to insure. Buyers most often acquire a fee simple in the property, but insurers also will insure leasehold interests, including ground leases.[6] In addition, this portion of the commitment should state the amount of insurance that the title company is agreeing to provide. The buyer typically wants insurance in an amount equal to the purchase price.

*Comment:* The buyer that is purchasing unimproved land on which it intends to erect a building at a later date should be certain that the title insurance company will issue additional insurance to cover the cost of the improvements.

Schedule B of the title commitment sets forth a list of specific exceptions and exclusions to coverage, reflecting the liens, encumbrances, and other matters that the title company discovered during the course of its search of title. By discovering these matters and listing them as exceptions to title, the insurer is telling the buyer that it will not insure the buyer against any title problems that arise as a result of these matters. In other words, the insurer is telling the buyer, "These are your problems, not ours."

Schedule B usually starts off by listing several standard exceptions that vary from jurisdiction to jurisdiction. To this extent, the schedule is not unique to the property. These standard exceptions may exclude from coverage such matters as the rights of parties who occupy the premises under unrecorded agreements; the rights of parties under unrecorded easements; matters that can be discovered only by an accurate survey or a physical inspection of the premises; mechanics' liens; real property taxes; and mineral rights.

*Comment:* As discussed later, it is common for the title insurance company to delete standard exceptions upon request. The title company typically will insist that the seller provide adequate information or an affidavit that satisfies the company that the matters to be deleted will not pose title problems.

Following this list of standard exceptions, Schedule B will list all matters that the searcher discovered during the examination of title. While the other sections of the policy contain form language or specific facts that should have been known to all parties beforehand, Schedule B may reveal some matters that the parties did not anticipate and will help the buyer's lawyer continue the due diligence investigation into the quality of the seller's title. Because Schedule B is unique to each transaction, it will serve as the jumping-off point for the next portion of the lawyer's due diligence work.

It is essential that the buyer's lawyer review each of these Schedule B exceptions thoroughly. In some cases, it will be possible to address the exception before closing and have it removed. In other cases, it will not be possible to remove the exception. If the buyer has committed to accepting title anyway, then it will be acquiring title subject to the exception. The lawyer now begins to see why it was so important to set forth in the contract the exact quality of title that the buyer is entitled to receive.

*Comment:* The buyer's lawyer may not be able to convince the title insurance company to remove some of the Schedule B exceptions to coverage. If this happens, the buyer's lawyer must assess the significance of each of these exceptions individually. This is the lawyer's task and not the title company's.

Schedule B of the title commitment lists title exceptions in summary fashion. The commitment typically includes a brief description of each exception and refers to the book and page of the recorded document that gives rise to the title exception. The buyer's lawyer should *always* review the document itself and not rely on the title company's summary description. When the lawyer orders the commitment, she should make clear that she expects to receive photocopies of these referenced documents and not just a bare commitment, and she should be sure that she receives and reviews every document to which the title commitment refers.

*Comment:* The title searcher will review the Uniform Commercial Code (UCC) records to see if any relevant financing statements have been filed. Be very careful to give directions to the title company as to whether it is to perform a UCC search as well as a search of matters in the land records. Some title companies provide UCC searches as a matter of course, while others do not. If the contract covers personal property—as it almost always does—then it is absolutely critical that the title company also search for UCC financing statements.

## §3.08—The Form Title Insurance Policy

Real estate lawyers will become quite familiar with the ALTA 2006 Owner's Policy over the course of their careers, but the newcomer to real estate transactions needs to read the policy carefully and understand the provisions of this form. The lawyer should review the form policy before her first closing so that she is aware of its terms and limitations and knows which provisions to question or to seek to modify. Technically, the title commitment is the document that the lawyer needs to address as part of her due diligence obligation; the title insurance policy is not issued before the closing. However, the lawyer must contemplate now the problems that might arise at closing, and a thorough familiarity with the policy form is important even at this earlier stage in the transaction.

The first two pages of the title policy state exactly what is being insured and refer the reader to the exclusions from coverage, the exceptions from coverage, and the conditions that appear later in the document. The ALTA form policy covers the insured against loss or damage sustained or incurred by reason of ten enumerated types of title problems, up to the amount of insurance. These potential title problems include:

1. Title being vested in someone other than the party listed in the policy.
2. Any defects, liens, or encumbrances.
3. Unmarketability of title.
4. Lack of access to the property.
5. Violations of certain land use laws, plus several other specified governmental actions, to the extent that there is a public record of these matters.
6. Certain bankruptcy claims.
7. Any defects arising between the policy date and the date on which the deed is recorded.

These pages also confirm the insurer's obligation to pay the costs of defending any claim, including attorneys' fees and expenses. The bottom of the second page contains a signature line. The buyer's lawyer must remember to confirm that an authorized representative of the insurer has signed the policy.

The next section of the ALTA form lists five exclusions from coverage. Because these matters are expressly excluded from coverage, the buyer needs to assure itself in other ways that none of these matters poses a problem. The exclusions listed in this section are:

1.  Land use laws, including zoning and environmental laws, and other exercises of the governmental police power, except to the extent that there is a public record of any violation.
2.  Rights of eminent domain, except to the extent that there is a public record of any exercise.
3.  Defects that the insured has created or agreed to, or knows of even though they are not matters of record.
4.  Certain bankruptcy claims.
5.  Real estate tax liens attaching between the policy date and the date on which the deed is recorded.

*Comment:* If the buyer is acquiring an entity that owns real estate rather than purchasing the real estate directly, it runs a heightened risk that the title insurer might deny coverage under the third of these five exclusions. Even though the buyer may not have undertaken any actions that fall within this exclusion, the entity it is acquiring may have, and the entity's actions (and knowledge) will be imputed to its new owners. For this reason, the buyer would be wise to request a so-called non-imputation endorsement from the title insurance company.

This section of the title insurance policy also excludes from coverage most matters that arise after the policy date, reminding the lawyer that title insurance, unlike other forms of insurance, insures the policy holder against past events and not future ones. The presence of a valid title policy gives the owner comfort that someone has searched title carefully (or, more accurately, that the company is insuring the policy holder against those defects that are not specifically excluded in the policy). At the same time, the exclusions section serves to emphasize to the lawyer that title insurance is not all-encompassing.

Schedule A of the policy contains certain important information specific to the transaction. This schedule sets forth the amount of insurance, the date and time of the policy, the name of the insured, the type of estate that will be insured, the name of the title holder, and the legal description of the land. These matters parallel those described in Schedule A of the title commitment. Recall that the title commitment sets forth the state of title as of the commitment date, while the policy should describe the state of title as of the closing date. Because of this temporal difference, the date, the time, and the name of the title holder will differ from the commitment to the policy, and some of the other information may change as well.

Schedule B is the portion of the title policy to which the real estate lawyer will devote the most attention. This section lists exceptions from insurance coverage that are specific to the property, and it should track the corresponding section of the title commitment. To the extent that matters disclosed in the commitment have been resolved, the lawyer must be sure that the policy accurately reflects the resolution of these matters. To the extent that matters disclosed in the commitment remain unresolved, the lawyer must help the buyer determine whether these title defects are acceptable, whether the title the seller will deliver complies with the terms of the contract, and whether the buyer will proceed to close. The buyer also must ascertain whether any new exceptions have arisen since the insurer prepared the commitment.

The ALTA form title policy ends with a lengthy list of conditions. This list defines certain terms that are used in the document, sets forth procedures for enforcing rights under the policy, and addresses other matters that are intended to be treated consistently in all title policies.

The next sections of this chapter discuss common title problems in more detail. These sections should help the lawyer learn how to read a title commitment, how to identify title problems from the commitment, how to begin to address these problems, and what to do if these problems are not resolved satisfactorily.

### §3.09—Real Property Taxes and Assessments

Death and taxes may be life's two great certainties, but the title insurer, unlike the life insurer, is concerned with only the latter. The buyer's chief concerns are that all real property taxes have been paid through the most recent payment due date and that taxes accruing for the current payment period are prorated between the seller and the buyer at the closing.[7] The searcher's first task is to confirm that taxes for all past years have been paid in full, along with any interest and penalties. The title searcher gathers this information by searching the real property tax records, usually found in the tax assessor's office.

> *Comment:* The person conducting this tax search also should determine whether there are any federal or state tax liens filed against the seller that may constitute liens on the property.

If past years' taxes have not been paid, the searcher will list the years and amounts as a special exception in Schedule B of the commitment. Unless the seller disclosed these arrearages to the buyer in advance and the parties factored this amount into the sale price, the seller should be required to pay these overdue taxes before the closing or, if necessary, at the closing from the sale proceeds. In either event, the buyer's lawyer should be sure that the taxes are paid by the closing and also should verify that the title company has insured this fact by omitting the tax exception from the commitment and the title policy. If there are overdue taxes that the searcher failed to discover and list on Schedule B, then the policy provides coverage.

> *Comment:* In many jurisdictions, the deed cannot be recorded until all real estate taxes that currently are due have been paid.

The next step for the buyer's lawyer is to determine the status of the property taxes for the current tax year. The mechanics of achieving and insuring this result depend on the jurisdiction and its method of levying taxes. In many localities, taxes are assessed at the beginning of the tax year and immediately become a lien on the property but are not due until later in the tax year. The title searcher will discover this lien and will appropriately list it on Schedule B of the commitment. This title exception reminds both parties that the taxes will become due soon and also reminds the buyer to apportion the current year's taxes at the closing: The buyer will eventually pay the taxes for the entire tax year and needs to be sure that the seller reimburses it for that portion of the taxes attributable to the time when the seller still owned the property.[8]

Other jurisdictions do not officially place a lien on the property until later in the tax year. For example, if a county uses the calendar year as its tax year, the lien for the tax year may not officially appear until October, with taxes due at the end of December. If the title searcher performs the tax search in March, he will not find a tax lien, even though taxes for the current year are accruing. Nonetheless, Schedule B will contain a general standard exception for current taxes, reminding the buyer's lawyer to determine how the jurisdiction times the assessment and required payment of taxes and to confirm that no payments are overdue. Once again, the buyer's lawyer should remember to prorate the amount of these taxes at the closing, because the buyer ultimately will have to pay the amount for the full year.

Still other jurisdictions collect taxes at the beginning of the tax year. If the seller has already paid these taxes, then the buyer should make sure that any Schedule B exception notes the payment of these taxes, and the seller should be certain to demand a prorated reimbursement from the buyer at the closing.

Other quirks may arise, reminding the buyer's lawyer to become familiar with local law and practice. In many jurisdictions, the property tax year will not coincide with the calendar year, and the parties need to know when this year commences so that they can correctly calculate arrearages, advance payments, and apportionments. Some jurisdictions collect tax payments more than once per tax year, either by using a more frequent assessment and collection cycle or by allowing installment payments of annual taxes.

In some locales, the penalty for late payments or bonus for early payments is set at a level that encourages payment after or before the official due date. The buyer may determine that the seller's latest tax payment is overdue because the seller, like many other property owners in the jurisdiction, regularly pays its taxes three months late to take advantage of a low-interest loan from the county. If the buyer's lawyer is comfortable that this practice creates no worrisome risks for her client, she may accept it but must remember to calculate the apportionments correctly. In a similar way, a substantial discount for early payment may have induced the seller to prepay taxes not yet due, and the seller must be sure to demand reimbursement for these early payments. In all of these cases, the Schedule B exception in the commitment should remind the buyer's lawyer of this issue. The lawyer must become knowledgeable as to local law and practice and must make sure that the title commitment and title policy are accurate and protect her client properly.

In some cases, the parties may not be sure of the exact amount of the taxes that are not yet due. The lien will appear in the records and in the title commitment, but the assessed valuation of the property or the tax rate may be unsettled. From a title insurance perspective, this uncertainty should have little effect on the matters just discussed. However, the parties may be unable to calculate their reimbursements and apportionments accurately. In these cases, the parties should agree (and the contract already should provide) that they will make their calculation based on either the previous year's actual amount or their estimate of this year's amount. If one party believes that this number will differ substantially from the actual amount ultimately due, that party also may ask for a post-closing adjustment when the number has been firmly set, with the title company or escrow agent holding in escrow an amount sufficient to make this adjustment.

### § 3.10—Caution: Real Estate Taxes, Local Law, and Nonlocal Lawyers

Unauthorized practice of law standards may prevent a lawyer who is not admitted to the bar of a given state from representing a party in that state in connection with the purchase of property. In addition, a lawyer should have some obvious practical concerns about representing a client in a jurisdiction if the lawyer is unfamiliar with that state's law. For example, a lawyer who is not licensed in California would have a very difficult time understanding the impact of Proposition 13 on property tax calculations in that state. Even if the lawyer is admitted in the state in which the property is located, local law and practice vary so widely that a lawyer who does not regularly represent clients in the area in which the property is located should rely on someone with local knowledge.

### § 3.11—Covenants, Servitudes, Easements, and Reciprocal Easements

If any recorded covenants, servitudes, easements, or reciprocal easements affect the property, references to them should appear on Schedule B of the title commitment. The buyer's lawyer should ask the title company to deliver photocopies of these recorded documents and should be sure to review each document in full, rather than relying on the summary information that appears on Schedule B.

Unlike the tax exception, which can be removed by payment, covenants and other similar documents are a permanent part of the land records and cannot be removed as exceptions unless they have terminated. The title company will not delete these matters from Schedule B of the policy because they are exceptions to title. As to these matters, the primary role of the title company is disclosure. The company provides the insured with information about the items it is excepting from coverage and commits to insure only that its search was thorough. Once the buyer's lawyer is aware of these property interests and can review the operative documents, she can determine the extent to which these interests violate the representations and conditions contained in the contract.

In some cases, such as utility easements, the physical location of the easement will be the buyer's primary focus. The buyer may have known from the outset that the electric company has a right-of-way across the property so that an abutting owner can connect to the main line running along the street. The only uncertainty remaining for the buyer is the location of the easement. Once the title company turns the easement document over to the buyer, the buyer can deliver it to its surveyor and the surveyor usually can use the legal description in the document to locate the right-of-way on the survey. The buyer can decide from the survey depiction of the easement whether it is a problem. If it is not, then the buyer will proceed to close. If the easement does pose a problem, then the buyer should look to the representations and conditions in the contract and examine what remedies are available in response. The lawyer again can see that careful forethought in drafting the contract will prove to be important when the inevitable but unpredictable title problems appear weeks later.

> Comment: Unfortunately, some easements of record will turn out to be so-called blanket easements. These are easements that have been given to a party such as a utility company without identifying their specific location. The result is that the easement covers the entire property. Usually, the location of blanket easements can be fixed more precisely by negotiating with the utility company. Blanket easements can, however, present challenging problems in some instances.

In other cases, the substance of the agreement may demand the bulk of the buyer's attention. A recorded reciprocal easement disclosed in Schedule B may state that the seller has agreed with a neighbor that they and their successors will keep their parking lots open to one another at all times. If the buyer plans to open a nursery school and the neighboring owner is operating a tavern, this reciprocal easement would prevent the buyer from erecting the fence it had planned. This knowledge is worthless to the buyer who has already signed a contract unless the contract provides it with useful rights. At the same time, effective rights do the buyer no good unless it learns of the easement before closing, by reviewing the title commitment and then the easement document itself. The obvious lessons to the buyer's lawyer are to negotiate the contract with care; to read every word of every document disclosed in the title commitment, including all attached exhibits; to decide whether any of these property interests will harm the client in any way, including the client's ability to sell the property when it wishes to; and to address any problems before the closing.

While the title company's primary role with regard to easements and similar documents is to discover and disclose them, the company also will insure against some of the negative effects of these documents in certain cases. Title companies often will insure, free of charge, that breach of a restriction will not lead to forfeiture of title, although they usually provide this coverage only if the insured requests it. If the nursery school operator decides to build the fence anyway and see how the tavern owner responds, or if the fence is already there in violation of the agreement and the buyer does not want to remove it, the title company would not cover the insured's damages or the cost of any equitable relief but would insure against any failure of title.

The title company may be willing to go one step further and insure the buyer against any losses it suffers if a court orders enforcement of the restriction. The insurer is most likely to provide this coverage when enforcement of the restriction is unlikely and the cost of compliance is slight. If a recorded agreement requires that all property owners leave a ten-foot setback along the sides of their lots and the seller's air conditioning unit encroaches by four inches, the title company may be willing, upon request, to insure the buyer against the costs of complying. This is particularly true (and least useful) in cases in which the restriction probably is not enforceable at all, as with a racially restrictive covenant.

If the title company is willing to provide any insurance of this type, the buyer should ask it to include this additional coverage in the commitment and should confirm that the title policy reflects the revised commitment. The title company that is willing to provide any of this affirmative insurance will either modify the relevant exceptions in Schedule B or add endorsements at the end of the commitment and the policy that specify the additional coverage it is providing. An endorsement of this type sometimes is known as a CC&R endorsement, for "covenants, conditions, and restrictions."

### §3.12—Caution: Reviewing Covenants, Servitudes, Easements, and Reciprocal Easements

It is essential that the buyer's lawyer examine each provision of any covenants, servitudes, easements, and reciprocal easement agreements that affect the property the buyer is acquiring. It is difficult or impossible to review and understand the impact of these agreements without also having copies of each of the plats and site plans that are customarily attached to them. Review of a current survey will provide additional essential information.

### §3.13—Existing Mortgages

The title commitment should disclose all unsatisfied mortgages and deeds of trust of record. In some cases, the parties will be aware of these interests and will intend for them to continue. The buyer may be buying subject to existing financing or may be assuming an existing mortgage. Schedule B will confirm the existence of these documents and will allow the buyer to examine their precise terms. The final title policy will continue to list these matters as Schedule B exceptions.

The buyer will not be concerned with the content of mortgages that the seller plans to satisfy out of the sale proceeds. Schedule B of the title commitment will disclose these documents, but they will have no legal effect after the closing. The final policy of title insurance should not list these matters as exceptions to title because they will be satisfied at the same time that the buyer acquires title and the insurer issues the title policy. The mechanics of this flow of funds will be discussed in connection with the closing,[9] but if everything proceeds as it should, these exceptions to the title commitment will not lead to corresponding Schedule B exceptions in the title insurance policy and, therefore, should not worry the buyer.

Sometimes the title commitment will reveal mortgages that neither party was aware of. The seller is responsible for delivering title that meets the contractual standard—most likely marketable title— and the seller must figure out who holds the outstanding mortgage and must pay that party as much as it is entitled to. In many of these cases, it will turn out that the debt was paid off long ago but was never satisfied of record. Nonetheless, it can take weeks or months to receive a recordable satisfaction from the correct party, assuming that the party can be found at all. If the document is old enough or the amount small enough, the title company may be willing to provide affirmative insurance to the buyer that it will not suffer any financial loss as a result of the mortgage. The company will not omit the exception from Schedule B of the title policy, because the mortgage still is an exception to title, but it will add language to the exception or in an endorsement that provides this affirmative coverage.

> *Comment:* It may be difficult or impossible to obtain a release if the lender no longer exists, as is the case with many banks and savings and loan institutions. In addition, the mortgagee of record may have assigned the mortgage without recording an assignment, which could mean that there is no practical way of determining the party to which the mortgage was assigned. This problem is even more common if the parties used a deed of trust.

The title commitment and policy will exclude from coverage any mortgages that the buyer executes in connection with its acquisition of the property, whether they are in favor of the seller or a third-party lender. Technically, these exceptions arise after the buyer's acquisition of title (by a few seconds, most likely). In addition, they are items to which the buyer has agreed, and for these reasons they already are addressed in the standard exclusions contained in every policy. The buyer should not object to these exceptions but should confirm that they are described accurately.

### §3.14—Caution: Existing Mortgages and Prepayment Fees

Certain mortgages are not prepayable or are prepayable only upon payment of a substantial prepayment fee. Both the seller and the buyer should carefully review the prepayment provisions of all existing mortgages. If the seller is required to deliver title free of all liens, as usually is the case, then the seller will have to pay any prepayment fees.

### §3.15—Tenant Leases and Parties in Possession

If a lease or a memorandum of lease has been recorded, then a reference to the lease should appear on the Schedule B list of title exceptions. The searcher also may learn of a tenant from other recorded documents. If a contractor who performed work for a tenant has filed a mechanics' lien, that document will appear on Schedule B and will serve, in turn, to provide notice of the tenant's interest. The information revealed in Schedule B should coincide with the lease information that the seller has provided to the buyer,[10] although the information in the title commitment will probably be less extensive and less detailed.

Title insurers know that other parties may be in possession under unrecorded leases or other unrecorded arrangements or may even occupy space without authorization. They naturally are reluctant to insure that the only occupants of the property are the parties whose interests were revealed by the title search. For this reason, the form of title policy may include a more general exception for parties in possession of the premises under unrecorded leases. By including this general exception, the title company is advising the buyer that the exception to coverage goes far beyond the parties specifically listed in Schedule B. In fact, the buyer is not receiving insurance against the occupancy of any party except for parties with recorded interests that are not expressly excepted on Schedule B.

The buyer may not wish to accept a title policy that includes a broad exception for any party in possession, because the buyer has no idea as to the identity of some of these parties or the scope of their interests. For this reason, the buyer should ask that the title company omit this exception from its commitment and issue a title policy that lacks this exclusion. The title company will want some additional comfort before it is willing to omit this exception, and it can obtain this comfort in two different ways.

The buyer or the title company can physically inspect the property on its own. If the property is a shopping mall, for example, someone can walk the halls and make a list of every party in occupancy, including those not previously revealed by the title search. Although the scope of inquiry notice varies from state to state, the bona fide purchaser may be protected against the rights of any occupant that has not either recorded its interest or provided constructive notice of its interest to the buyer by virtue of its occupancy of the space. The buyer's chief concern is with actual possessors whose presence is not noted in the land records.

---

*Comment:* In most states, occupancy by a tenant imparts constructive notice of the tenant's lease. In many cases, evidence short of physical possession may suffice, such as the presence of construction materials or a "Coming Soon" sign.

The title insurance company can also ask the seller to provide it with an affidavit and indemnity listing all parties that have the legal right to occupy space in the mall. In fact, the title company will often make this demand in addition to inspecting the premises. The affidavit should list all parties in possession and should state that there are no other parties with rights of occupancy. It also should indemnify the insurer against any loss that it suffers as a result of any inaccuracy in the affidavit.

If the title insurer receives occupancy information in either or both of the ways just described, it may be willing to strike out the standard exception for parties in possession and replace it with a list of the specific tenants it has discovered. The insurer must except all the tenants who have legal occupancy rights, because those rights often take priority over the ownership interest of the buyer and truly are exceptions to the buyer's title. By eliminating the blanket "parties in possession" exception, however, the company assures the buyer that no one beyond these listed parties has any right to possession and promises to cover the buyer's losses if this assurance proves to be inaccurate.

If any occupant disclosed by inspection or affidavit does not have the right to possess any portion of the premises, the buyer should advise the seller that the seller must remove this occupant. The title policy will not insure against the occupancy of this party, so the buyer must force the seller to resolve the problem before the closing. Parties falling into this category might include holdover tenants, illegal subtenants or assignees, adverse possessors, and other trespassers.

To the extent that the seller's affidavit and indemnity contains inaccurate or incomplete information that causes the insurer to omit a specific exception that it otherwise would have included, the insurer will have recourse against the seller. Meanwhile, the buyer can recover directly from the insurer without having to worry whether the seller will be available and capable of satisfying a judgment, without having to face the defense that the seller's contractual representations as to occupancy have merged into the contract, and without having to pay its own legal costs. The buyer recovers from the insurer when it discovers the surprise occupant, and the insurer then must pursue the seller.

> Comment: It is very important that the buyer and its lawyer become aware of the rights that tenants in possession under unrecorded leases may have. If a tenant is in possession, it is imperative that the buyer read the tenant's lease and make due inquiry as to the rights of the tenant, including rights of first refusal and options to purchase the property.

## §3.16—Mechanics' Liens

Recorded mechanics' liens are treated just like other recorded interests. The title searcher should discover them and list them on Schedule B, thereby excepting them from coverage. The buyer will learn of these interests when it reviews the commitment and will demand that the seller take the steps necessary to remove these liens. This should impel the seller to pay each mechanic the amount it is owed on or before the closing. To the extent that any lien arises from a disputed matter, the seller should provide alternative security to the mechanic, commonly in the form of a bond, or the buyer should insist that an amount sufficient to satisfy the lien be held in escrow after the closing until the dispute is resolved. The buyer's lender must approve the bond or escrow. If the title insurer is satisfied with the bond or escrow, it should remove or insure over the exception.

Mechanics' liens that have not yet been recorded and potential mechanics' liens raise much knottier problems. Recall that contractors, subcontractors, and suppliers have the right in many states to file liens that relate back to an earlier date for purposes of establishing their priority under the recording statute. Although the specifics of these laws vary greatly from state to state, the end result in many states is that a mechanic may file a lien after the closing that relates back to a date before the closing and that thereby encumbers the buyer's title. There is no way for the buyer to discover this lien in the course of its title search, because the lien has not been recorded yet. Title companies, well aware of this problem, typically include an exception for unrecorded mechanics' liens, thereby placing the problem squarely back in the buyer's lap.

> Comment: State mechanics' lien laws vary so widely that it is absolutely essential that the buyer's lawyer understand local law, practice, and custom. Many states allow mechanics' liens to relate back, as just noted, while other states, such as Maryland, do not. The buyer's lawyer simply must become aware of local law, practice, and custom, or must work with local counsel that is.

Concerns about mechanics' liens, like concerns about parties in possession, can be addressed by a physical inspection of the property and, more critically, by an affidavit and indemnity from the seller. The physical inspection is useful because it can tip the inspector off to any recent work at the property. Of course, some types of work may not be evident to the inspector, and even the obvious presence of new construction does not tell the observer whether the mechanic has been fully paid for its labor and materials.

An affidavit from the seller forces the seller either to disclose the existence of any unpaid mechanics or to state affirmatively that there are no unpaid parties entitled to file a mechanics' lien. On the strength of the seller's affidavit, the insurer will strike the blanket mechanics' lien exception and replace it with any specific unrecorded mechanics' liens of which it has become aware. The buyer will immediately object to these enumerated liens and insist that the seller remove or otherwise address them by the closing date. The end result is that the buyer receives title insurance against unrecorded mechanics' liens and the insurer can seek indemnification from the seller if it needs to.

### § 3.17—*Violations*

The buyer needs to learn if the property is in violation of laws, ordinances, or regulations enforced by any governmental entity with jurisdiction over the property. To obtain this knowledge, the buyer must request that the searcher check the records of any office in which violations are documented. This inquiry may already constitute a part of the standard title search, but the buyer should remember to ask the searcher specifically to look for any violations.

If Schedule B of the commitment reveals any violations, the buyer once again must ask that the seller address these exceptions before the closing so that the insurer can omit the exceptions from the title policy. In some cases, addressing these matters will involve nothing more than correcting a mistake by a government official or paying some money. If the violation is erroneous or has been remedied, then the seller must demonstrate to the relevant official that it should remove the violation. If the municipality has taken corrective action on its own and levied a fee against the property, then the seller must pay that fee or the buyer must ensure that this amount is paid out of the sale proceeds.

Other violations may be more difficult to correct. If the structure violates building codes or fire and safety codes, the buyer may determine that expensive modifications are necessary and may have to solicit construction estimates from contractors. Depending on the terms of the contract, the seller may not be required to make these repairs. Even if the seller is not required to remedy the violation, the violation should give the buyer the right to refuse to close, and the buyer is likely to advise the seller that it will exercise its right to terminate the contract unless the seller remedies the violation. The buyer may wish to inform the seller that there is nothing to be gained by refusing to make the repair, because any subsequent buyer is likely to discover the violation and make the same demand. If the buyer would prefer to perform the work itself after the closing, it might be willing to accept the property with the violation as long as it can deduct the estimated cost of the work from the sale price.

In the worst case, the building may suffer from a violation that cannot be corrected. Unless the buyer is willing to purchase the property anyway, it must advise the seller that it will not close unless the seller receives a waiver or variance. If the seller cannot obtain this document by the closing date, then the buyer's goals have been irremediably frustrated and the buyer must withdraw from the deal. This potential problem demonstrates once again how important it is for the buyer to obtain suitable representations and closing conditions when it negotiates the contract of sale and to perform its due diligence obligations thoroughly.

The buyer will be insured against any violations that are matters of public record and that have not been excepted from the coverage of the title insurance policy, so its goal is to make sure there are no excepted violations. Any unacceptable violations that the insurer discloses on Schedule B of its commitment should be remedied by the seller and then omitted from the commitment and title policy by the insurer. Note that in some jurisdictions, it may be difficult to ascertain the existence of violations, or title companies might not routinely search for them. If this is true, then the buyer or its lawyer must find other ways to determine whether there are any current violations.

### §3.18—Caution: Discovering Violations

Although the buyer wants to be aware of violations of laws, ordinances, and regulations that are matters of record, a request for a certificate from a local authority may lead to an inspection by the local authority, which could have unwanted consequences for either or both of the parties. Therefore, this matter must be approached with great caution. In addition, when dealing with older properties, be certain that someone investigates whether the property is on a national or local historic registry.

### §3.19—Judgments and Lis Pendens

If the seller has failed to satisfy a judgment rendered against it, that judgment may appear as a lien on title. If the judgment was rendered in the county in which the property is located, then the judgment may automatically constitute a lien on the property by operation of the state's judgment lien law. If this is not the case, or if the judgment was rendered in another county in the state or in another state, then the successful litigant probably will have to record a certified copy of the judgment in the land records in the county in which the property is located. Either way, the searcher must remember to check the appropriate court dockets and property records. Any unsatisfied judgment that has achieved the status of a lien should appear on Schedule B of the title commitment.

The buyer that learns of a judgment lien will insist that the seller remove it by the closing date. This may require the seller to satisfy the lien out of the sale proceeds or to post a bond. If the matter still is in dispute, the buyer must ensure that the lien is removed from the property and that it attaches instead to another asset of the seller, such as the sale proceeds. Once the lien has been removed, the title commitment and policy should omit this matter, and the buyer will be insured that there are no judgment liens affecting the property.

If litigation that may affect title to the property is ongoing at the time of the transaction, the buyer may discover that the property is subject to a lis pendens. Unlike a judgment lien, which may arise from litigation that had nothing to do with the property itself, a lis pendens arises only if the property itself is the subject of the dispute. In some states, the lis pendens arises automatically at the time the lawsuit is initiated, which means that the searcher must examine court records in search of relevant pending disputes. In other states, the plaintiff must affirmatively file a notice of lis pendens in the land records. This latter method means that the plaintiff initially bears the burden of notifying potential buyers rather than the buyer bearing the burden of discovering any relevant disputes.

Lis pendens problems may be more difficult to resolve than judgment lien matters, because the amount of any potential liens may be unsettled. The litigation giving rise to the lis pendens may even dispute the seller's title to and right to convey the property. The buyer must be sure that the lis pendens is omitted from the title commitment and the final title policy. The seller may be able to satisfy the plaintiff and accomplish this result by settling the suit or by providing the plaintiff with alternative security for the satisfaction of any resulting judgment. If the seller cannot persuade the plaintiff to release its lis pendens, the insurer will not omit it from the title policy, and the buyer will probably choose to withdraw from the transaction.

### §3.20—State and Federal Tax Liens

State and federal entities with taxing authority have the legal right to impose liens against the property if the seller has failed to pay taxes that it owes, such as income, employment, estate, or inheritance taxes. These liens, unlike property tax liens, do not arise on a regular and periodic basis and generally do not achieve superpriority status. Rather, they function like other liens and take their place in the priority sequence ordained by applicable recording laws. The searcher that discovers any tax liens of this type will list them on Schedule B, and the buyer then will demand that the seller take the steps needed to satisfy these liens.

The holder of any of these liens is a government entity and the method of enforcing these liens probably differs from the method of enforcing mortgages, mechanics' liens, or judgment liens. However, the buyer's concerns are the same here as with any lien that is senior to the buyer's interest. The buyer will advise the seller that Schedule B of the commitment has revealed a lien for unpaid taxes and that the buyer will not close until the seller takes the steps needed to have this lien removed. If the seller owes these amounts, it must pay them, perhaps out of the proceeds of sale. If the seller disputes these amounts, it must provide the taxing authority with alternative security that is satisfactory to the holder of the lien and to the title company, so that the title company will remove the exception from Schedule B. The buyer should refuse to close unless the exception is removed from the title policy or unless the seller reduces the price or places in escrow funds that are sufficient to pay any lien that survives the closing.

---

*Comment:* Removing tax liens is not always an easy thing to do. In a transaction with which one of the authors is familiar, the seller was involved in a major dispute with the state over millions of dollars in personal property taxes. This dispute led the state to impose a lien on all the property of the seller, thereby creating serious problems for the parties.

---

### §3.21—Air Rights and Development Rights; Mineral Rights

If air rights or development rights are an important part of the transaction, the buyer must be sure that these matters are appropriately addressed in the title commitment. It is important to distinguish between these two different concepts. A party that purchases a fee simple interest in land owns not only the plane of dirt but also the cube of air directly over that dirt. The new owner of the property can develop these "air rights," subject to applicable laws such as zoning restrictions on height. Sometimes, a buyer purchases someone else's air rights. A hospital that wishes to connect two noncontiguous buildings with an elevated walkway over an intervening building will need to acquire air rights from the owner of that intervening fee. The buyer must be careful that the title policy insures the buyer's title to these air rights. The title commitment should describe these rights with sufficient specificity (a legal description will not suffice unless it is three-dimensional!) and should clarify how the owner of this elevated cube of air can access it.

Development rights differ from air rights. Some jurisdictions limit the height and lot coverage of structures that an owner may build. If an owner builds less intensively than it is allowed to under these laws, it may be allowed to transfer its unused "development rights" to other property owners. A developer that wishes to build a twelve-story office building in a ten-story zone may be able to buy two floors of development rights from a neighbor with an eight-story building. Similar issues arise in less urbanized contexts, such as heavily restricted resort communities. Once again, the title commitment and policy should clearly describe and insure these development rights, which may be an important and expensive component of the deal.

Cubes of property extend downward as well as upward. Just as some owners may be buying the cube of air above someone else's fee, others may be buying or leasing subsurface rights. If the buyer's right to mine, drill, or quarry is an important aspect of the transaction, the buyer must be sure that the title commitment and policy adequately describe and insure these subsurface rights.

Laws pertaining to air rights, development rights, and mineral rights are highly state-specific, and these issues do not arise in every deal. The lawyer whose transaction raises these issues must remember to familiarize herself with state law and to confirm that the title policy addresses these matters to her satisfaction.

> *Comment:* Air rights and development rights are not the only nontraditional property rights that may arise in a transaction. Other, similar rights include those created by conservation easements and wetlands remediation easements. An agreement creating rights such as these may provide that conservation or remediation on one parcel frees up another restricted parcel for development. All such rights need to be carefully investigated and should be insured.

### § 3.22—Permitted Encumbrances

Schedule B will disclose every recorded matter that the title searcher has discovered, but not all of these matters will trouble the buyer. The seller may have disclosed certain title encumbrances to the buyer in advance, and the buyer may be satisfied or even happy to accept them. The title search may reveal other encumbrances that the buyer finds acceptable. These satisfactory matters are commonly referred to in the contract as "Permitted Encumbrances."

One obvious case in which the buyer will not object to a Schedule B exception is when the buyer is purchasing subject to existing financing or is assuming that financing. The searcher will discover the prior mortgage in the records and enumerate it on Schedule B, and the buyer will not object. The buyer's reaction is likely to be similar when the searcher excepts reciprocal easement agreements, utility rights-of-way, and tenant leases that the buyer already was aware of. These matters constitute title encumbrances, but they are acceptable and may even be beneficial.

The seller knows that the title searcher will discover these matters, and it should disclose them to the buyer in advance and address them in the contract. There are at least two related reasons why this is true. First, the mere existence of these title encumbrances is enough to render title unmarketable in some cases. The buyer will have the right not to close under a standard marketability closing condition and also may have recourse against the seller if the seller has provided a marketability representation. If the seller neglects to list these matters as exceptions to its more general representation and closing condition, it is allowing the buyer to back out of the deal for free and perhaps even to recover damages from the seller.

Second, the contract typically will provide that the buyer need not close unless it receives a title insurance policy free of Schedule B encumbrances. If the seller fails to disclose these matters and list them as exceptions to this requirement, the buyer again will have the right to terminate the contract without penalty and also may be able to recover contract damages from the seller. For these reasons, the seller should be sure to include a list of permitted exceptions in the contract, perhaps in an exhibit.

There is another reason the seller should disclose these matters to the buyer. Although they may technically render the property unmarketable, many of these encumbrances actually increase the value and desirability of the property. The buyer may have been anxious to buy the property because of the presence of good rent-paying tenants, an assumable mortgage at a below-market interest rate, and a cross-easement agreement with a successful project next door. Not only should the seller disclose these matters in the contract, it should emphasize their importance and value.

Even undesirable title encumbrances may be permitted under the contract. The buyer may have agreed to accept the property even though a holdover tenant has refused to vacate its space. The seller may have disclosed this matter and may have persuaded the buyer to accept the property anyway, perhaps by offering the buyer additional consideration such as a price reduction. If the presence of this holdover tenant is one of the terms of the deal, the parties should document that fact in the contract and the buyer should agree that it cannot refuse to close when this matter appears on Schedule B of the title commitment and policy.

### § 3.23—*Title Endorsements*

The ALTA form title policy provides the buyer with fairly extensive coverage, particularly if the buyer persuades the insurer to modify or omit some of the standard exceptions and exclusions to coverage. Even so, the form policy does not cover all risks, and some buyers may have particular concerns that arise from the individual characteristics of a given deal. Buyers and their lawyers need to be aware that title companies offer endorsements to their policies that provide additional coverage beyond that contained in the standard form.

The scope and availability of these endorsements vary widely from state to state. Some states regulate title insurance heavily and may limit endorsements to title coverage or prohibit them altogether. In other states, title insurers can and do offer a wide array of endorsements. The lawyer for the buyer needs to become familiar with the range of endorsements available and then needs to decide if any of these endorsements are warranted. If the lawyer decides that the buyer will need to obtain endorsements to the title policy, she should be sure to advise the insurer of this fact when she initially orders the title commitment. In this way, she will learn early in the process whether these endorsements are available, whether any conditions need to be met before the title company will provide them, and whether the title insurer will charge a fee for this additional coverage.

### §3.24—Checklist: Title Endorsements

See Appendix F for a Checklist of Title Endorsements.

### §3.25—Zoning and Subdivision Laws

As part of the investigation of the property, the buyer's lawyer needs to confirm that local zoning laws permit the use that the buyer intends to make of the property. The buyer does not wish to buy raw land for an industrial park and then discover that the land is zoned for residential use only. The buyer should address zoning matters in the representations and the closing conditions of the contract.

To the extent that the buyer's planned use will not comply with existing law, the lawyer needs to ascertain whether a variance, a special use permit, or a rezoning of the parcel is likely to be available. If one of these options is feasible, the lawyer needs to make sure that the buyer pursues this option in accordance with the terms of the contract. This may entail enlisting the cooperation of the seller, who still is the record title holder. If the parties have executed a real estate sales contract with a lengthy list of closing conditions and a sufficiently long executory period, the buyer should have the time it needs to address its land use concerns. This contract should allow the buyer to withdraw without penalty if it cannot obtain the necessary permits and will require the seller to cooperate with the buyer in its pursuit of these permits. An option contract can achieve the same result.

> *Comment:* Zoning inquiry should not be limited merely to permitted uses. The buyer's lawyer must also examine other restrictions commonly included in zoning ordinances, such as setback requirements, height restrictions, parking requirements, and restrictions applicable to residential units.

The buyer needs to recognize that the form title policy specifically excludes zoning and other land use matters from coverage and that title insurers are reluctant to omit this exclusion from the title policy. In many cases, the solution for the buyer's lawyer is to examine applicable land use laws herself or to retain zoning counsel to undertake this investigation. Zoning law is a highly technical and localized component of commercial real estate practice, and many lawyers are reluctant to render zoning opinions, particularly if the property is physically located outside the area in which their practice is based. Whether the buyer's real estate counsel undertakes this zoning investigation herself or brings in a qualified zoning lawyer, the investigation will involve a careful examination of applicable law and a clear understanding of the buyer's intended use of the property.

> *Comment:* The local zoning authority often will issue a letter setting forth the zoning classification of the property and sometimes even its permitted uses.

Title companies may be reluctant to omit the zoning exclusion from the form title policy, but they sometimes will issue a zoning endorsement to the policy. The buyer's lawyer needs to review the language of any proffered zoning endorsement with great care and will likely take little comfort even if the insurer is willing to issue the endorsement. Zoning endorsements often contain highly qualified language and may simply state that the insurer has examined the applicable zoning and has determined that the property is located in a stated zone, without any assurance that this zone permits the buyer's planned use. These endorsements may be quite expensive, and some states will not allow insurers to issue them at all. Even in states in which an insurer can issue a zoning endorsement, it may refuse to do so. The insurer may be uncertain as to the effect of the zoning laws and may fear the substantial liability that could result if it issues the endorsement.

The buyer also needs to determine if the property has been subdivided. If it has, the property most likely has been assigned a lot number on a subdivision plat. The buyer will need to determine whether the property must be legally described by that lot number and plat name or by metes and bounds.

---

*Comment:* Lenders are sensitive to subdivision issues. They recognize that the improper subdivision of a lot can lead to conveyancing problems later on. Subdivision irregularities may also indicate that the parcel does not have an accurate tax lot number, suggesting that the proper real estate taxes have not been paid. As a result, lenders generally will refuse to lend if the parcel in question appears to have been subdivided from a larger lot without meeting all state and local legal requirements.

---

The buyer should be aware that other land use laws can raise similar concerns. Counsel for the buyer needs to familiarize herself with historic preservation laws, environmental restrictions, and other similar land use controls, and not just with zoning and subdivision laws.

### § 3.26—Coinsurance and Reinsurance

On extremely large deals, the buyer may be concerned that the title company will be unable to satisfy a claim under the policy. Even the largest and most stable companies have only limited reserves for payment of claims, and there is no reason for the buyer to purchase more insurance from the company than the company will be able to pay if title should fail entirely. For this reason, buyers of expensive properties may prefer to divide their title insurance up among two or more companies, thereby reducing the risk of nonpayment of a valid claim.

Title companies facilitate this process by coinsuring or reinsuring title among themselves. The insured party need not contact multiple companies and arrange for numerous partial policies. Instead, one company serves as lead insurer and then finds other companies to share in the risk. If this lead company coinsures, then it essentially is setting up numerous fractional policies for the insured party and retaining only a part of the liability for itself. The insurers divide the premium and are responsible for paying claims pro rata. If the lead insurer instead reinsures, it serves as lead insurer for the entire amount but purchases insurance from other companies to cover portions of the risk. It is insuring the entire amount but also is purchasing insurance of its own for that portion of the total amount that it could not cover out of its own reserves.

ALTA recognizes the need for coinsurance and reinsurance and provides forms for these purposes. The buyer needs to make it clear when it wants its title company to coinsure or reinsure. This insured party should verify that no one company is bearing more risk than the insured party is comfortable with.

### §3.27—Survey

The legal description of the property will often be a lengthy and confusing metes and bounds description; occasionally it may use imprecise language or may refer to a monument that no longer exists in its original form (". . . proceeding from Old Man Brown's oak tree for about 30 feet toward the river bed. . . ."). Even if the property is described by block and lot numbers or by reference to a filed subdivision plat, this description does not tell the buyer everything it needs to know about the property and its physical appearance. For this reason and others, the buyer should order a survey of the property and should review it as part of the buyer's due diligence review. This section discusses some of the more important survey issues, but the lawyer should understand that survey review is a more complex task than this section can address in full.

The survey should be prepared by a surveyor or engineer who is licensed by the state and who meets all required professional standards. The surveyor should include a signed certification on the survey that verifies the accuracy of the survey and that sets forth the standard to which the survey has been prepared, typically the ALTA standard.[11] The survey should also include a statement confirming that the buyer, its lender, their title insurer, major tenants, and other interested parties may rely on the survey's accuracy. This statement clarifies that, in the event of an error, these parties will have the right to bring a personal claim against the surveyor for negligence.

Comment: In most instances, the lawyer will request that the surveyor prepare a survey that meets ALTA standards. Not all surveys meet ALTA standards, and if the survey must meet a different set of standards, the lawyer should specify what the survey requirements are. In all cases, the buyer's lawyer should let the surveyor know the identities of the parties to whom the survey must be certified.

The lawyer should be sure to order the survey well in advance, particularly in northern states where surveying may be difficult during the winter months. The surveyor will probably ask the lawyer to provide copies of the last deed of record and any other documents affecting title. If the lawyer becomes aware of additional relevant documents after receiving the title commitment, the lawyer should remember to send copies of these documents to the surveyor.

When reviewing the survey, the lawyer should begin by confirming that the boundaries of the surveyed land conform to the legal description in the last recorded deed. The description's point of beginning will probably be described by reference to some fixed monument, such as an iron pin or a street corner, and this point should be identified on the survey as the "Point of Beginning," or "POB." As the lawyer reads each consecutive "call" (statement of distance and direction) from the written description, she should trace the perimeter of the surveyed property and check that the lines on the survey appear to follow the words of the description. The final call should bring the boundary of the property back to its point of beginning, closing the perimeter of the surveyed property.

When record bearings, angles, or distances, differ from measured bearings, angles, or distances, both the record and measured information should be clearly indicated. If the record description fails to form a mathematically closed figure, the surveyor should so indicate. In either event, both the record title description of the property (or the description provided by the client) and any new description prepared by the surveyor should be included on the face of the plat or map or otherwise accompany the survey in order to conform to current ALTA standards.

Comment: It is not uncommon for the depiction of the property in the survey that is prepared for the buyer to differ from the legal description in the deed by which the seller obtained title to the property. In these instances, the title insurance company, the seller, and the buyer should be certain that all the property that is supposed to be conveyed to the buyer actually is conveyed at the closing. The seller may be willing to deliver a warranty deed to the property described by the older deed and a quitclaim deed to the property depicted by the new survey. Some sellers will go further and will deliver a warranty deed to the entire property, particularly if they receive assurances from the surveyor that the new survey and the older legal description actually represent the same property. Similarly, upon receipt of assurances from the surveyor, many title companies will insure that the survey and the legal description represent the same property.

The lawyer next should confirm that all physical structures and all significant natural features are shown on the survey. Buildings and outbuildings; all ways of access, including driveways and alleys; parking lots and other paved areas; utility poles and connections; landscaping; roadways and curb cuts; fences; waterways (including ponds, lakes, springs, and rivers bordering on or running through the property); and natural features such as ridges and canyons all should be portrayed. The location of these features should be indicated by measurements perpendicular to the nearest perimeter boundaries. This portion of the lawyer's survey review may involve consultation with the client, who is likely to be more familiar with the physical features of the property than the lawyer is, or examination of recent photographs of the property.

The reviewer of the survey should confirm that all structures and other improvements that the seller is supposed to convey are located entirely on the property. If there are no buildings, the survey should bear the statement, "No Buildings." In addition, no structure or improvement belonging to a neighbor should encroach on the seller's property. The survey should display enough detail about the surrounding property—including streets and sidewalks, natural boundaries such as rivers, and the edges of neighboring property and the names of those lots' owners—that the reader can get her bearings. The survey also should show proper street numbers where available.

The lawyer's next step is to locate all known easements on the survey. Any easement that is revealed in the title commitment should be turned over to the surveyor, who should locate each of these interests on the survey. If the county has the right to pave sidewalks along the edge of the property or the electric utility has the right to service an existing power line, these interests should be shown clearly. The buyer's lawyer needs to confirm that these rights-of-way do not interfere with the buyer's current uses or planned future uses of the property. If the telephone company has the right to service a buried cable that runs right through the center of the property, the buyer's office building plans may be rendered impossible or more expensive. If the surveyor has knowledge of any easements or servitudes that are not observable at the time the survey is made, the surveyor should note this lack of observable evidence. If there is any recorded or otherwise known property interest that the lawyer believes should be noted on the survey but is not, the lawyer should advise the surveyor that the survey is incomplete and needs to be corrected.

By the same token, if any easement or other matter that appears on the survey is not reflected in a document, the buyer needs to investigate this unexpected interest. The survey should display observable evidence of any easements and servitudes, including those created by roads; rights-of-way; water courses; drains; telephone, telegraph, or electric lines; and water, sewer, oil, or gas pipelines. This is true if these features are observed on or across the surveyed property or on adjoining properties if they appear to affect the surveyed property. The survey also should note if there are any surface indications of underground easements or servitudes. A visible but undocumented pathway through a vacant lot may be evidence of a prescriptive easement that the buyer needs to know of before closing. Crops growing on land that was thought to be vacant may reveal an unexpected tenant, thereby putting the buyer on constructive notice of all terms of the tenant's lease. In these instances, the survey discloses new information to the buyer that the buyer must address before the closing.

## §3.28—Access to the Property

During the course of her review of the title commitment and survey, the buyer's lawyer must confirm that access to the property is both available and adequate for the buyer's intended purposes. The ALTA form title policy insures that there is access to the property but does not insure that this access is satisfactory for the buyer's needs. The curb cut on a main street that currently is in use may not be authorized, and property that appears to front on a main street may not have legal access to that street. Vehicles may have to take a long and roundabout route to enter property that appeared to be more easily accessible. The survey should show where all access points to the property are located, and the lawyer must remember to confirm that the important access points are legally permitted. The title company may be willing to insure the location and legal propriety of specific access points by endorsement.

Sometimes the only access to the property may be by right-of-way over the property of another. A fast-food restaurant that is owned in fee simple may be located in the middle of a shopping center parking lot, with the only access to the eatery by easement across the lot. In cases such as this, the original easement must be in writing and recorded; a description of the easement should be included in the legal description of the deed that the seller delivers to the buyer and that the buyer records; this same legal description must appear as part of the insured estate on Schedule A of the title insurance policy; and the easement must be shown on the survey. This legal right of access is an essential part of what the buyer is acquiring, even though neither the seller nor the buyer ever has a fee simple interest in the underlying land.

> *Comment:* The fact that the property includes a right to an easement does not necessarily imply that the buyer can use the easement for the buyer's intended purposes. For example, an easement that provides access for residential use may not be able to be burdened with access for a commercial use or even for a multi-family residential development, as these uses may generate a great deal more traffic. The buyer must be attentive to the easement's scope and limitations.

### § 3.29—*Utilities*

What is true for access for visitors also is true for access for necessary utility services. If the property can provide for its own needs, as with well water or a septic system, the buyer must confirm that these systems comply with all applicable laws, are in good working order, and are adequate to meet the needs of the property. If the property must receive service from outside its borders, as with electricity and telephone service in most cases, the access points should appear on the survey. The buyer should confirm that it has the right to connect to the public supplier of these services. If the property connects to these utilities via a right-of-way over another party's property, the buyer also needs to confirm that it has the legal right to continue to use this easement. The buyer also will want the survey to show the easement and the title policy to insure it.

### § 3.30—*Torrens Registration*

Several American jurisdictions follow the Torrens system of title registration. In Torrens jurisdictions, the recording office is not just a repository of documents open to public inspection. These jurisdictions also issue title certificates, similar to automobile titles, setting forth the name of the owner, the legal description of the property, and a list of all recorded encumbrances. In theory, the municipality is liable for errors, but this liability usually is quite limited, and the buyer will still want to obtain title insurance in case of title problems.

When Torrens property changes hands, the seller needs to deliver its certificate of title to the buyer at the closing and indicate on the certificate that it is conveying the property. The buyer will then bring this certificate to the appropriate public official, who will replace it with a new certificate that indicates the name of the new owner and that updates the list of title encumbrances. The seller's mortgage will probably be omitted from the certificate and will be replaced by the buyer's new financing, and any obsolete liens will be removed.

The main concern for the lawyers for the parties is that the seller remember to bring the original certificate to the closing. Torrens certificates display an amazing tendency to disappear, and the sooner the seller begins looking for it, the more likely it is that the certificate will find its way to the closing. Lost certificates can be replaced, but the process may be slow enough and cumbersome enough to delay the closing.

## §3.31 Lease Review and Estoppels

So far, this chapter has examined title and survey due diligence matters that are relevant in nearly every commercial real estate transaction. Commercial real estate buyers ordinarily care about far more than just the title to the property, and for most buyers the due diligence obligation does not end with title and survey issues. Most commercial buyers are purchasing income-producing property and need to verify that the property is capable of producing the income that the buyer expects. Because this income most commonly takes the form of tenant rents,[12] the buyer will need to review every lease affecting the property and will probably want to contact at least some of the property's tenants directly. The following sections describe the ways in which the buyer and its lawyer can obtain information about tenants and tenant leases, the problems that typically arise, and the ways in which the parties can respond to these problems.

As was true with the previous sections, each of the following sections serves at least two purposes. First, each section reminds the lawyer of her obligations to her client during this important due diligence phase of the transaction. These sections advise the lawyer how to gather information that she and her client need and how to use that information. If the client wants to be sure that a major tenant is obligated to remain in place and pay rent for the next twelve years, she can confirm these matters by reviewing the lease now. Second, these sections remind the lawyer of the issues that she needs to have addressed earlier in the transaction, when she negotiated the contract. If it turns out that the major tenant has the right to terminate the lease early or that the lease actually has only one year to run, then the lawyer had better have remembered to address the duration of this lease in the seller's representations—with adequate remedies for breach—and in the closing conditions. Once again, the lawyer must anticipate in the contract the due diligence problems that might arise later.

### § 3.32—Obtaining Tenant Leases

The first step in the lease review process is for the buyer to obtain exact copies of the leases themselves, including all exhibits. While the seller may have boasted to the buyer during the negotiation phase about the more desirable terms of these leases and will have already provided the buyer with a rent roll and lease summaries, the buyer needs to learn more than just the good news. The contract should require the seller to provide the buyer with copies of all leases promptly so that the buyer and its lawyer can begin their due diligence review of these documents.

The buyer may worry that the seller will neglect to turn over a complete set of these important documents, either because of a desire to mislead the buyer or out of simple carelessness. It is important for the buyer to have received a covenant that the seller will deliver a complete set of these documents, including all exhibits, amendments, modifications, extensions, and renewals, so that the buyer will have remedies for any omissions by the seller. This covenant should be accompanied by a closing condition that allows the buyer to refuse to close if it has not received a complete and accurate set of these these documents in advance of the closing. Once the parties sign the contract, the buyer's lawyer needs to be persistent in requesting a complete set of these documents.

Buyers must remember—and need to remind their sellers— that lease amendments and renewals may appear in informal correspondence and not just in official-looking documents with the words "Lease Amendment" in large type at the top. If a tenant regularly sends a monthly check for less than the stated rental amount along with a cover letter explaining that the tenant had to pay someone to provide janitorial services because the landlord failed to do so, the tenant may argue that the landlord's regular acceptance of a reduced amount of rent constitutes a lease amendment. The buyer will not become aware of this issue unless it reviews the correspondence, which the seller may not think of as part of the lease. In some cases, these omissions will be obvious from the documents themselves, as with the expired lease where the tenant still is in possession. When the buyer's lawyer asks the seller why this tenant still is in possession, the seller may suddenly remember the letter agreement extending the lease for five years at an increased rent. In other cases, the only way for the buyer to be sure that it has received a complete set of documents is to ask pointed questions.

Remember that there are two parties to each of these leases, and it will be possible for the buyer to confirm that it has received a complete set of documents by asking each of the tenants. This confirmation normally is handled in a tenant estoppel letter.[13]

---

*Comment:* It is absolutely essential when the lawyer obtains copies of the leases and related documents that she also receive copies of all exhibits to these documents, including site plans. These exhibits are incorporated into the documents and may contain essential information. Without this important information, for example, it may be impossible for the buyer to determine whether it can improve, expand, or modify the structures on the property.

---

## § 3.33—Reviewing Tenant Leases

As soon as the tenant leases begin to arrive, the buyer's lawyer needs to start reviewing them thoroughly. "Thoroughly," in this context, means that the lawyer must read every word of every lease. Even leases that appear to be standard forms are likely to vary in their particulars, and the lawyer should not assume that these leases are identical in their details. Under the recording statutes of many states, a subsequent buyer is deemed to be on notice of the rights of any prior tenant of which it has actual or constructive notice, and those rights include all rights set forth in the lease. Depending on the scope of the state's recording statute, the buyer may be deemed to be on notice of the terms of leases that it has not received, but it quite plainly is on notice of the terms of every document in its possession.

---

*Comment:* It is increasingly common for the seller to transmit the leases to the buyer in electronic format, particularly in more complex transactions involving many leases.

---

The buyer will primarily be interested in the business terms of each lease, but the lawyer also should be concerned with the more technical legal terms of these documents. Buyer's counsel must determine exactly what rights each tenant has and exactly what obligations the buyer will be undertaking when it accepts title to the property. Thus, the lawyer's review will encompass both the legal terms and the business terms of each lease.

---

*Comment:* Although the buyer may ask the lawyer to confirm the accuracy of the exhibits to the contract that pertain to the leases, such an investigation is difficult or impossible for the lawyer to undertake. The lawyer can confirm that the terms of the leases correspond to the terms of the exhibits that the seller appended to the contract. However, the lawyer is not in a position to verify that any of this information actually is correct. The buyer's lawyer must caution the buyer to undertake its own investigation of these matters.

---

Counsel to the buyer will probably find it helpful to prepare a standard lease review summary form that sets forth the major terms of each lease in a way that is easy for the client and the lawyer to use—in fact, experienced real estate clients may already have forms of their own that they use for this purpose. This form should set out, in a user-friendly way, the name of the tenant; the location of the premises; the uses permitted and prohibited at the space; the duration of the lease, including any renewal or extension options; the rental rate, including base rent, percentage rent, periodic increases, and pass-throughs of operating costs; any obligation of the landlord to provide allowances for renovation in the future; any rights to expand or contract the amount of space that the tenant will occupy; any rights to terminate the lease or to purchase the property; restrictions on assignment and subletting; the amount and type of any security deposit; and any other significant or unusual terms. The lawyer then can turn these lease summaries over to her client, highlighting any unexpected or worrisome matters. With these summaries in hand, the buyer will be able to review the significant terms of each lease without having to wade through the original documents.

The lawyer will also find these lease summaries useful for her own purposes. If questions about the leases arise as the transaction progresses, she will be able to refer to these standardized lease summaries rather than having to go back and comb through individual leases over and over. In addition, she will have highlighted on these summaries any troublesome matters, as a means of reminding herself of those problems that must be addressed before the closing. Of course, the lease summaries will serve these valuable purposes only to the extent that the lawyer prepares them with care.

The following sections of this chapter look at some of these lease terms in more detail and offer suggestions as to how the lawyer can recognize and respond to some of the more common lease issues that arise.

### §3.34—Form: Lease Review Summary

See Appendix G for a Lease Review Summary Form.

### §3.35—Permitted Uses; Radius Restrictions; Covenants of Continuous Operation

Commercial leases customarily limit the uses for which the tenant may occupy the space. In some cases, these use restrictions will be very general, perhaps limiting the use of the space to "general office purposes" or "retail use." More often, the leases will be more specific so that the landlord can ensure that its tenants will not be competing against one another or engaging in businesses that the landlord deems undesirable.

In addition, larger tenants often negotiate for restrictions on the use to which other space in the project or other nearby space may be put. A supermarket may insist that the landlord agree not to lease other space in the shopping center to a drug store so that it will not have any competition for its own lucrative pharmacy and cosmetics departments. The landlord may even agree that it will not lease any space that it owns within a one-mile radius to any drug stores. Landlords who are anxious to sign desirable tenants may have no objections to these "exclusive clauses" or "radius restrictions."

*Comment:* Radius restrictions present many dangers and risks. These clauses can make it difficult for the buyer to sell the property later, as some potential buyers may already own other property in the area with existing tenants that would violate the radius restriction. This issue is of particular concern to lenders, because potential foreclosure purchasers (including, perhaps, the lenders themselves) may be unable to bid on the property.

The buyer needs to be aware of the use restrictions, exclusive clauses, and radius restrictions contained in all leases. To begin with, it needs to verify that the seller is not in violation of any of these clauses. If the supermarket's landlord has, in fact, just leased space in the center to a drug store, the supermarket is likely to object, and the new owner may find itself facing litigation and the possibility of vacant space. Beyond this, the buyer needs to be aware of these clauses so that it will not violate any of them in the future. If the buyer had been hoping to sign a drug store lease in the center, the existence of the radius restriction in the supermarket's lease puts an end to those plans, unless the buyer can persuade the supermarket to modify its lease. If the radius restriction extends beyond the perimeter of the subject property, the buyer may find its ability to use other nearby land impaired.

*Comment:* Reviewing and keeping track of use restrictions, exclusive clauses, and radius restrictions can be quite a difficult matter and may present judgment calls as to how particular clauses might apply. All such clauses found in all leases should be compiled in a single summary, which the buyer reviews carefully. In this way, the buyer can determine the collective impact of these restrictions on its future leasing and development plans for the center and nearby property.

The buyer also should note whether any of the leases require the tenant to remain open for business. This issue is particularly important for those tenants that calculate some or all of their rent as a percentage of gross or net sales and for those large, high-volume anchor stores that draw a significant number of patrons to the property. If a tenant that pays percentage rent closes its doors, the rent obviously will fall off unless the minimum base rent is high enough. If a regional superstore goes dark, the center's other tenants will suffer as traffic drops. The extent to which these types of tenants are implicitly obligated to operate, and the standard to which they must operate, is a developing area of the law in many states, but the buyer needs to learn whether the relevant leases resolve this issue one way or the other.

### §3.36—Duration of Leases

The buyer must determine how long each tenant is obligated to remain in place and pay rent. If the buyer is basing its business plans on the assumption that specific, high-quality tenants are obligated to remain in place and pay a stated rent, it needs to confirm the duration of those tenants' obligations. If the lease to the largest tenant in an office building expires in six months, the buyer may soon find itself with empty space and a much-reduced cash flow.

The flip side of this issue is that the buyer will want to know how soon it can be rid of unwanted tenants. If the buyer hopes to upgrade the quality of a shopping center or gut and rehabilitate an apartment building, the presence of an adult entertainment establishment with ten years left on its lease or dozens of residents with rent-control protections may undermine those plans. If a large and desirable law firm tenant has made it known that it will exercise its lease renewal option only if it can add two contiguous floors to its space, the buyer needs to determine when the current occupants of those floors must vacate their space. All of this information is available in the leases.

### §3.37—Caution: Determining Lease Commencement Dates

It is sometimes impossible for the lawyer to determine when the term of a particular lease will end. Even if the lease states the length of the term in years, it may be impossible to establish the commencement date from the document itself. For example, the lease may state that the tenant's ten-year term began "ten days after receipt of a certificate of occupancy" but may not specify the date on which this event occurred. Only a tenant estoppel can confirm this date, unless there is a commencement date confirmation or memorandum in the file.

### §3.38—Renewal Options

Renewal options raise other issues. Renewal options benefit the tenant more than they benefit the landlord, in that the tenant may retain its space at a pre-agreed rent if it so desires but is under no obligation to do so. These options are given by the landlord at the beginning of the lease, as an inducement to the prospective tenant that wants the assurance that it can stay without being required to remain beyond the base term of the lease.

The buyer must be aware of any outstanding renewal options because they restrict the buyer's ability to lease the space that is subject to those options. The buyer cannot lease space that is subject to an option until the holder of the option allows the deadline for exercising it to expire. If the holder of the option decides instead to exercise its rights and renew or extend its lease, the buyer may find itself saddled with a tenant paying a preset rent that is lower than the current market rent. While there is probably little that the buyer can do about any outstanding unexercised options (unless a tenant is willing to relinquish those rights gratuitously or for consideration), it needs to become aware of them during its due diligence review of the leases.

> *Comment:* Tenants that are concerned about missing their important renewal deadline may request a so-called fail-safe clause. Under this type of provision, the tenant will not lose the benefit of its renewal option until it receives notice from the landlord that the tenant has failed to exercise its option on time and a short grace period. These clauses are particularly important in those states where the courts are not inclined to bail out tenants who miss their deadlines. The buyer must learn whether any leases at the property contain such clauses.

## § 3.39—Expansion Options

Just as tenants may have the right to extend the duration of their leases, they may also have negotiated for the right to expand the physical boundaries of their space. A business that expects to grow may lease a modest amount of space at the outset of its lease but may agree with its landlord that it will have the periodic right to add to the size of its leased space. Expansion options can become quite complex, with tenants enjoying periodic rights to add certain amounts of space. Sometimes, the ability to exercise future expansion rights is contingent upon the exercise of earlier ones.

Once again, these tenant rights are granted by the landlord as an accommodation and inducement to new tenants, and the buyer will probably be unable to persuade a current tenant to give up those rights. The buyer does, however, need to know exactly which tenants hold which rights. It must confirm that the seller has not granted contradictory or inconsistent rights to two or more tenants. The buyer also needs to be sure that it will not violate any tenant expansion rights itself. It does not want to lease space to a new tenant and then discover that a current tenant has the right to expand into that space during the new tenant's term. The only way to discover existing problems and avoid future ones is to read each lease carefully.

### §3.40—Caution: Expansion Options

Expansion options can be a major problem for the landlord. Particularly in office leases, expansion options held by different tenants may overlap, and the buyer may find that the seller made inconsistent promises to two or more tenants. It is important that the buyer identify these problems at the time it reviews the leases and before it closes on the property.

### §3.41—Termination Options

Some tenants may have bargained for the right to terminate their leases early. To induce a tenant to sign a lease, the landlord may have afforded it the right to leave before the stated termination date, either free of charge or upon payment of a termination fee. In many ways, termination options differ little from renewal options, because, in either case, the tenant is bound to the landlord only for the shorter time span but has the right to stay longer if it wishes. The buyer needs to be sure that it is not assuming a particular tenant will remain in place and pay rent if that tenant may terminate its lease. Once again, a careful lease review will disclose any tenant rights of this nature.

> *Comment:* Termination options in retail leases are sometimes conditioned on the tenant's achieving or failing to achieve a certain level of gross sales. An understanding of the effect of these options may require detailed analysis on the part of the buyer, which must determine when the landlord or any tenant may exercise any of these options.

### §3.42—Purchase Options; Rights of First Refusal; Rights of First Offer

The seller may have granted one of its tenants the option to purchase the property at a price set forth in the lease. This is particularly true if the tenant is a large tenant with considerable economic leverage or if the tenant will be spending a substantial amount to improve its space. If a tenant holds a purchase option, the buyer needs to become aware of the terms of this option. An option of this type allows the tenant to enjoy the benefit of appreciation of the property without any of the risk of depreciation: if the value of the property ever exceeds the option price, then the tenant can exercise the right or sell the right back to the landlord, while if the value of the property remains below the option price, then the tenant simply remains as a tenant. Any consideration that the tenant may already have paid to the seller for this option will not necessarily inure to the buyer's benefit.

Purchase options raise many of the same concerns for buyers that tenant expansion options raise, but to an even greater degree. An option of this type caps the buyer's potential gain from the property without limiting its loss and also makes the property more difficult to finance. To many buyers, the presence of a purchase option will be a deal breaker. If the seller cannot persuade the tenant to relinquish the option, the buyer may choose to exercise its right to terminate the contract (assuming, of course, that the buyer's counsel remembered to include such a right in the contract). In some instances, the seller's contract with the buyer may itself violate the terms of the option.

Rights of first refusal allow the holder of the right to match any offer to purchase the property that the owner receives from a third party. In theory, the buyer should be less troubled by a lease that contains a right of first refusal, because if a tenant holds such a right and exercises it, the buyer still receives the price it wants but receives it from the tenant rather than from the third-party offeror. Nonetheless, rights of first refusal contained in tenant leases are undesirable from the buyer's perspective. They inevitably delay future sales of the property, because the holder of the right will enjoy a certain amount of time to decide whether it wishes to exercise the right. In fact, the mere presence of a right of first refusal may discourage third parties from making offers on the property. They know they will have to wait for the tenant to make up its mind, and they also know that the tenant is more likely to match a favorable offer than an unfavorable one. The prospective buyer knows that it could spend a great deal of time and money investigating the transaction, only to lose the property to the third party.

If a tenant holds a right of first offer, the owner must allow the tenant to make the first offer on the property before the owner places the property on the market. If the owner rejects the tenant's offer, it may not accept a lower price from a third party. Rights of first offer, though less worrisome to a buyer than purchase options and rights of first refusal, may still raise concerns with the buyer. The buyer may worry that, as the future owner of the property, if it rejects the tenant's offer, its flexibility in negotiating with other prospective buyers will be limited. For example, if the owner offers concessions to third parties in areas other than price, the tenant might argue that the owner undercut the tenant's right of first offer.

> *Comment:* Rights of first offer, in which the owner gives the tenant the first right to buy the property, have become increasingly common. Rights of first offer contained in a tenant's lease have less of a chilling effect on sales by the owner. It is far more difficult for the owner to locate a buyer if a tenant's lease contains a right of first refusal.

The buyer needs to become aware of the presence of any rights of this type and also needs to become familiar with their precise terms. Careful review of all leases will allow it to accomplish these goals.

> *Comment:* The seller may have granted one of its tenants any of these purchase rights in a recorded document or in an unrecorded lease. The buyer almost certainly is on constructive notice of an unrecorded lease because of the tenant's possession of the premises. Here, careful due diligence is required: the tenant's obvious possession places the buyer on notice of the tenant's lease, and the buyer then must obtain and review the tenant's lease.

### §3.43—Assignment and Subletting Rights

The buyer will want to know whether it has control over the selection of all occupants of the property. Owners may want their property to have a certain identity, whether it is a luxury office building or a discount mall. They may want to avoid competition among tenants. They will probably want to reject occupants in whom they have little confidence. This landlord control can be undercut by existing tenants if these tenants have the unrestricted right to sublet their space or assign their leases to third parties. While it may be impossible for the seller to modify the terms of leases that predate this transfer of the property, the buyer certainly needs to know before the closing exactly what assignment and subletting rights each tenant at the property holds. The buyer also needs to know if any original tenants have already subleased or assigned and must review any documents effecting such a transfer.

---

*Comment:* The buyer needs to determine whether the parties that are currently in possession are the original tenants under the leases or are subtenants or assignees of these original tenants. If the current occupant is not the named tenant, the original tenant may or may not remain liable under the lease. The named tenant's liability will depend on the original lease, the document of transfer, and the law of the jurisdiction.

---

Assignment and subletting rights are not an all-or-nothing proposition, and leases differ widely. The seller is likely to have negotiated this clause heavily in each of its individual tenant leases, and different tenants are likely to have received different rights to assign and sublet. Even if the seller has attempted throughout its ownership to convince tenants to accept the landlord's form lease, this is one of the provisions most likely to have been modified on a tenant-by-tenant basis.

The range of possibilities for these clauses is broad. Tenants with a strong negotiating position may demand and receive broad rights to sublet or assign without limitation. Leases that are silent on the point lead to the same result. At the other extreme, a lease may prohibit subletting and assigning outright or may permit such transfers only at the unfettered discretion of the landlord. Most subletting and assignment clauses fall between these extremes. The landlord may permit subletting and assignment only with its consent, which it will agree in advance not to withhold unreasonably. The parties to the lease may establish objective standards that a proposed subtenant or assignee must meet before the landlord is required to consent to the transfer. These standards may address such matters as the creditworthiness of the proposed new occupant, the type of business that it plans to run, and the new occupant's assumption of the lease.

The landlord may agree in the lease that it will accept assignments to entities that are affiliated with the named tenant or may agree in advance that it will accept subleases of certain limited portions of the property. Whatever the parties have agreed to, the buyer's lawyer needs to note these terms on each lease summary and draw her client's attention to them, to be sure that the buyer is satisfied with the range of occupants it later may find itself dealing with. Note also that some leases may treat subletting differently from assignment.

The buyer's lawyer also needs to be aware of the relationship between rights to sublet and assign, on the one hand, and use restrictions, exclusive clauses, and radius restrictions, on the other. If the subletting and assigning clause in one lease does not clearly limit the new occupant in the same way that it limits the original one, the buyer may find itself with a subtenant or assignee that is competing with another tenant of the buyer, perhaps in violation of the buyer's obligations under the other tenant's lease.

Landlords are concerned with more than just the tenant mix at the property. They also may worry that tenants whose rentals have proven to be bargains will turn around and assign or sublease their space at a profit, perhaps even competing with the landlord for occupants. The landlord's position will be that the tenant should not be making a profit on the landlord's space. The tenant's response will be that it took the risk of rental values dropping unexpectedly, so there is no reason it should not profit if rental values have increased unexpectedly. Sophisticated parties will sometimes agree in the lease that the landlord will consent to a future sublease or assignment only if a specified portion of any rental profit is turned over to the landlord. If the subtenant's rent to the tenant exceeds the tenant's rent to the landlord, or if the assignee is paying the tenant a fee in return for the assignment of the lease, the landlord will be entitled to share in this gain. A lease that is even more pro-landlord than this may effectively allow the landlord to retain all of this profit. For example, if the landlord has the unrestricted right to reject subleases or assignments, the law in many states may not prevent the landlord from turning down a tenant's request and then attempting to lease other space at the property directly to the proposed new occupant.

### §3.44—Security Deposits

A tenant will often provide a security deposit to its landlord as a way of assuring the landlord that the tenant will pay its rent, maintain its space, and meet all its other leasehold obligations. These deposits are most often cash deposits but may also take the form of a note, letter of credit, or other form of security. Some states regulate the manner in which the landlord must hold these deposits, at least in residential settings. For example, a state may require that the landlord pay interest on the deposit and keep the deposit separate from its other funds.

If the tenant meets its leasehold obligations, it will expect the landlord to return the deposit at the end of the lease. If the tenant does not meet its obligations, the landlord will want to draw against the deposit to pay the costs of the tenant's default. Once the property changes hands, the buyer, rather than the seller, is entitled to enjoy the benefits of the security deposit and must also meet the corresponding responsibility of returning any amount remaining when the lease expires. For these reasons, the seller should transfer all security deposits to the buyer at the closing.

The buyer can determine the amount of these deposits from the leases and from the tenant estoppels and must remember to demand that the seller turn these amounts over to the buyer at the closing. In the case of cash deposits, a transfer of funds is easy to implement. If the deposit takes another form, the parties must be sure that the benefit of the deposit is transferred to the buyer, such as by endorsing the tenant's note or by asking the issuer of the letter of credit to issue a new letter of credit for the benefit of the new owner.

### § 3.45—Guarantees

Landlords sometimes demand that a third party guarantee the performance of a tenant's leasehold obligations. If the tenant is a brand new entity or is thinly capitalized, the landlord may require a guarantee from a creditworthy principal or from a more established parent corporation. Counsel to the buyer needs to determine whether any lease guarantees exist and needs to confirm that the guarantee will benefit the new owner after the seller transfers the property. A well-drafted guarantee will automatically benefit the new owner without any further action on the buyer's part. If the guarantee was less thoughtfully crafted, the buyer should make sure that the seller contacts the guarantor and asks the guarantor to modify the guarantee appropriately.

*Comment:* Under the law of many jurisdictions and under general principles of suretyship, any change in the legal or economic terms of a lease may relieve the guarantor of its obligations. Thus, one of the most difficult problems for a buyer and its lawyer is determining whether guarantees remain in effect. If a guarantee is an important element of any lease, the buyer should seek assurances from the seller and the guarantor that the guarantee remains effective.

### §3.46—Landlord's Construction Obligations; Improvements by Tenants

As an inducement to a prospective tenant, a landlord will sometimes agree to pay a portion of the tenant's cost to build out or renovate the leased premises. The landlord may perform the tenant's work itself, particularly if the structure is a new one and the landlord's contractors can finish the interior of the space while they are constructing the building itself. In other cases, the tenant will arrange on its own to have the work performed and then will be entitled to reimbursement from the landlord for some of the costs, either directly or in the form of reduced rent for some future period of time.

The buyer's lawyer needs to determine during her lease review whether the seller still has outstanding construction obligations to any tenant. If so, the buyer's lawyer then needs to determine the extent to which the buyer will become liable for these costs. If the seller will remain responsible, the buyer should be sure that the seller sets funds aside for this purpose, perhaps by establishing an escrow account to be used solely to meet tenants' construction costs. If the buyer will become responsible for these expenses, then the buyer should be sure that the sale price is adjusted to account for this cost, unless the seller disclosed this fact in advance and the parties already have factored it into the sale price.

---

*Comment:* An unwary buyer will be in for an expensive surprise if it has to put up a substantial allowance for construction or renovation costs by an existing tenant. Careful lease review can determine whether the seller still has any outstanding financial obligations to tenants for which the borrower may become responsible.

---

Whether or not a tenant's improvements have already been paid for in full, the buyer and the seller may disagree as to how these costs should be allocated. The seller may believe that the costs should be amortized over the life of the tenant's lease and that the buyer should reimburse the seller for a portion of the costs the seller has already incurred. The buyer may take the position that the value of the property, reflected in the price the buyer agreed to pay for it, already factored in all improvements to the building. To the extent that a tenant still enjoys the right to pay a reduced rent, the buyer may even argue that the seller should compensate the buyer for this differential. The parties will need to resolve this issue, unless their contract already foresaw and addressed this possible conflict. While the resolution of this disagreement is a matter for the seller and the buyer rather than for their lawyers, the buyer's lawyer can determine what the facts are by reviewing the lease or leases in question.

*Comment:* The buyer may have agreed with its acquisition lender that the cost of these tenant improvements will be paid from the borrowed funds. If this is the case, the buyer's lawyer must be certain that the loan documents reflect this agreement. The loan documents probably will set forth the requirements the buyer must meet before the lender will disburse these funds.

### § 3.47—Leasehold Financing

Tenants' interests in leases are mortgageable. If a tenant plans to spend a large sum to improve or renovate its space, it may decide to borrow some portion of this amount and give its lender a mortgage or deed of trust on its leasehold interest. The lender has a security interest in the leasehold. If the tenant fails to pay the amount it owes its lender, the lender can foreclose on its borrower's interest—the leasehold—and step into the shoes of the tenant. This obviously will be an issue only in major leases with lengthy terms on which the tenant plans to spend a significant amount in design and construction costs.

Most courts will probably view a leasehold mortgage or deed of trust as a transfer of an interest in property, and all courts will view a foreclosure as a transfer. This means that the tenant should have complied with any requirements contained in the assignment clause at the time it granted the leasehold mortgage to its lender. If the landlord has agreed to a leasehold mortgage or never had the power to deny its consent, then the analysis here is similar to the discussion of assignments and subleases, and the buyer may find itself with a new occupant following a foreclosure.

Leasehold mortgagees have concerns that mortgagees of fees do not face. If the tenant breaches its lease, the landlord may be able to terminate the lease and wipe out the lender's security. The lender knows from the outset that its leasehold security is not a perpetual interest in the way that a fee simple is and that the landlord's rights are superior to its own. For this reason, leasehold mortgagees will not extend loans of this type unless the borrower's landlord agrees to accommodate the lender in certain ways.

Practically speaking, leases are not considered mortgageable unless the landlord agrees that it will send copies of all default notices to the lender; will afford the lender an adequate grace period during which it may cure any tenant defaults; and will accept the lender, any foreclosure sale purchaser, or any assignee of either of these parties as a substitute tenant. If the lease is terminated, the lender must have the right to enter into a new lease directly with the landlord on substantially similar terms within a specified period of time.

If there is a leasehold mortgage in place, then the seller has probably agreed to accept certain constraints not present in other leases. The buyer's lawyer can determine the extent of these constraints from the lease, which it should have received, and from the leasehold mortgage, which should be recorded. Her task now is to review these provisions, to explain them to her client, and to make sure that the client is willing to accept these constraints.

### §3.48—Caution: Leasehold Financing

Leasehold financing is a complex topic that extends beyond the purview of this book. There are established standards in the real estate industry as to the specific lease clauses that need to be included before a lender will make a loan that is secured by a leasehold. Different lenders may have additional requirements that tenants and their landlords must meet in order for the tenant to qualify for leasehold financing.

### §3.49—Tenant Estoppels

So far, the ability of the buyer's lawyer to perform her lease review properly has depended entirely on her examination of documents and other information provided to her by the seller. If the seller fails to provide all of the documents that the contract requires, the buyer may have a claim against the seller for breach of a representation, warranty, covenant, or indemnity, or may have the right under a closing condition to withdraw from the transaction without penalty.

If the buyer does not learn of the seller's breach until after the closing, however, the buyer may have a problem. The closing condition no longer has any value, and the representations, warranties, covenants, and indemnities create a contract claim against an entity that may be hard to find or may be judgment-proof, assuming that these provisions even survive the closing. Thus, the buyer should worry that the seller will fail to provide accurate lease information and turn over all of the relevant lease documents, either intentionally or through inadvertence.

There is a way to verify that the seller has turned over all of the relevant leases and related documents. The buyer can confirm the terms of any landlord–tenant relationship by checking with the other party to the relationship, namely the tenant. This confirmation normally takes the form of a tenant estoppel letter or tenant estoppel certificate.

In a tenant estoppel letter, the seller or buyer contacts the tenant and asks the tenant to verify the terms of the landlord–tenant relationship in writing. The seller should prepare this letter in consultation with the buyer and should be sure that the letter addresses any specific concerns that the buyer may have.[14] A typical estoppel letter will ask the tenant to confirm the identity of the leased premises; the duration of the lease, including exercised and unexercised renewals and extensions; the rental rate; the amount of any security deposit; whether the lease has been modified or amended in any way; that the tenant has not assigned the lease or sublet any space; that neither party is in breach of its leasehold obligations; that the tenant has not prepaid any rent; that the landlord has either made or paid for all improvements to the space for which the landlord is responsible under the lease; and any other facts about which the buyer has concerns, including, perhaps, some of the other issues already discussed in this chapter.

To the extent that the tenant cannot confirm any of the preceding information, the letter will ask the tenant to list and explain any exceptions to these statements. Prudent buyers sometimes ask the seller to attach a copy of the lease to the estoppel letter and to have the tenant confirm that the attached document is true and complete. The letter also should emphasize that the buyer will be relying on the accuracy of the tenant's statements in the letter and that the tenant will be estopped from later denying the accuracy of the letter.

Why would a tenant ever sign such a letter? After all, the tenant cannot safely sign the letter until it confirms the accuracy of many

technical statements. Once it signs the letter, the tenant will probably no longer be able to raise any claims it might previously have
had unless it has listed these disputed issues in the letter itself. The
answer lies in the lease: commercial leases usually contain provisions requiring the tenant to provide an estoppel letter upon request.
The tenant that fails to respond to a request for an estoppel letter
probably is breaching its lease and may cause significant damage to
the seller.

> *Comment:* Sophisticated tenants will require that the obligation to furnish
> estoppel letters bind the landlord as well. The tenant may need to pro-
> vide an estoppel letter to its own lenders or to other parties.

This does not mean that the buyer's lawyer should expect a 100
percent response rate when it requests estoppel letters. If there are
fifty tenants at the property, perhaps ten will respond to the initial request, another twenty-five will respond to follow-up letters
and phone calls, and fifteen will never be heard from. A landlord is
unlikely to terminate a lease over a default of this type, as some tenants well know. Even if the receipt of estoppel letters from all tenants is a closing condition, the buyer and its lawyer should assume
that they will not receive all estoppels in time and should decide in
advance exactly which leases are important enough that the buyer
will refuse to close until those tenants respond. The buyer also
should be sure that it and its lenders are satisfied with the wording of the estoppel requests, that the requests go out as soon as the
contract is signed, that the seller pursues all estoppels vigorously,
and that the buyer reviews the content of all estoppels that tenants
return to the seller.

Tenant responses to estoppel letter requests may disclose problems that the seller has not revealed and of which it perhaps is not
even aware. These letters provide a useful check on the seller's disclosures to the buyer, which is why the buyer's lawyer must be careful to review the estoppel letters thoroughly. If an estoppel reveals
a problem between the seller and one of its tenants, the buyer then
can figure out whether the problem is a significant one and whether
the seller needs to resolve it before the closing.

> *Comment:* A tenant will occasionally attempt to use the estoppel letter
> request as a weapon to force the settlement of an ongoing disagreement
> with the seller. If a known claim by a tenant still is unresolved when the

> sale closes, the buyer may insist that a portion of the purchase price be placed in escrow to cover any possible losses.

### §3.50—Form: Tenant Estoppel Certificate

See Appendix C for a Form of Tenant Estoppel Certificate.

### §3.51—Subordination, Nondisturbance, and Attornment Agreements

The relative priorities of interests in real property are determined, at first, by state recording laws. Mortgage lenders must be sure that their mortgages and other security documents are recorded promptly so that any subsequent interest holder will be deemed to be on record notice of the previously recorded mortgage documents. Tenants would be wise to record their leases, or memoranda summarizing the major terms of their leases, for the same reason.[15] In many states, a tenant can also protect its interest by taking possession of its space, and subsequent interest holders are deemed to be on constructive notice of the tenant's interest by virtue of the tenant's prior possession. The scope of this constructive notice varies substantially from jurisdiction to jurisdiction.

> *Comment:* Some states impose substantial transfer taxes and recording costs when a party records a lease. These fees obviously discourage parties from recording leases or lease memoranda in those states.

The parties are free to modify their initial priorities by agreement, as long as their agreement does not prejudice the rights of third parties. Landlords, tenants, and mortgagees frequently accomplish this result by executing a "Subordination, Nondisturbance, and Attornment Agreement," or "SNDA."

It is important to understand the differences among these three terms. A party *subordinates* its interest when it agrees to demote the priority to which it is otherwise entitled under the state's recording statute. If a tenant executes a lease and takes possession of its space and the landlord then executes a mortgage that its lender records, the lease enjoys priority and would survive a foreclosure of the mortgage. If, however, the tenant were to subordinate its lease prior to foreclosure, the parties would be reversing the original priority of the documents and the mortgage would become senior to the lease.

The tenant voluntarily weakens its position, the mortgagee benefits, and no third party is affected. If the lender were to foreclose properly after this subordination, the tenant's lease would terminate automatically.

---

*Comment:* Note that some states follow the so-called pick-and-choose rule, which permits the lender to omit junior leases from a foreclosure intentionally, thereby allowing desirable tenants to survive foreclosure.

---

A *nondisturbance* agreement is an agreement by which a mortgage lender promises, on behalf of itself and any foreclosure sale purchaser, that it will not disturb the possession of a tenant whose interest otherwise might be terminated by a foreclosure of the mortgage. In the preceding example, if the tenant's subordination agreement is accompanied by a nondisturbance agreement from the mortgagee, the lease that has just been subordinated to the mortgage would not technically survive the foreclosure, but the new owner of the property would have to recognize the original tenant on the same terms as those contained in the original lease.

---

*Comment:* The parameters of any nondisturbance agreement must be defined by the parties with care. In a technical sense, the use of this term means that the tenant will not be wiped out in a foreclosure. This does not necessarily imply, however, that the tenant can look to the new owner to perform all the obligations of the original landlord under the lease. For example, a foreclosure sale purchaser will not necessarily be required to meet the original landlord's responsibility to pay for a portion of the tenant's improvement costs. Issues such as this should be resolved clearly in the SNDA, and the tenant that is relying on the landlord to perform certain important obligations should be sure to raise these issues when negotiating the SNDA.[16]

---

The nondisturbance agreement protects the tenant against the effects of a foreclosure, but it does not obligate the tenant to remain. The tenant is free to leave, even though the new owner is required to accept the tenant on the original terms. Lenders balance the one-sidedness of a nondisturbance agreement by insisting in advance that the tenant *attorn* to the lender or its successor, or recognize that party as its new landlord. Attornment derives from the feudal process by which a party transferred homage and service from one lord to another. The combined effect of a nondisturbance agreement and an attornment agreement is to create a new lease between the original tenant and the foreclosure sale purchaser. Note that while subordination, nondisturbance, and attornment provisions generally appear together, there is no legal reason parties cannot agree to some, but not all, of these terms.

> *Comment:* Although it is true that subordination, nondisturbance, and attornment need not all be included in a single agreement, it is a rare tenant that will agree to subordinate to a lender without also receiving nondisturbance protection.

SNDA agreements, like other agreements respecting property rights, are subject to state recording laws. Parties that are considering taking an interest in the property later, including prospective purchasers of the relevant property, are deemed to be on notice of all documents of which they have actual or constructive notice. In other words, they are on notice of previously executed SNDA agreements as long as those agreements appear in the tenant's lease (if the lease or a memorandum of the lease is recorded or, in most states, if the tenant is in actual possession of the premises), the recorded mortgage, or a separate agreement of which they have actual or constructive notice. Stated differently, the parties to an SNDA agreement must make sure that this agreement either is recorded or is contained in an unrecorded document of which a subsequent party will be deemed to have constructive notice. The lawyer who is conducting due diligence review for a buyer should receive all recorded documents from the title insurer and all leases from the seller. If these documents or any of the tenant estoppel letters refer to unrecorded SNDAs, the buyer's lawyer must locate and review these additional documents as well.

In many cases, the buyer will not be disturbed by the presence of SNDAs, although it certainly needs to review every word contained in every one of them. These documents are often given as inducements to large tenants, which may be unwilling to lease their space unless they have assurances that the lease will survive any inability of the landlord to meet its own financial obligations. If a major department store chain tells its prospective shopping center landlord that it will sign a lease only if the landlord's lender executes an SNDA, the lender should be only too happy to comply and thereby induce the tenant to move into the center, and the buyer will be happy that this matter was resolved to everyone's satisfaction.

The buyer should be aware of the relative priorities of tenant leases and any financing on the property that will remain after the closing, and it should review all these documents for any unexpected provisions, but it probably will not be surprised or troubled by what it finds.

The buyer should review the content of any agreements among the seller, the tenants, and any lenders whose interests will survive the closing. A tenant may have insisted that its interest remain superior to all mortgages, including those executed and recorded after the lease was signed. If this is the case, the buyer must satisfy itself that its own lenders will be willing to lend on those terms and will not insist that leases that are senior to their mortgages be subordinated. Similarly, if an earlier mortgage loan is to remain in place, the buyer must examine the SNDA provisions that the surviving loan documents contain. The loan may require the lender to grant nondisturbance protection to tenants who lease a certain amount of space, which may make it easier for the buyer to locate new tenants later.

The buyer's lawyer must be sure that any agreements to which the buyer will become subject leave it with some flexibility in the future. The buyer needs to be able to locate tenants and give them the protection they reasonably seek, and it needs to be able to obtain mortgage loan financing and give its lenders the security they demand.

### §3.52—Form: Subordination, Nondisturbance, and Attornment Agreement

See Appendix H for a Form of Subordination, Nondisturbance, and Attornment Agreement.

## §3.53 Condition of Property and Improvements

This chapter so far has focused on legal matters that the buyer's lawyer must investigate before she can competently advise her client whether to close. Some property matters are beyond the scope of a lawyer's expertise, however. In particular, the lawyer probably is not qualified to advise the client whether the land and structures are physically acceptable. Other experts, such as engineers, architects, or geologists, must address those matters. The lawyer's task with respect to these issues is to ensure that the contract contains appropriate representations, conditions, and remedies. The buyer's lawyer also must remind her client to retain persons who are competent to investigate these matters during the due diligence period. The next sections examine these matters along with some related legal issues.

### §3.54—Suitability for Intended Use

The buyer needs to confirm that the land and buildings are suitable for their intended use. If the buyer plans to put the structure on the property to the same use as the seller, this probably means nothing more than retaining someone who is competent to inspect it and make sure it is in good condition. The buyer might hire an engineer or an architect who will examine the building, test it for structural soundness, and confirm that all building systems are in proper working order.

If the buyer is more concerned with the land than with the structures on it, as is the case with agricultural or mineral property, the buyer again needs to confirm that the property is appropriate for its planned use. This might entail hiring a soil expert or geologist to examine the land itself so that the buyer minimizes the risk of post-acquisition surprises.

In either case, it is unlikely that the lawyer herself will perform this investigation. The lawyer's job is to protect her client's rights in the contract, to remind the buyer to undertake this investigation during the due diligence period, and to address any problems that these inspections reveal.

### §3.55—Caution: Responsibility for Ordering Inspections

Unsophisticated buyers often believe that it is the task of the lawyer to arrange for various inspections. The lawyer should be careful to point out which inspections need to be undertaken, but it is up to the buyer to arrange for these inspections. The lawyer should not assume responsibility for having these inspections performed.

The lawyer also should advise the client whether any unexpected omissions in the contract and the other documents raise questions. For example, the failure of the lawyer to note the absence of an exhibit to a document, such as an alarm system contract, may expose the lawyer to a claim for negligence on the grounds that she should have known from this omission that such a system did not exist.

## § 3.56—Suitability for Construction

In some situations, the buyer will be acquiring undeveloped land for the purpose of building on it or will buy an older structure that it plans to renovate or replace. In these settings, there may be little need to inspect the existing structure, even if there is one, unless environmentally hazardous substances such as asbestos may be present. Instead, the buyer will need to confirm that the land itself is suitable for the project that the buyer has in mind.

This will probably entail hiring soil experts, geologists, or structural engineers with the expertise to determine whether the subsurface is appropriate for the buyer's intended use. At one extreme, the buyer hardly can expect to construct a sports arena on land that is riddled with limestone caverns and sinkholes. At the other extreme, the buyer may find it prohibitively expensive to excavate a foundation for a skyscraper if the subsurface rock is unexpectedly hard and dense. The buyer's lawyer cannot discover this information on her own, but she can remind the buyer to hire people who can.

---

*Comment:* Buildings to be erected on fill present many unique problems. The buyer must investigate the quality of the fill and must determine whether structures that will be built on the fill will require special foundations.

---

## § 3.57—Availability of Necessary Permits

Federal, state, and local authorities impose a wide range of restrictions on land use. Even if the buyer plans to continue the seller's use of the property, the buyer is likely to need to acquire or update an array of permits and certificates. The problem is magnified if the buyer intends to change the use of the property or to engage in excavation, construction, or demolition at the site.

These matters may lie at the interface between the lawyer's work and that of other professionals. Some of these permits should be on the lawyer's regular checklist. She needs to remember, for example, to confirm the existence of a valid certificate of occupancy that permits the uses that the buyer plans to continue at the property. Other documents fall within the domain of the architect or the contractor, who more commonly deal with construction law issues and the public officials who issue the needed permits. The lawyer's job here is to make sure that none of these matters falls through the cracks.

This may involve coordinating her checklist with those of the other professionals involved and ensuring that every necessary issue is addressed by someone on the buyer's team.

### § 3.58—Environmental Matters

One subset of these permits is sufficiently important and complex to merit special mention here. Governments at all levels have become sensitive to the need to protect the environment and may impose stringent limitations on the uses that owners can make of their property. The "environmental law" umbrella is a broad one, covering matters ranging from protection of wetlands, to maintenance of the habitat of endangered species, to proper handling of hazardous substances. The buyer's lawyer must be particularly careful to confirm that the buyer's intended use of the property will comply with all federal, state, and local environmental laws.

> *Comment:* The buyer that hopes to build in or near areas where there may be wetlands will need to make a wetlands determination and obtain the necessary permit from the Army Corps of Engineers.

If the buyer's lawyer is experienced in environmental matters, she is likely to be aware of the range of issues that demand investigation. Discussion of these matters is beyond the scope of this book, but this section serves as a reminder to the lawyer to address environmental concerns during the due diligence phase. If the buyer's lawyer is unfamiliar with the environmental matters that deserve attention at this point, she would be well advised to work with co-counsel more familiar with these issues.

> *Comment:* The buyer generally cannot rely on environmental reports furnished by the seller to the buyer without the consent of the company that issued the report to the seller.

### § 3.59—Caution: Liability for Hazardous Waste

In the environmental arena, it is difficult to protect the parties and their principals from personal liability, regardless of the entity status of the property owner. Therefore, it is absolutely essential that the buyer determine the potential environmental liability with care. If the property truly is "dirty," the buyer should consider staying away from the property unless it can obtain all necessary assurances as to both the steps required for cleanup and the cost of that cleanup. The parties then can allocate responsibility for performing this work and paying for it. Environmental insurance, when available, may be extremely expensive.

### §3.60—Assignability of Contracts and Licenses to Buyer

The discussion of the contract of sale emphasized the importance to the buyer of maintaining certain existing contracts and licenses.[17] To the extent that assignment of these agreements to the buyer requires the consent of a third party, the buyer must be sure that the seller initiates and completes the process of obtaining those consents. If the buyer plans to continue the seller's use of a trademark, then the owner of that trademark probably must consent to the buyer's use of the mark. If the buyer plans to continue to retain the seller's cleaning service on the same terms as the seller, then that service provider probably must consent.

The seller is the party that initially established these business arrangements, so the seller should be the party to initiate contact with its counterparts. The role of the buyer's lawyer is to be sure that the seller pursues these consents or, if the seller agrees, to pursue these consents herself. Once the consents arrive, the buyer's lawyer must review them to make sure they are substantively acceptable.

> Comment: Standard forms of architect's and engineer's contracts are not assignable without consent.

In some cases, assignment of these rights will not require the consent of any third parties. The buyer's lawyer must confirm that this is the case by reviewing the appropriate contracts and verifying that they are assignable without consent.

### §3.61  Corporate, Partnership, and Limited Liability Entity Matters

In many cases, one or both of the parties to the contract will be a business entity. The other party must verify that this entity has a valid legal existence and has taken all the steps necessary to perform under the contract in accordance with law. The following sections provide guidance to the lawyers as to how they can accomplish these goals.

These sections focus on corporations, general and limited partnerships, and limited liability entities, including limited liability companies and limited liability partnerships. Similar entity issues may arise in connection with contracts involving trusts, estates, and state-specific entities such as the Illinois land trust, and the discussion in these sections should be adaptable to these types of entities with only minor modifications. In other cases, one or both of the parties may be an individual, a tenancy in common, a joint tenancy, or a tenancy by the entirety. Strict compliance with the following sections for these parties probably is unnecessary but is unlikely to be harmful.

### § 3.62—Due Organization of Parties

If one of the parties is a corporation, a partnership, or a limited liability entity, the other party needs to confirm that this entity was duly formed and validly exists in accordance with the law of a particular state, that it is in good standing in that state, and that it is qualified to do business in the state in which the property is located. This matter is of particular importance to the buyer, which does not wish to deliver the funds in exchange for a deed that turns out to be invalid because the grantor does not legally exist.

The buyer can confirm the legal existence and good standing of the seller by obtaining a certificate of good standing from the state in which the seller is organized. All states will provide these certificates and, in many states, this information can be confirmed online or by fax on the closing date.[18] If the entity is organized in a state other than the one in which the property is located, the buyer also should obtain a certificate from the state in which the property is located confirming that the seller is authorized to conduct business in this state, has paid all required fees and taxes, and has designated a resident agent for service of process within this state. Each party also can confirm the legal existence of the other party by asking that the other party's lawyer provide a confirmatory legal opinion.[19]

### § 3.63—Authority of Parties

The fact that the other party exists legally does not provide any comfort that this party has taken all necessary entity steps to authorize the transaction. Corporations act by the authority of their board of directors at a meeting that has been properly called. Some partnership actions may be authorized by just one partner, while others require more than this, with the law varying from state to state. Each party—and the buyer in particular—needs to confirm that the other has taken every step necessary to authorize the transaction in accordance with its own internal documents and the laws of the state under which it has been formed.

If one of the parties is a corporation, the other party will request a corporate resolution authorizing the transaction. This resolution should be accompanied by a waiver of notice of the board meeting at which the directors authorized the transaction that has been signed by all directors. If one party is a partnership, it may argue that no authorizations of this type are required and that any one general partner has the authority to bind the entity. Even if this is true—and that is a question to be resolved by reference to state partnership law and the entity's internal documents—the other party would be wise to ask for a copy of the partnership agreement and an authorization signed by all of the general partners, rather than get into a dispute later as to the scope of the signing partner's actual or apparent authority to bind the entity. The forms of consent that a limited liability entity must deliver will parallel these corporate and partnership forms. Note that in many instances, the title company also will insist on receiving corporate resolutions or other similar documents from both the seller and the buyer.

Each entity also should deliver an incumbency certificate that lists all the officers or partners who are authorized to sign the operative documents on behalf of the entity, along with a statement of each person's title and a specimen of each signature. These documents, certified by the secretary of the entity, allow the other party to confirm that the person who appears at the closing for the first party has been authorized by that entity to execute the documents. The parties also must recognize that these authorized representatives may need to negotiate last-minute changes to the documents and that some of these changes may be of great substance. The resolution should clarify which persons have the authority to make these changes without returning for an expanded authorization, and the incumbency certificate will confirm that the person executing the amendment is the person authorized to do so in the resolution.

*Comment:* It can sometimes be difficult to obtain the necessary corporate authorizations, particularly from large corporations, which rarely pass specific resolutions dealing with specific properties. In these cases, a certificate of incumbency that confirms the authority of the party signing the various documents may be sufficient. Alternatively, the corporation may have passed a blanket corporate resolution giving certain parties sufficient authority to sign the documents to complete the transaction, or the corporate secretary may specifically certify that these parties possess the requisite authority.

Ordinarily, there will be no way for either party to rule out the possibility that the performance of the other requires the approval of a third party or violates another agreement to which that entity is a party. However, either party can ask for a contract provision requiring an affidavit from the other confirming that no other approvals are required. In some cases, one party may disclose in the contract or in one of these affidavits that the consent of a third party is needed. In these cases, receipt of this consent should be a condition precedent to closing.[20]

### §3.64—Opinions of Counsel

Each party can request an opinion of the other party's counsel to verify that the other party exists legally and has taken all the necessary entity actions just discussed. By requesting an opinion letter, the demanding party is asking the responding party's law firm to put its own reputation (and malpractice insurance) on the line, and a misstatement by the party that is confirmed by its lawyer places both the party and the law firm at risk of legal liability. The popularity of opinion letters varies from place to place, and one or both of the parties may decide that opinion letters are not warranted.

*Comment:* Even if counsel to the buyer and the seller are reluctant to deliver opinion letters to each other, an opinion letter from borrower's counsel is almost always required by the lender as a part of the loan transaction.[21]

### §3.65 Financing Matters

The final matter to be addressed during the due diligence period is one of the most important, at least from the buyer's perspective. The buyer must use the due diligence period to obtain commitments for the financing it will need to complete the transaction. If financing is available, then the buyer can close, but if it is unavailable, then the buyer must be sure to exercise its contractual right to terminate the contract without loss of its down payment in strict accordance with the terms of the pertinent closing condition.

Previous sections described the financing condition that the buyer wishes to receive in the contract.[22] If the buyer learns that it will not be obtaining the funding that it needs, then it must be certain to comply precisely with any deadlines and notice requirements contained in that closing condition. The buyer that fails to do so will see the financing condition expire. If this happens, the buyer must find the funds elsewhere or it will be in default under the contract.

Until that deadline arrives, the buyer should energetically pursue its financing. The loan transaction between the buyer and its lender parallels, in many ways, the sale transaction between the seller and the buyer. This loan transaction is a separate, overlapping business deal, and is sufficiently unique and complex to merit a discussion of its own. Part III provides this discussion.

## Notes

1. Closing conditions differ from representations in important ways. A seller that provides its buyer with a closing condition is not making a statement about the current condition of the property and is not promising anything about the future condition of the property. Rather, this seller is telling the buyer that if the condition is not met, the buyer need not close. The buyer may opt not to close, but it has no personal recourse against the seller if a closing condition is not met. Once the closing occurs, the closing condition becomes meaningless: the buyer cannot refuse to close if it has closed already.

2. These sections are intended to provide the reader with a basic understanding of title and survey due diligence and are not intended as treatises on title insurance. For more thorough examinations of this area of the law, *see generally* D. Barlow Burke, Law of Title Insurance (3d ed. 2000 & Supp. 2007); Joyce D. Palomar, Title Insurance Law (1994 & Supp. 2007).

3. Note that in some parts of the country, title opinions from lawyers and title abstracts may be used at this early stage.

4. *See infra* §§ 7.11, 8.06.

5. Most ALTA forms, including the ALTA Commitment Form, are available electronically at *http://www.alta.org/forms/#3* (last visited Feb. 25, 2008).

6. The lender's policy of title insurance is considered in §§ 5.03–5.05, *infra*.

7. Assessments, unlike taxes, may be paid entirely by the seller. *See supra* § 2.115; *infra* § 7.19.

8. *See supra* § 2.115 (discussing how to address this apportionment in the contract).

9. *See infra* Chapter 8.

10. *See supra* §§ 2.42–2.43.

11. *See supra* §§ 2.86.

12. Other sources of income may include parking fees, vending machines proceeds, crop shares, and mineral royalties. Much of the following discussion of lease review and estoppels applies to these other income sources, with some obvious modifications that reflect the differing nature of these various types of income.

13. *See infra* §§ 3.49–3.50.

14. *See supra* §§ 2.90–2.92.

15. Landlords and tenants may prefer not to record the entire lease because of its length and because of their mutual desire to keep some terms of the lease out of the public records. In many states, a memorandum of lease serves to put subsequent parties on notice of the terms of the entire lease without revealing all of those terms. The presence of the memorandum in the land records informs the searcher that there is a more detailed document somewhere with which it must become familiar. State law varies as to what information the memorandum must contain in order to impart this constructive notice. The recording of a lease or a memorandum of lease may trigger an obligation to pay transfer taxes and recording fees. If these taxes and fees are substantial enough, the tenant may choose not to record and will have to rely instead on constructive notice imparted by its possession of the premises.

In addition, many landlords prohibit their tenants from recording a lease or memorandum of lease because of the reasonable concern that the tenant's recorded interest might later impair the marketability of the landlord's title.

16. For a more detailed discussion of subordination, nondisturbance, and attornment agreements, see Morton P. Fisher, Jr. & Richard H. Goldman, *The Ritual Dance Between Lessee and Lender—Subordination, Nondisturbance, and Attornment*, 30 REAL PROP. PROB. & TR. J. 355 (1995).

17. *See supra* §§ 2.53, 2.55–2.57.

18. If the seller is a general partnership, it may not have any formal organizational documents and the secretary of state may not be able to confirm its existence. The buyer can ask that the seller register with the secretary of state before the closing, if state law so permits, or can rely on affidavits from the general partners and an opinion letter from the seller's counsel. *See infra* § 3.64.

19. *See infra* §3.64.

20. In some cases, the parties will know in advance that a third-party consent is needed but cannot be obtained. For example, if the seller is conveying a restaurant, it may not be able to transfer its liquor license to the buyer, and the buyer will have to obtain one on its own. Any blanket representations and closing conditions addressing third-party consents need to include exceptions for matters of this type. The buyer also may want to include a post-closing obligation on the seller's part to cooperate in the buyer's pursuit of these consents. This obligation should not merge into the contract at closing.

21. *See infra* §4.17.

22. *See supra* §§2.76–2.77.

# Part III
# Loan Transactions

# CHAPTER 4

# The Loan Commitment

## § 4.01 The Need for a Loan Commitment

Part II of this book examined sales transactions, discussing the issues that are likely to arise when an owner wishes to sell its property to a buyer. In most instances, that buyer will be borrowing some of the funds it uses to acquire the property. Most buyers do not have enough money to buy real property without borrowing funds, and even if they do, the use of borrowed funds offers attractive tax benefits and leveraging opportunities. Part III turns to a discussion of loan transactions.

Keep in mind that a sales transaction need not be accompanied by a loan transaction. An investor, for example, can purchase real estate entirely with his own funds. Similarly, a loan transaction need not be accompanied by a sales transaction, as when a property owner refinances property it already owns at a lower interest rate. The discussion in Part III, however, assumes that the loan transaction is taking place at the same time as an acquisition of property, as a means of addressing those issues unique to acquisition loans. Thus, while the text that follows usually refers to the parties to the loan as "the lender" and "the borrower," it should be evident that the same party is filling the roles of both borrower and buyer.

If you are representing a borrower that is refinancing property that it already owns, or a lender that is providing money to a party that already owns the property it will mortgage, this discussion will still be valuable to you, but some of the issues discussed here may not be pertinent to your transaction. It also is worth remembering that the seller sometimes furnishes the buyer with some or all of the needed financing by accepting a note and mortgage at the closing as part of the consideration for the property. In these cases, the seller and the lender are the same entity.

The buyer needs to make sure that the seller is obligated to sell the property and that the lender is obligated to lend the acquisition funds. If the buyer contracts to buy the property but cannot obtain a loan, then it may have to breach the contract and pay damages to the seller, perhaps by forfeiting its down payment. If the buyer receives a loan commitment but cannot close on the property, it may lose its loan commitment fee even though it does not receive the property. From the buyer's perspective, the acquisition and lending transactions are contingent upon each other, which means that the buyer must enter into two different agreements that provide it with some flexibility in the event that something goes wrong.

The most common way for the buyer to protect itself against these overlapping uncertainties is by signing a contract of sale that contains a financing condition. This closing condition in the sales contract should state precisely what type of commitment the buyer must receive before it is obligated to close so that the parties understand exactly what types of nonperformance will be legally excused.[1] The buyer then should make sure that it attempts to meet this financing condition during the due diligence period.[2] If the buyer meets this condition, it must close. If it is unable to satisfy the financing condition, however, it can exercise its contractual right to terminate the sales contract without penalty and without forfeiting its earnest money deposit. Less commonly, the buyer may be able to secure a commitment for a line of credit in advance and then contract to acquire the property. In a case such as this, the parties will execute the loan commitment first, and the commitment will contain numerous conditions addressing the property that the buyer may acquire with these funds.

Neither the buyer nor its lender will want to rely on a verbal promise to make a loan. The buyer will want to be sure that if it decides to close, the lender must make the acquisition funds available at the closing. In fact, the buyer is likely to face a preclosing contract termination deadline, after which it will be unable to withdraw from the contract of sale without penalty. The lender wants to know that it will be compensated if it sets funds aside for the buyer's use. The lender may have passed up other lending opportunities or may itself be borrowing the funds from another source, and it does not wish to lose money as a result of the seller's unexpected withdrawal from the transaction. Each party, then, wants to execute a loan commitment in advance that places obligations on the other party if certain enumerated conditions are met.

> *Comment:* Many contracts of sale condition the buyer's obligation to close on the receipt of a loan commitment and not on the actual receipt of the funds. Sellers are reluctant to agree to condition the closing on the actual receipt of the funds, because they wish to know in advance whether the closing is going to occur. A buyer in this situation needs to be confident that it can satisfy all conditions contained in the loan commitment.

## §4.02 Similarities to and Differences from the Contract of Sale

The loan commitment is an executory contract in which the lender agrees to lend the acquisition funds to the buyer if all the conditions contained in the loan commitment are met. In many ways, the loan commitment parallels the contract of sale, which also is an executory contract. Both documents set forth the legal and financial obligations of two parties and the conditions that each of these parties must meet. Each document includes representations, warranties, and covenants that each party makes in favor of the other. The contract and the loan commitment each contain closing conditions so that the failure or inability of one party to perform for certain pre-agreed reasons will be excused. Each document states what events constitute defaults and sets forth remedies for those defaults. The two documents provide for the disclosure of information and the allocation of risks. Finally, each of these documents sets out a road map to the closing and explains how the parties meet their obligations at the closing. If much of the discussion in this chapter sounds familiar, it is because the buyer will have attempted to address similar issues in its contract with the seller.[3]

The role of the seller in the sales contract parallels the role of the borrower in the loan commitment. Each of these parties is requesting money from its contract counterpart, the seller in the form of the sale price and the borrower in the form of the loan proceeds.

Each of these parties is offering to provide an interest in real estate in consideration for that money, with the seller promising to deliver title to the buyer and the borrower offering to deliver a mortgage or deed of trust to the lender. Each of these parties must provide whatever information its contract counterpart demands before that counterpart will agree to part with money and accept a piece of paper in return.

Similarly, the role of the buyer in the contract is analogous to the role of the lender in the loan commitment. Each party is acquiring an interest in real estate about which it initially knows very little. Each party must use its written agreement and the due diligence period as a means of eliciting as much of this unknown information as possible so that it can decide whether it is comfortable proceeding to the closing. Each party knows that its bargaining leverage will largely disappear after the closing: its chief role in the deal is to provide a significant amount of money, its most credible threat is to refuse to produce that money, and that threat becomes nearly meaningless after the closing.

The sale transaction and the loan transaction are not complete mirror images of one another, however. The sale transaction is intended purely as a conveyance of real property. The whole point of the sale is for the seller to terminate its interest in the real estate, and the operative document of transfer—the deed—conveys the seller's entire interest to the buyer. While the deed may include warranties, and while post-closing litigation is far from unheard of, the sale transaction is designed to end the relationship between the seller and the land and also the relationship between the seller and the buyer.

The loan transaction does not end at the closing, and the operative loan documents—including the note, the mortgage, the assignment of leases and rents, and any Uniform Commercial Code (UCC) financing statements—create an ongoing relationship between the borrower and the lender that may last for decades. The two parties are, in essence, sharing the bundle of property rights that used to belong to the seller. The buyer has become the owner of the property but has immediately conveyed a security interest in that property to its lender, and the lender may find itself foreclosing on the real estate, and perhaps buying it, years after the closing. Thus, the loan commitment not only governs the parties' relationship between the time of its execution and the time of the closing, it also establishes the terms of an ongoing post-closing relationship.

## §4.03 Lender's Perspective

As the previous section suggests, the lender's perspective on the loan commitment is fairly similar to the buyer's perspective on the contract of sale. The lender can address the loan issues that concern it in much the same way that the buyer addresses its concerns about the acquisition of the property. The lender should review the loan transaction carefully before deciding whether to extend the loan; should agree to a loan commitment that provides it with necessary information about the transaction and the property and that allocates risk in an acceptable way; should perform all necessary due diligence; and should accept loan documents at the closing that will fairly govern its ongoing relationship with the borrower.

Bear in mind that the seller ordinarily knows far more about the property than the borrower does. The seller has probably owned the real estate long enough to know of its problems, may have participated in the creation of some of the title encumbrances, and will have executed many of the leases. The borrower, in contrast, is probably as new to the property as the lender is. It is about to buy the real estate and then immediately mortgage it to the lender. This means that the borrower may have little firsthand knowledge of the property and may be doing nothing more than turning the seller's disclosures over to the lender. The borrower may prefer to limit many of its disclosures by clarifying that it is making statements only to the best of its own knowledge. This means that the lender is receiving less valuable representations and will have to expand its own investigation accordingly.

Unlike in a sales transaction, the parties to a loan do not possess equivalent bargaining leverage. When the buyer and the seller negotiate their contract, each party is anxious to consummate the sale, and they will probably compromise on many of the more important issues. Obviously, there will be exceptions to this general statement, depending on market conditions, the identity of the parties, and the uniqueness of the property, but it is fair to state that neither party is likely to hold all the good cards.

In a loan transaction, by contrast, the lender is typically in a far stronger position than the borrower. Some of that strength may emanate from federal or state lending regulations that mandate or prohibit certain behavior by the lender, but most of this bargaining clout simply reflects the fact that the lender will be in the position of greater risk once it extends the loan. The lender gives up money and receives in return documents that allow it to recover from the borrower or foreclose on the property. Once the money has changed hands, the lender is relying on the value of the property and the skills of the borrower, so the lender must make itself comfortable with that value and those skills before the loan closes. If the lender is not comfortable (or if it is not receiving consideration adequate to compensate it for its remaining discomfort), then it will not wish to make the loan. Moreover, the number of willing lenders tends to be smaller than the number of willing sellers, so borrowers may find that their loan options are limited. In the end, the lender is likely to dictate many of the terms of the final agreement, and the borrower may find itself fighting an uphill battle to make a small number of changes in the lender's standard form documents.

---

*Comment:* Although the lender will usually be in a far stronger bargaining position than the borrower, sometimes it will not have the superior position. Moreover, lenders, and not just borrowers, have been known to default. During the savings-and-loan crisis, for example, lenders defaulted on loan commitments more frequently than they had in prior years.

---

*Comment:* One of the chief differences between the lender and the borrower is that the lender almost always has deep pockets, while the borrower often does not. If the borrower defaults, a single-purpose entity may be liable, but if the lender takes over the property, the lender may become responsible for the borrower's obligations under leases and other agreements.

---

## §4.04 Borrower's Perspective

The borrower's perspective, predictably enough, is just the opposite. Once it signs the contract of sale, the buyer will be anxious to secure satisfactory financing and will probably spend the next several weeks scrambling to find an acceptable loan and to turn over to prospective lenders whatever information they request. All potential lenders will be examining the same factors—the value of the property, the quality of title, the status of tenant leases, and the skills and experience of the borrower—and the borrower knows that if one lender rejects its application out of dissatisfaction with one of these factors, other lenders may reach the same decision for the same reason.

The borrower is likely to be extremely accommodating to potential lenders and is also likely to recognize the difficulty of exacting major concessions from any lender. Many lenders will prove to be fair parties that are willing to accommodate reasonable concerns of the borrower, but the borrower should not expect any lender to respond to every one of its requests or to make dramatic modifications to its regular documents. Perhaps the largest developer in town can dictate the terms of a loan from a bank that wants its business, but most borrowers are smaller players with far less negotiating power.

## §4.05 Terms of the Loan Commitment

The sections that follow focus on those portions of the loan commitment that differ from the contract of sale. Before highlighting these important differences, however, it is important to emphasize the many terms of these two documents that are similar. This chapter has already noted the great degree to which the loan commitment tracks the conceptual format of the contract of sale.[4] The remainder of this section focuses on some of the key textual similarities between the loan commitment and the contract of sale.

The summary contained in this section is not intended to be a comprehensive treatment of issues already addressed earlier; rather, it should remind the lawyer to review the earlier discussion of the contract of sale, as well as the contract of sale itself.[5] To the extent that an issue is not specifically discussed here, the lawyer needs to consider the parallel discussion of the sales contract and to determine the extent to which that discussion raises concerns that also must be addressed in the loan commitment. The lawyer should also review all provisions of the contract of sale itself and confirm that the loan commitment addresses all the relevant issues that the sales contract raises.

The loan commitment must be in writing and must set forth the essential terms of the loan transaction. The commitment must identify the parties and the property and must state that it contains the lender's agreement to lend on the terms specified in the commitment. It must state the principal amount of the loan, the interest rate or the manner in which the rate is to be determined, and the repayment terms. The loan commitment needs to clarify that the real property that the borrower is acquiring will also serve as security for the repayment of the loan.

Like the contract of sale, the loan commitment will contain representations and warranties, and these provisions will address many of the same issues that the contract addresses. The lender, like the buyer, uses these provisions as a way of learning about the property, allocating as many risks as possible to the other party, and setting up remedies for breach. The lender recognizes that if the borrower cannot operate the property successfully, the lender may have to assume that operational role, either before or after a foreclosure. Therefore, the lender evaluates the property in much the way that a buyer does, and the representations in the loan commitment will often parallel the representations in the contract of sale.

The same can be said for the loan commitment's closing conditions. The lender will want the same types of assurances from the borrower that the buyer received from the seller, and the lender will insist on the right to terminate the transaction before the closing if its due diligence reveals material problems. While the documentation of the loan will differ from the documentation of the sale—and thus the closing conditions addressing document delivery will have to be modified accordingly—the closing conditions in the two documents should be tightly coordinated.

The loan commitment will also address closing mechanics. The commitment will set forth an outside date and a location for the closing, and it will allocate responsibility for meeting closing conditions, delivering information, and preparing documents. In addition, the loan commitment will contain a remedies section that explains the rights of each party should the other party breach.

The remaining sections of this chapter focus on those portions of the loan commitment that are significantly different from provisions of the contract of sale and are thus unique to the borrower–lender relationship. The next chapter builds on this chapter's discussion by turning to an examination of the lender's due diligence.

### §4.06—Caution: Loan Commitment Issues and Loan Document Issues

The lawyers should recognize that many of the issues addressed in the loan commitment—an executory contract—will be implemented in the note, the mortgage, and the other security documents later. The parties agree in the commitment that they will take certain actions, and they actually take those actions in the loan documents. For this reason, lawyers who are drafting and negotiating a loan commitment would be well-advised to read Chapter 6 now and be sure that their loan commitments address the issues discussed there in connection with the loan documents. Many of the issues addressed there, including prepayment rights, rights to seek junior financing, and due-on-transfer limitations, could appropriately be discussed here. Just as the loan commitment will track the contract of sale, the loan documents will track the loan commitment, and the lawyers need to take these similarities into account when they prepare the loan commitment.

The more detailed discussion of these additional matters is deferred until later, because these provisions may be drafted with greater specificity in the operative loan documents than in the executory loan commitment. In many cases, however, the language addressing these issues in the two documents will be identical or nearly identical. The current chapter discusses items that are more in the nature of closing conditions, while the chapter that addresses the loan documents focuses more on the terms of the loan itself. This division is an artificial one, because there is significant overlap between the two groups of clauses. The drafter would be wise to review both sets now rather than realizing later that the loan commitment lacks an essential term. The drafter also should keep in mind that once the parties execute the loan commitment, they are under an obligation of good faith and fair dealing to consummate the closing of the loan in accordance with the terms of the commitment.

### § 4.07—Form: Loan Commitment

See Appendix I for a Form of Loan Commitment.

### § 4.08—Tenant Leases; Lease Priorities

The lender, like the buyer, must confirm that creditworthy, rent-paying tenants are in possession of space and that they are obligated to pay rent well into the future. The lender's interest in these leases is somewhat different from that of the buyer, and this section focuses on the concerns that are unique to the lender.

The buyer's primary concern is to operate the property successfully. The lender is just as concerned that the buyer succeed in operating the project but also is worried about what happens to the property if the buyer fails to meet its obligations. If the project is unsuccessful, the lender will have to exercise its pre-foreclosure remedies and then may have to foreclose on the property. In other words, the lender looks into the future and anticipates the possible consequences of owning the property after the borrower's association with it has ended.

When the buyer acquires the property, it steps directly into the seller's shoes. The buyer becomes the owner, the tenants begin to pay the rent to their new landlord, and there should be little legally significant change in the operation of the project. If the lender should need to exercise its mortgage remedies later, however, there may be changes of great legal significance at the property.

The lender is specifically interested in learning the relative priorities of its own mortgage and the various tenants' leases under the state's recording statute. These priorities will determine whether the leases will survive or be terminated if there is a foreclosure. If some or all of the tenant leases are junior to the mortgage, a successful foreclosure, and perhaps even the exercise of certain pre-foreclosure remedies, may terminate these leases automatically or afford the tenants the option to terminate their leases. Conversely, if some or all of the tenant leases are senior to the mortgage, a foreclosure may not result in the termination of these leases, and the foreclosure sale purchaser will be left with these tenants even if they are undesirable.

The relative priorities of leases and mortgages can be determined by reviewing the relevant documents, by becoming familiar with the state's recording laws, and by understanding the ways in which the state permits enforcement of the various remedies contained in the mortgage. The leases, the mortgage, and any SNDA agreements[6] will establish the initial priorities. These documents may also provide the lender with the option to rearrange these priorities as it chooses or may set forth priorities that cannot be changed without the consent of the tenant in question. The state's recording laws may clarify the extent to which tenants without recorded leases nonetheless enjoy priority by virtue of their prior obvious possession of their space. The state may or may not allow foreclosing lenders to omit certain junior tenants from the foreclosure process strategically as a way of preserving junior leases that otherwise would terminate at foreclosure.

Counsel to the lender will not be able to figure out the relative priorities of these leases and mortgages before undertaking a due diligence review of the documents and becoming familiar with the state's recording statute and foreclosure procedures. Meanwhile, the parties will wish to execute a loan commitment before the lender has completed this due diligence investigation. The loan commitment therefore must contain closing conditions that allow the lender to review the relevant documents after the commitment is signed and address any problems it discovers.

For example, lender's counsel may insist that the borrower deliver a first mortgage to the lender that is senior to all leases. Borrower's counsel might respond by noting that all the leases to existing tenants will be senior to the mortgage under state law, but that all but three of these senior leases contain provisions allowing the lender to subordinate the lease to the mortgage by giving written notice to the tenant. The remaining three tenants, the borrower might point out, are the largest and most desirable tenants. The parties may ultimately agree to a loan commitment in which the borrower represents that all leases for less than 5,000 square feet of space are junior to the mortgage or can be made junior to the mortgage, and that all leases for larger space are senior to the mortgage. A closing condition will mirror this statement and will provide the lender with the option not to close if the statement is untrue. By reaching this compromise, the lender learns some critical information about the property and removes much of the risk of the loan. The lender receives assurance that it is senior to all leases that it is likely to want to terminate, and the borrower ensures that the lender will be obligated to fund the loan at the closing.

### §4.09—Environmental Matters

Buyers and lenders both are concerned about liability for the costs of remediating environmental problems. Liability of this type may arise under federal, state, or local law. For many buyers and lenders, the most obvious source of concern is the federal Comprehensive Environmental Response, Compensation and Liability Act of 1980 (CERCLA),[7] although both parties need to become familiar with the full array of applicable environmental laws.

The lender's concerns differ somewhat from those of its borrower. Most obviously, the borrower will have far more control over the operation of the property than will the lender during the time that the borrower owns the property. The borrower knows that it will own and operate the property and that it cannot avoid potential responsibility for cleanup costs under CERCLA and similar statutes,[8] while the lender anticipates that it will neither operate nor own the property unless something goes very wrong with the borrower. CERCLA provides a statutory exemption from liability for secured parties, and the lender will want to be certain that both parties act in a way that allows the lender to retain this valuable insulation from liability.

The lender should demand in the loan commitment that the borrower demonstrate that the property is free of hazardous substances as of the closing date. If this is true, the lender ensures that neither party is inheriting any preexisting liability. The lender should also insist in the loan commitment that the buyer covenant to continue to operate the property in a manner that will not lead to future environmental liability. This protection needs to appear in the operative loan documents as well. By insisting that the borrower give these covenants, the lender is taking steps to make sure that the property remains clean while the borrower owns it. If the lender ever needs to foreclose on the property, any prospective buyer (including itself) will want to avoid liability for cleanup costs, and contaminated property will sell for far less than property that is free of environmental liability.

The lender may also want the loan commitment and the operative documents to provide additional assurances that the borrower will operate in compliance with all environmental laws and will not subject the lender to liability for cleanup costs. The lender may insist that the borrower obtain insurance or that the principals of the borrower provide personal guarantees to this effect. The extent to which the lender demands these extra assurances is likely to depend on the type of business that the borrower plans to operate: a lead-recycling facility will obviously worry the lender more than an apartment house will.

> *Comment:* Because of the potential for enormous liability, lenders want to assume virtually no risk whatsoever with regard to environmental matters. Lenders often demand an environmental carveout from any nonrecourse protection and a separate environmental indemnity. The carveout and the indemnity must be backed up by individuals or entities with sufficient net worth to pay the cost of remediation or other liability costs. This is one of the most difficult issues in the loan transaction on which to reach agreement, because individuals and entities with high net worth are reluctant to indemnify for such obligations personally.

## § 4.10—Insurance

Both parties have an interest in seeing that the property remains adequately insured against casualty loss. If uninsured or underinsured improvements were to be destroyed or significantly damaged by fire or other casualty, the borrower would be more likely to default on the loan, the lender then might be forced to foreclose on property that is worth far less than the outstanding principal, and both parties could suffer substantial losses.

The interests of the parties with respect to casualty insurance are likely to differ somewhat, for several reasons. Lenders tend to be more risk-averse than borrowers. The borrower may wish to save money on insurance, which it will be paying for, but the lender will want the broadest possible coverage. In addition, the lender's risk usually is greater than the borrower's for the simple reason that the lender often has provided 80 to 90 percent of the funds for the purchase of the property. If the building burns down and the project is not adequately insured, the lender will probably lose more money than the borrower.

The lender's insurance concerns will be particularly acute if the project is not successful or if the loan is nonrecourse. If the project struggles, the value of the property is likely to drop, and the borrower's equity may soon be even lower than it was when the loan closed. At some point, the borrower may have no equity left in the project and may assume that it is going to lose its entire investment no matter what happens. Once the borrower reaches this conclusion, it may see no reason to spend any of its scarce funds on insurance premiums. If the loan is nonrecourse, the lender has agreed from the outset that, subject only to any carveouts from the nonrecourse provisions, it will look solely to the property for satisfaction of any unpaid debt and will not seek recovery from the borrower or any of its principals.[9] The nonrecourse borrower believes—not always accurately—that its losses are capped at its investment and that it need not worry about any additional personal liability.

The lender must receive adequate evidence that the borrower has insured the property in sufficient amounts with reliable companies as of the closing date. It addresses this concern in the loan commitment, which should contain a covenant and a closing condition to this effect. The commitment should also specify that the loan documents will require the borrower to maintain this insurance throughout the life of the loan. Lenders often insist that the borrower make monthly escrow deposits to the lender in the amount of one-twelfth of the annual insurance premium, with the lender agreeing to pay the premium to the insurer when the bill comes due.[10] In this way, the lender receives early warning if the borrower is experiencing financial distress and also knows for certain that funds have been set aside to cover at least part of the insurance premium. Borrowers often object to such escrow provisions and seek to omit them or to require the lender to pay interest on the amounts held in escrow. The parties may compromise by agreeing that the lender will demand an escrow only after the borrower shows evidence of financial distress, such as by defaulting.

The lender must be certain that the insurer is aware of the lender's interest in the property and that the coverage will not be voided by any act of the borrower. The parties ordinarily address this concern by agreeing to use an insurance policy that contains a standard mortgage clause, known in some areas as a union mortgage clause. This clause does more than simply name the lender as payee under the policy. It also compels the insurer to pay the proceeds to the lender even if the borrower would have forfeited its coverage because of its intentional or reckless acts on the property. The lender must be sure that the form of the policy will be acceptable, and it achieves this goal first by including appropriate language in the closing conditions of the loan commitment and then by making sure that the actual policy meets these conditions.

The lender should also verify that after a casualty loss, the insurer is obligated to pay the insurance proceeds to the lender alone or to the borrower and the lender jointly, and may not pay them to the borrower alone. This reassures the lender that it will retain control over the insurance proceeds. Even after the lender receives the insurance proceeds, the parties may differ as to how they wish to use these funds. The borrower may want to rebuild the property, while the lender may prefer to retain the proceeds and credit the amount against the principal balance. This disagreement could reflect tensions between the parties over their past relationship, or it may indicate nothing more than an unexpected change in the prevailing interest rate. The parties would be wise to address this issue with care in their loan commitment and loan documents.

---

*Comment:* The interests of the borrower's tenants also must be considered. The lender may want to have the right to apply the insurance proceeds toward the loan balance, but major leases may require that the proceeds be applied to restoration of the property. The borrower needs to be careful not to enter into loan documents that conflict with the leases.

---

Lenders are concerned with other types of insurance as well. The lender will want to be sure that the borrower obtains adequate amounts of liability insurance, so that deaths, injuries, or other damage at the site will not lead to a huge judgment against the borrower. The borrower should also carry other types of insurance, including workers' compensation insurance; rental interruption insurance; and, where appropriate, environmental liability, flood, wind, earthquake, or terrorism insurance. The parties and their lawyers would be wise to consult with knowledgeable insurance experts, because these issues are often beyond the training and expertise of many lawyers. Whatever coverage the parties agree to, however, must be documented in the loan commitment, implemented at the closing, and maintained thereafter.

Insurers generally will not issue completed policies at the closing. Rather, they ordinarily provide binders, which summarize the major terms of the coverage but supply little detail. The insurer then forwards full policies some time after the closing. The parties would be wise to review the full policy forms in advance so that they know before the closing exactly what coverage the insurer plans to provide and can raise any concerns.

> Comment: This issue was brought into stark relief following the destruction of the World Trade Center, which came just a few weeks after the buildings had changed hands. Disagreement over the precise language of the full policies, which had not yet been issued, led to litigation disputing $3.5 billion in coverage.[11]

## §4.11—Assignability of Contracts and Licenses

An operating real estate project is a business, and the borrower will be managing various aspects of this business throughout its ownership of the property. The borrower, acting on its own or through various agents, hires and dismisses employees; maintains, secures, and insures the premises; ensures that essential services are provided; leases space to new tenants; collects rent and pays bills; and shoulders all the other burdens of running a business.[12]

The lender will have great interest in the borrower's ability to maintain good working relationships with tenants, employees, and other parties, because the lender is more likely to be repaid if the borrower's project is successful. The lender's concern extends beyond the borrower's period of ownership. If the borrower defaults and the lender must foreclose, the lender will want to maximize the price for which the property can be sold. Any new owner, whether it is a third party or the lender itself, will place great value on maintaining ongoing relationships with suppliers, tenants, and employees, particularly if the relevant contracts contain favorable terms. The new owner will not want to spend its first weeks of ownership desperately seeking new landscaping service providers, custodial staff members, and bookkeepers and will want to ensure that the contracts that establish the most important relationships are assignable to it. This issue is of particular importance in a construction loan, in which the borrower will have established critically important relationships with design and construction specialists.

The lender should ask for a representation that lists and describes all the major contractual relationships, licenses, and other agreements to which the borrower will be a party. Disclosure of these documents will allow the lender to examine them as part of its due diligence investigation of the property. The lender should also seek closing conditions in the loan commitment that state that the lender must be reasonably satisfied with major contracts, that the borrower has the power to assign these contracts, and that the borrower will assign its interest in these contracts to the lender as additional security for the borrower's performance of its loan obligations. If the borrower defaults on the loan, the lender can step into the borrower's shoes whether the lender forecloses or merely takes possession. Security assignments of this type will also permit the lender to transfer these contracts to any successor owner, such as a foreclosure sale purchaser. Some of these relationships may prove to be of only minor importance to the lender or may be "at will" relationships, but in other cases these contracts may be of great value to the lender.

### §4.12—Real Property Taxes and Assessments

The lender, like the buyer, must be certain that all real property taxes and assessments that become due before the closing are paid by the seller and that the borrower will continue to make these payments after the closing. Once again, the interests of the lender and the buyer largely parallel each other, but the lender has additional concerns. The lender may worry that if cash is tight, the borrower will fail to pay its real estate taxes. Taxing jurisdictions often wait months or years before attempting to enforce tax liens, while other creditors rarely provide this much leeway. This concern is particularly great if the loan is nonrecourse, because the borrower's failure to pay effectively devalues the lender's security, and the lender has given up much of its ability to recover personally from the borrower.[13]

---

*Comment:* Prudent lenders always insist that the mortgaged property consist of one or more separate tax parcels. The lender does not want to receive a mortgage on property that is only a portion of a larger tax parcel.

---

The parallels between real property taxes and insurance premiums should be apparent. In both cases, the borrower has the ability to devalue or demote the priority of the lender's security by not paying an amount that the borrower is responsible for paying. Real property tax liens are always prior to mortgage loans, even if the mortgage was recorded before the taxes accrued, and the borrower that fails to pay its taxes makes the lender's security that much less valuable. Insurance premiums remove the risk that the lender will suffer a loss because of the destruction of some or all of its security. It is essential to the lender that the borrower pay both of these bills.

Just as the lender may insist on an escrow for payment of insurance premiums,[14] it also may demand an escrow for payment of real property taxes and assessments. The borrower will be required to pay to the lender one-twelfth of the actual or estimated annual taxes each month, and the lender then will turn the payments over to the taxing authorities as they come due. To the extent that the parties are unsure of the exact amount, they can use the prior year's amount or their best estimate of the current year's amount, with an adjustment when the actual amount is fixed. The borrower is likely to make the same objection here as it made when the lender asked it to escrow insurance premiums, and the parties must reach an acceptable resolution with respect to taxes and assessments, just as they did with respect to insurance.

The loan commitment should clarify the parties' obligations. If, for example, the lender commits to lend on the condition that the borrower make monthly escrow payments of taxes, the loan commitment must spell out that condition, and the operative loan documents should effect the transaction the parties have agreed to.

### § 4.13—Prior Mortgages

If the lender will be making a junior loan, it will have some obvious concerns about all senior debt. It will want to know the status of this senior debt as of the closing, including the outstanding principal, the interest rate, and the due date. The junior lender will also want assurances that there are no defaults on any senior debt. These matters can be addressed by including borrower representations in the loan commitment, which the junior lender will then confirm during the due diligence period, and by including parallel closing conditions.

Just as important, the junior lender will have concerns about the status of its own mortgage should any senior lender exercise any of its own mortgage remedies in the future. A senior lender might seek the appointment of a receiver or might exercise its rights under an assignment of leases and rents, thereby reducing the borrower's ability to meet its obligations to the junior lender. A senior lender might even foreclose, which would wipe out the junior lender's mortgage and leave it with only the surplus cash from the foreclosure, if any, and a personal claim against the borrower.

To reduce the risk of any of these unsatisfactory outcomes, the junior lender is likely to condition the funding of its loan on receipt of agreements from all senior lenders that they will provide it with notice of any defaults on their loans and with the opportunity to cure those defaults. This requirement will force the borrower (or the seller, if the property is being purchased subject to senior debt) to approach these senior lenders and ask them to amend their documents, to the extent those documents do not already provide junior lenders with these protections. From the junior lender's point of view, it is essential that the loan commitment contain a closing condition mandating that all holders of senior debt protect the junior lender in this way.

---

*Comment:* Many lenders simply will not make a junior loan. The lender that agrees to make a junior loan may find itself in a position in which, in order to protect its own interest, it has to redeem the senior debt if that debt goes into default.

---

*Comment:* Mezzanine loans, in which there is a pledge of ownership interests in lieu of a second mortgage, are frequently used in situations in which the senior lender will not permit a junior loan.

---

### § 4.14—Appraisal

The lender typically begins its analysis of the borrower's loan application by assuming that the price set forth in the contract of sale accurately reflects the value of the property. However, the lender may also insist that an independent appraiser place a value on the property and that this appraised value equal or exceed the contract price. If the lender has agreed to lend an amount that is close to the maximum that its internal loan-to-value guidelines or applicable lending regulations allow, then the appraisal must confirm the accuracy of the sale price set forth in the contract of sale. If the loan is for less than this amount, however, the lender may be willing to accept a lower appraisal, because the lender will be oversecured even if the appraisal suggests that the property is worth somewhat less than the purchase price.[15] The loan commitment should specify the appraisal method that the parties will instruct the appraiser to use, because different methods can lead to different valuations. The commitment should also clarify whether the borrower must pay for this appraisal, as it nearly always will.

The loan commitment will usually provide the lender with the right to terminate the commitment without penalty or to reduce the principal amount pro rata if the appraiser determines that the value of the property is too low. If the appraisal comes in low, the borrower will often have the right under the contract of sale to terminate the contract without penalty and may thereby gain some leverage for reducing the purchase price set forth in the contract. If the seller refuses to agree to a price reduction, the buyer may choose to close anyway but will probably have to accept a loan in a lower amount than it had hoped for.

### §4.15—Creditworthiness Matters

Before the lender enters into the loan commitment, it will assess the borrower's professional experience, financial condition, and borrowing history and will examine the property itself, as a means of deciding whether the borrower merits a loan in the amount it has requested. The loan commitment should contain representations from the borrower as to these issues, along with corresponding closing conditions. These provisions will address matters such as the lender's receipt, review, and acceptance of the borrower's financial statements. The commitment may also require the acceptance of similar statements from the borrower's principals and any guarantors. If the borrower's initial disclosures prove to be untrue, or even just overly optimistic, the lender needs the ability to terminate the loan commitment without penalty.

The lender's lawyer is unlikely to perform these reviews himself. Unlike legal matters such as title and lease review, these are matters about which the client has the greater expertise. The lawyer's task is to address these matters in the loan commitment and to be sure that he receives the appropriate documentation during the due diligence period and turns it over to his client for its own review. The lawyer also must be sure that the contract contains appropriate remedies should these documents reveal any significant problems.

> *Comment:* To be sure that their borrowers remains in sound financial condition throughout the term of the loan, lenders increasingly seek financial statements and annual reports from borrowers during every year of the term.

### §4.16—Loan Guarantees and Other Forms of Credit Enhancement

Every lender is concerned that the real estate will prove not to be adequate security should the borrower fail to meet its loan obligations. The project may be risky, market conditions may be uncertain, the borrower may be involved in a business that could lead to environmental liability, the borrower may be a thinly capitalized entity, or the loan might be nonrecourse. For these and other reasons, the lender may insist on additional security.

One common form of additional security is a personal guarantee. If the borrower is a corporation or a limited liability entity, the lender may demand that a creditworthy principal of the entity serve as a "backstop," promising to pay some or all of the loan balance if a foreclosure followed by a claim on the note should fail to lead to full repayment of the debt. If the borrower is a single-purpose entity that is affiliated with a more creditworthy entity, the lender may seek a guaranty from that related entity.

Guarantees may cover all or only part of the debt, they may last for the entire term of the loan or may expire after a fixed period of time, they may terminate or spring into existence upon the occurrence of a stated event, and they may guarantee the lender's recovery following any type of default or after only specifically listed defaults. The lender may prefer some other form of credit enhancement, such as a letter of credit. Whatever form of additional security the lender desires, the loan commitment must state expressly that the lender's obligation to fund the loan is conditioned on the borrower's delivery of the appropriate document, collateral, or other form of credit enhancement.

> *Comment:* Sometimes the lender agrees to accept a partial guarantee. In these cases, the parties must be clear as to exactly what is being guaranteed: A 20 percent guarantee might refer to the first 20 percent of the loan, the last 20 percent, or twenty cents of every dollar.

### §4.17—Opinion of Borrower's Counsel

The loan commitment will condition the lender's obligation to close the loan on its receipt of a satisfactory legal opinion from borrower's counsel. This opinion will contain many of the same provisions as the opinions discussed in connection with the contract of sale.[16] The lender will want the borrower's counsel to confirm that the borrower is properly organized and licensed to do business, that it has authorized the transaction in accordance with all applicable laws and governing documents, that the transaction does not violate any third-party agreements, and that the individuals who will be executing the documents have the authority to do so.

The opinion from the borrower's lawyer often goes beyond these issues. The lender may ask the borrower's counsel to opine that the mortgage and the other loan documents are enforceable in accordance with state law. The lender may also request a zoning opinion. These opinions are often heavily negotiated, perhaps in large part because the law firm delivering the opinion is responsible for any misstatements contained in the letter. During the past few years, several bar organizations have developed standard forms for some of these legal opinions.[17] Even if these forms are not acceptable in every transaction, they should serve to highlight some of the issues the parties may need to address.

### §4.18—Nonrecourse Provision

Commercial borrowers often seek nonrecourse loans, in which the lender agrees that it will look only to the mortgaged property for satisfaction of the debt and will not seek a deficiency judgment against the borrower or any of its principals. If the lender agrees to a nonrecourse loan, the borrower knows that it can lose no more than it commits to the property initially. This is particularly important to partnership borrowers, whose general partners face potentially unlimited personal liability. The borrower also may enjoy tax benefits as a result of borrowing on a nonrecourse basis.

In spite of the greater risk posed by nonrecourse loans, lenders often agree to provide them. Lenders are aware of the tax and liability concerns that borrowers face, they know that there will be an equity cushion at the time they extend the loan, they may have factored the greater risk into the financial terms of the loan, they may demand guarantees or other forms of credit enhancement, and they know whether competing lenders are offering nonrecourse loans.

If the loan is to be nonrecourse, the borrower must be certain that this provision appears in the loan commitment. Simply stating that the loan is "nonrecourse," however, is not enough, because the scope of a nonrecourse loan is subject to much negotiation. For the borrower's protection, the loan commitment should specify exactly what the parties intend. If the borrower is a partnership that owns other significant assets, for example, the borrower must be sure that the exculpation extends to the borrower partnership and not just to the general partners of that partnership.

---

*Comment:* In many loan transactions, the lender insists that the borrower be a single-purpose bankruptcy-remote entity. Note also that there are few partnerships in commercial real estate practice in which the general partner is not itself an entity.

---

Lenders also have concerns about the precise meaning of the term "nonrecourse." Even a lender that is willing to lend on a nonrecourse basis must exclude certain matters from the broader exculpatory language. For example, the borrower should not be permitted to make misrepresentations in its loan application, or to commit waste at the property, and then defend against the lender's suit for damages by arguing that the loan is nonrecourse. Nonrecourse provisions can become quite lengthy and complex, containing many of these lender carveouts, and the parties should define this term with care in the loan commitment.[18]

---

*Comment:* Lenders frequently include nonrecourse carveouts for items such as fraud or other misconduct; misappropriation of insurance proceeds; environmental liability; and the actual costs and expenses of foreclosing the mortgage, including attorneys' fees. The borrower thus would be responsible for payment of these amounts even though the loan is otherwise nonrecourse.

---

### §4.19—Loan Commitment Fee

The interest that the lender charges serves as consideration for the borrower's use of the borrowed funds, but the lender also is likely to charge an additional fee as compensation for the transaction costs of initially extending credit and documenting the deal. This compensation typically takes the form of a loan commitment fee, and this fee can be substantial. The loan commitment must state the exact amount of that fee, how it is to be paid, when it is to be paid, and the conditions upon which it is fully or partly refundable.

The borrower will most likely deliver this sum to the lender at the time the parties execute the loan commitment, and the lender will take the position that it has earned the fee by agreeing in writing to extend the loan. It has invested its time and energy, it has arranged to have the loan proceeds available, and it has earned this fee whether or not the loan ultimately closes. The borrower may claim that it should receive a refund if the lender breaches or if the loan fails to close through no fault of the borrower's. The lender should concede the first of these points, and the parties are likely to negotiate the contours of the second one. The commitment needs to be clear as to how the parties have resolved these issues.

### § 4.20—Loan Expenses

The borrower will also have to pay most of the lender's other expenses associated with the loan. Prominent among these is the lender's cost for outside counsel, including out-of-pockets costs and travel expenses. The borrower is likely to pay for the lender's title insurance policy, the appraisal, the survey, and the recording costs, although local custom varies as to these matters and some of these costs may already have been paid by the seller. Local custom (and perhaps state law) also varies as to whether the borrower will be responsible for paying mortgage recording taxes.

The parties should be clear in the loan commitment as to precisely which costs the borrower must bear and when they must be paid. Unlike the commitment fee, many of these costs probably will not need to be paid until the closing.

In some cases, the lender may insist that the borrower sign a letter agreement before the parties negotiate the loan commitment, in which the borrower agrees to pay the lender's major costs—most notably its legal fees—in the event the parties cannot agree on the terms of the commitment. By insisting on this agreement, the lender knows that its costs will be covered even if the loan falls through before the commitment is signed.

## *Notes*

1.  *See supra* §§ 2.76–2.77.
2.  *See supra* § 3.65.
3.  *See supra* Chapter 2.
4.  *See supra* § 4.02.
5.  *See supra* Chapter 2; *infra* Appendix B.
6.  *See supra* §§ 3.51–3.52; *infra* § 5.11.
7.  42 U.S.C. §§ 9601–9675 (2000 & Supp. IV 2004).
8.  *See id.* § 9607(a).
9.  *See infra* §§ 4.18, 6.18. Note that the failure to pay insurance premiums commonly appears as a nonrecourse carveout.
10.  For a discussion of escrow requirements, see *infra* § 6.20.
11.  *See* SR Int'l Bus. Ins. Co. v. World Trade Center Props., LLC, 467 F.3d 107 (2d. Cir. 2006) (concluding that different insurers provided different coverage).
12.  Note that in many cases, the buyer will continue relationships that the seller has already established. *See generally supra* §§ 2.53, 2.55–2.57.
13.  Note, however, that the failure to pay real estate taxes typically is included as a nonrecourse carveout.
14.  *See supra* § 4.10.
15.  In either case, of course, the lender must be sure that it does not overlook the outstanding principal amount of any senior debt that is to remain in place after the closing.
16.  *See supra* §§ 2.95–2.96, 2.106, 3.64.
17.  *See supra* § 2.95.
18.  For a form of nonrecourse provision, see *infra* Appendix I, Section 8(d). *See generally* Gregory M. Stein, *The Scope of the Borrower's Liability in a Nonrecourse Real Estate Loan*, 55 WASH. & LEE L. REV. 1207 (1998) (discussing scope of general nonrecourse language in absence of more specific provision in documents). *See also* John C. Murray, *Carveouts to Nonrecourse Loans: They Mean What They Say!*, PRAC. REAL EST. LAW., May 2003, at 19; Joshua Stein, *Lender's Model State-of-the-Art Nonrecourse Clause (with Carveouts)*, PRAC. LAW., Oct. 1997, at 31, 40–54 (offering detailed form nonrecourse clause, along with shorter alternative form); Joshua Stein, *Nonrecourse Carveouts: How Far Is Far Enough?*, REAL EST. REV., Summer 1997, at 3, 6–9 (listing items for which lenders might demand carveouts from nonrecourse treatment and other items for which lenders ordinarily would not demand carveouts); John G. Wharton, *Negotiating Carveouts to Non-Recourse Loan Documents*, PRAC. REAL EST. LAW., Nov. 1997, at 47 (discussing issue and offering form language).

# CHAPTER 5

# Post-Loan Commitment
# Due Diligence

## §5.01 Due Diligence and the Loan Commitment

When the lender extends the loan, it makes available a significant amount of money in reliance on the skill and expertise of the borrower and the value of the mortgaged property. The lender assumes that the borrower will be a capable property manager that can develop and operate the property successfully and produce cash flow that is adequate to repay its debt. If the borrower is not sufficiently skilled (or lucky), and thus is unable to meet its obligations to the lender, the lender needs to be confident that the property can be sold for enough money to satisfy the debt. The lender knows from the outset that it needs to be comfortable with the ability and experience of the borrower; with the physical, legal, and financial attributes of the property; and with the quality of the legal documents and the remedies they contain. The loan commitment should have already addressed all these issues.

After the parties have executed the commitment, the lender will obtain additional information during the due diligence period. This information helps the lender decide whether all conditions precedent have been satisfied, thereby requiring the lender to provide the funds to the borrower at the closing. The due diligence responsibilities that the lender faces parallel, to a great extent, those that the buyer confronts between the date of the contract and the date of the closing. In each case, the party that is spending money or extending credit in exchange for an interest in property must learn all that it can about the property so that it does not face unpleasant surprises later. Once the buyer or the lender parts with its own funds, its options become far more limited. These parties can no longer threaten not to close and instead must rely on their remaining contractual remedies, which may not lead to complete satisfaction. Before the closing, the lender, like the buyer, must maximize its knowledge of the property and of the party with which it has contracted so that it can decide whether to proceed.

---

*Comment:* The lender's due diligence standards may exceed those of the buyer in many respects. Buyers are not as risk averse as lenders: a buyer may be willing to take certain risks when acquiring property that a lender will refuse to take when making a loan. Thus, the lender's level of caution in scrutinizing tenant leases, for example, may be greater than that of the borrower.

---

The review of the loan application and the negotiation of the loan commitment constitute the first steps in the lender's due diligence. The lender will usually require that the borrower complete a loan application and furnish the lender with extensive materials regarding the borrower and the property. Then the lender will include a wide variety of representations, warranties, covenants, indemnities, and closing conditions in the loan commitment. By executing a commitment that includes these provisions, the borrower discloses information about itself and the property. If this information turns out to be inaccurate, the commitment will place the lender in a position to pursue the remedies set forth in the commitment and to refuse to close.

A prudent lender will not rely solely on these disclosures from the borrower and will use the post-commitment period to undertake an independent due diligence review of the borrower and the property. During this period, the lender will confirm the information that the borrower has provided to it, will gather new information on its own, and will decide after evaluating this information whether to proceed to close the loan.

It already should be evident that the work the lender's counsel must undertake here is similar in some respects to the task the buyer's counsel must undertake when advising the buyer whether to proceed to acquire the property. Because of these similarities, this chapter highlights the distinctions between the due diligence burdens of the buyer and the lender and focuses on those aspects of due diligence work that are unique to the lender's position. Counsel to the lender should review the previous discussion of the buyer's due diligence responsibilities and should use that discussion as the basis for preparing the lender's due diligence checklist.[1] Lender's counsel should also review the loan commitment, along with the previous chapter discussing the loan commitment,[2] as a means of remembering whether there are unique issues in this transaction that merit investigation during the critical due diligence period.

Borrower's counsel should remember that the borrower must perform due diligence work of its own under the loan commitment. Although the borrower's due diligence burden under the loan agreement may be lighter than its burden under the contract of sale, borrower's counsel should review the earlier due diligence chapter, this due diligence chapter, and the loan documents as a means of determining the work it must perform under the loan commitment before the closing.

## §5.02 Loan Commitment Remedies for Problems Unearthed during Due Diligence

The lender's preclosing remedies fall into two categories. If the borrower breaches a representation, warranty, or covenant contained in the loan commitment, then the commitment will provide the lender with contractual remedies. If the borrower fails to meet a closing condition contained in the commitment, then the lender has the right to refrain from funding the loan without incurring any liability. The lender almost always will prefer this second option, which allows it to avoid extending a loan that has proved to be out of accord with the lender's original expectations. The reason for the termination will also determine whether the lender may retain the commitment fee,[3] which compensates the lender for the commitment that it made but no longer must keep; whether it may recover its costs associated with the loan, including its legal fees; and whether it may recover damages.

Recall that many of the same matters that the parties address in representations will also be covered in the closing conditions section of the loan commitment. This means that the lender may be able to make use of both sets of remedies, by terminating the loan commitment and seeking damages. It is evident that the lender's position during the due diligence period will be strongest if it previously negotiated for an expansive array of representations, warranties, covenants, and closing conditions. Receiving these concessions will not be enough, however, because these provisions are valuable only if the lender uses them appropriately, and the lender can use them to its best advantage only if it undertakes its due diligence obligations thoroughly. The lender also must remember that many of the representations will survive the loan closing only if they are also incorporated into the operative loan documents, as they usually are.

> *Comment:* In most circumstances, if the borrower breaches a representation, warranty, or covenant during the due diligence period, it also has failed to meet a closing condition. If the breach is material, the lender will typically refuse to fund the loan; retain the commitment fee; and require the repayment of its outside expenses, such as legal, engineering, and appraisal fees. If the borrower has defaulted intentionally, however, the lender may decide to pursue damages or other remedies as well. For example, if the borrower fails to close so that it can take advantage of a different loan commitment at a lower interest rate or on otherwise preferable terms, the lender may seek damages.

## §5.03 Title and Survey Matters

The lender will be concerned about title and survey matters for two related reasons. First, the lender wants to be absolutely satisfied that the borrower owns good, marketable, and unencumbered title to the property. If the borrower were to close and then discover that it had inadequate access to a public road and needed to acquire an expensive right-of-way, the borrower's financial position would suffer and the lender's might suffer as well. Second, the lender recognizes that it might someday have to operate, foreclose on, or even acquire the property and thus must review title and survey issues with the eyes of a potential future owner.

The lender's concerns about title and survey matters are not quite the same as the borrower's, however. In some ways, the lender's worries are not as acute as the borrower's, while in other ways, they may be even greater. For example, the borrower may be far more concerned than the lender is about minor title encumbrances. If there is a slight boundary dispute over land worth a small amount, the borrower might become incensed, while the lender realizes that it is substantially oversecured even if the borrower loses the dispute. Given that the lender may have provided a loan worth only 80 percent of the value of the property and given that the loan principal should drop over time even as the value of the property appreciates, the lender may not be as concerned about a minor detail of this type as the borrower is.

At the same time, the lender's concerns may extend well beyond those of the borrower. Lending institutions, as a group, tend to shy away from business risks more than entrepreneurial buyers do. In addition, the lender is concerned about its rights under the loan documents and not just its rights under the deed and other title documents. The borrower wants an acceptable survey, deed, and owner's policy of title insurance. The lender wants all of this but also wants valid and enforceable mortgage documents and title insurance on the mortgage. The borrower will care about these last matters only until the lender funds the loan at the closing; after that, the loan documents are the lender's concern.

> *Comment:* A lender will have one specific concern that differs from the concerns of the borrower. If, for any reason, the lender's lien does not cover all the property owned or controlled by the borrower, the lender may not be able to protect itself in the event of an improper act by the borrower or a tenant occurring on the portion of the property on which the lender has no lien. Activities on this unencumbered land may be addressed in another document, such as a reciprocal easement agreement, and the lender should consider making a default under that agreement a default under the mortgage as well.

The following sections look at title and survey matters that affect the lender and the buyer in significantly different ways. Once again, the lawyer should remember to refer to the earlier sections addressing title and survey matters in connection with the sale transaction.[4] Those sections are as relevant to the loan transaction as they are to the sale transaction, and the lawyer should be able to adapt that discussion to the loan with only some minor and obvious modifications. Once the lender's lawyer has undertaken this task, however, he must also remember to think about those issues that are specific to loan transactions and that are discussed in the sections that follow. Finally, the lawyer must remember to review the loan commitment and the other loan documents, in case they are atypical in some way.

### §5.04—The Title Commitment to Lender and the Form Title Insurance Policy

Like the buyer of the property, the lender is concerned that the buyer acquire good title subject to no encumbrances other than those agreed to in advance or at the closing. Unlike the buyer of the property, the lender is also concerned about receiving a valid and enforceable mortgage on the buyer's property. The lender's concerns about title thus extend beyond those of the buyer, and the lender will require a policy of title insurance that reflects those differences. For this reason, the American Land Title Association (ALTA) offers a different form title commitment and a different form title insurance policy for lenders.

Schedule A of the lender's commitment is similar to Schedule A of the owner's commitment. The lender should be listed as the party to be insured, and the interest to be insured will be that of a mortgagee rather than that of an owner. The amount of the insurance should be equal to the principal amount of the loan. Note that the insurer will not pay the lender an amount greater than its loss, which means that the value of the title insurance will shrink over the life of the loan as the principal is repaid. In this respect, the lender's insurance is less of a risk for the title company than the owner's insurance, which lasts indefinitely.[5] Note also that any recovery by the lender will reduce the amount that the owner may recover: if the owner suffers a total loss of title at a time when the mortgage is still outstanding, every dollar that the insurer pays to the lender is a dollar less that the borrower has to repay to its lender under the note.

The contents of Schedule B should not differ from one form to the other. Counsel to the lender nonetheless should be every bit as careful as the buyer's lawyer is about reviewing each exception, including all backup documentation.

ALTA promulgated a new loan policy form in 2006, which parallels the new form of lender's title commitment. Under the lender's policy, the title company insures the lender's mortgage on the property and not just the owner's title. The lender's lawyer should be sure to become familiar with this important form and to understand all its terms. As with the owner's policy, the insurer will not issue the lender's title insurance policy until the closing, but the lender's lawyer should address any title problems during the due diligence period so that issuance of the policy will not delay the closing. The lender's lawyer should be certain to verify that all matters that appear in the lender's policy track the corresponding sections of the lender's title commitment.

---

*Comment:* The form of lender's title insurance policy differs from the form of owner's title insurance policy. Moreover, a lender's policy insures only the lender and not the borrower. The borrower must be certain that it receive a separate owner's policy of title insurance.

---

### §5.05—*Mechanics' Liens*

The lender will be particularly concerned about the statutory right of mechanics—including contractors, subcontractors, and suppliers—to place liens on property for work for which they were not paid. If a construction project has already commenced before the mortgage is recorded, then a lien recorded after the mortgage will, in most states, relate back to a date before the recording date of the mortgage. Such a lien may be large enough to jeopardize the lender's security. The lender has no conclusive method of determining whether there are any unpaid mechanics or how large these mechanics' claims are. Like the buyer, the lender should be able to persuade the title insurer to remove the mechanics' lien exception from Schedule B of its title insurance policy on the basis of an affidavit and indemnity from the seller to the insurer.

Mechanics' liens are a particular concern in a construction loan, in which the lender may be disbursing funds in numerous installments over a period of months or years. The reasons for this are twofold. First, mechanics' liens are more likely to arise in connection with construction loans, because the proceeds of these loans are being used to improve the property. In contrast, in a loan to acquire improved property, there may have been little or no recent work at the property, and thus there are no unpaid mechanics to worry about. Second, depending on state law, the lender may discover that different installment payments under the construction loan enjoy different priorities for recording purposes.

A number of states distinguish between obligatory and optional advances. An "obligatory advance" is a loan installment that the lender must make if certain objectively defined criteria have been met. If the borrower has satisfied this list of conditions, the lender is required to fund the installment. An "optional advance" is one over which the lender has a greater amount of discretion. For example, if the contract allows the lender to refuse to advance funds if the lender is not satisfied that the project is progressing appropriately, state law may hold that the lender is not obligated to advance the funds and the installment thus is optional.

The problem for the lender is that these two types of advances may have different priorities under state recording law. In states in which this distinction matters, obligatory advances enjoy the priority of the mortgage recording date. The lender agreed as of that date that it would advance the funds, and the borrower's subsequent compliance with all the necessary conditions for each advance does not change the fact that the lender's commitment was made, for recording purposes, at the beginning of the loan. Conversely, each optional advance is treated as a separate loan, and each has its own priority date for recording purposes.

If all advances are obligatory, then the lender will know at the outset whether the loan has priority over all mechanics' liens. If the state's lien law holds that all mechanics' liens relate back to "visible commencement of construction," for example, and the mortgage is recorded before that time, then the entire loan is senior to all liens. If loan advances may be considered optional, however, then some advances may be junior to mechanics' liens that were filed during the course of construction. In this case, the lender must be sure that the title company searches title before each advance; confirms that no new liens have been recorded; receives an affidavit and indemnity from the borrower stating that no mechanic has the right to place a lien on the property; and updates the title policy to the date of the latest advance, with the exception for mechanics' liens omitted. This increases and extends the lender's due diligence burden, but state law may provide no better option.

## §5.06 Lease Review

The lender recognizes that the borrower's ability to operate the project successfully is largely a function of the cash flow from the property and the quality of the tenants' leases. As a result, the lender will want to review these leases with care to satisfy itself that the project will be successful. The lender is also well aware that someday it may have to sell the property to a third party that will decide how much to bid on the basis of the content of these leases, or that it may buy the property itself and become the landlord to the tenants under these leases. For these reasons, the lender will review all tenant leases during the due diligence period and will exercise its right to withdraw from the loan if the leases do not meet the standards set forth in the loan commitment.

Remember that every provision of an existing tenant's lease will probably be deemed senior to the lender's mortgage under state recording laws unless the lease contains subordination language. If the lease, or a memorandum of the lease, is recorded, then there is no dispute that the terms of the lease are senior. Even if the lease is not recorded, the presence of the tenant in the space probably affords constructive notice of the tenant's rights to the lender, and the lender will be deemed to be on notice of every provision of the unrecorded lease.

The lender's review of tenant leases should mirror the buyer's review of these documents, with the lender focusing on the same issues that the borrower examines. Therefore, the lender's lawyer should recall the earlier discussion of lease review and should undertake a similar assessment.[6] The lender's emphasis will often be on different provisions of these leases, however, and the sections that follow highlight leasing matters that are of particular concern to the lender.

> *Comment:* In reviewing the leases, the lender should be attentive to obligations it may have to undertake later if it becomes the owner of the property, such as paying for future renovations or improvements. The lender will have to pay these costs out of its own pocket.

### §5.07—Renewal, Expansion, and Termination Options

Tenant leases often provide the tenant with options to renew or extend the term of the lease, to expand the amount of space that the tenant is occupying, or to terminate the lease before the stated expiration date. Provisions of this nature can have an enormous impact on the value of the lease and, if the tenant is a large one, on the value of the entire project. Thus, lenders should be particularly attentive to provisions of these types that appear in any tenant leases. The lender wants the borrower's investment to succeed and also wants some assurance that the project will retain significant value if the lender must foreclose.

If an anchor tenant negotiated aggressively for the right to renew, the buyer and the lender may feel some confidence that the tenant eventually will do so, even though it is not obligated to renew. More important, if the rent for the renewal period turns out to be considerably lower than the then-going rate for comparable space, the tenant may be inclined to exercise its renewal right to take advantage of this bargain. The space will be occupied, but the tenant will be paying a submarket rental rate. A similar analysis applies to expansion space: even though the tenant is not required to expand, the fact that it bargained for this right suggests that it is entertaining the possibility with some seriousness. Once again, if the rent turns out to be low, the tenant will be more inclined to exercise its expansion right.

Termination rights represent the flip side of renewal options. If the tenant's lease contains a termination option, the tenant has the right to shorten the term of the lease, although it may have to pay some consideration to exercise this right. The higher the tenant's rent is in relation to prevailing rates and the lower the termination fee is, the more likely the tenant is to exercise its termination right. If the lender is banking on the income stream from a particular lease but the tenant has the right to terminate that lease, then the lender must adjust its analysis of the property.

Buyers, of course, are extremely concerned about the presence of these provisions, but the nature of the lender's concern differs somewhat from that of the buyer. The lender is most concerned with what might happen to the property if the borrower experiences financial difficulties. A distressed borrower may allow maintenance to lapse, and the project may develop a reputation for shoddy management. It is precisely at this time that the dissatisfied tenant will be most likely to exercise any lease provision that allows it to escape from the lease: an unhappy tenant is less likely to renew or expand and more likely to terminate. Just when the lender needs the tenant most, the tenant will be most inclined to make use of any escape hatches the lease provides. Even if the tenant does not immediately exercise a right to end the lease, every potential bidder will presume that the tenant remains uneasy and may exercise that right soon. Each bidder will reduce its bid accordingly.

This concern, like every other due diligence concern, should also serve to remind the lender's lawyer to include appropriate language in the loan commitment. The lender must have the ability to terminate the commitment if the major occupancy agreement that the borrower described as "a twenty-year lease" turns out to contain termination options every five years.

### §5.08—Purchase Options and Rights of First Refusal

Purchase options and rights of first refusal that cover the entire project are considerably more troublesome to the lender. If a purchase option is contained in a lease or other document that is senior to the mortgage, then the holder of that option enjoys rights that are prior to those of the mortgagee. A tenant that exercises its purchase option needs only to pay the stated purchase price to the lender. If the principal amount of the loan exceeds the option price, the lender may be left holding an unsecured note from the borrower for the excess. Lenders will obviously be extremely concerned about the content of any purchase option agreements, and a sufficiently one-sided purchase option might make the property unmortgageable.

Rights of first refusal also pose significant problems for the lender. A right of first refusal allows the holder of the right to match any offer to purchase that the owner receives from a third party. This could affect the borrower's ability to sell the property later and might also impair the ease with which the lender can foreclose. A clause of this type could also affect the lender should it ever become the owner of the property and later seek to sell it. If a lease or other document contains a purchase option or a right of first refusal, the lender's lawyer needs to review the relevant provisions carefully during the due diligence period and determine whether they violate a representation or permit the lender to terminate the loan commitment.

### §5.09—Landlord's Construction Obligations

The lender needs to review each lease and determine whether the landlord under that lease is responsible for undertaking construction within the space or reimbursing the tenant for all or some of its own construction costs. To begin with, the lender must learn the extent to which the borrower will be assuming large financial obligations originally incurred by the seller. If the seller has previously agreed to pay a significant amount of a tenant's costs and if the borrower will become responsible for those payments, the lease, and thus the property, are less valuable than they otherwise would have been.[7] There is a difference between a ten-year lease at $20 per square foot and a ten-year lease at $20 per square foot with a $500,000 tenant allowance from the landlord toward tenant construction, and the lender might not learn of this allowance until it reviews the lease.

The lender also needs to determine whether it might become responsible for those costs itself should it become the owner of the property before the borrower meets all of its financial obligations to the tenant. The only thing worse for the lender than foreclosing on the property at a loss is foreclosing at a loss and then having to pay the $300,000 balance of this tenant allowance to the tenant. As with all other lease provisions, the lender cannot learn of the extent to which it is at risk until it reviews the lease itself.

Other tenant concessions can raise similar concerns, although the magnitude of other concessions will usually be smaller. For example, the seller might have granted the tenant a free-rent period. If the lender ever becomes the owner of the property, it might find itself bearing all the costs of having a tenant in possession without receiving any rent in return during this free-rent period.

---

*Comment:* The parties customarily address the rights of the lender and the tenant with regard to future funding obligations in the subordination, nondisturbance, and attornment agreement (SNDA).[8]

---

## §5.10—Tenant Estoppels

Tenant estoppel letters or certificates provide a wealth of information to the buyer of the property,[9] and the lender can also garner a tremendous amount of useful knowledge from these tenant estoppels. The lender, like the borrower, will want the comfort of knowing that each tenant is occupying its space and paying its rent without any claims against its landlord. Some of the provisions of the typical estoppel letter will be of particular interest to the lender, and lender's counsel should review the estoppel letters in detail, focusing on these provisions in particular.[10]

Each letter should verify that the lease has not been amended or modified. To the extent that a letter says otherwise and the lender was not previously aware of this fact, the lender has just learned that it must examine some additional documents. The tenant's estoppel should state whether the landlord is in breach of its obligations under the lease, thereby alerting the lender to any claims that the seller may be facing and that the buyer may inherit. In addition, the tenant should confirm in the estoppel letter that it has not prepaid any rent other than the next month's rent. Large rent prepayments suggest that the landlord is trying to raise cash from its tenants, and if a tenant has prepaid any rent, it presumably expects the buyer and the lender to honor these prepayments. The letter should also disclose any obligation on the part of the landlord to provide or pay for tenant improvements.

The lender needs to be sure that the owner of the property may not amend the lease so that the owner receives a disproportionate amount of the benefit in advance. To illustrate, if the borrower (or, for that matter, the seller) knows that it is facing financial problems and may lose the property, it might offer the tenant two years of "free" rent if the tenant makes a lump sum payment now equal to ten months' rent. The borrower presumably will receive and dissipate the advance payment immediately, and a foreclosure sale purchaser will later acquire a building with a tenant that believes it does not owe any rent for the next two years. The costs and benefits of being a landlord will have become uncoupled, with the landlord front-loading the benefits to its own advantage.

Not all such schemes will work, of course, and the tenant may find itself liable to the new owner for the future rent even though it paid the lump sum to the borrower.[11] The lender always would prefer avoiding disputes to prevailing in litigation, however, and it can use the tenant estoppel letter, along with the lease itself, as a way of determining in advance whether any rights of this type exist under the lease or any side documents.

> *Comment:* Many loan commitments provide that the lender is not obligated to fund the loan unless it receives estoppel letters from specifically named tenants, a specified percentage of the tenants, or tenants representing a specified percentage of the floor area of the mortgaged property.

### §5.11—Subordination, Nondisturbance, and Attornment Agreements

The previous discussion of subordination, nondisturbance, and attornment agreements (SNDAs) emphasized how important these agreements are to tenants, owners, and lenders.[12] The lender's lawyer must use the due diligence period to obtain and review any SNDAs and determine their legal effect. SNDA provisions can appear in freestanding SNDAs, but they may also be found in the leases. Thus, the lender's lawyer must remember to check all leases that will remain in place to determine whether these documents contain relevant language.

Once the lawyer has reviewed any SNDA provisions, his next task is to figure out what the relative priorities of all leases and mortgages are. The initial answer is determined by reference to the state's recording laws, which should describe how a subsequent party can obtain priority over a party with a prior interest. Keep in mind that it may not be possible to ascertain all of the relevant priorities simply by reviewing the documents, because recording statutes often determine priorities on the basis of a party's knowledge as of the date when it takes an interest in the property. In other words, even a lawyer who searches title carefully might not be able to determine all recording priorities with complete accuracy.

After the lender's lawyer establishes these initial priorities, he next must determine the extent to which the leases and SNDAs rearrange these priorities. The lawyer also must note whether any provision gives the lender or any other party the right to rearrange these priorities in the future and the method this party must follow to do so.

Lenders are extraordinarily concerned with these priorities because of the impact they can have on future foreclosures. The loan commitment should contain representations from the borrower addressing lease priorities and should also contain a closing condition that allows the lender to withdraw if the priorities are not what the commitment says they must be. The lender also needs to keep track of any resequencing possibilities that may be available in the future so that it can use these options to maximum benefit before employing any other remedies under the mortgage.

> *Comment:* Frequently, a new lender will seek to enter into new SNDAs with the tenants. Leases typically are drafted so as to require each tenant to enter into a new SNDA upon request from the lender. Working out the form of the SNDA can be an arduous process.

## §5.12 Creditworthiness Matters

The lender must make sure that it receives all financial information that the borrower agreed to provide to the lender in the loan commitment. The lender needs to review items such as financial statements as a way of confirming that its preliminary decision to lend was a wise one. If these statements reveal that the borrower's financial house is not in order, the lender may want to exercise its right to withdraw from the loan commitment before the closing. While the lawyer himself probably will not be able to assess the creditworthiness of the borrower, he should be sure that the borrower provides all the required documentation to his client in a timely fashion.

## §5.13 Environmental Matters

Lender liability for hazardous wastes has become an important subspecialty within commercial real estate law. While this section can only begin to scratch the surface of this critically important issue, it should serve to remind lender's counsel to consider environmental matters during the due diligence phase. The buyer, too, will have concerns about environmental matters and will be reviewing these matters on its own.[13] In addition, the lender's lawyer already should have included appropriate environmental provisions in the loan commitment.[14]

The primary role for lender's counsel at this stage is to make sure that his client has received any environmental reports to which it is entitled and to work with the client in reviewing these reports. The lender may need to retain environmental experts of its own to determine the significance of these reports and to decide whether the lender should request some sort of action by the borrower or the seller before it will extend the loan. The lender does not want to fund the loan until these matters are addressed to its satisfaction, because once it provides the funds, exercise of its mortgage remedies may expose it to environmental liability of its own.

---

*Comment:* In most instances, a lender will not even consider making a loan on property that it considers to be environmentally risky or that might lead to potential environmental liability.

---

## §5.14 Insurance

The due diligence period provides the lender with the time it needs to review the insurance coverage that the borrower plans to provide and to confirm that this coverage will be satisfactory. The loan commitment should specify the types and amounts of coverage that the borrower is required to obtain,[15] and the lender now must verify that the coverage will actually meet these requirements. The lawyer's role here is to make sure that the lender receives and reviews the documents that are necessary to determine whether the insurance meets the conditions set forth in the loan commitment.

The lender's lawyer must confer with his client and verify that the insurance companies are acceptable, that the amount and scope of the coverage meet the loan commitment's requirements, that the policy forms are adequate, and that the insurance will be effective as of the closing date. The policies should also provide that the insurer will not cancel or terminate them without first notifying the lender and providing it with an opportunity to resolve the problems leading to the notice.

---

*Comment:* The lawyer must make clear to the lender that matters of insurance should be carefully reviewed by the lender itself or the lender's insurance agents and advisers. Most lawyers are not sufficiently knowledgeable about insurance issues to determine whether the borrower has addressed these matters adequately and completely.

---

*Comment:* In most instances, the buyer will want the seller to have its existing insurance coverage endorsed as soon as the contract is signed so that the buyer is protected during the due diligence period "as its interests may appear." Although the buyer and the lender probably would not be obligated to close following a casualty loss, this language should protect both parties in the event of an insured loss during the due diligence period.

---

## §5.15 Contracts and Licenses

The loan commitment should provide that the lender must be satisfied with all major contract and license agreements and that the owner's interests in all such agreements are assignable to the lender and any successor owner. The first portion of this provision allows the lender to review and approve all agreements of this type. If the borrower will be operating a franchise of a national hotel chain, for example, the lender should confirm that the terms of the franchise agreement are satisfactory. The lender wants to be sure that the borrower can operate successfully within the terms of the agreement and also needs to know whether any successor owner, such as a foreclosure sale purchaser, can operate effectively if it must step into the borrower's shoes.

The second portion of this provision confirms that the successor owner can continue to enjoy the benefits of the agreement without the need to renegotiate its terms or the risk of losing its benefits entirely. For example, if a foreclosure sale purchaser is forced to relinquish the rights to the hotel chain's well-known name, the property may drop in value, and the bidder that is aware of this fact will bid less at the sale.

> *Comment:* There also is a question as to whether the lender will make the loan if it cannot cancel the franchise agreement in the event of a foreclosure. Various well-known fast-food restaurant chains and hotel chains will not readily agree to such a cancellation right, even in the event of a foreclosure.

The lender's lawyer must review all major contracts and licenses during the due diligence period. He should satisfy himself that they are acceptable, that they meet the requirements of the loan commitment, and that they are assignable. If any consents are required for either the transfer to the buyer or a subsequent transfer to a foreclosure sale purchaser, the lender's lawyer should be sure that the borrower receives these consents before the closing. It is the borrower's responsibility to procure these consents, but the lender's counsel must confirm that they have been received and are acceptable to the lender.

The loan commitment should also provide the lender with the right to approve all permits that affect the property. These permits should be assignable to the lender and to successor owners.

> *Comment:* Frequently, all required consents can be obtained before the closing, and the contracts, licenses, and permits can be assigned at the closing unilaterally.

## §5.16 Prior Mortgages

During the due diligence stage of the transaction, counsel to the lender must review all prior mortgages that will remain of record after the closing. Chapter 4 noted how the loan commitment should address the issue of prior mortgages.[16] The lawyer for the lender must review each of these senior mortgages and all related loan documents and must determine whether the security that its own client is to receive will be acceptable in light of the terms of these prior documents. At a minimum, the junior lender's lawyer will want to confirm certain facts about the senior debt, such as the amount of principal outstanding, the interest rate, the term, and the fact that there are no defaults.

To the extent that the junior lender demands modifications of these senior mortgages, the junior lender's lawyer must ensure that the borrower's lawyer or the seller's lawyer approaches these prior lenders and requests these modifications. These modifications are likely to address such matters as a requirement that the senior lender provide notice to the junior lender of defaults on the senior mortgage, along with an opportunity to cure these defaults. If the senior lenders have not already included provisions to this effect in their documents and are unwilling to add them now, the junior lender is unlikely to accept the encumbered property as security and probably will withdraw from the transaction without funding the loan.

### §5.17—Caution: Prior Mortgages

In many instances, a lender simply will not enter into a loan transaction if there is a prior mortgage. To do so might place the lender, as the junior lienholder, in a position in which it has to pay off the first mortgage or make payments to keep the first mortgage current in order to avoid foreclosure of the senior loan.

Similarly, senior lenders may prohibit their borrowers from entering into junior mortgages. Even though the senior lender enjoys superior priority, it may worry that the junior lender will be able to impair the senior lender's ability to foreclose, perhaps by invoking the doctrines of equitable subordination or marshaling of assets.

### §5.18 Appraisal

The lender will order and review the appraisal during the due diligence period. The lender should satisfy itself that the appraiser has prepared the appraisal properly and that the amount of the appraisal is at least equal to the amount that the lender used when making its credit decision. If there are problems with the manner in which the appraisal was prepared, the lender can inform the appraiser that it needs to correct the appraisal. If the amount comes in lower than the parties anticipated, then the lender must decide whether applicable regulations permit it to extend the loan anyway and whether it wishes to do so. Should the lender decide that it cannot lend the full amount, it may offer to lend a reduced amount or it may inform the borrower that it wishes to terminate the commitment, and the commitment itself should clarify which of these courses the lender may follow. The borrower that learns that the appraisal has come in too low often will decide to approach the seller and seek a price reduction.[17]

## Notes

1. *See supra* Chapter 3.
2. *See supra* Chapter 4.
3. *See supra* § 4.19.
4. *See supra* §§ 2.41, 2.82–2.87, 3.06–3.30.
5. The lender's policy is assignable, which means that if the lender sells the loan, the transferee also acquires the transferor's rights under the policy of title insurance. However, the loan will eventually be paid off. The owner's insurance, in contrast, is not assignable to successor owners, who must purchase their own policies, but the insurer may still be liable after the insured party transfers the property. If the successor owner were to recover from the insured party under a deed warranty for a matter that was covered by the insured party's title insurance, the insurer would be responsible to the insured party.
6. *See supra* §§ 3.31–3.52.
7. *See supra* § 3.46.
8. *See supra* §§ 3.51–3.52; *infra* § 5.11.
9. *See supra* §§ 2.90–2.92, 3.49–3.50.
10. A form of tenant estoppel certificate appears at *infra* Appendix C.
11. *See* 11 U.S.C. § 548 (2000) (allowing bankruptcy trustee to set aside certain constructively fraudulent transfers); Prudential Ins. Co. of America v. Allied Tower, Ltd., 874 P.2d 36, 40–41 (Okla. 1993) (rejecting improper lease amendment between distressed borrower and its tenant); RESTATEMENT (THIRD) OF PROPERTY: MORTGAGES § 4.4 (1997) (allowing receiver to disaffirm this type of "sweetheart" agreement if it contravenes provisions of senior mortgage or if mortgage was in default when agreement was made and agreement is not commercially reasonable).
12. *See supra* §§ 3.51–3.52.
13. *See supra* §§ 2.52, 3.58–3.59.
14. *See supra* § 4.09.
15. *See supra* § 4.10.
16. *See supra* § 4.13.
17. *See supra* § 4.14.

# CHAPTER 6

# Loan Documents

## §6.01 Document Preparation

In addition to the due diligence responsibilities discussed in chapter 5, the parties also have to agree on the language of the operative loan documents. Recall that the loan commitment itself is nothing more than an executory contract in which the lender agrees to lend the funds on specified terms. The lender does not actually fund the loan until the closing and will not do so unless the borrower executes and delivers acceptable loan documents. The parties must negotiate these loan documents after they sign the loan commitment so that the documents will be ready for execution when the closing date arrives.

If the parties are unusually concerned about the terms of these documents, they may accelerate this schedule and attempt to agree on the exact wording of the documents, or certain key provisions of the documents, before they even execute the loan commitment. If they are able to do so, they can then attach the agreed documents to the commitment, undated and unsigned, and reference them in the body of the commitment itself. Instead of saying that "the borrower will execute a note that is reasonably acceptable to the lender," the commitment will state that "the borrower will execute a note that is substantially identical to the form note attached to this loan commitment as Exhibit A." This procedure also means that the parties' closing preparation will be relatively easy: they simply prepare copies of these agreed documents and sign and date them at the closing.[1]

The advantage to executing a loan commitment of this type is that the parties eliminate the possibility that they will be unable to agree on the critical terms of the loan documents after they sign the commitment. The primary disadvantage is that the parties may negotiate a long list of documents before they execute the commitment itself and before each is fully confident that the other is firmly committed to the loan. In other words, the parties might negotiate a lengthy list of documents only to have the deal come apart. For this reason, the parties are more likely to sign a loan commitment that does not establish the precise language of the operative loan documents, deferring those negotiations until later.

> *Comment:* Even if the loan documents are not attached to the loan commitment, key provisions often will be spelled out or summarized in the commitment or in exhibits to the commitment.

That "later" arrives after the parties execute the commitment, when, in addition to all their other responsibilities, they must also agree on the language of the documents they will sign at the closing. In most cases, the lender will prepare these documents and will use its standard forms. These forms, not surprisingly, tend to be pro-lender documents, and the borrower will spend much of its time trying to persuade the lender to make changes to accommodate the borrower's chief concerns. The borrower should not expect the lender to agree to all changes that the borrower wants and may have little negotiating leverage. At the same time, to the extent that the lender has already made concessions in the loan commitment, the borrower must be sure that the loan documents reflect those concessions.

> *Comment:* Although the loan commitment will not usually specify all the terms of the loan and the precise language of the loan documents, the doctrine of good faith and fair dealing applies to the negotiation of the loan documents in some jurisdictions. Therefore, it is incumbent upon each of the parties to include those provisions that are most essential to it—particularly if these provisions are unusual—in order to avoid a claim that its failure to close on the loan was a violation of this doctrine. There are a number of cases that deal with this issue, including the well-known case of *Teachers Insurance & Annuity Association v. Butler.*[2]

The remainder of this chapter examines the most important loan documents and the terms they ordinarily contain. This chapter assumes that the lender prepares the initial drafts and that the borrower then must negotiate these documents from a position of relative weakness.

## §6.02 Note

The note is the document that evidences the debt. It is the borrower's IOU to the lender. Many nonexperts in real estate law believe that the mortgage or deed of trust document,[3] in which the borrower grants a security interest in the property to the lender, is the central element of a real estate loan transaction. This belief is incorrect. In most jurisdictions, a note without a mortgage creates a valid—if unsecured—debt, while a mortgage without a note is meaningless.[4]

---

*Comment:* In states such as Maryland, a mortgage (but not a deed of trust) serves as evidence of the debt. In these states, a note may be unnecessary, and if the mortgage is inconsistent with the note, the terms of the mortgage will usually govern.

---

The note must state the name of the borrower, the principal amount that the borrower has borrowed, the maturity date by which the note must be paid in full, and the frequency of payment. If the loan is to be repaid at a fixed interest rate, the note should set forth that rate. If the loan is to be repaid at an adjustable interest rate, the note should state the manner in which the rate will be calculated, the frequency with which it will be adjusted, and any caps on these changes.

The note also should state what events will constitute defaults and should describe the remedies for these defaults. For example, the note might provide that if a payment is not received within five business days of its due date, the borrower is in default and the interest rate shall increase to a stated default interest rate. Lenders frequently have the right to assess late fees, and the note also is likely to require the borrower to pay any legal fees that the lender incurs in enforcing its rights under the note.

---

*Comment:* Another provision that is important to include in the note (and in the loan commitment) is the provision addressing the conditions on which prepayment will be permitted. The absence of this very provision was the subject of the *Teachers Insurance & Annuity Association v. Butler* case just noted.

---

The lender will often want the note to be negotiable. If so, the lender must be sure that the note complies with the negotiability requirements set forth in Article 3 of the Uniform Commercial Code (UCC). A negotiable note is easier for the lender to transfer to another lender on the secondary mortgage market, and any lender that may wish to transfer the loan later on should decide at the outset whether the note needs to be negotiable.

If the loan is a nonrecourse loan or a loan with partial recourse, the note must contain a provision that establishes the extent to which the lender may hold the borrower personally liable. Nonrecourse provisions can become extremely complex. They are addressed later, in the context of the mortgage.[5]

The note may contain a wide array of other provisions reflecting the specific transaction that the parties have agreed to. The lawyers should be sure that the note provisions accurately reflect the terms of the deal. Keep in mind that the presence of these more deal-specific terms may affect the negotiability of the note.

### § 6.03—Form: Promissory Note

See Appendix J for a Form of Promissory Note.

## § 6.04 Mortgage

The real estate lender will not be content to receive only a note. The lender needs more than just the borrower's promise to repay the loan; it also needs security that the borrower will keep that promise. The lender already has investigated the borrower's credit and, in many cases, has confirmed that the only asset of any significant value that the borrower owns is the real estate itself. In fact, that is one of the reasons many borrowers need to borrow funds in the first place. The lender is willing to extend the loan only because it knows that the funds will be used to purchase or refinance an asset with a value that exceeds the amount of the loan and that the lender will have access to that asset if the borrower fails to repay its debt. If the borrower defaults, the lender needs to be confident that it will be entitled to be repaid from the property itself before any other creditor is paid. The mortgage gives the lender that assurance.

A mortgage is a security interest in real estate. The borrower mortgages the property to the lender as security for repayment of the debt and thereby creates certain property rights in the lender. The borrower may receive the loan, but it grants an interest in the real estate and thus is the transferor in the mortgage transaction. This means that the borrower is the "mortgagor" and the lender is the "mortgagee," terms that laypersons frequently confuse with one another.

In addition to receiving the mortgage, the lender must also record it and thereby notify the world that it holds a security interest in the borrower's property. Mortgage priorities are governed by state recording laws, and the lender assures its place in line by recording the document promptly.[6] Borrowers may grant other interests in the real estate, including other mortgages, and the proceeds of any foreclosure sale will be distributed in accordance with the creditors' priorities under state law.

---

*Comment:* As will be discussed later in this chapter, the lender's security interest in personal property and fixtures should be perfected in accordance with Article 9 of the Uniform Commercial Code.

---

Mortgage law is highly state-specific, and it is critical that the real estate lawyer become knowledgeable about the mortgage law of the state in which he practices. Contract law and negotiable instrument law may not differ much from location to location, but mortgage law does. The mortgage must comply with, and will be enforced according to, the laws of the state in which the property is located.[7] This point will become acutely important if the borrower defaults on its note obligations, because methods of enforcing mortgages vary dramatically from state to state. If the lawyer is not familiar with the laws of the state in which the mortgaged property is located, or is not licensed to practice there, the lawyer must consult with a competent local lawyer.

---

*Comment:* Although they are similar to mortgages, deeds of trust differ from mortgages in some significant ways. For example, a deed of trust will contains provisions addressing such issues as the appointment of a substitute trustee and the mechanics of a power-of-sale foreclosure that involves a trustee.[8]

---

The following sections discuss the more important provisions contained in a typical mortgage. These sections examine the manner in which these provisions ordinarily address recurring mortgage issues. Given the profound differences in the states' mortgage laws, the lawyer must remember that these discussions are necessarily general.

### §6.05—Similarities to and Differences from the Loan Commitment

The loan commitment is an executory agreement in which the lender promises to lend funds to the borrower if the borrower meets certain conditions. The borrower agrees, among other things, that it will provide the lender with a note evidencing its debt and a mortgage and other security documents that secure its obligation to repay this debt. The loan commitment, then, is an agreement under which each party must perform in the future.[9] Nothing in the commitment gives the lender any legal interest in the borrower's real estate.

The mortgage, in contrast, is an operative real estate document. By executing and delivering the mortgage, the borrower grants the lender a legal interest in the real estate. The lender now holds a security interest in the property. In title theory states, the lender nominally holds title to the property, while in lien theory and intermediate theory states, the lender receives only a lien on the property. Note, however, that the differences among these three types of states have begun to blur, and it is probably accurate to say that in every state the lender obtains an interest in the borrower's real estate that allows it to exercise certain remedies, including the right to foreclose, upon the occurrence and persistence of certain events of default. The mortgage, like the deed and some of the other security documents, but unlike the contract of sale and the loan commitment, is a document of conveyance.

### §6.06—Form: Mortgage

See Appendix K for a Form of Mortgage.

### §6.07—Granting Clause

The granting clause appears at the beginning of the mortgage. This is the clause that effects the mortgagor's transfer of an interest in the real estate to the mortgagee. The granting clause reads much like the corresponding clause in a deed, and in many ways the mortgage will sound like a deed. In title theory states, this similarity is more than coincidental, and the courts still purport to follow the common law principle that the borrower actually has deeded the property to the lender as security for the debt, with a condition that the lender will reconvey it to the borrower upon payment of that debt. While no modern court would actually enforce a mortgage in this way, this does explain why the granting clause of a mortgage appears to grant title, and not just a security interest in the property, to the lender.

The mortgage may sound like a deed, but it is not. Somewhere in the mortgage, whether in the granting clause itself or in a subsequent provision of the document, will be language stating that the grant lasts only until the borrower repays the debt or that the lender will reconvey the property to the borrower upon repayment of the debt. The lender's mortgage interest is a temporary interest that persists only until the debt and all other loan obligations have been satisfied. In contrast, the borrower's fee simple interest endures perpetually.

---

*Comment:* Sellers in some jurisdictions are unwilling to provide general warranty deeds to their buyers, because these deeds warrant against title exceptions that predate the seller's period of ownership. Many lenders, however, will require a general warranty in the mortgage, thereby making the borrower responsible to the lender for title exceptions that the borrower did not create during its period of ownership. Although this may seem inconsistent or unfair, the lender may insist on receiving greater protection than the buyer.

---

---

*Comment:* It is incumbent upon the lender and its counsel to be certain that all of the property to be secured by the mortgage is included in the legal description of the mortgage. This description should include easements, appurtenances, rights to public ways, and any other rights the lender or a foreclosure sale purchaser will need in order to own and operate the entire property.

---

### § 6.08—Due-on-Transfer

The lender has many concerns when it extends a mortgage loan. One of its worries is that the borrower may transfer the property to a successor owner that lacks the skills and abilities of the borrower.

Another concern is that interest rates will increase and that the lender will be stuck with a long-term loan at a rate that has turned out to be well below the market rate. This second fear is obviously more of a concern with a fixed-rate loan, and lenders frequently respond by lending money at an adjustable rate that is tied to an acceptable index, with frequent adjustments.

Another way for the lender to address these two problems is for the parties to agree that the loan becomes due in the event that the borrower conveys the property to another owner. The parties accomplish this result by including language in the mortgage stating that the entire principal amount of the note will come due immediately upon a transfer of the property. This provision is commonly known as a "due-on-transfer" clause.

If the borrower decides to convey the property and the transferee would like to leave the existing financing in place, they will have to request permission from the lender, and the lender will be under no obligation to consent. The lender will have the opportunity to assess the expertise and creditworthiness of the proposed transferee and will also have the chance to increase the interest rate to the market rate if the prevailing rate is higher than the rate set forth in the note. Stated more bluntly, a due-on-transfer clause allows the lender to terminate the loan upon conveyance of the property if it finds the new owner unacceptable and allows the lender to increase the interest rate (or terminate the loan and re-lend the funds at a higher rate) if the stated rate seems too low at the time of the transfer. The lender in this position has a great deal of flexibility but should be aware of the extent to which state law imposes a duty of good faith and fair dealing.

The borrower may object to a due-on-transfer clause. It will contend that the lender has already committed to lending the funds at the stated rate for the term of the loan and should not be permitted to earn extra profit solely because the borrower has decided to convey the project. Moreover, the borrower will argue that the lender's primary—and sometimes its only—source of repayment is the mortgage on the property, so the lender will not suffer any economic loss as a result of a transfer as long as the property continues to be worth more than the amount of the debt. The parties ought to have resolved this issue during the negotiation of the loan commitment, and the mortgage should reflect that resolution.[10]

Borrowers and lenders sometimes refer to this type of clause as a "due-on-sale" clause, but that term is too narrow. A properly drafted clause of this type will apply to more than just an outright sale of the property. The lender may want the restriction to apply to long-term leases of all or substantially all of the property, to junior financing of any significant size, to other material junior interests, and to transfers of interests in the entity that owns the property. If the borrower makes a transfer of any of these types, the lender will want the ability to accelerate the due date of the debt. The borrower, in turn, will want to clarify the types of transfers that do not trigger an acceleration. These may include space leases of significant size and junior financing of certain types. The borrower will also want to make it clear that certain other changes in ownership are exempted. If the borrower entity conveys the property to a related entity or merges with another entity, the borrower will want the loan to remain in place, because the transfer is merely a change in form. If an individual owner transfers property to a family member or if she dies and the property passes through her estate, the borrower will not want her successor to have to refinance.

If the lender is willing to agree that some transfers will not trigger the due-on-transfer clause, it may want to demand in exchange that the transferee assume the loan. This will allow the lender to seek a deficiency judgment from the transferee in the event that a foreclosure sale does not produce funds equal to the amount of the debt and will also give the lender some assurance that the transferee will devote its attention to the project. This demand will be difficult for the lender to justify, however, if the original loan was nonrecourse.

### § 6.09—Prepayment

The issue of prepayment is the mirror image of the due-on-transfer concern just discussed. The lender may require the inclusion of a due-on-transfer clause as a way to get out of a low-rate loan. The borrower may seek the right to prepay the loan whenever it chooses as a way to get out of a high-rate loan. If the borrower borrows the funds at the stated rate and the prevailing rate then drops, it will want to be able to refinance at a lower rate and use the proceeds of the refinancing to pay off the original loan. Once again, this issue is less significant if the interest rate on the loan is adjustable. Borrowers also need to know that they have the right to prepay the loan if they seek to sell the property before the loan is fully repaid.

The lender will worry that it is entering into a one-sided transaction in which it must suffer if rates increase but the borrower may exit if rates decrease. In response to this concern, the lender may charge the borrower a fee to prepay the loan. This fee is sometimes referred to as a "prepayment penalty," but the lender would be wiser to refer to it as a "prepayment fee" or "prepayment charge." Some courts might refuse to enforce a "penalty" under contract principles when, in fact, the lender seeks only to charge the borrower for the right to have an additional, early, payment option.

Parties sometimes agree to fairly complex prepayment fees. They might agree that the loan cannot be prepaid at all for the first year[11] and that the prepayment fee shall be equal to 5 percent of the outstanding principal during the second year, 3 percent during the third year, 1 percent during the fourth year, and zero thereafter. A structure of this type is a rough attempt by the parties to compensate the lender for its actual losses if the borrower pays off the loan more quickly than the lender had anticipated.

Partial prepayments may or may not merit different treatment. The borrower that prepays part of the loan may be trying to get out of a high rate incrementally, or it may simply be using unexpected cash now to reduce its carrying costs later. If the lender insists on charging for prepayments and the borrower thinks that it might want to prepay a small portion of the loan later on, the parties might be able to agree on some maximum amount of prepayment that is permitted without charge.

---

*Comment:* The lender should not be entitled to charge a prepayment fee if it uses the proceeds of a casualty insurance policy or a condemnation award to reduce the outstanding principal of the debt. Lenders also will generally agree to waive all prohibitions on prepayment during the last ninety days of the term so that the borrower will have some flexibility in refinancing.

---

### § 6.10—Technique: Yield Maintenance and Defeasance

A form of prepayment fee that is common in large commercial loans is known as a "yield maintenance fee." Under this type of charge, the borrower that wishes to prepay the loan also must pay the lender an amount that, when invested along with the principal in some agreed conservative investment, will yield to the lender a total return equal to the return that the lender would have received had the borrower not prepaid the loan. Because a yield maintenance fee approximates the lender's actual loss more closely than a flat fee does, the use of a yield maintenance fee reduces the risk that a court might treat the prepayment fee as an unenforceable penalty. When drafting yield maintenance clauses, the lawyers must be aware of state law limits on the enforceability of provisions of this type.

An alternative to the prepayment of a loan is the "defeasance" of a loan. In a defeasance, the loan remains in place, but high-grade, income-producing securities serve as substitute collateral. The securities must generate a continuous income stream equal to the remaining debt service payments over the life of the loan. Additionally, a new single-purpose borrower is created whose sole asset is the newly purchased securities, and the new borrower assumes the existing borrower's obligations under the loan. The intent behind a defeasance is to give the lender the same return on its investment regardless of the form of collateral.

The benefits of this approach to the borrower are that it is released from its ongoing payment obligation and its real property is released as collateral securing the loan. The drawback to the borrower is the potential cost. The costs associated with purchasing securities that produce a sufficient level of income may be prohibitively high. Although the concept of defeasance is easy to understand, the process has many technical requirements that will require the use of additional specialists, such as lawyers, accountants, rating agencies, and possibly defeasance consultants. The use of these specialists will add to the existing borrower's defeasance costs.

In certain instances, a loan may not be open to prepayment or the prepayment fee may be extremely large. In those cases, the ability to defease the loan, as opposed to prepaying the loan, may serve as a viable alternative that provides additional flexibility to the parties.

### § 6.11—Limitations on Junior Financing

At first glance, there might seem to be little reason for the lender to care whether the borrower later borrows additional funds from another lender and gives that junior lender a second mortgage on the property. The original lender's first mortgage will retain its priority from the moment it is recorded, and the subsequent lender will always be junior to it. If the original lender forecloses, it will receive its last penny before the second lender receives anything. Nonetheless, the lender may have good reasons for wanting to prohibit or place limits on junior financing. Once again, the parties should have addressed this issue when they negotiated the loan commitment, and the mortgage needs to reflect that agreement.[12]

Junior lenders will typically refuse to lend unless all senior lenders agree to provide them with notice of any defaults on the senior debt and a reasonable opportunity to cure those defaults.[13] The junior lender will fear that a default on the senior debt will lead to a potentially devastating foreclosure of its subordinate interest and may be willing to cure the default rather than risk losing its own security.

The borrower, which should be aware of this common demand from junior lenders, may ask the senior lender to agree in the first mortgage that it will provide these accommodations. If the senior lender agrees to provisions of this type, however, this language may impede or delay its ability to enforce its own mortgage later on. The longer the first lender is forced to wait before it can exercise its remedies, the more the property may depreciate, and the smaller the chance that the first lender will be made whole. If the senior lender does not agree to include these protections for junior lenders, the whole issue of junior financing may be moot, because the borrower may be unable to find junior lenders that are willing to lend without these protections.

The senior lender will have other concerns. Junior mortgages are likely to contain the same remedies as the first mortgage, and a junior lender's exercise of those remedies may work to the detriment of the senior lender. If the junior lender activates its assignment of leases and rents before the senior lender does, the borrower's ability to meet its obligations to the senior lender could be further impaired. If the junior lender seeks the appointment of a receiver before the senior lender does, that receiver may be appointed without any obligation to look after the first lender's interests.

Most worrisome of all to the senior lender is the fact that it has little or no control over the junior lender's timing of any foreclosure sale. One of the chief benefits of being the only lender is having the luxury of choosing which remedies to use and when. Once the borrower grants a junior mortgage to another lender, that benefit is reduced significantly. The junior lender, which is in a shakier position to begin with by virtue of its junior status, may have less patience with any defaults and may choose to foreclose at a time the senior lender views as inopportune. After this sale, the first lender may suffer as the project and its tenants cope with the discontinuity of ownership and management. If the first lender is the only lender, it avoids this problem and has complete control over the timing of any foreclosure sale. The senior lender may even insist that junior lenders be prohibited from foreclosing for as long as the senior mortgage remains in place, effectively eliminating the possibility of junior financing.

The first lender may have other concerns about the borrower that later seeks junior financing. The lender may believe, perhaps with some justification, that the owner that is forced to seek a second loan is in the early stages of distress. According to the borrower's initial application, the project should have been successful with just the first loan. Now, though, the borrower is seeking additional funds, most likely at a higher interest rate, so something must be wrong. The first lender may want to have the exclusive right to work with the borrower or to pull the plug before things get any worse. The senior lender also may have concerns that the borrower is using junior financing as a way of pulling some of its equity out of the project.

The borrower may respond to many of these arguments by observing that no one can predict the future and that the borrower may need additional funds for a variety of reasons that the lender would find acceptable. The borrower may wish to upgrade the property, may want to accommodate a tenant that needs expensive renovations, or may need to pay a large brokerage fee as the up-front cost of attracting a desirable long-term tenant. The lender may have no objection to these reasons but may have greater concerns about many of the other reasons why borrowers seek junior financing. The parties may be able to compromise by agreeing to allow junior financing only in certain limited amounts for purposes that are specifically listed in the first mortgage. The senior lender also may ask that the borrower seek additional financing from it first, before turning to other lenders, or may state that it will have the right to match the terms that any third-party lender is willing to offer.

---

*Comment:* Some lenders simply will not permit junior financing under any circumstances. Their concerns are many, but one of their principal worries arises under the doctrine of "marshaling of assets." Under this doctrine, a court, whether in bankruptcy or otherwise, may force the senior lender to pursue other assets of the borrower if the court believes that the senior lienholder can be satisfied out of these other assets, thereby preserving the mortgaged real estate for the junior lienholder.

---

---

*Comment:* One common circumstance in which a junior lien might arise is the case in which the seller finances a portion of the purchase price and takes back a second mortgage. This scenario might occur, for example, if the appraisal comes in low and the borrower is forced to borrow some of the acquisition funds from the seller. This type of junior financing may be easier to address because both mortgages are created at the same time. The third-party lender should be careful in this setting, however, because seller financing sometimes enjoys senior priority under state law unless the seller expressly subordinates its own mortgage to that of the third-party lender.

---

## §6.12—Cross-Default

If the lender agrees that some types of junior financing are acceptable, or if the lender's mortgage itself is a junior loan, the lender may worry that the borrower will default on its obligation to another lender while remaining current on all its obligations to the lender in question. At first, this might not strike the lawyer as a problem. If the borrower somehow can continue to make its payments to the lender even as it defaults on its other obligations, why should the lender be anything less than thrilled? There are at least two reasons. First, the fact that the lender cannot meet its other obligations suggests that a cascade of financial problems is about to begin. Second, the lender does not want to see the borrower's other creditors begin to exercise their most useful remedies at a time when the lender's own right to do so has not yet been triggered. The lender may find that by the time it actually can make use of the valuable remedies that it insisted on including in the mortgage—which is to say, after the borrower defaults on the lender's loan—those remedies will have lost much of their value.

For these reasons, the lender should insist that the mortgage contain a cross-default provision. Under a provision of this type, a default by the borrower on any of its loans from other lenders also constitutes a default under the lender's loan. This provision allows the lender to exercise its mortgage remedies as soon as the borrower gets into trouble with any of its other lenders. The lender could even expand this provision to include other major obligations in addition to mortgage loans so that a default on those other obligations constitutes a simultaneous default on the lender's loan. Whether or not the lender takes this last step, the parties must clarify whether the cross-default provision applies only to the borrower's other debt with respect to this real estate or also to the borrower's other debt with respect to the borrower's other assets.

One problem the lender will face is that it may not know if the borrower is in default on another obligation, and there is no incentive for the borrower to disclose this fact to the lender. The lender may decide to ask these other lenders to provide it with notice of any defaults. It should be obvious that the lender's ability to wrest this concession from other lenders will be greater if those lenders are junior. Senior lenders have the power simply to refuse, and they may do just that.[14]

---

*Comment:* If a lender extends a single large loan that is secured by mortgages on multiple parcels owned by the borrower, the lender may require a cross-default in each of the mortgages. The lender needs to know that if the borrower defaults with respect to one property, the lender will have the right to pursue remedies under all the mortgages. In these circumstances, it is important that the legal descriptions of all the properties that are cross-defaulted (or references to the cross-defaulted loans) be included in each of the mortgages.

---

### §6.13—Maintaining the Property

The lender wants the borrower to maintain the property adequately. The mortgaged property is the lender's primary security, and the lender needs to know that if the borrower defaults on its obligation to repay the debt, the property will be worth more than the amount of the debt that is then outstanding. If the borrower intentionally harms the property, or even if the borrower merely allows the property to deteriorate, the lender may discover that it is undersecured. The depreciated property might sell for less than the amount of the debt, leaving the lender with an unsecured claim for the shortfall. This concern is particularly acute for the nonrecourse lender, which has agreed not to seek a deficiency judgment from the borrower.[15] Similar problems arise in states with antideficiency legislation.

Real estate that is subject to a mortgage presents a classic case in which waste can arise. Waste may occur whenever two or more parties have an interest in the same real estate. Here, the borrower may determine that it is in its own best interests to allow the property to deteriorate, even though the parties collectively will suffer, because most or all of the damage falls on a party other than itself.

The lender addresses the problem of waste in the mortgage by requiring that the borrower maintain the property. A simple statement to this effect is insufficient, however, and the document should explain exactly what the term "maintain" means. This clause should distinguish between regular maintenance and capital expenses and should clarify exactly what the borrower's responsibilities are with respect to each type of upkeep. This clause should also address both active and permissive waste. The former type of waste should only rarely be permitted, as there are few acceptable reasons for the borrower to damage the property intentionally.

Permissive waste is a trickier problem, because the borrower may choose to let maintenance slip if it is in distress and is trying to get through a dry spell. The prudent lender will include specific maintenance standards, just as a major tenant will. The lender may also want the borrower to establish a reserve fund or an escrow to ensure that funds are available later for repairs and capital improvements.

The parties should be clear as to whether the obligation to maintain the property refers only to physical matters or also to financial ones. The borrower's failure to pay real estate taxes, insurance, or ground rent can harm the lender's security just as much as its failure to repair a leaking roof. The careful lender should be sure that the borrower's maintenance responsibilities are defined to include financial matters as well as physical ones.

---

*Comment:* As will be discussed later, waste generally is a carveout from any clause exculpating the borrower in a nonrecourse loan. The same is true for the borrower's failure to pay real estate taxes, insurance premiums, and ground rent.[16] One type of waste that may be permitted but that should be carefully controlled is the right of a borrower to raze the improvements on the property and restore the property with new improvements. Generally, the documents include provisions ensuring that a party that wishes to raze and restore the improvements has adequate financial resources to do so.

---

## §6.14—Events of Default

The lender must be sure to specify exactly what its remedies are if the borrower fails to meet any of its obligations under the note and mortgage. In achieving this objective, the lender must answer two questions. First, it must state when the borrower's failure to satisfy an obligation—a default with a lower-case "d"—rises to the level of an "Event of Default," thereby allowing the lender to use its arsenal of remedies. Second, it must specify what those remedies are.[17]

The borrower is likely to point out that many defaults are minor or readily curable and that it might not even be aware of some defaults. It will ask the lender to provide it with notice of default and a reasonable opportunity to cure. The lender's response to this request is likely to be highly nuanced, with its willingness to agree dependent on the type of default the borrower is referring to.

Some defaults truly are minor, and the lender may be willing to agree that only material defaults place the lender in a position in which it can use its stronger remedies. A prolonged failure to repair a cracked window technically constitutes waste, but the borrower will argue, with some justification, that it is not a significant enough example of waste that the lender should be permitted to foreclose. The parties are likely to agree that only material or continuing defaults rise to the level of an Event of Default.

As for the borrower's request for notice of default and a cure period, the lender may respond that different types of default merit different answers. Intentional and incurable defaults should instantly rise to the level of an Event of Default, because the borrower knew that it was violating the document and now cannot remedy that breach. For example, notice and a cure period are unwarranted if the borrower transfers the property in violation of a due-on-transfer clause.

The borrower's case is stronger for other types of default. If the borrower is late with a monthly payment, the cause may be administrative carelessness, and the appropriate remedy may be the imposition of a late fee. This is a minor breach, the borrower will argue, and should become an Event of Default only if it persists for a stated period after the lender notifies the borrower. The lender may agree, and the default clause may state that it is an Event of Default if the borrower fails to make a required monthly payment within five business days after receiving written notice from the lender that it is overdue. If the lender is worried that the borrower will regularly make use of this built-in extension, the lender can still impose the late fee as of the original due date and can also state that it will agree to provide this notice and cure period only three times during the life of the loan.

---

*Comment:* Some lenders today will not provide notice of monetary defaults, arguing that the borrower already knows when payments are due.

---

> *Comment:* Courts are often reluctant to enforce remedies for nonmonetary defaults, except in cases where waste has been committed.

The reasonable lender will probably agree to provide cure periods of different duration for different types of default. The result may turn out to be a lengthy Events of Default clause, with various defaults grouped together on the basis of their seriousness. Once a material default remains uncured after notice and the applicable cure period, the lender next must turn to the remedies section of the mortgage and decide how to respond to this Event of Default.

> *Comment:* After a default, it is essential that the lender follow the notice provisions of the default clause carefully and give proper notice to each party entitled to it.

> *Comment:* As will be discussed later, it is important that the default clause or the remedies clause provide a right of acceleration.[18]

## § 6.15—Caution: Lender Advances to Cure Defaults

Unless the mortgage specifically provides, advances by the lender to remedy certain defaults by the borrower, such as the failure to pay a mechanics' lien or real estate taxes, may not automatically be added to the mortgage debt. Even if they are, they may not enjoy the same mortgage priority as the principal unless the mortgage specifically secures these future advances. The mortgage must be carefully drafted to protect the lender, clarifying that the lender may advance these funds, that the advances will be added to the principal, and that the advances will be given the same priority as the principal.

## § 6.16—Pre-Foreclosure Remedies

The lender will customarily include a broad array of remedies in the mortgage document. The lender should be sure the mortgage states that its exercise of any one remedy does not impair its ability to elect to employ any other remedy later and that no action or inaction on its part will constitute a waiver of its ability to exercise its remedies in the sequence it chooses.

Once a default has ripened into an Event of Default, the lender will ordinarily have several options. Before deciding to foreclose, the lender may seek the appointment of a receiver, may make use of its rights under the assignment of leases and rents, may seek to take possession of the property, or may choose to cure the default itself.

A receiver is a third party appointed to operate the property in the borrower's stead. Theoretically, the receiver is neutral, but in many states the lender has significant input into the selection of the receiver. The judicial order appointing the receiver will place limits on the actions that he may take and will provide for his compensation and his insulation from liability. From the lender's perspective, a third party operating under court supervision will have replaced a borrower that has demonstrated its inability to operate the property successfully. If the receiver is successful, the lender may find that it never has to foreclose; if the receiver is unsuccessful, the foreclosure option remains available in the future.

The decision whether to appoint a receiver is made by a judge and not by the lender. States vary widely in their willingness to appoint receivers, and no language in the document can force a judge to make such an appointment. At the same time, the lender should be sure that the document supports its request for a receiver to the greatest extent possible. The absence of receivership language in the remedies section may lead a judge to refuse to make such an appointment, and the presence of such language may be an important factor in the judge's decision to appoint a receiver. The lender's lawyer should become familiar with state statutes and case law on this point and should be certain to include language that will strengthen its argument for a receiver should the need arise later.

Another pre-foreclosure option available to the lender is the exercise of its rights under the assignment of leases and rents.[19] Language assigning the borrower's rights under tenant leases to the lender needs to be included in the mortgage or in a separate "Assignment of Leases and Rents" to which the mortgage refers.

The lender also may consider taking possession of the property itself. In lien theory states, this option is likely to be available only if the borrower agrees to turn possession over to the lender. In title and intermediate theory states, by contrast, the lender has the ability, at least in theory, to have the borrower ousted from its property upon the occurrence of a default. Remember that possession does not equal title, and a mortgagee-in-possession does not own the property.

This last point emphasizes the chief problem the lender will face if it becomes a mortgagee-in-possession: it bears most of the responsibilities of an owner but enjoys few of the benefits. The lender may be responsible for operating the property prudently, for insuring it, and for securing it. It must strictly account for all funds received and spent and must return to the borrower any funds beyond those needed to meet the borrower's debt to the lender. It may be responsible for torts and may become responsible for environmental cleanup costs. The lender, which may have little experience in operating real estate projects, will suddenly find itself running a project that is deeply troubled.

### §6.17—Foreclosure

If none of these pre-foreclosure options appears likely to succeed, the lender will begin considering whether it needs to ratchet up its response to the borrower's default. Its choices at this point boil down essentially to two options: a suit against the borrower directly on the note (unless the note is nonrecourse or state law restricts the use of this option) or foreclosure. The lender also may consider working with the borrower to restructure the loan or accepting a deed in lieu of foreclosure, but these last options are more likely to be addressed after the default than in the mortgage documents themselves.

---

*Comment:* Some lenders will not accept deeds in lieu of foreclosure as a matter of policy, because a deed in lieu of foreclosure will not wipe out any junior liens. Only by foreclosing properly can the lender be certain to wipe out all junior liens. If the lender decides that it will accept a deed in lieu of foreclosure, it must pay special attention to the title search and to the content of the title policy to establish and insure that there are no junior liens.

---

Whether the lender decides to sue the borrower on the note or to foreclose, it must remember to accelerate the debt in accordance with the terms of the note. If the lender fails to accelerate, it can recover only the amounts that are due as of the time of the suit or the foreclosure and will probably be unable to recover those amounts that have not yet come due. Once the lender accelerates, the entire principal amount of the note becomes due immediately. When drafting the note, the lender's lawyer must be sure to include effective acceleration language.

A suit on the note has the benefit of being quicker and easier in many states. The matters that must be factually established are easy to prove, and the defenses available to the borrower are limited. The problem arises with the remedy. If the lender wins, it will receive a personal judgment against the borrower that it next must enforce. If the borrower's principal asset is the real estate, then the lender will ultimately have to force the sale of the property anyway and may find that it has lost time rather than saved it. Thus, a suit directly on the note makes the most sense if the borrower has substantial liquid assets beyond the real estate, which will not often be the case.

Three other points are worth keeping in mind. First, a suit on the note is not an option if the note is nonrecourse or if antideficiency legislation limits the availability of this alternative. Second (and subject to the limitations in the previous sentence), a suit on the note may be inevitable if the property is worth less than the debt, because the lender will have to sue the borrower personally for the deficiency. Finally, lender's counsel must become familiar with state law as to the timing of this action on the note; in some states, the lender must combine its foreclosure action and its suit on the note.

The lender is more likely to decide that it will foreclose. In some states, the only method of foreclosure that is available is foreclosure by judicial sale. The mortgage should clarify that the lender may opt to foreclose in this way. The lender that decides to foreclose judicially should be sure that it follows state law and procedure to the letter, and these laws and procedures are highly state-specific. If the foreclosure proceeds properly, the lender will name all necessary parties in the judicial proceeding, the property will be sold at auction, and the proceeds will be distributed to the lienholders in order of their recording priority and then to the borrower. If the foreclosure sale proceeds are inadequate to satisfy the borrower's entire debt to the lender, then the borrower remains liable for the deficiency.

---

*Comment:* Remember that antideficiency statutes are in effect in some states, limiting the lender's remedies to the borrower's interest in the real property. If an antideficiency statute applies, the lender will be unable to obtain a deficiency judgment.

---

More than half the states also allow the lender to foreclose privately, by power of sale. In these states, the lender can follow the procedures spelled out in the relevant statute and can foreclose without any court involvement. In order for the lender to make this election, the mortgage must state that the lender may foreclose by power of sale. A foreclosure by power of sale should be quicker and less expensive than a judicial foreclosure, and in those states in which this option is available, lenders often prefer it. The notice requirements in power-of-sale states tend to be much easier for the lender to satisfy, and junior parties (and the borrower) may find that their interests are not as well protected in these states.

Some states provide other options, including strict foreclosure in certain instances. While a handful of states still may allow strict foreclosure of the mortgagor's interest, this method of foreclosure is most commonly used in cases in which an earlier foreclosure failed to name a necessary junior party, whose interest thus survives. If a court orders strict foreclosure, a junior lienholder that does not redeem a senior lien within a stated time period will see its own lien foreclosed without a sale of the property. This procedure, which is useful for cleansing the land records of omitted interests, is highly unfavorable to junior lienholders. If the property is located in a state that permits strict foreclosure, the mortgage should permit the lender to pursue this remedy if it so chooses. Even if the lender does not anticipate using this method of foreclosure, it should leave the option open in case it changes its mind later.

### §6.18—Nonrecourse Provision

During the course of negotiating the loan commitment, the parties will have agreed whether or not the lender will extend the loan on a nonrecourse basis. In the absence of nonrecourse language, the party that signs the note is personally liable for repaying the entire debt and, in a state that permits deficiency judgments, will need to make up any shortfall if a foreclosure sale produces insufficient funds. If the lender has agreed to a nonrecourse loan, the borrower needs to be sure that both the note and the mortgage include appropriate exculpatory language that reverses this default rule of full borrower liability. If the borrower is a partnership, the parties also need to clarify whether the borrower entity itself will be shielded from personal liability or if only the general partners of the borrower will be so protected.[20]

The precise language of this nonrecourse provision is critically important. If the lender agrees to language simply stating that it will look solely to the property and will not seek recourse from the borrower, the lender may be giving up more than it intends to. In a full recourse loan, the borrower has every incentive to manage the property with care, even if the project is not doing well, because the borrower knows that any decrease in the value of the property will lead to a lower foreclosure sale price and a larger deficiency. That incentive vanishes if the lender includes the nonrecourse language just described. Once the project appears to be unsalvageable, the borrower has every reason to allow the property to deteriorate further. It will see no reason to invest any additional funds of its own in a doomed project, and it need not fear increasing the size of the deficiency judgment. The lender that agrees to a nonrecourse loan must be sure to word this provision in a more restrictive way, to give the borrower an incentive to maintain the value of the property even if things go badly.

The lender accomplishes this result by including exceptions to the nonrecourse language, frequently referred to as "carveouts." The carveouts expressly describe certain types of default for which the otherwise nonrecourse borrower will remain personally liable, along with the extent of that remaining liability. The loan still is nonrecourse in the sense that the borrower will not be personally liable for certain defaults—including nonpayment of principal and interest—if the project is unsuccessful. The carveouts, however, should ensure that the borrower continues to manage the property with care and does not commit certain acts that reduce the value of the security. The list of potential carveouts is long, and the lender should insist on all that it believes appropriate.[21] The lender should also be sure that it drafts the nonrecourse provision with care. Any nonrecourse provision will reduce the value of one of the lender's most powerful remedies, and the lender must be sure that it does not relinquish any more of this remedy than it planned to.

Two carveouts in particular merit discussion. First, the lender should be sure to include a carveout for the borrower's waste and failure to maintain the property. The fully nonrecourse borrower that is in financial trouble will see little reason to maintain the premises once foreclosure appears inevitable. Every dollar that it spends on maintenance increases the value of the lender's security, which the borrower soon will lose, while every dollar that it saves is an extra dollar that it keeps for itself. The borrower to which the lender has full recourse would not reason in this way, but the presence of nonrecourse protection gives the borrower every incentive to allow the property to deteriorate. A carefully worded nonrecourse carveout will make the borrower personally liable for lapses of this sort, removing the borrower's incentive to ignore the condition of the property and giving the lender extra confidence that the security will maintain its value.[22]

A second and related carveout that the lender should demand is personal liability on the borrower's part for nonpayment of real estate taxes. Just as the borrower can devalue the property by failing to remediate physical deterioration, it can also reduce the value of the property by failing to pay real property taxes. The taxing authority always has the power to place a lien on the property that is senior to the lender's first mortgage, and the presence of a lien for unpaid taxes increases the chance that the foreclosure sale proceeds will be inadequate to satisfy the debt. The distressed nonrecourse borrower has little motivation to pay its real property taxes unless the mortgage contains a nonrecourse carveout for these taxes. The borrower that knows it will have to make up for any deficiency is more likely to pay the taxes in the first instance. A carveout for nonpayment of insurance premiums is warranted for similar reasons.

---

*Comment:* In addition to the carveouts just noted, environmental liability is almost certain to be a carveout. A lender will wish to look personally to the borrower, and possibly even to the borrower's principals, should the lender incur any environmental liability. The lender may even seek a separate environmental indemnity agreement.

---

### §6.19—Releases and Partial Releases

The borrower may ask the lender to agree in advance that it will release all or part of the property from the lien of the mortgage if the borrower satisfies certain conditions. Two examples will illustrate this point.

If the borrower is acquiring undeveloped land with the intention of subdividing it and selling off lots, it must be sure that the lender agrees to release these lots from the mortgage as the borrower sells them. No knowledgeable purchaser will agree to accept title subject to the blanket mortgage on the entire property, so the borrower will be unable to sell the lots sequentially unless the lender agrees to this provision. In return, the lender will require that the borrower repay a portion of the loan in return for any partial release. For example, if the borrower sells one of twenty lots of equal value, the lender will demand that the borrower repay at least one-twentieth of the debt in return for the lender's release of that lot from the lien of the mortgage. The borrower should be receiving funds in excess of this amount from the purchaser of the lot and can turn over a portion of these funds in exchange for the lender's partial release.

---

*Comment:* In actual practice, the lender may require a premium to release certain specified lots, in order to guard itself against the "good lot/bad lot" problem. The lender may worry that the borrower will ask it to release all the more desirable lots first, leaving the lender with a mortgage on the less desirable (and less valuable) lots.

---

Another example arises in the context of a shopping center. A borrower that plans to operate a shopping center may need partial releases at different times. A major department store chain that is considering a location in the center may decide that it would rather own than lease its store and may insist that the owner of the center sell it a portion of the shopping center, along with an easement to the common areas. The owner may have no objection but will be unable to convey marketable title unless its lender agrees to release the site from the mortgage lien. The shopping center owner may wish to convey an outparcel, such as a portion of the parking lot, to a restaurant, a gas station, or a hotel operator. Its ability to convey marketable title is contingent on its lender's partial release of the lien. The lender will demand repayment of a portion of the principal in return for a partial release, but the borrower should have no objection to this reasonable demand.

The borrower should be sure that the parties agree in advance as to exactly what conditions the borrower must meet before the lender is obligated to release a portion of the property from the lien of the mortgage. By addressing this issue before the loan closes, the borrower ensures that it will have less trouble obtaining a partial release when it needs one later.

---

*Comment:* Other circumstances in which advance agreement on partial releases might be warranted include common ownership parcels in subdivisions that are required to be used for swimming pools, recreation centers, and other amenities; and easements for utilities, roadways, and other similar public improvements. In some of these cases, the lender should provide a partial release even if the borrower does not repay any principal. If the lender objects, the borrower can respond that the presence of these facilities has increased the value of the remaining, encumbered, portions of the property.

---

### §6.20—*Escrows for Payment of Taxes and Insurance*

One of the lender's chief concerns is the adequacy of its security. If a lien senior to the mortgage somehow materializes, then the lender's likelihood of being repaid is reduced. If the property is destroyed by fire or other casualty, then the security may be worth less than the debt. The lender will insist that the borrower pay its real estate taxes on time to avoid the first of these problems and that it purchase adequate amounts of casualty insurance to reduce or eliminate the impact of the second problem. A lender that is sufficiently worried that the borrower will not meet these obligations will try to establish a mechanism to make sure that these amounts are paid on time.

The most common method to ensure that the borrower makes these payments is the use of an escrow account. The lender may require in the loan documents that the borrower pay the lender one-twelfth of the annual real property taxes and insurance premiums each month. The lender will hold these amounts in escrow and pay the bills when due. The lender thus will know that the bills actually have been paid on time and will also have early warning of any nascent financial problems that the borrower faces.

---

*Comment:* A retail lease may require that the tenant pay its pro rata share of the landlord's real estate taxes. If this is the case, and if the mortgage requires the borrower to pay monthly installments of real estate taxes into escrow, then the borrower must be certain to require a similar escrow payment under each of its tenant's leases. If the borrower fails to do so, it will have to pay these amounts to its lender before receiving the corresponding payments from its tenants.

---

The issue of escrows for payment of taxes and insurance already has been discussed in connection with the negotiation of the loan commitment.[23] The main point for the lawyer to remember here is to include language in the loan documents that conforms to the parties' prior agreement. The borrower may object to the use of an escrow account. It may ask that the lender pay interest on the escrowed amounts and that the lender commit to take advantage of any bonuses for early payment of taxes. The borrower may also argue that the lender should not enter into the transaction assuming that the borrower will default on these obligations and that the lender should use an escrow account only after the borrower demonstrates an inability to meet its obligations, such as by defaulting once. These matters all are subject to negotiation by the parties, but the mortgage document must reflect the resolution of these discussions.

### § 6.21—Usury

State usury laws differ widely, and in some jurisdictions, commercial lenders may have good reason to worry that they will run afoul of these laws. The penalty for violating usury limits can be devastating, ranging from reduction of the interest rate to the highest permissible level, to forfeiture of interest, perhaps even to forfeiture of principal. This issue is of particular concern if the loan is at an adjustable rate with no lifetime cap, because the parties will not know at the outset how high the interest rate might climb.

The lender should be able to address this concern by including appropriate usury language in the loan documents. This language should confirm that in the event the loan rate ever exceeds the legal limit, the loan rate will automatically be reduced to the maximum amount that is permissible under state law. A properly worded usury clause should be able to head off any problems, but the lender must remember to include this important provision in the loan documents.

### § 6.22—Bankruptcy

Lenders always need to be attentive to bankruptcy matters. At first, this statement might seem counterintuitive. The first mortgage lender has already placed itself at the head of the line of creditors and is more likely than any other creditor to be made whole if the borrower files for bankruptcy protection. This view, while accurate, overlooks some of the strategic and procedural difficulties the lender may face if the borrower ends up in bankruptcy. These concerns suggest that the lender should address bankruptcy matters in the loan documents.

Keep in mind that the lender's ability to draft around bankruptcy matters successfully is somewhat constrained: bankruptcy is governed by federal law, which may trump whatever language the lender has been able to include in the mortgage and the other loan documents. In some ways, then, this section highlights a problem that the lender should be aware of, even though careful drafting may be unable to avoid it entirely.

The commercial lender is most likely to be concerned with Chapters 7 and 11 of the Bankruptcy Code.[24] Chapter 7 provides for the liquidation of the debtor. All of the debtor's assets will be sold, and the proceeds will be distributed to creditors in the order of their priority. Chapter 11 seeks to provide for the reorganization of the debtor. The debtor will be permitted to propose a plan that may involve the sale of some assets to strengthen the remaining business of the debtor. Under Chapter 11, the lender's loan might or might not survive the bankruptcy proceedings.

Under either chapter, the borrower benefits from the automatic stay provided by Section 362 of the Code.[25] All foreclosures, whether pending or merely contemplated, are put on hold until the court lifts the stay. In other words, the federal filing stops the state foreclosure process in its tracks. While it is easier for the lender to have the stay lifted under Chapter 7 than under Chapter 11, the stay is sure to delay the lender's exercise of its foreclosure remedies under either chapter.[26] The Bankruptcy Reform Act of 1994 has made it somewhat more difficult than it previously was for mortgagors that own just a single real estate asset to use Chapter 11 to delay a foreclosure.

Under Chapter 11, the lender that is unable to have the stay lifted will have to participate in the process of approving the reorganization plan. Even if the lender does not accept the plan, the borrower may be able to force acceptance of the plan upon the lender in certain instances.[27]

The drafter of the mortgage must do his best to plan for these bankruptcy possibilities while recognizing that the documents cannot overrule the law. At minimum, the lawyer must be sure that any bankruptcy filing constitutes an Event of Default, thereby allowing the lender at least a chance to employ its full arsenal of remedies.[28] This provision will permit the lender to accelerate the loan and seek to foreclose, but only to the extent permitted by the Code and the court.

The lender also should recognize that the exercise of some of its other remedies may be delayed or curtailed by a bankruptcy filing. For example, courts are divided over the extent to which a lender may exercise its rights under an assignment of leases and rents after the borrower declares bankruptcy.[29] The answer to this question revolves around state law issues of property and perfection of security interests, a fact that will remind the drafter that bankruptcy law is federal law but incorporates state law property concepts.

*Comment:* Note that bankruptcy clauses in any documents, including loan documents and leases, will be unenforceable in the short run if the event of default that activates the lender's rights is the filing of a bankruptcy. The bankruptcy triggers the lender's right to act while simultaneously preventing the lender from proceeding. For this reason, if there are other clauses that give the lender the ability to exercise its remedies prior to bankruptcy, such as by employing its rights under an assignment of leases and rents, the lender should seek to exercise these rights before the bankruptcy filing. The courts may not give effect to any attempt to take advantage of these rights after a bankruptcy has been filed.

### § 6.23—Caution: Bankruptcy Stays

In the event of a bankruptcy filing, the lender must immediately cease any and all actions pertaining to the borrower or the property, including a foreclosure sale. The lender that fails to do so may find itself in contempt of the bankruptcy proceeding, because a bankruptcy filing stays all such actions.

## § 6.24 Deed of Trust

This chapter has used the term "mortgage" to include both mortgages and deeds of trust, but there are some instances in which these two different security devices can operate in different ways. Some states permit the use of just one of these security interests, while other states permit the use of both. Even in these latter states, there may be practical reasons for preferring one security device to the other, and these reasons will vary from place to place.

A mortgage is a two-party document. The owner, or mortgagor, mortgages its property to the lender, or mortgagee, as security for the repayment of its debt. The mortgagor still owns fee simple title to the land while the mortgagee holds a security interest.[30]

A deed of trust (known in Georgia as a deed to secure debt) is a three-party document. The owner, referred to as the grantor or trustor, deeds the property to a third party, the trustee, to be held in trust for the benefit of the lender, or beneficiary. Title is nominally held by the trustee, whose actions are governed by the document and by state law. If the grantor repays the debt, the beneficiary will notify the trustee that it should reconvey the property to the grantor. If the grantor defaults, the beneficiary will instruct the trustee to begin employing the remedies set forth in the document.

The difference between these two security devices is most pronounced when the lender decides to foreclose in a state that permits foreclosure by power of sale. In a mortgage state, this private sale will be organized and run by the lender, which is thereby precluded from bidding at the sale. In contrast, in deed of trust states, the foreclosure sale is ostensibly under the control of a disinterested trustee, although this trustee acts at the request of the lender and rarely is completely impartial. Technically, the lender is not involved in the process of foreclosing and is thus free to bid on the property. The law is highly state-specific on these remedial matters, and this discussion does not fully explain the reasons the deed of trust is preferred in some states that permit its use, but one of the principal goals of the deed of trust is to permit lenders in power-of-sale states to bid at their own foreclosure sales.

Note that the states vary tremendously in the degree of independence they require from their trustees, particularly during a foreclosure. In some states, the trustee's level of fiduciary responsibility is low, and a bank officer or lawyer for the beneficiary may serve successfully as long as the sale is conducted properly. Other states have stricter standards, and in these states an interested trustee would be wise to resign if foreclosure seems imminent, particularly if the beneficiary is considering bidding at the sale.

## §6.25 Assignment of Leases and Rents

If the mortgaged property produces rental income—as most commercial property does or will—the lender should receive an assignment of leases and rents from the borrower. During the course of negotiating the loan commitment, the parties almost certainly will have agreed that the borrower must execute such a document, and the parties will now have to decide on its language. Some states permit this language to appear in the mortgage itself, but in most states the assignment of leases and rents will be a freestanding document that the lender will record immediately after the mortgage.

The assignment of leases and rents allows the lender, rather than the borrower, to receive all tenant rents directly from the tenants upon the borrower's default. As long as the borrower continues to meet its obligations, it may retain the tenant rents. If the borrower misses a payment or fails to meet one of its other loan obligations, the lender may declare a default and activate its remedies under the assignment of leases and rents. The lender can accomplish this result in some states simply by sending written notice to the tenants instructing them to begin paying their rent to the lender rather than to the borrower.[31]

Individual tenants that receive a notice of this type from their landlord's lender may properly wonder what they should do next. They may fear that the notice is inaccurate or perhaps even fraudulent, and they will have genuine concerns that if they pay the wrong party they may end up paying their rent twice. A properly drafted assignment will protect tenants by setting forth the conditions under which the tenant can rely on a notice from the lender, even if the lender's notice proves to be mistaken.

The assignment of leases and rents provides the lender with a powerful pre-foreclosure remedy. If the borrower defaults, the lender probably would prefer to resolve the problem without resorting to foreclosure. The assignment of leases and rents allows the lender to take control of some or all of the cash flow from the property and thereby ensure that it receives money to which it is entitled. The lender can also prevent the borrower from using this cash flow for inappropriate or unwise purposes, such as distributions to its equity holders. The lender can accomplish these results without undertaking the risks of owning or operating the property and without the expense and difficulty of having a receiver appointed.

---

*Comment:* Another reason the lender wants to get its hands on the rents as soon as possible is so that the borrower cannot use the rents as a war chest to finance its fight with the lender.

---

There are some drawbacks to the use of an assignment of leases and rents. The money that the lender is receiving is money that the borrower might otherwise have used for the maintenance of the property. If the problem is that business conditions have suffered and the property cannot operate at a profit, rather than dishonesty or poor management on the borrower's part, the lender will be taking from the borrower the scarce funds that the borrower needs to keep the project afloat. The use of an assignment of leases and rents also cannot solve certain other problems. If the borrower has been having trouble courting new tenants, the lender cannot address that issue simply by taking control of the rents from existing tenants, and exercise of some other remedy might be warranted. Moreover, the assignment of leases and rents has little value to the lender if there are few or no rent-paying tenants in occupancy.

### §6.26—Form: Assignment of Leases and Rents

See Appendix L for a Form of Assignment of Leases and Rents.

## §6.27  Security Agreements and Financing Statements; Fixture Filings

The lender often requires that the borrower provide it with a security interest in the borrower's personal property, to furnish additional assurance that the borrower will repay the loan. In some cases, this personal property may be of relatively modest value but may be necessary to keep the property running after it changes hands. For example, the lender may insist on a security interest in the borrower's office equipment, cleaning supplies, and lawn care equipment. This personal property may represent only a tiny fraction of the value of the debt, but the foreclosure sale purchaser will find it easier to step into the borrower's shoes if it does not have to replace all of this personalty as soon as it acquires the property.

In other cases, the borrower's personal property may represent a significantly larger proportion of the loan amount. The clearest example may be the case of a hotel mortgage. If the foreclosure sale purchaser acquires the land and improvements but not the furnishings and equipment, it will have to go to enormous expense before it can use the property for its intended purpose: an unfurnished hotel will produce no revenue, and furnishing it will be costly. The lender and its lawyer must be attentive to personal property matters and must not forget about the interrelationships between real and personal property.

The method of obtaining a security interest in personal property differs from the method used for real property. The creditor acquires its interest by having the debtor pledge a security interest in this personal property to the creditor. This pledge is accomplished by the debtor's execution of a simple security agreement, which is analogous to the real property mortgage. Rather than recording this interest, as the lender would with a mortgage, the creditor must perfect it in accordance with Article 9 of the Uniform Commercial Code.

For most types of personal property, perfection will mean that the debtor must execute a UCC-1 financing statement, which then must be filed in accordance with the requirements of Article 9 and any other applicable state laws. Note that, unlike mortgages, financing statements generally expire after five years unless they are extended by the filing of a continuation statement. If the financing statement expires, the creditor is left holding an unperfected security interest, which is much like a lender holding a note secured by an unrecorded mortgage. For some types of property, such as motor vehicles, the method of perfecting a security interest will differ, and the lawyer would be wise to review the provisions of Article 9 before attempting to perfect a security interest. The lawyer should also recognize that the Uniform Commercial Code is not completely uniform: some states have modified certain provisions before adopting various articles of the UCC.

Fixtures fall into the gray area between real and personal property. When personal property becomes permanently affixed to real estate, it is deemed to be a "fixture" under state law. For example, a heating system is personal property when it is on the contractor's truck but becomes a fixture after it is installed in a building. Priority battles can arise between the holder of a security interest in the fixture—in this case, the heating contractor or a third-party lender—and the lender that holds a mortgage on the real property to which the heating system has become affixed. The UCC addresses fixtures as well as personal property, and the lender should be careful to comply with the fixture filing provisions of Article 9, which incorporate state principles of property law.[32]

---

*Comment:* Despite months, if not years, of attempting to agree on a uniform definition of the term "fixture," the drafters of Article 9 were unable to settle on a definition that did not incorporate state law. This is true for two reasons. First, the definition of the term varies greatly from state to state. Second, as has been noted by a number of commentators, the meaning of the term varies from one setting to another and depends on what the parties intended with regard to the specific items of property in question.

---

### § 6.28—Form: Security Agreement

See Appendix M for a Form of Security Agreement.

## §6.29 Guarantees

Lenders sometimes insist on receiving personal guarantees as additional security for the repayment of the loan. The lender can not only foreclose the mortgage and sue on the note (unless it is a nonrecourse note or state law prohibits deficiency judgments) but can also seek satisfaction from the guarantor in accordance with the term of the guarantee. The parties will have agreed at the loan commitment stage whether someone will guarantee the borrower's performance; at the document drafting stage, the parties must settle on the terms of a guarantee that conforms to this earlier agreement.

The lender is more likely to demand a guarantee if it is worried about the adequacy of its other security. If the property is highly risky or if the borrower's financial status suggests that it is unlikely to be able to satisfy a personal judgment, then the lender may refuse to lend without receiving the additional comfort of a third-party guarantee. Borrowers that are thinly capitalized corporations or limited liability companies pose greater risks than borrowers that are partnerships with creditworthy general partners; nonrecourse loans pose greater risks than full recourse loans; and environmentally risky security poses a greater risk than a run-of-the-mill apartment house.

Borrowers and their guarantors often ask to have the guarantees limited in different ways. The responsible party may ask for a dollar cap on its potential liability or for a time limit after which the guarantee will expire. The parties may agree that the guarantor will be personally liable only for certain types of losses, such as those arising from the failure to complete a construction project or from the release of hazardous substances. The negotiating range here is wide, and the parties will need to agree to an arrangement that suits the specific parties and specific type of land in question.

---

Comment: A particularly lethal clause for a lender to include in a guarantee is a "confession of judgment" clause. In some jurisdictions, these clauses are enforceable and commonly used. A confession of judgment clause permits the lender to have a court enter judgment against the guarantor immediately following a default under the note or mortgage: The guarantor has "confessed" in advance that it must pay when the lender makes a demand. It then becomes incumbent upon the guarantor to enter court to attempt to set the judgment aside. The immediate effect of the judg-

ment can be devastating to the guarantor, which in most instances is an
entity that is related to the borrower and often is its parent.

### § 6.30—Form: Loan Guarantee

See Appendix N for a Form of Loan Guarantee.

## § 6.31 Participation Agreements

Lenders sometimes sell participation interests in their mortgage
loans, particularly if the principal amount of the loan is large. Rather
than assuming all of the lending risk itself, the lender is able to share
the risk with other willing lenders. The participants commonly enter
into a participation agreement under which each lender receives a
participation certificate that evidences its fractional interest in the
loan. The lead lender usually retains the original note, administers
the loan, collects funds from the borrower and distributes funds to
the participants, and enforces any remedies if that becomes necessary. The borrower will probably have little to say about any loan
participations. It has few reasons for objecting if the lender decides
to share the loan risk with other lenders.

If the lender plans to participate the loan, it will want to enter
into agreements with its participants before committing to the loan
or funding it. These agreements should clearly delineate the authority of the lead lender to make decisions binding on all participants
and should clarify the extent to which the lead lender is assuming
any fiduciary responsibility toward its participants. Participation
agreements are complex arrangements that raise issues beyond the
scope of this book. However, if the lender plans to participate the
loan, it should address these issues during the commitment and
document stages of the mortgage loan transaction.

### § 6.32—Caution: Loan Participations

The borrower should note whether the commitment requires participation as a condition of the lender's funding of the loan. The
lender may have the right to refuse to fund the loan if it is unable to
obtain the necessary participants. The borrower should also negotiate for the right to deal with only the lead lender so that it will not

have to work with any of the other participating lenders during the life of the loan.

## §6.33 Seller Financing

In Part III of this book, we have assumed that the seller and the lender are two different parties, but sellers occasionally serve as lenders. In some cases, the seller is anxious to dispose of the property and may be willing to provide the buyer with favorable financing terms as an inducement to enter into the contract. In other cases, the buyer may have difficulty procuring a loan on its own and may turn to the seller as the lender of last resort. Even if the buyer is able to obtain a third-party loan, the amount of this loan may not be large enough, and the seller may agree to fill the gap with second mortgage financing. Sellers may have their own reasons for preferring to receive the sale proceeds in installments rather than all at once. If the parties are willing, they are free to agree that the seller will serve as the lender or as one of the lenders.

If the seller agrees to provide this type of purchase money financing, the parties will probably incorporate the terms of the loan into the contract of sale, rather than executing a separate loan commitment.[33] Some of the issues previously discussed in connection with the loan commitment become immaterial.[34] For example, it would be pointless for the lender to demand copies of the tenant leases or estoppel letters from the tenants, because the lender is also the current owner and already has full information about tenant leases. Other issues discussed in connection with the loan commitment probably will be addressed directly in the contract of sale. If the seller insists on receiving a guarantee from a third party and the buyer requests nonrecourse protection, those issues can be addressed in the contract, which now serves the dual function of sales contract and loan commitment.

The operative mortgage documents themselves will differ little whether the lender is the seller or a third party. The seller will deliver the deed to the buyer, and the buyer will deliver the note, the mortgage, and the assignment of leases and rents to the seller. These documents, except for the note, will ordinarily be recorded in the sequence just stated. If the buyer also is borrowing some of the funds from a third-party lender, both mortgages should expressly state which is to have priority over the other. This language—effectively, a subordination clause—should assist in resolving any confusion that might arise if the documents are accidentally recorded out of sequence or if the state applies a presumption that seller financing receives first priority.

## §6.34 *Assumption of Existing Financing*

The buyer may find it advantageous to assume the seller's existing financing. Assumption of existing financing allows the buyer to enjoy the benefits of the original interest rate—even if rates have increased since the loan was extended—and all the other terms of the original loan. In some jurisdictions, the buyer that assumes existing financing will not become subject to mortgage recording tax, even though the buyer would have to pay this tax if it granted a new mortgage to its lender. The buyer also will save the time and expense of negotiating new loan documents. Of course, if the terms of the existing financing are undesirable, the borrower may decide that this disadvantage outweighs the benefits of assuming the existing loan. The buyer's lawyer should emphasize to her client that, by assuming the loan, the buyer becomes responsible for repaying it, just as if the buyer had signed the note itself.

The buyer and the seller must confirm that the seller's loan documents permit the buyer to assume the existing financing. If the documents prohibit assumption or limit the ability of the buyer to assume the financing, then the parties will need to obtain the lender's consent to this transfer. For example, if the loan contains a due-on-transfer clause and the parties close without receiving the lender's consent, the loan will go into default at the moment of the transfer. The parties must be sure that their contract of sale specifies what the parties' rights are if the lender denies its consent to the assumption. If the primary reason for assuming the existing financing is to preserve a below-market interest rate, then the lender is unlikely to consent; it will see the sale as a fortuitous event that allows it to escape from a low-rate loan. Stated differently, the very factor that makes the buyer wish to preserve the loan will make the lender wish to terminate it. If, however, the buyer wishes to assume the existing financing primarily to save on its closing costs, taxes, and legal fees, the lender may be more accommodating, particularly if it receives a fee for allowing the assumption.

The lender may be perfectly happy to permit the buyer to assume the loan. If prevailing rates have not changed or if the loan is an adjustable-rate loan, there will be no significant economic consequences to the sale. The lender's decision then becomes a credit decision, and the lender must decide whether the buyer is as good a credit risk as the seller was. The lender will probably examine the creditworthiness and business expertise of the buyer just as it would if it were extending a new loan to the buyer. The lender does enjoy one added benefit if the buyer assumes the seller's financing, in that the seller remains liable for repayment of the debt even after the buyer's assumption. This contingent liability may provide little practical benefit to the lender, however, if the seller owns no other assets beyond the subject property or if the seller will be difficult to locate once it sells the property. At the same time, the seller must remember that if its buyer defaults, it may be called on to make up any deficiency that the buyer cannot pay.

Sellers are sometimes under the mistaken impression that the buyer's assumption releases them from personal liability on the debt. Counsel to the seller must be sure to correct this erroneous belief: the seller remains liable for repayment of the debt even after the buyer assumes. Only the lender can release the seller from this liability. The seller may request a release of this type, and the lender occasionally may agree, but absent such an agreement, the seller remains personally liable.

The difference between the sale price of the property and the outstanding principal amount of the existing financing may be large enough that the buyer still needs to borrow additional funds to acquire the property. The buyer then will turn to a third-party lender or to the seller and seek to borrow funds to fill some of this gap. This lender then becomes a second mortgagee, with an interest subordinate to that of the lender that holds the original mortgage.

If the buyer and the seller agree to a sale with an assumption, they must modify their documents to reflect this fact. The contract of sale should clarify that the buyer will pay part of the consideration by assuming the seller's debt and should list the existing mortgage as a permitted exception to marketable title. Any warranties in the deed also should except the prior mortgage.

## §6.35 Acquisition Subject to Existing Financing

Instead of assuming existing financing, the buyer may purchase the property subject to existing financing. The principal difference between these two structures is that the buyer that assumes becomes liable for repayment of the debt, but the buyer that purchases subject to existing financing does not. While a nonassuming buyer cannot be called on to pay the outstanding principal, the mortgage remains as a valid encumbrance on the buyer's title. If the buyer fails to make the required payments to the original lender, the lender can exercise all its mortgage remedies—including foreclosure—but cannot recover any deficiency from the buyer. The buyer thus has every incentive to keep the loan payments current if it still wants to retain the property but loses most of that incentive if the property's value drops below the amount of principal still outstanding on the loan. If the seller was liable on the note originally, it remains liable after the conveyance, even though the buyer is not liable.

The buyer would clearly prefer to purchase subject to, rather than assuming. It enjoys all of the interest rate benefits and all of the transaction cost savings of an assumption but ends up in a position much like that of a nonrecourse borrower. The seller, however, would prefer that the buyer assume the mortgage. Even though the seller will remain liable in either case, the seller is less likely to be called on to pay if the buyer assumes. The buyer will be primarily liable for any deficiency, and the seller effectively serves as a surety rather than as a principal debtor.

The lender would also prefer that the buyer assume the mortgage, because an assumption provides the lender with one extra responsible party in the event of a default. If the loan documents require that the lender consent to any transfer of this type, the lender may decide to grant its consent on the condition that the buyer assume. Absent such restrictions in the loan documents, the seller and the buyer are free to negotiate whatever resolution they desire.

The nonassuming buyer should be aware that it still may be financially responsible for certain actions at the property. The fact that it has not assumed means that the buyer cannot be called on to pay principal, interest, or any other amounts contractually required under the note and mortgage. The buyer may, however, be held liable for torts. If the buyer damages the property, perhaps simply by failing to maintain it, the lender may sue the nonassuming buyer for waste, and the buyer may be responsible for paying damages to the lender. The buyer's failure to pay real property taxes and insurance premiums may also constitute waste.[35]

As with an assumption, the buyer still may need to borrow additional funds from another lender or from the seller. In addition, if the buyer is purchasing subject to existing financing, the buyer and seller need to clarify this point in the contract of sale and in the deed.

## §6.36 Subordinate Lending

Sometimes the lender in question will be a junior lender. The buyer may be borrowing its acquisition funds from two different lenders, and the lawyer will find himself in the role of counsel to a second mortgage lender. The buyer may be assuming existing financing or may be acquiring the property subject to existing financing, and then may borrow additional funds from a junior lender. Or the seller may be providing some of the financing itself and becoming a second mortgage lender.

All of the lending issues discussed in Part III apply with equal force to a junior lender. The lender will enter into a loan commitment with the borrower, will perform due diligence, and will insist on satisfactory documents. If anything, the junior lender is in a more precarious position and should be even more concerned with the sufficiency of its remedies than the first lender is. The junior lender must also consider some additional issues and may need to address these in the loan documents.

The junior lender should take the steps necessary to ensure that it will receive notice of any defaults on the senior debt along with an adequate opportunity to cure those defaults.[36] It does not want the senior lender foreclosing, and potentially wiping out its own junior mortgage, without at least having the opportunity to decide whether it wishes to spend additional money to protect its own interest. If the senior debt is to be negotiated at the same time as the junior debt, the senior lender will be aware of this issue from the outset and may be willing to work with the junior lender, but if the senior debt already is in place, the senior lender may refuse to modify its loan documents. In this latter instance, the junior lender will simply have to decide whether it would rather enter into a risky loan or walk away.

The junior lender also should seek a cross-default provision, under which a default on any other debt constitutes a default on its own loan.[37] The junior lender will worry that a senior creditor will begin to exercise its remedies at a time when the junior lender's hands are tied because the junior loan has not yet gone into default. The presence of a cross-default provision allows the junior lender to begin exercising its remedies even if the borrower has otherwise managed to remain current on its obligations to the junior lender.

### Notes

1. Contrast this with the way in which the parties must prepare for a more typical closing. *See infra* Chapter 7.

2.  626 F. Supp. 1229 (S.D.N.Y. 1986).

3.  Deeds of trust, which are similar to mortgages, are discussed below. *See infra* § 6.24.

4.  On occasion, a mortgage will secure some other type of document, such as a bond or a guarantee. But the mortgage must secure some obligation.

5.  *See infra* § 6.18.

6.  Some state recording statutes treat mortgagees somewhat differently from fee simple owners, so the lawyer must become familiar with the recording laws of the state in which the mortgaged property is located.

7.  The note may be enforced under the law of another state, but the mortgage or deed of trust will be enforced under the law of the state in which the property is located. Thus, the parties can execute a note that is to be enforced in accordance with Maryland law, but if this debt is secured by real estate located in Tennessee, the deed of trust must comply with Tennessee's requirements and will be enforced under Tennessee's laws.

8.  *See infra* § 6.24.

9.  The borrower also delivers consideration to the lender at the time it executes the loan commitment, by paying the commitment fee. *See supra* § 4.19.

10.  *See supra* § 4.06.

11.  Lenders must be aware of the interactions between prepayment clauses and due-on-transfer limitations. If the prepayment clause prohibits prepayment of the loan for, say, the first year, and the due-on-transfer clause makes the loan immediately due if the borrower sells the property, then there is a contradiction: if the buyer sells the property quickly, the loan is due but cannot be paid. At best, the court will view this inconsistency as confusing. At worst, the court may treat it as an unreasonable restraint on alienation. Either way, the court may refuse to enforce the prepayment limitation.

12.  *See supra* § 4.06.

13.  *See supra* §§ 4.13, 5.16–5.17.

14.  *Cf. supra* §§ 4.13, 5.16–5.17.

15.  *See supra* §§ 2.113, 4.18; *infra* § 6.18.

16.  *See infra* § 6.18.

17.  These remedies are discussed at *infra* §§ 6.16–6.17.

18.  *See infra* § 6.17.

19.  *See infra* §§ 6.25–6.26.

20.  If the owner is a corporation or a limited liability entity, the interest holders will be immune from liability by operation of law, and the only issue is whether the lender can recover from the entity. If the owner is an individual, then the distinction described in the text is inapplicable.

21.  *See supra* § 4.18.

22.  Note how the wording of this provision must dovetail with the language of the section addressing the borrower's obligation to maintain the property. *See supra* § 6.13. This carveout needs to address both

ordinary maintenance and capital expenses, and should discuss both matters in some detail. *See id.*

23. *See supra* §§ 4.10, 4.12.

24. 11 U.S.C. §§ 701–766, 1101–1174 (2000 & Supp. IV 2004).

25. *Id.* § 362 (2000).

26. *See generally* GRANT S. NELSON & DALE A. WHITMAN, REAL ESTATE FINANCE LAW 770–73, 780–84 (5th ed. 2007).

27. *See* 11 U.S.C. § 1129 (2000); NELSON & WHITMAN, *supra* note 23, at 787–98.

28. If the borrower is forced into involuntary bankruptcy, the lender may agree to provide a brief period of time for the borrower to cure before the bankruptcy becomes an Event of Default.

29. *See infra* §§ 6.25–6.26. *See generally* UNIFORM ASSIGNMENT OF RENTS ACT (2005); R. Wilson Freyermuth, *Of Hotel Revenues, Rents, and Formalism in the Bankruptcy Courts: Implications for Reforming Commercial Real Estate Finance,* 40 UCLA L. REV. 1461 (1993); Patrick A. Randolph, Jr., *Recognizing Lender's Rents Interests in Bankruptcy,* 27 REAL PROP. PROB. & TR. J. 281 (1992).

30. Recall, however, that some states may still purport to subscribe to the fiction that the mortgage actually is a conveyance of the property to the mortgagee. These title theory states may hold that the lender nominally has legal title to the real estate.

31. The states are not unanimous on this point. In some states, it may be possible for the lender to prepare a "self-activating" assignment of leases and rents. Under this approach, the tenants would be obliged to send rent to the lender immediately upon their landlord's default, without any further action on the lender's part. In other states, the lender may have to take some stronger action to activate the lease assignment, such as commencing foreclosure or seeking the appointment of a receiver. In all states, however, the lender should send notice to the tenants, who might have no other way of learning that the borrower has defaulted.

32. Fixtures are defined in Section 9-102(a)(41) of Article 9, but the definition incorporates state real estate law concepts.

33. *See supra* §§ 2.19–2.21 (discussing seller financing).

34. *See supra* Chapter 4.

35. *Cf. supra* §§ 6.13, 6.18.

36. *Cf. supra* §§ 4.13, 5.16–5.17, 6.11.

37. *Cf. supra* § 6.12.

# Part IV
# The Closing

# CHAPTER 7

# Preparing for the Closing

## § 7.01 The Need for a Closing

The contract of sale and the loan commitment are executory contracts. The parties to each of these documents promise to perform in the future if certain conditions are met. Neither of these documents has the effect of conveying a legal interest in property. The seller can convey legal title to the buyer only by executing and delivering a deed, and the buyer can convey a mortgage to the lender only by executing and delivering a mortgage. All of the negotiations so far have been preparation for the moment when the parties deliver these operative documents and effect the transfer they have been planning for weeks or months.

The closing is the point at which this formal transfer of title occurs. One reason for having a closing is to underscore the legal significance of what is happening. In this sense, the closing replaces the common law concept of "livery of seisin," which required the seller to give the buyer a ceremonial handful of dirt from the land. Modern sellers and buyers can accomplish the same result more conveniently by reviewing, executing, and delivering the documents at the closing.

A more important modern reason for having a closing is to ensure that all closing conditions are met concurrently. Neither party wishes to carry out its obligations without knowing that the other party will perform in return. The buyer will be unwilling to hand over the sale proceeds to the seller if there is no way to be certain that the seller will deliver the deed, and the seller will be just as unwilling to deliver the deed without assurance that the buyer will pay the balance of the purchase price. By having a closing, each party can ensure that all the others perform and that all conditions precedent are met before anyone leaves the room with any documents or funds. Closings can be conducted without gathering all the parties and their lawyers around a conference table,[1] but all closings should be designed to attain this legal effect.

The remainder of this chapter discusses closing preparations. The ideal closing will proceed smoothly, with the various parties signing documents and departing quickly and happily. The more the lawyers prepare for the closing in advance, the more likely they are to achieve that goal and satisfy their respective clients. Careful preparation does not guarantee a flawless closing, but poor preparation often leads to a dreadful one.

## §7.02 The Closing Checklist

The first step for the lawyer is to prepare a closing checklist. This checklist should enumerate every matter that someone must address before the closing and should allocate responsibility for attending to these items. Often, one of the lawyers will take responsibility for preparing a closing checklist and will distribute it to all the other parties as a means of ensuring that everyone has agreed to the same division of labor. The fact that a lawyer receives a closing checklist from another party does not absolve that lawyer of responsibility for verifying its completeness from the perspective of that lawyer's client. Each lawyer is concerned about protecting only one client's interests, and someone else's checklist may overlook matters of particular importance to your own client, including internal matters that your client may want to keep confidential. In other words, each lawyer should think about these closing matters carefully—and perhaps prepare an internal closing checklist—rather than relying on someone else to complete this task.

The contract of sale forms the starting point for preparation of the closing checklist. The contract typically contains a lengthy list of representations, warranties, covenants, and conditions. Every party with an interest in the proper performance of the contract should review its terms carefully and should include every unresolved matter on the checklist. If the buyer needs to verify the accuracy of a representation or the performance of a covenant, it should be sure to note this fact on its checklist.

The closing conditions section of the contract, in particular, will probably form the backbone of the closing checklist. Each party's obligation to perform is conditioned on a variety of uncertain events occurring first, and each party's lawyer must confirm that all of these events have occurred by the closing date. Many of these closing conditions involve the delivery of closing documents, and the inclusion of each of these items on the closing checklist will remind the lawyer to make sure the document is drafted, negotiated, completed, and ready for execution by the closing. Other closing conditions may focus on review of external documents or approval of certain matters. It is most comforting to the lawyer if each of these open matters can be resolved before the closing and checked off the list. However, problems often arise with seemingly routine matters, and some items—such as execution of the operative documents themselves—will probably have to be deferred until closing day.

Each lawyer that is preparing a closing checklist must remember to review other documents that are relevant to that lawyer's client in addition to the contract of sale. The loan commitment ordinarily follows a format similar to that of the contract and will contain its own representations, warranties, covenants, and conditions. If the matters described in the loan commitment are not addressed before the closing, the lender will not be willing to fund the loan and the loan will not close. The title company undertakes certain obligations in the title commitment, and other documents create similar responsibilities in other parties. Each lawyer must review each of these documents to ensure that his or her closing checklist is complete. In fact, the experienced lawyer probably begins to compile this checklist early in the transaction, updating it regularly to reflect changes that develop along the way and the content of newly drafted documents.

The closing checklist should also help the lawyer supervise the responsibilities of other parties. The buyer's lawyer cannot produce a payoff letter from the seller's lender, but she can remind the seller's lawyer that he needs to pursue this document.[2] If each of the lawyers helps the others remember their respective roles, the closing is more likely to proceed without a hitch.

Some of the items on the closing checklist will involve the payment of funds. The most obvious examples are the payment of the purchase price by the buyer and the advancing of the loan proceeds by the lender, but there are others. The buyer and the seller will have to apportion certain expenses related to the property, and various other parties will need to be paid. The lawyers probably cannot calculate these amounts until shortly before the closing, but they should list these items on the checklist and should specify the acceptable methods of making these payments.

### § 7.03—Checklist: Due Diligence and Closing Checklist

See Appendix E for a Form of Due Diligence and Closing Checklist.

## § 7.04 Document Preparation

One of the lawyer's principal responsibilities before the closing is to prepare, negotiate, and approve the various documents that the parties must execute and deliver at the closing. Chapter 6 discussed the documents that are specific to the loan transaction, but the lawyers need to prepare other documents as well. Some of these additional documents pertain to the seller's delivery of title to the buyer, while others effect the transfer of personal property or address more general matters.

The lawyer should be attentive to formal requirements when preparing these documents. If a particular document must be acknowledged before a notary public, then the parties must include an appropriate acknowledgment form.[3] If the local recording office requires that documents meet certain color and size requirements, then the lawyers must prepare documents that meet those requirements.[4] The lawyers also should begin considering how many originals of each document the parties will need to execute.[5]

The following sections address the most significant of the documents that have not been discussed in previous chapters. The lawyer should remember to review all previous chapters and should be sure that someone prepares all relevant documents discussed there. The lawyer also should remember that every transaction is unique and that no list of documents can be viewed as all-encompassing.

### § 7.05—Caution: Reliance on Form Documents

Many lawyers rely on forms prepared by other lawyers or on forms published in various journals and books as the basis for preparing their own documents. The lawyer should exercise great caution when using any form prepared by anyone else. The drafter must take care to modify the form to fit the particular transaction and the jurisdiction whose law will govern.

## § 7.06—Deed

The deed is the operative document that the seller must use to convey legal title to the property to the buyer. If the seller does not execute and deliver a deed in proper form, then the seller may not have effectively transferred title to the property. If the deed is valid but is not in recordable form, then the buyer will be unable to record it and provide notice to the world of the transfer of title. The deed, then, is the central document in the entire transaction and must be prepared with care.

Most states recognize three types of deeds, although not every state uses the same names for these three types. In a "general warranty deed," the seller not only conveys title but also warrants against defects in title arising during or prior to the seller's period of ownership. If any of these title imperfections should arise, the seller must make the buyer whole, up to the amount of consideration the buyer paid. A "special warranty deed" is similar to a general warranty deed, but the seller takes responsibility only for title problems arising during its period of ownership. If the seller executes a "quitclaim deed," it includes no warranties and merely conveys to the buyer whatever title the seller has, if any. The parties will have already agreed on a type of deed at the outset, and the lawyers must now be sure that the seller delivers the appropriate deed at the closing.

---

*Comment:* Where a general or special warranty deed is used, it is wise for the grantor to state that it is giving its warranties subject to all matters of record.

---

*Comment:* Quitclaim deeds are customarily delivered by entities such as personal representatives and trustees. However, quitclaim deeds may not be sufficient to satisfy title insurance company requirements in other situations.

---

Customs vary from state to state as to which party prepares the deed. The language of these three types of deed is brief and standardized, and the preparation of the deed will constitute only a minor burden and expense. Some states still employ common law language in their deeds, while others have adopted statutory language that accomplishes the same result. Whichever approach the state in question follows, and whatever type of deed the parties have agreed on, this is not a drafting project that will demand enormous creativity on the part of the lawyers. The deed should follow the common law or statutory language closely, and there should be little for the parties to negotiate. The parties should also be sure that the title company and the lender find the language and form of the deed acceptable—in fact, in many jurisdictions the title insurer will provide a blank form and the parties simply will have to fill in their names, the date, and a legal description of the property. The deed will probably turn out to be one of the few documents in the transaction for which a standard form will suffice.

Both the buyer and the seller should confirm that the legal description is correct. It should match the descriptions found in the deed that conveyed title to the seller, the contract of sale, and the title commitment (which, in turn, is the description that the title company used when it searched title and committed to insure). The legal descriptions in the survey, the mortgage, and the assignment of leases and rents also will need to match exactly.

---

*Comment:* The description in the contract of sale and the description actually shown in a new survey prepared at the request of the buyer may differ, based on the surveyor's actual examination of the site. In these circumstances, the buyer may want to use a new legal description prepared to reflect the more recent survey, while the seller will be reluctant to use (and warrant) anything but the old description. It is best if this issue is addressed in the contract of sale. In some cases, the title company may be willing to issue a policy endorsement insuring that the two descriptions depict the same property.

---

If the parties have agreed that the buyer will accept title subject to certain permitted encumbrances, then the deed customarily lists these exceptions specifically, although practices in some states differ.[6] Permitted exceptions might include existing mortgages that the buyer is assuming; existing mortgages to which the buyer's deed will be subject; ground leases; tenant leases; and covenants, servitudes, easements, and reciprocal easements. If the seller has disclosed the existence of these title encumbrances to the buyer and the buyer has agreed to accept title subject to these encumbrances, then these exceptions are ordinarily enumerated in the deed and thereby removed from the scope of the seller's deed warranties.

The parties must be particularly attentive to state and local formal requirements applicable to deeds, a point that the title insurer can usually clarify. The parties need to know in advance if the county accepts only deeds that are signed in black ink, on 8½ x 11-inch paper, with the name and address of the buyer's lawyer stated at the bottom of page one, and with a 3-inch-square blank space for the recorder's stamp in the upper-right-hand corner of the first page. The parties should also be sure that the document contains the proper language for acknowledging the deed before a notary public. Errors of this type can usually be corrected after the closing, but it is easier and less embarrassing to avoid them before the closing. In the end, preparation and review of the deed should prove to be one of the lawyer's easier tasks in connection with the transaction.

### § 7.07—Corporate, Partnership, and Limited Liability Entity Documents; Power of Attorney

Frequently, one or more of the parties taking part in the transaction will be a business entity. Unlike individual persons, who may appear at the closing in person and sign the documents, business entities have no physical existence. The corporation, partnership, or limited liability entity (whether a limited liability company or a limited liability partnership) must meet certain legal formalities and establish that the individual signing on its behalf has the authority to do so. Previous sections have noted the legal matters that these entities must address in the contract of sale and in the loan agreement.[7] This section reviews that discussion in brief but focuses on how to draft the documents necessary to comply with those requirements.

Each party must confirm that all other parties with which it is dealing are properly formed in some jurisdiction and legally authorized to conduct business in the state in which the property is located. Each of these entities must next authorize its own role in the transaction and must verify that its counterparts have done the same. The board of directors of a corporation, for example, must pass a resolution authorizing the transaction and designating those persons who are permitted to sign documents on its behalf. This resolution should be accompanied by a waiver of notice of the meeting at which the resolution was passed, signed by all directors, to avoid any subsequent claim by a disgruntled director that the meeting was improperly convened. The resolution should clarify the degree to which each person who will attend the closing possesses corporate authority to modify documents, just in case the terms of the deal should continue to evolve until the last minute. The corporation also should provide an incumbency certificate that lists these authorized signatories, states their titles within the organization, and includes specimens of their signatures. In some cases, larger entities may pass blanket resolutions authorizing all transactions of a certain type rather than authorizing each transaction individually. Similar authorizations are required of partnerships and limited liability entities that are involved in the transaction.

---

*Comment:* If a party wishes to confirm that its counterpart is legally authorized to conduct business in the state in which the property is located, it should order a good standing certificate for the other entity from that state. This certificate will verify that the entity is in good standing there.

---

Special board meetings can be difficult to schedule. The lawyer must be sure to prepare these documents sufficiently far in advance that the principals of the entity will have time to meet, to consider whether to authorize the transaction, and to grant the entity's approval. Opposing counsel will want to review and approve the language of these entity documents, and it might be wise to provide the proposed language to all other parties before your entity client grants its approval, just in case one of the other parties has a legitimate objection to the proposed language. If state law and the entity's organizational documents permit, these matters may be handled by unanimous written consent without the need to convene a special meeting.

To the extent that any outside party must grant its consent to any aspect of the transaction, the lawyer should be sure to include this approval on the closing checklist. Lenders, ground lessors, bankruptcy trustees, tenants, utilities, franchisors, and municipalities may all need to approve portions of the transaction, and the lawyer should contact these parties as soon as possible. The lawyer may need to pursue these consents relentlessly, as outside parties have far less incentive to act speedily than do the parties to the transaction. In some cases these parties will prepare their own documents, while in others they may ask the requesting party to prepare a draft for them.

Ordinarily, there will be no need for authorizations of this type with respect to any individual who is a party to the transaction.[8] One issue that occasionally arises is the method of participation of an individual who will be unable to attend the closing and execute the necessary documents in person. In some cases, this party may be content to execute the documents in advance and entrust them to his lawyer or to an escrow agent for delivery at the closing. The other parties may agree to such an arrangement, but this approach will probably preclude the parties from making any changes to the documents after the absent party becomes unavailable. A preferable alternative may be to have the individual execute a power of attorney, authorizing someone else—perhaps his lawyer, a family member, or a friend—to modify and execute documents on his behalf at the closing.

---

*Comment:* An individual can give a power of attorney, but a corporation or other entity cannot. Entities must provide different types of authorizations, such as corporate resolutions.

---

It should be apparent from this discussion that the power of attorney serves many of the same functions as the entity authorizations described earlier. The power of attorney should clearly state how much latitude the attorney-in-fact has with respect to modifying documents so that there is no dispute at the closing if the documents must be changed. The parties must also be sure that the form of the power of attorney complies with state law requirements. This last point is important, because the power of attorney may have to be recorded in the land records so that subsequent searchers of title can establish the validity of a recorded document executed by an apparent stranger to title. In other words, the lawyer for the absent party must be sure that all other parties approve the form and the language of the power of attorney before this party executes it and becomes unavailable.

---

*Comment:* Forms of power of attorney vary greatly from state to state. If an individual intends to send a representative who is authorized to execute documents on his behalf, the parties should take great care to verify that the form of power of attorney meets all legal requirements and satisfies the title insurance company. In addition, the authorization is ineffective unless it can be shown that the person giving the power is

alive and of sound mind as of the time of the closing and that he has not
revoked the power of attorney.

## §7.08—Form: Certificate of Secretary, with Attached Resolutions

See Appendix O for a Form of Certificate of Secretary, with Attached
Resolutions.

## §7.09—Bill of Sale

The deed conveys real property but not personal property, and the
seller will also need to execute a bill of sale to convey most types of
personal property. The bill of sale is, in essence, a deed to the personal property, and it accomplishes the same result as the deed. The
bill of sale should contain a list of all the personal property that the
seller is conveying. This list is analogous to the legal description in
the real property deed and defines the personal property that the
seller is transferring to the buyer.

Some personal items cannot be conveyed by a bill of sale. The
clearest example is motor vehicles, for which the state issues a certificate of title. The seller must sign this certificate and deliver it to the
buyer, who must then have a new certificate issued in its own name.
Personal property of this type is more like real property in Torrens
jurisdictions, and the transfer should be just as easy to accomplish
(once the seller locates its title certificate, of course).

The lender will have its own concerns about the personal property. It not only will want assurances that the seller has conveyed
all significant personalty to the buyer, but also will want to perfect a security interest in that personal property. The buyer grants
this security interest to the lender by executing a security agreement, and the lender perfects its interest by filing a properly executed UCC financing statement (UCC-1). Once again, the method
of perfection will differ for motor vehicles and some other types of
personal property, as established by Article 9 of the Uniform Commercial Code.[9] This discussion also should remind the buyer and
the lender to perform their own UCC search, to confirm that no
other lender already holds a perfected security interest in this personal property.

The role of the lawyers here centers on document preparation.
The bill of sale is a short document, and the UCC financing statement is a one-page form that must meet state filing requirements.

The security agreement may be somewhat lengthier but largely is analogous to the mortgage. The lawyers also need to be sure that the list of property is accurate, which probably means conferring with their respective clients and reviewing any listing of items contained in the contract of sale.

In addition, the lawyers must remember to be attentive to any sales tax consequences of this aspect of the transaction. The contract should have already addressed responsibility for paying these costs.[10] Any potentially liable parties must be sure that the party that is contractually responsible for paying these taxes delivers the correct amounts to the appropriate taxing authorities.

### § 7.10—Form: Bill of Sale

See Appendix P for a Form of Bill of Sale.

## § 7.11 Title Insurance

Earlier sections of this book introduced title insurance matters in different contexts. These sections discussed title insurance in general,[11] described title insurance matters that concern the buyer,[12] and noted the related issues that worry the lender.[13] These discussions pointed out that the parties can resolve many title matters before the closing: the title search should reveal any title problems, and due diligence work by the seller and others may clear up the problems that the search revealed. This section discusses how the parties prepare for those aspects of the closing that pertain to title insurance, how they resolve last-minute title insurance issues, and what happens when they cannot resolve these issues.

The main concern for the buyer and the lender is to make sure that someone has addressed each of the outstanding problems disclosed in the title commitment. By offering the initial commitment, the insurer has stated its willingness to provide insurance on the terms contained in that commitment. To the extent that those terms were not yet acceptable, the buyer and the lender should have voiced their objections, and the seller, the buyer, and the title company should have taken the steps necessary to address each concern. If all of these problems have not been resolved by the closing, then the buyer or the lender may refuse to close, assuming that the contract and the loan commitment contain closing conditions that protect their interests adequately. The buyer and the lender will not proceed to close until each of them receives either an acceptable and irrevocable commitment from the title company or an actual policy of title insurance on acceptable terms.

The primary focus of each of these parties will be the list of title exceptions that appears in Schedule B of the commitment. To the greatest extent possible, the buyer and the lender will seek the removal of every exception that these parties did not agree in advance to accept.[14] If an old mortgage still encumbers title to the premises, then the seller should locate the record holder or its successor and obtain and record a satisfaction. If a mechanic has placed a lien on the property, then the seller should pay the mechanic or obtain a bond that serves as substitute security for the mechanic's claim. If the title documents or the survey disclose a boundary dispute with a neighbor, the seller and the neighbor should resolve it. The only exceptions remaining on Schedule B should be those that the parties agreed in advance would remain—such as mortgages to be assumed by the buyer or acceptable reciprocal easement agreements—or any newly discovered matters that the buyer and the lender deem to be acceptable. The insurer should also remove those standard exceptions that it has promised to remove and should provide any endorsements requested by the buyer or the lender and agreed to by the title company.

---

*Comment:* As noted previously, a list of permitted exceptions is frequently attached as an exhibit to the contract of sale. This exhibit specifies those items the buyer is willing to accept as exceptions to title. Schedule B of the title commitment should parallel this list of permitted exceptions.

---

The title company should update Schedule A of the buyer's and lender's title commitments at the closing to reflect the new owner, the new lender, their respective interests in the property, and the date and time of the last title search. This information will differ from that contained in the initial title commitment. Schedule A of the policy also should reflect any changes in the amounts of insurance resulting from adjustments to the sale price or the loan amount.

Note finally that if the parties are unable to resolve a material title matter before the closing, they will have to postpone the closing, come up with an acceptable way of handling the problem after the closing, modify the terms of the transaction, or terminate the transaction. In some cases, a postponement will give the seller the time it needs to resolve an ongoing dispute or to locate a missing document. In other situations, the seller may convince the buyer to live with the unexpected risk in return for a reduction in the sale price or the seller's promise to resolve the problem later. The buyer may not be comfortable employing this last option unless the seller gives it some security, such as an escrow fund, on which it can draw if the seller fails to perform its new post-closing obligation. If none of these solutions works, the buyer and the lender may decide to exercise their contractual right not to close because of the seller's failure to deliver marketable title.

This worst-case scenario highlights once more the importance of beginning the title investigation promptly after the parties sign the contract. The sooner the insurer delivers its title commitment, the more time the parties will have to resolve any problems by the closing. If the parties cannot resolve a title issue, they will learn this fact early on and can modify or terminate their contract.

## §7.12 Payoff Letters and Satisfactions of Existing Mortgages

The seller, like most property owners, may previously have mortgaged the property to its own lender. In many transactions, the buyer plans to obtain new financing of its own and does not want the existing financing to survive the closing. The existing mortgage will appear on Schedule B of the title commitment, but no one should be surprised to find this financing listed as an exception, and the seller will plan to pay this loan off at the closing out of the sale proceeds.

---

*Comment:* Both the seller and the buyer should carefully ascertain whether the existing loan is prepayable. If the loan can be prepaid, the parties need to determine whether there is a prepayment fee and what that fee is.

---

The seller probably cannot pay its loan off in advance, which means that the existing lender will be unwilling to deliver a satisfaction of the mortgage or a reconveyance of the deed of trust before the closing. The events necessary to remove the lien and transfer title to the buyer must all happen simultaneously, and until they do, the mortgage remains unsatisfied of record and continues to appear as an exception in the title commitment.

The buyer, the buyer's lender, and the title insurer may not be terribly concerned about this typical cloud on title, but the buyer and the buyer's lender must be certain that the title company insures over this exception or removes it from the commitment at or before the closing. In a very large transaction, the existing lender may send a representative to the closing to return the seller's note and to deliver a mortgage satisfaction immediately upon repayment, but in the overwhelming majority of cases the existing lender will not want to be troubled to this degree.[15] As a substitute, the seller should seek an acceptable payoff letter from its existing lender. The lender also may be willing to deliver a satisfaction of the mortgage in escrow.

A "payoff letter" is a letter from the existing lender that states the amount the lender must receive before it will return the seller's note and execute and deliver a recordable satisfaction of mortgage. The payoff amount is a moving target because interest accrues daily. The letter thus should state the principal and accrued interest as of a specific date along with a per diem interest amount, so the parties can come up with a precise number even if they postpone the closing. The parties must be sure to remit these funds to the existing lender promptly to stop further interest from accruing.

Payoff letters may contain qualifications, and the existing lender may state that it is not responsible for calculation errors or other mistakes. The seller should attempt to obtain as unqualified a letter as it can. If the title company is comfortable with the payoff letter and with the identity of the existing lender, as it often is, it may be willing to insure over the existing mortgage on the basis of the payoff letter once it knows that the funds necessary to satisfy the mortgage have been delivered. The mortgage will continue to be listed on Schedule B until the satisfaction is recorded, because it still is an exception to title, but the title company will agree to make the buyer and the buyer's lender whole if the existing lender seeks recourse against the property. If the insurer is uncomfortable insuring over the existing mortgage on the basis of a payoff letter—as it might be if the lender is not an institutional lender—then the parties may have to place the closing documents and the funds in escrow until the existing lender receives its payoff and delivers the mortgage satisfaction.[16]

Once the parties receive the mortgage satisfaction, they should record it promptly. The recording of the satisfaction informs the world that the loan has been paid and that the mortgage no longer has any legal effect. At this point, the title insurer should remove the mortgage from Schedule B, as the mortgage no longer encumbers the property.

Existing lenders are sometimes slow to return original notes and to deliver mortgage satisfactions. Many states now have legislation requiring delivery of these documents within a stated time period. Some of these statutes impose stiff penalties on the existing lender if it fails to comply with these obligations.

---

*Comment:* In a world in which many mortgages have been securitized and many financial institutions have merged or been sold, it can be difficult to determine precisely which party must issue the mortgage satisfaction and to obtain the satisfaction from that party.

---

## §7.13 Opinions of Counsel

Previous sections have emphasized the important role that legal opinion letters play in real estate closings.[17] As part of the closing preparation, each lawyer should be sure that all of the required opinions are in progress, including letters to be prepared by others.

Drafting an opinion letter for a client can be a formidable and time-consuming task. The lawyer preparing the opinion may have to review many of the client's internal documents and may need to rely, in turn, on another lawyer's opinion letter.[18] Many law firms have strict internal review procedures for issuing legal opinions because of the enormous liability that can result from delivering an erroneous opinion. Moreover, these opinion letters are often long and complex, and opposing counsel will want to review them before the closing. The opinion itself may not be required until the closing, but the lawyer must initiate the process of producing the letter much earlier than that. In recent years, the real estate industry has developed standard form opinions, and lawyers have become more willing to provide and accept opinions that conform to these so-called Accords.[19]

---

*Comment:* The complex process of drafting and negotiating opinions is beyond the purview of this book. Opinions vary widely, depending on whether the opinion is issued to a seller, a buyer, or a lender, and forms of opinions vary from state to state. The matters to be addressed in each opinion of counsel should be carefully negotiated in the contract of sale or the loan commitment. As part of their closing preparation, the lawyers should review the opinion letters and verify that the opinions discuss these agreed matters.

## §7.14 Method of Payment

The contract of sale should list the acceptable method or methods for the buyer's payment of the purchase price. If the contract does not expressly state that payment in cash is prohibited, then the seller cannot refuse a cash tender without breaching the contract. In practice, buyers never pay the purchase price in cash, and any buyer that wished to do so would raise suspicions. Nonetheless, the seller should be sure that the contract is clear on this point.

In some cases, part of the purchase price will be paid in a manner that does not involve the transfer of funds. The buyer may be assuming existing debt, in which case its assumption constitutes part of the consideration. The seller may be providing some of the financing itself, in which case the buyer's execution of a note and mortgage in favor of the seller constitutes part of the consideration. To the extent that the buyer is paying consideration in one of these ways, the method of payment should be evident from the contract.

In most cases, however, the buyer will deliver funds either by certified check or by wire transfer. The contract should state which of these methods the parties have agreed to. If the seller is to receive a certified check, then the buyer must obtain the check before the closing. If the seller is to receive a wire transfer, then the buyer must arrange with its bank to wire the funds. This process may require some lead time. The buyer must be sure that it has sufficient available funds in its account with the bank that will certify the check or wire the funds and also must provide proper instructions to any third-party lenders that will be providing any portion of the purchase price at the closing.

The buyer must ascertain in advance whether the funds should be delivered directly to the seller. In many cases, an escrow agent or title company will receive the funds initially and will disburse them later. Once the buyer learns this information, it next needs to determine the name of the bank to which any funds should be wired, the number of the recipient's account, the method by which it must initiate the transfer on closing day, and the name of a contact person at each bank in case something goes awry.

*Comment:* The USA Patriot Act and laws prohibiting money laundering and drug trafficking can have a significant impact on real estate practice. While the law in this area is evolving and an in-depth analysis of this topic is beyond the scope of this book, lawyers must be attentive to these issues when conducting real estate transactions.[20]

The parties need to establish in advance the precise amount of the funds to be delivered at the closing so the buyer can be sure that the check or wire transfer is for the correct amount. The parties also should recognize that other funds will change hands at the closing. They most likely will have agreed to a number of closing adjustments and apportionments in the contract.[21] These amounts will usually be netted out against one another and then added to or subtracted from the purchase price, as appropriate. If the net amount of these adjustments is likely to be substantial, then the parties should attempt to calculate the adjustments far enough in advance that the certified check or wire transfer can reflect the net adjustment. If the parties delay making these calculations until the last minute, they will have to use a personal check for any adjustments.

Other parties are likely to demand payment at the closing. Title insurers, real estate brokers, lawyers, and escrow agents all need to be paid, and in many cases they will insist on receiving their fees at the closing. Once again, the party responsible for paying these service providers—most often the buyer—must be sure to pay the correct amounts in an acceptable manner.[22]

## §7.15 Insurance Coverage

The buyer should insist—and the lender will insist—that all required insurance be in effect as of the closing date. The lender will fear that an uninsured casualty loss will diminish the value of its security or that an uninsured personal injury will leave the borrower exposed to tremendous liability. Previous sections addressed the types of insurance that the lender should require in the loan commitment,[23] and the buyer and the lender need to be sure that all necessary insurance will become effective by the closing.

The buyer should have already contacted its insurer. The insurer will provide the buyer and the lender with binders that describe the insurance to be provided. The binders will summarize the coverage that the insurer agrees to provide, but the buyer and the lender would be well advised to look beyond the binders and to request copies of the insurance policies themselves. The specific terms of the policies generally take priority over the terms of the binders, and the only way to determine the content of the policies is to review them.

The lender is likely to have an insurance specialist who can review the policies. The buyer, however, may not, and the buyer's lawyer may not feel comfortable that she is knowledgeable enough about insurance matters to provide competent advice. For this reason, the buyer may decide to engage an insurance consultant who is more conversant with insurance matters and who can provide impartial advice. The insurance consultant can help the buyer determine the adequacy of the policies and the degree to which they comply with the requirements of the various documents.

---

*Comment:* Lawyers beware! Clients sometimes rely on their lawyers to provide advice as to insurance matters. Lawyers should be careful not to undertake this responsibility.

---

## §7.16  Employment Agreements, Service Contracts, Licenses, and Other Agreements

The buyer may wish to succeed to the seller's rights under employment agreements, service contracts, franchise agreements, and licenses, and may wish to continue the seller's use of intellectual property rights and visual artists' rights.[24] The effective transfer of any of these rights may require the consent of a third party. The buyer should have raised these matters when it was negotiating the contract of sale, and the parties should have reached a written resolution of these issues. During the due diligence period, the parties should have been pursuing the necessary consents and preparing the documents needed to effect the seller's transfer of these rights to the buyer.

As part of their closing preparation, the buyer and the lender must confirm that all required consents are in place and that all of these rights can be transferred at the closing. The buyer and the lender will want to see unconditional consents from any parties that have the right to withhold permission. These two parties also will have participated in the drafting of the documents of assignment and should reassure themselves that the language of these transfer documents is satisfactory.

Liquor licenses can pose special problems, as previously noted.[25] Licensing jurisdictions examine the holders of these licenses carefully, and the seller may lack the legal authority to transfer its license to the buyer. Similarly, the buyer may be unable to pledge any interest in the liquor license to its lender. If this is the case, the parties will need to familiarize themselves with the licensing process, attempt to learn if there are likely to be any problems or delays in securing a new license, and initiate the application process as soon as they can.

## §7.17 Permits, Certificates, Warranties, Plans, and Keys

The seller may possess other legal rights that the buyer wishes to acquire, such as rights under permits and certificates and rights to enforce warranties. These rights, unlike those described in the previous section, may not require the consent of a third party before the seller can transfer them to the buyer and the buyer can pledge them to the lender. Of course, the lawyers for the buyer and the lender need to confirm that consent is not needed, and they should not reach this conclusion without reviewing the relevant documents and legal requirements. If the consent of a third party is required, then the lawyers should follow the process described in the previous section; if not, then the parties need only to effect the transfer and the pledge at the closing.

---

*Comment:* The transfer or reissuance of certain permits, certificates, and licenses issued by public agencies may require the approval of these agencies.

---

At the closing, the seller also should turn over the plans for any structures on the property. The buyer will need the plans if it ever decides to modify the structure and will probably need them even if it expects only to operate and maintain the existing structure. Copies of the plans may be available from the local building department, but these filed copies may be outdated and are likely to be expensive to copy. The seller ought to have current plans in its possession and should deliver them to the buyer.

The seller should also turn over all keys, key cards, entry codes, and other related passwords. There is no reason for the seller to object, and this delivery will save the buyer considerable expense and inconvenience.

## *§7.18 Utility Readings*

The buyer will either take over the seller's existing utility accounts or establish new relationships with each provider of an essential service. In most cases, the buyer will prefer the second option, but the first option sometimes will make more sense.[26] Either way, the parties need to request that the appropriate utility companies read their meters at approximately the time of the sale. If the buyer is taking over the seller's account, a reading of the meter just before the closing will allow the parties to apportion the cost of service for the month that includes the closing. If the buyer is establishing a new account, a reading of the meter just before the closing will allow the utility to terminate the seller's account and charge each party only for its own use.

The lawyers should remind their clients to arrange these readings with the companies that provide electricity, gas, water, sewer, local and long-distance telephone, cable television, Internet, and any other similar type of service. Each party should confirm that it has not been billed improperly for any connection or disconnection fees that the other party should bear. If the property is heated by oil, the parties should remember to check how much oil is in the tank on the day of the closing.

## *§7.19 Calculating Closing Apportionments and Adjustments*

The preceding sections addressed a number of ongoing charges that need to be apportioned as of the closing date, ranging from franchise fees to the water bill. Several other significant items need to be added to this list, including real property taxes, ground rent, fees to any property owners' association or similar organization, principal and interest on any mortgage that will survive the closing, and incoming tenant rent. The contract should already list the items that will be apportioned and adjusted at closing, along with the agreed method of making these calculations.[27]

The lawyers need to make sure that they obtain all the information they need to make each of these calculations shortly before the closing. They will need to know the amount due for the period that includes the closing date, the length of the billing period, and whether the seller has made the payment in advance or the buyer will have to make the payment in arrears. After one of the parties has made these calculations, all other parties should review them and point out any disagreements so that there is no dispute as to the net amount necessary to settle all these matters at the closing.

---

*Comment:* Under some contracts, a service provider may have offered a discount for prepayment, an introductory "teaser" rate, or a reduced rate for bundling of services. This is particularly true with regard to cable television, Internet, and telephone services. The parties should be attentive to these issues when apportioning costs.

---

---

*Comment:* In certain cases, it may be necessary to make a post-closing adjustment. For example, some tenants, particularly in residential rental properties, may be delinquent in paying their rent. When the tenant ultimately pays, the parties must determine whether amounts received after the closing should be applied to delinquent rent obligations that accrued before the closing.

---

Some amounts will not need to be apportioned. Real property assessments other than taxes may be the responsibility of the seller, although the contract should resolve this issue. If it does not, the buyer will argue that it has already factored the value of the improvement for which the assessment was levied into its offer and should not be forced to pay for part of the improvement twice. If the seller is holding any security deposits from tenants, the seller should turn them over to the buyer, which will have to reimburse the tenants when their leases end. Similarly, if a ground lessor is holding a security deposit from the seller, the buyer should reimburse the seller for this amount. If any service provider is holding a security deposit and the buyer plans to continue the seller's account, the buyer should reimburse the seller for this amount.

Various other taxes, fees, and commissions are probably the responsibility of just one party and not both parties on a prorated basis. Some of these items are discussed in the next section.

## §7.20 Calculating Fees, Commissions, Taxes, and Other Closing Costs

Many of the service providers who participate in the transaction will insist on being paid at closing, and a variety of taxes and other fees may also need to be paid. To the extent that the buyer, the seller, and the lender have entered into arrangements with parties who must be paid at the closing, they should be aware of their own obligations through their agreements with these parties, although they may not know what obligations other parties have undertaken. Note as well that responsibility for making some of these payments may not be addressed in the documents but instead may be determined by local custom, and the lawyer must become familiar with these customs.

Each lawyer must make sure to include every required payment on his or her client's internal closing checklist and on the closing statement.[28] This will remind the lawyer to calculate in advance how much is owed to each payee and to be sure that each party delivers the sums for which they are responsible at the closing. In some cases, the payee of these amounts may not be obvious, and the payor must determine the name of the party to which its check must be payable. For example, the buyer may remit the amount of the mortgage recording tax to the title insurer or an escrow agent rather than paying it directly to the taxing jurisdiction, and that third party then will record the mortgage and pay the tax.

The title insurer is ordinarily paid at the closing. The insurer will provide a lender's policy to the lender and an owner's policy to the buyer. The fee for each policy should have been worked out ahead of time—and in many places is regulated by statute—so there should be few surprises as to the amount. The insurer also may charge extra fees for certain endorsements, which the parties may have requested after negotiating the original policy premium. It is likely that the buyer will pay the premium for both of these title policies. In addition, if an escrow agent participates in the closing, that party will need to be paid on closing day.

Real estate brokerage commissions will also be paid at closing, to the extent they have not been paid previously. Depending on the terms of the brokerage agreement, the broker may have earned some or all of the commission at an earlier point, such as when the contract was signed, and may have been paid then. Similarly, any mortgage brokers will demand payment at the closing to the extent they have not already been paid.

Some or all of the lawyers may insist on being paid at the closing. This is particularly true of the lender's counsel, who is probably being paid by the borrower and does not want to have to pursue payment later from this nonclient. In fact, the lender may have insisted on a closing condition in the loan commitment that mandates payment of the lender's legal fees by the borrower before the lender is required to close. If the lawyer for the buyer or the seller is representing a regular and reliable client, that lawyer may not be so insistent that its own client pay its legal fees at the closing.

The parties themselves may also be entitled to payment. This is particularly true of the lender, which may require that the borrower reimburse some of its costs. For instance, if the property is not located near an office of the lender, the lender may have demanded that the borrower pay the travel and lodging costs incurred by its representatives who attend the closing. The borrower also may still owe the lender some portion of the lender's commitment fee.

The closing of title and the lending of funds often lead to a variety of taxes, fees, and other charges imposed by government authorities. The nature of these charges, the amounts of the fees, and the identity of the person responsible for paying them may vary substantially from place to place, but the parties must make sure that all necessary amounts are accounted for at the closing. For example, the county recorder may be required to impose a transfer tax on the seller, a mortgage recording tax on the borrower, and a per-page recording fee on each party recording a document. The Internal Revenue Service may demand withholding of some of the purchase price because the seller is a foreign entity. The city may have imposed a lien for unpaid real property taxes, which must be paid out of the closing funds so that the seller can deliver marketable title. Some of these charges may be subject to interest and penalties for late payment. The parties must be sure to calculate these amounts ahead of time and see that the proper party pays them at the closing.

---

*Comment:* The buyer and the seller both need to take great care in determining who is responsible for paying transfer taxes, mortgage taxes, recording costs, and other similar fees. These costs can be substantial.

---

*Comment:* Some states have withholding requirements that apply if the seller is a nonresident. The parties must be extremely careful to comply with these withholding provisions.

---

Certain other parties probably will have been paid before the closing. These parties, who may have played a more minor role in the transaction, probably demanded payment at the time they provided a service. They completed their performance earlier in the process and earned their fee, and they wanted to be sure they were paid even if the deal did not close. Surveyors, appraisers, and inspectors such as architects and engineers may fall into this category.

## §7.21 Notices

The fact that title is changing hands probably means that someone needs to send official notices to a variety of affected parties. The parties most obviously affected by the sale are the tenants at the property. They will need to make their rent checks payable to their new landlord and may need to mail them to a new address, and the new owner will become the party the tenants must contact in the event of a problem. Notice of this change in ownership should come from the seller, and any tenant who receives a notice signed only by the buyer—a stranger to them—may refuse to treat it as valid until the seller confirms its validity. These notices should comply with the notice provisions contained in the various tenant leases and should be delivered in accordance with those provisions. The lawyers should include these notices on their checklist and should prepare them before the closing.

Other parties also may be entitled to notice. If the buyer is succeeding to the seller's rights under any employment agreements, service contracts, or franchise agreements, the seller must send notices to the other parties to these contracts. These parties probably know that the sale is pending, and may have had to consent, but they will not know whether title has passed to the buyer until the seller so notifies them. These notices need to be prepared for the seller's signature ahead of time and should be included on the closing checklist.

## §7.22 The Walk-Through

The buyer and the lender should perform a final inspection of the property as close to the closing date as possible. This inspection should take the form of a careful "walk-through," and representatives of each of these parties should examine the property thoroughly. One purpose of this walk-through is to ensure that the seller has made all repairs that it is supposed to make, including those set forth in the contract and those that became necessary as a result of the buyer's and lender's due diligence. A second purpose is to make sure that no new problems have arisen since the parties last examined the premises. Any problems that still need to be resolved should be enumerated on the "punch list," and items later can be removed from this list as they are addressed.

If the parties perform the walk-through just before the closing, the seller may not have time to resolve all the punch-list items before it conveys title to the buyer. The buyer, however, will want these repairs charged to the seller. There are two ways to accomplish this goal, and the parties should have stated in the contract which method they will use. The buyer can agree to make these repairs and can receive a credit against the purchase price for the estimated cost. Some buyers prefer this approach because they can oversee the repairs themselves rather than relying on a seller with an obvious incentive to cut corners. Other buyers may not wish to assume this responsibility or may fear that the cost estimate will prove to be low.

A second way to ensure that the punch-list items are addressed is to leave the responsibility for them with the seller. The seller can agree contractually that it will make these repairs after the closing. Remember that the contract of sale may merge into the deed at the closing, so the buyer and the lender will want to be sure that the seller's obligation to make these repairs survives. In some cases, they will achieve this goal by entering into a separate agreement before the closing, often referred to as a "post-closing agreement," that addresses the matters that the seller must resolve after the closing. The buyer would be wise to ask that some of the purchase price be held in escrow until these repairs are made so that it can draw against these funds if the seller breaches the post-closing agreement and the buyer ends up making the repairs. If this is how the parties resolve the problem, then the lawyers will have to include escrow provisions in the post-closing agreement setting forth how much money is to be held and by whom, along with the conditions under which these funds can be released to the appropriate party.

---

*Comment:* In some cases, the seller will wish to retain possession of the property after the closing. This occurs most commonly in residential transactions. In these circumstances, the parties should work out an agreement as to responsibility for insurance, maintenance, upkeep, and repair. The buyer also should have a right of reinspection when the seller turns the premises over to the buyer.

---

*§ 7.23—Form: Post-Closing Agreement*

See Appendix Q for a Form of Post-Closing Agreement.

## § 7.24 The Closing Statement

The parties should prepare a closing statement that lists all of the amounts that are to be paid at closing and the party to whom each of these payments will be made. The statement should also list all payments that have been made prior to the closing. The closing statement serves several different functions. Years later, the parties may have only the cloudiest recollection as to who paid what sums to whom, and the closing statement memorializes all of these transfers in writing in a single document. The closing statement also will be helpful when auditors and accountants review the parties' books and assist them in preparing their tax returns. This statement is essential to the seller, which now must calculate its gain or loss on the property, and will serve a similar function for the buyer when it ultimately disposes of the property. If the parties later suspect that one of the closing amounts was incorrect, they can establish exactly what happened at the closing by reviewing the closing statement. The closing statement also helps the parties calculate a single net amount that must change hands at the closing, rather than passing numerous checks back and forth to account for various minor closing adjustments and apportionments.

Some parties may prefer to use a formal closing statement that is signed by all parties, while others may favor a simple and less formal memorandum that they retain in their files. In addition, some parties might prefer that certain closing costs, such as their own legal fees, not appear on the closing statement for confidentiality reasons. These amounts can be documented in a separate memorandum rather than in a closing statement available to everyone at the closing, but they should be memorialized in some form.

---

*Comment:* The Department of Housing and Urban Development has prepared a form, known as the HUD-1, that must be used for this purpose in residential transactions. Parties to commercial real estate transactions may find that this form can serve as a useful guide and reminder, and may even choose to use the HUD-1 form itself.

---

## Notes

1. *See infra* §§ 8.01–8.03.
2. *See infra* § 7.12.
3. *See infra* § 8.07.
4. *See infra* § 7.06.
5. *See infra* § 8.08.
6. Such a list probably is unnecessary in a quitclaim deed, in which the seller is not warranting the quality of its title.
7. *See supra* §§ 2.32–2.34, 2.65–2.67, 2.78, 2.105, 3.61–3.63, 4.05–4.06, 5.01.
8. If this individual should happen to be a minor, the beneficiary of a trust, someone who is legally incompetent, or a married person whose spouse may have marital interests in the property under state law, then the guardian, trustee, or spouse may need to execute or consent to the operative documents.
9. *See supra* §§ 6.27–6.38.
10. *See supra* §§ 2.26, 2.28.
11. *See supra* §§ 2.82–2.85, 3.06–3.08.
12. *See supra* §§ 2.82–2.85, 3.06–3.29.
13. *See supra* §§ 5.03–5.05.
14. For a more detailed discussion of Schedule B matters, including a listing of common encumbrances and methods of addressing them, see *supra* §§ 2.82–2.85, 3.06–3.29, 5.03–5.05.
15. If the existing lender is an individual, such as a principal of the buyer entity or of the seller entity, then this person may attend the closing.
16. *See infra* § 8.03 (discussing escrow closings).
17. *See supra* §§ 2.95–2.96, 2.106, 3.64, 4.17.
18. For example, if a Texas lawyer is opining as to the propriety of actions taken by his own client, a Texas limited partnership, and the sole general partner of this partnership is a Missouri corporation, the Texas lawyer may have to rely on an opinion letter from a Missouri lawyer. The Texas lawyer probably cannot opine as to matters of Missouri law, such as whether the corporation has taken all actions required to authorize the transaction.
19. *See supra* § 2.95.
20. *See infra* Appendix B.
21. *See supra* § 2.115; *infra* § 7.19.
22. *See infra* §§ 7.20, 8.09.
23. *See supra* §§ 4.10, 5.14.
24. *See supra* §§ 2.53, 2.55–2.57.
25. *See supra* § 2.27.
26. For example, if the sale is a stock sale rather than an asset sale, the seller will be transferring stock in the owner entity rather than transferring title to the property itself. The same entity will own the property before

and after the sale; the only difference will be that the buyer will now own all the shares of stock in that entity. From the point of view of the electric company, nothing has changed, and the same customer is receiving service and paying its bill.

27. *See supra* §2.115.
28. *See infra* §7.24.

# CHAPTER 8

# Running the Closing

## § 8.01 Structure of a Typical Closing

The closing is the event that formally marks the passage of title from the seller to the buyer. Unlike the contract of sale and the loan commitment, which are executory contracts, the deed that the seller delivers to the buyer at the closing is more than just a promise of future performance: it operates to convey the property legally. The closing also provides an opportunity for all closing conditions to be met simultaneously so that no party must meet its obligations without knowing whether its counterparts also will perform.[1] As noted in the previous chapter, the structure of the closing should be designed to meet these two goals, by reminding the parties of the significance of their actions and by ensuring that all parties perform concurrently. The next two sections discuss the structure of the closing in more detail.

## § 8.02—The Table, or New York–Style, Closing

The more traditional type of closing takes the form of a gathering in a conference room, often at the office of the title company or one of the lawyers. Each of the parties to the transaction sends a representative who is authorized to execute documents on that party's behalf, and the other service providers, such as title company representatives and lawyers, perform their designated roles. This type of closing is sometimes referred to as a "table closing" or a "New York–style closing."

If all of the parties are located near each other, a table closing is a convenient way of finalizing the transaction. The table closing also allows all unmet closing conditions to be satisfied simultaneously. The buyer will not want to tender the purchase price to the seller until the seller's current lender delivers either a satisfaction of the current mortgage or a payoff letter stating exactly how much money the seller must repay before the current lender will deliver this satisfaction. The buyer's lender does not want to tender the loan proceeds to the buyer until it is confident that the mortgage the buyer is delivering in return will be the only mortgage on the property. The seller does not want to execute and deliver the deed until the buyer delivers a certified check or wires the funds. If all the documents and parties are in the same room at the same time, everyone can keep an eye on the events that are unfolding and can make sure that everyone else is fully performing their obligations.

### § 8.03—The Escrow Closing

In many cases, it may be impossible or impractical to hold a table closing. The parties may be located in different parts of the country or different parts of the world. One of the conditions precedent may have to be met by a third party, such as a government permitting body, that cannot or will not perform until it is certain that another party has performed first. A necessary document, such as an old note, may be missing, and the parties may wish to complete all the closing formalities without actually transferring title until the missing document is found. Or the parties might simply have conflicting schedules and may find it more convenient and less expensive to dispense with a New York–style closing. For any of a number of reasons, the parties may prefer an alternative closing structure.

In cases such as this, the parties may decide to hold an "escrow closing," a structure that has become increasingly common. The parties select an escrow agent or closing agent and entrust the documents and the funds to this agent. This escrow agent may be the title company, the lawyer for one of the parties, or a representative of an escrow company. In some areas in which escrow closings are common, escrow companies perform this function on a regular basis. In these parts of the country, table closings may be rare even when the parties are available.

---

*Comment:* It is dangerous for any lawyer involved in the transaction to act as the escrow agent. Unless there is a clear agreement setting forth the role of the lawyer in the event of a dispute, it is possible that she will not be able to represent her client after a dispute arises: her role as escrow agent, in which she was acting for the benefit of both parties, will disqualify her from representing one of them.[2] For this reason, most lawyers prefer that a title company or an escrow company serve as the escrow agent.

---

The parties and the escrow agent will enter into a written agreement that defines the responsibilities of each of them, or the parties will provide the agent with a detailed closing instruction letter.[3] The agreement or letter will list all the conditions that the buyer, the seller, the lender, and all other parties must meet before they are deemed to have performed their obligations. If everyone performs as they are supposed to, the escrow agreement or instruction letter will authorize the escrow agent to release all documents and funds to specified parties. Once this happens, the closing will be complete, and title will have passed as effectively as if the parties had held a table closing. If one or more of the parties does not perform, the agreement or letter will instruct the escrow agent what to do next to protect the rights of the nonbreaching parties.

The escrow closing allows the parties to effect the transaction without the need to assemble everyone in the same room at the same time. For this reason, the parties may find this structure more convenient to use. The disadvantage of the escrow closing is that there may be a period of days or weeks during which the outcome is uncertain. If one of the parties has not performed but the escrow period has not yet expired, then everyone simply must wait.

The contract of sale and the loan commitment should each state when, where, and how the closing will occur. These documents should also clarify how the parties must meet their closing conditions. The closing checklist, which should track these documents, will assist the parties in closing in accordance with their chosen method.

The remainder of this chapter discusses some of these closing mechanics in more detail. This discussion assumes that the parties have agreed to use a table closing, but it will be obvious how to modify the discussion if the parties have decided to close in escrow instead.

## § 8.04 Following the Closing Checklist

If the parties and their lawyers have prepared for the closing properly, then the closing itself should flow smoothly. Each lawyer will follow his or her closing checklist and will instruct his client to perform only if all other parties meet their concurrent obligations. The seller will be content to execute the deed and place it on the table if it knows that the deed will remain on the table until the buyer delivers the purchase price, while the buyer will be willing to deliver the purchase price because it sees the seller's executed deed sitting on the table. At the closing, the parties and their lawyers should need only to follow the checklist, ensure that all parties meet all of their obligations, and confirm that everyone leaves the room at the end with the correct documents and funds.

Of course, problems may arise. A last-minute title update may reveal an unexpected mechanics' lien, a promised satisfaction of an old mortgage may not be received in time, a tenant estoppel may arrive on the day of the closing and disclose a dispute with the landlord, and an opinion letter from one of the lawyers may not provide the other party with the level of comfort it wants. The fact that these problems arise at the last minute does not change their nature, although it may change the urgency with which the parties must resolve them. In other words, the parties will probably have to address these problems in much the way they would have had the problems surfaced earlier but with modifications to reflect the abbreviated time schedule they now face. If the title company is confident that the old mortgage has been paid in full, it may be comfortable insuring over the mortgage until the satisfaction arrives and can be recorded. If the seller does not have time to resolve its dispute with its tenant, the parties may decide to hold a portion of the purchase price in escrow until the buyer can resolve it. On rare occasions, the parties may have to postpone the closing in the hope that they will be able to satisfy the remaining closing conditions with some extra time. On even rarer occasions, the parties may have to terminate the contract altogether.

> *Comment:* If the contract contains a "time is of the essence" clause, then the closing may not be postponed over the objection of one of the parties. If the contract does not contain such a clause, then courts will generally find that a party may postpone the closing even if another party objects.

If the closing is a table closing, each lawyer will follow his or her own checklist at the closing, as described in the remaining sections of this chapter. If the closing is an escrow closing, then the lawyers must provide instructions to the escrow agent. In some cases, all parties will enter into a single escrow agreement, while in other cases, each party will provide its own set of instructions to the escrow agent. These individualized sets of instructions typically appear in closing instruction letters from each party.

### § 8.05—Form: Closing Instruction Letter from Buyer

See Appendix R for a Form of Closing Instruction Letter from Buyer.

## § 8.06 Title Insurance

The buyer and the lender should not leave the closing without each receiving either an acceptable policy of title insurance or an acceptable and irrevocable title commitment conditioned only on performance of matters entirely within the insured party's control.[4] If the insurer provides an actual title insurance policy at the closing, this policy will probably not be in a clean and unmarked format. More likely, the title agent will mark up the most recent title commitment, updating the Schedule A information and omitting or insuring over some of the Schedule B exceptions. When the commitment is in final form, the agent will write the word "insured" on the policy and sign it. After the closing, the insured party will receive a clean version of this policy, which should be identical in all material respects.

Alternatively, the buyer or the lender may accept a marked-up version of the commitment if the only conditions precedent to the company's issuance of a title policy are matters entirely within the insured party's control. This is particularly likely in those locales in which title companies do not customarily issue actual insurance policies at the closing. If the title commitment is in acceptable form and the only condition that the buyer still must meet to obtain the final policy is payment of the premium, it can pay the premium at the closing or it can leave the closing without paying, as long as it remembers to meet this condition before the commitment expires. There obviously is less risk in meeting the condition at the closing, and there probably is no reason not to finalize this important matter at the closing. Once again, the insured party must confirm that when the insurance policy arrives, it conforms to the commitment.

The lawyers for the buyer and the lender also need to confirm that the final commitment and the final policy include all necessary endorsements and that the insurer has correctly calculated the cost for the title insurance. This last matter is of particular concern to the buyer, which probably is paying for both policies.

---

*Comment:* When the final title insurance policy arrives, the lawyers for the buyer and the lender should check carefully to be sure there are no exceptions for open mortgages that were to be satisfied out of the proceeds of the sale or the loan.

---

*Comment:* Almost as important as the title policy may be the receipt of a so-called insured closing letter from the title insurance company. When the parties are working with a title agency rather than with the title insurance company itself, the insured closing letter confirms that the title company stands behind the policy. Unless there is such a letter in the file from the title insurance company, the company may not be responsible for defalcation, theft, or fraudulent acts by the agent. On rare occasions, the lawyer may even find out later that the agent had actually been suspended prior to the closing.

---

## §8.07 Execution and Acknowledgment of Documents

One of the principal activities that the parties undertake at the closing is the execution of documents. Shortly before the closing, the lawyers should confirm that the documents are in their final form. They should verify that all exhibits have been attached, all blanks filled in, and all documents dated. The lawyers then should make sure that the correct number of copies of each unsigned document has been prepared[5] and that the signature lines and acknowledgment blocks of each document are tabbed for easy access. If the client is an entity, it may require the lawyer to initial the signature line as a means of confirming that the lawyer reviewed the document before the entity's authorized representative signed it. The lawyers should take care that any documents to be recorded or filed comply with the technical requirements of the office that must accept them.[6]

At the closing, the lawyer for each party should hand each copy of each unsigned document to the person who is to sign on behalf of that lawyer's client. The lawyer should be careful that this person signs every document in the correct place and does not miss any copies of any document. The lawyer should also be sure that all other parties to the document execute it properly and that a notary public is present to observe the necessary signatures.

---

*Comment:* In some states, a lawyer who is admitted to practice in that state must sign certain documents to certify that they were prepared under his supervision.

---

Operative documents are generally valid when they are executed and delivered, but some documents must also comply with additional requirements established by state or local law. The most important of these requirements are those applicable to documents that will be recorded or filed. The deed, the mortgage, the assignment of leases and rents, subordination agreements, memoranda of leases, and satisfactions of existing mortgages must all be recorded in the recording office of the county or counties in which the property is located. In addition, Uniform Commercial Code financing statements and termination statements will have to be filed in accordance with state law.

Any document that is to be recorded must be acknowledged before a notary public who is properly licensed in the state in which the party executes the document. If the closing takes place in Tennessee and the property is located in Colorado, then any signature placed on the document in Tennessee must be acknowledged before a notary public licensed by the state of Tennessee. If the closing is an escrow closing and the other party will be signing the document beforehand at its office in Illinois, then that party's signature must be acknowledged before an Illinois notary public. However, the language used in the acknowledgment form must comply with the requirements established in Colorado, because the recording official who accepts the document will be a Colorado official. State forms vary, and the states are not uniform in their willingness and legal authority to accept forms that differ from their own. The lawyer also should be aware that the acknowledgment forms for individuals, corporations, partnerships, and limited liability entities may differ. Title company officials are familiar with acknowledgment requirements and are useful resources for lawyers who are uncertain how to handle these matters.

The lawyer should make sure that the notary public affixes any necessary stamps or seals to the document if state law requires more than just the signature of the notary. The lawyer must also be certain that the notary actually witnesses the execution of the document.[7] If the acknowledgment is incomplete or inadequate as to form, or if the notary does not witness the signature, the acknowledgment may be invalid. A document with an invalid acknowledgment may be deemed to be unrecorded under state law. In addition, states can impose hefty penalties on notaries who certify in writing signatures that they did not actually witness.

---

*Comment:* In some states, the date of the instrument may not be later than the date of the last acknowledgment, while in other states, the date of the instrument may not be earlier than the date of the last acknowledgment. The rules pertaining to the dating of documents can be complex, and the lawyers need to be familiar with the laws of the state in which any document is to be recorded.

---

## § 8.08 Multiple Copies

The lawyers should consider in advance how many signed originals of each document they will need. Each party to the document should receive an original that has been signed by all parties, and the lawyers for these parties often want originals for their own files. Any document to be recorded or filed with a public official must be an original, and the title company may wish to receive originals as well. Thus it will not be unusual for the parties to choose to execute multiple originals of many of the closing documents.

There are two important exceptions. One of these is obvious. There should be only one original of each check or certified check to be delivered at the closing. The second exception may not be quite as apparent to the lawyer with less experience: the borrower should *never* sign more than one original note, and this unique original note should be delivered to the lender. The note may well be a negotiable instrument, and if two or more original negotiable notes end up in the hands of holders in due course, whether by accident or by fraud on the part of the original holders, the borrower—or, more likely, the malpractice insurer for the borrower's lawyer—is responsible for paying the claims of all holders in due course and then seeking recourse from the parties that improperly negotiated the instruments to some of them. The defenses of prior payment or lack of consideration will not defeat the claim of a holder in due course. Any party other than the lender that wants a copy of the note for its files should be satisfied with a photocopy that is clearly marked as a copy. For related reasons, if any existing debt is paid off at the closing, the maker of the note should be sure that the original note is returned to it and marked "paid."

---

*Comment:* Lost original notes are a huge problem in the real estate industry. Every state has a procedure for enforcing lost notes, but these procedures can be slow and cumbersome. Title companies may be willing to accept affidavits as to lost notes or copies of original notes that have been marked "paid."

---

Some lawyers for sellers balk at delivering multiple originals of the deed, and some lawyers for borrowers have similar reservations about delivering duplicate originals of the mortgage or deed of trust. There probably is little reason for concern about executing multiple originals of these documents. Unlike original notes, where physical possession of the piece of paper has important legal consequences, originals of the deed and mortgage generally have no special significance. This is not universally true, however, and the lawyer needs to become familiar with state law on this point.

---

*Comment:* In some states, the mortgage serves as the actual evidence of the indebtedness. It is very important in these states that the borrower execute only a single mortgage.

---

Note also that the law in some states requires production of the original deed of trust before the public trustee will release the deed of trust in the land records. In these states, the beneficiary of the deed of trust should treat it in the same careful way that it treats the grantor's note.

Once a document is recorded, the copy in the land records is admissible in evidence if a legal dispute arises later. The buyer and the lender will not usually face any significant problems if they cannot locate the original documents that were delivered to them at the closing.

## §8.09 Delivery and Distribution of Funds

Any party that is entitled to be paid at the closing, and in particular the seller, will probably insist on receiving its funds at the closing. If the closing is a table closing, a party that is entitled to receive funds will not allow other parties to leave with their documents until it receives a certified check or confirmation that wired funds have found their way into the correct bank account. If the closing is an escrow closing, the instructions to the escrow agent will direct it to retain the documents until these funds have arrived. Other participants in the closing, such as real estate brokers, mortgage brokers, title company officials, and some of the lawyers, may be similarly insistent.

The person running the closing, whether it is a title company official, an escrow agent, or someone else, must be sure to carry out this disbursement function with care, and the lawyers for each of the parties should confirm that this person is disbursing all funds correctly. The closing checklist and the closing statement will be helpful in this regard. The closing checklist should list all matters to be addressed at the closing, and the closing statement should specify the amounts of any required payments and should net them out against one another.

There are numerous advantages to wiring funds: the parties need not worry about large quantities of cash and need not fuss with a check, and the recipient knows that the funds are in the bank earning interest almost immediately. However, wires sometimes go astray, and the parties should prepare in advance for problems that occasionally arise when funds are wired. When this occurs, the lawyers must promptly enlist the assistance of officials at the wiring bank and the recipient bank, who should attempt to figure out what happened to the money. The explanation may be as simple as an incorrectly typed account number, but the lawyers need to make this determination quickly, particularly if the parties are sitting impatiently in a conference room waiting to collect their documents and leave.

For this reason, the parties may want to avoid scheduling closings late in the day, especially on Fridays, when bank offices may close for the night or for the weekend before the funds can be traced. Lawyers and their clients should also be aware that the number of wire transfers, and thus the likelihood of misdirected funds, increases dramatically late in December, as parties around the country rush to close deals before the end of the year.

If something does go wrong with the wiring of the funds, the lawyers may find themselves converting a table closing into an escrow closing at the last minute. They will agree to appoint someone as escrow agent to hold the documents until the funds reappear and then to distribute the documents in accordance with the instructions they gave to that escrow agent.

### §8.10—Caution: Confirming That Funds Have Been Wired

The fact that the buyer has placed a telephone call to its bank instructing the bank to initiate a wire transfer does not mean that the buyer has provided good funds and met its closing condition. One of the authors is aware of a closing in which a party that ordered funds to be wired then went down the hall and made another telephone call—out of the presence of those who heard the first telephone call—revoking the wire instructions before the bank had initiated the transfer.

The bank that initiates the transfer will receive a federal wire number, which can be used to track the wired funds and to confirm when they were sent and received. Only the receipt of the federal wire number can serve as confirmation that the funds actually have been wired.

### Notes

1. *See supra* §7.01 (discussing purposes of closing in more detail).
2. *See supra* §2.25 (discussing these conflict of interest problems).
3. *See infra* §§8.04–8.05.
4. *See supra* §7.11 (discussing title insurance in context of closing preparation).
5. *See infra* §8.08 (discussing appropriate number of copies to be executed at closing).
6. *See, e.g., supra* §7.06 (discussing requirements applicable to deeds).

7. It is simple for a lawyer to become a notary public, and some lawyers do so in case they must serve this role in a pinch. However, the lawyer for each party is likely to have other important matters to attend to during the closing and would be better off arranging to have someone else serve as the notary. Many law firms have members of their support staff obtain their commissions as notaries so that these persons can perform this role at closings.

# CHAPTER 9

# Post-Closing Matters

## §9.01 Recordation of Documents

The parties' first order of business after the closing should be to see that all documents that must be recorded are delivered to the county recording office. In most cases, the title insurance company or escrow agent will assume responsibility for performing this task. The title insurer has a significant personal interest in ensuring that these documents are recorded correctly and promptly. It probably has issued policies of title insurance or irrevocable commitments that assume that all of these documents will be recorded, and under the current American Land Title Association form of title insurance policy, it bears the risk if other documents are recorded between the policy date and the time it records the deed.[1] The title insurer will not want to entrust this important responsibility to someone else.

---

*Comment:* It is very important that the lawyer follow up with the title company to be sure that all documents have been recorded and that they have been recorded in the proper sequence. Title agents—and even title companies—have been known not to record documents promptly, a failure that can lead to serious problems later. Even if a party has received title insurance, its lawyer should verify that recordation has occurred in a timely manner.

---

If, for some reason, the title insurer does not take responsibility for recording the documents, the buyer must take care that the deed is recorded, and the lender must be sure that all of its security documents are recorded or filed in the proper places.[2] If the buyer has granted more than one mortgage on the property, the senior lender must make sure that its mortgage and related documents are recorded first, or the various lenders must enter into a subordination agreement (if they have not already included one in their mortgage documents) that clarifies the relative priorities of the mortgages.

The recording office should stamp all the documents it receives with a date and time stamp as soon as these documents are delivered to the appropriate official and all taxes and fees are paid. The official will retain the documents for the time being and will eventually give each one a book and page number that corresponds to the location in the records at which that document can be found. The official records will include only copies of these documents; the originals will be returned to the parties designated in the deed or the mortgage—most commonly the buyer and the lender, respectively, or their lawyers—after the recorder makes and retains copies of the originals. The recorder will also index these documents as required by state law so that title searchers can locate them.

---

*Comment:* In many cases, it takes the recorder weeks—or even months— to return the original documents. The lawyer often must follow up to confirm that the documents are recorded, indexed, and returned. In a Torrens jurisdiction, a new Torrens certificate also must be issued.

---

## §9.02 Distribution of Documents

At the end of the closing, or shortly thereafter, the lawyers must make sure that all remaining documents are distributed to the proper parties. The lender's lawyer must be sure that the lender receives the original note, which the lender should secure in a safe location. The lender should also receive originals of the mortgage, the assignment of leases and rents, all UCC financing statements, all other documents to which it is a party, and any other documents it might need in the event of disputes or litigation. In addition, the lender should receive copies of any other documents that may be relevant to its role in the transaction. To the extent that these documents have been recorded or filed, the lender may be content to wait for the government official to return the originals to it, with recording information affixed, but should keep photocopies handy for reference in case the recording official is slow to return them.

The buyer's lawyer should make sure that the buyer receives an original deed, a copy of the note, originals of all the loan documents, originals of any other documents to which it is a party, originals of any other documents that it could need later if disputes or litigation arise, and copies of any other relevant documents. Once again, the buyer may be willing to accept photocopies of some of these documents for the time being if it knows that the recording official will return the originals to it with all recording information indicated directly on them.

All other parties will want copies, and sometimes will want originals, of those documents that are pertinent to their own roles in the transaction. For example, the seller should keep any paid notes that its own lender returned to it and should retain the originals of any mortgage satisfactions that accompanied these notes after the satisfactions are recorded. The title company should receive originals of any affidavits and indemnities delivered to it. The lawyers may each want originals of those documents that were executed by their own clients.

## §9.03 Following Up

There are usually some loose ends after a closing. Some of the problems that arose at the last minute may have been resolved temporarily by an agreement that requires one of the parties to meet additional obligations after the closing. The seller may have to resolve a dispute with a tenant and modify the terms of an easement for utility lines, and the escrow agent may be holding a portion of the purchase price in escrow to ensure that the seller will perform these obligations. The parties must remember to follow up with these matters after the closing.

It is easy for the parties to let these responsibilities slide. Once the urgency of the closing deadline passes, each party and each lawyer moves on to the next transaction and may place this matter at the bottom of an ever-expanding "to do" list. The lawyer should try to remember that some of these matters may be quite important and may merit some additional attention even though the deal has closed.

The lawyer must also remember that the types of matters that will need to be cleared up after the closing vary widely from transaction to transaction. Contracts, loan commitments, mortgages, and closing checklists may not change very much, but the range of unexpected problems that can arise is wide. The lawyer is unlikely to have a standard form of post-closing checklist to parallel the closing checklist. Rather, the lawyer should keep careful track of any matters that are unresolved at the closing and should take the steps necessary to resolve these matters later.

## §9.04 Organizing the File

This chapter has already discussed the distribution of all the original closing documents. One or more of the lawyers should probably take on the responsibility for organizing a more formal closing binder after the deal has closed, at least for larger transactions. This closing binder, which may take the form of an electronic file of scanned documents, a hardcover bound volume, a softcover volume, or a carefully organized file of papers, should include copies of every closing document in a sensible sequence. For example, the closing binder may group the sale documents together, followed by the loan documents, the title insurance documents, the corporate authorizations, the legal opinions, and other miscellaneous documents.

The closing checklist can serve as a useful tool for organizing the closing binder. It should be easy to revise the closing checklist so that it can serve as the table of contents for this volume. The lawyer may want to prepare a brief narrative summary of the transaction, including a list of all persons who attended the closing and their respective roles, and place it at the beginning of the binder. The lawyer also should be sure to include the closing statement in this binder.

The closing binder will serve as a useful resource after the closing. The parties and their lawyers will not want to risk losing or damaging original documents if they need to review them later. They can keep the originals in a safe storage location and can consult the closing binder whenever they need to review the content of the documents. The closing binder will also be useful when parties new to the deal must refer to the documents. The table of contents, the narrative summary, and the closing statement can help these parties reconstruct the deal, and the documents themselves will be useful as the buyer's ownership of the property progresses over time. It is easy to procrastinate in organizing this file, but the lawyer should make every effort to prepare the closing binder promptly; to review it for accuracy; to make copies for itself, its client, and other interested parties; and to close the book on this transaction. Then comes the best part of the transaction: the closing dinner. And after that, it's time for the next deal!

## Notes

1.  Suppose, for instance, that the insurer delays recording these documents for a week. During that week, the seller still will appear from the records to be the owner of the property and could sell it again to someone else or mortgage it to a lender. If the new party has no actual notice of the prior unrecorded documents, the new party may be entitled to priority under state recording laws. Under the most recent ALTA form of title insurance policy, the insurer would be liable to its insured buyer and then would have to seek recompense from the seller that sold the property twice.

2.  UCC financing statements, for example, may have to be filed in the office of the secretary of state.

# Appendix A

# Form of Letter of Intent

Dear _____:

This letter (the "Letter of Intent") serves as an outline of the terms and conditions under which _____ proposes to sell to _____ all of Seller's [fee] [leasehold] interest in the real estate and improvements constructed thereon generally known as _____, which have a collective address of _____, and which consist of approximately ____ acres more or less (collectively, the "Property").

It is our intention that the terms and provisions set forth in this letter be set forth in greater detail in a purchase and sale agreement for the Property ("the Agreement"). The language used in this letter is not necessarily to be incorporated verbatim in the Agreement, and additional terms and provisions not set forth herein may be added to the Agreement as mutually agreed upon by the parties.

1. <u>Buyer.</u> The Buyer shall be _____ and its permitted assigns ("Buyer").

2. <u>Seller.</u> The Seller shall be _____ ("Seller").

3. <u>Property.</u> The Property is as described above. The Property shall be conveyed "as-is," "where-is," subject to the representations and warranties set forth in the Agreement.

4. <u>Purchase Price.</u> The Purchase Price shall be $_____. The [initial] deposit will be $_____, and shall be deposited with an escrow agent mutually acceptable to Buyer and Seller (the "Escrow Agent") within ____ days after the execution of the Agreement [, and the additional deposit will be $_____, and will be deposited with the Escrow Agent within ____ days of the expiration of the Study Period, if the Agreement is not terminated by Buyer prior to the expiration of the Study Period]. The [initial] deposit [and the additional deposit], together will all interest thereon, shall be referred to as the "Deposit."

5. <u>Representations.</u> The Agreement will contain limited representations regarding the condition of the Property of the nature customary in transactions of the nature herein described. Each of Seller and Buyer shall represent to the other that it has the necessary authority to enter into the transaction contemplated by the Agreement.

6. <u>Conditions Precedent to Closing.</u> The Agreement will provide for limited conditions to closing including, but not limited to, the following (the "Conditions"):

(a) That all of Seller's representations and warranties will be remade as of the date of Closing, subject to information learned by Buyer either from Seller or during its investigations of the Property, with the same force and effect as if made on and as of such date;

(b) That at Closing, a title company reasonably acceptable to Buyer and Seller will be irrevocably committed to issue a title insurance policy insuring Buyer's title to the Property in the condition required by the terms of the Agreement, with no monetary liens or encumbrances against the Property (other than those created or assumed by Buyer) and subject only to Permitted Exceptions (to be defined in the Agreement);

(c) That Seller shall have delivered to Buyer tenant estoppel certificates in form reasonably satisfactory to Buyer from tenants leasing not less than ___ of the rentable square footage of the Property;

(d) That Seller shall have delivered to Buyer an estoppel certificate in form reasonably satisfactory to Buyer from any declarant or association under any recorded covenants against the Property; and

(e) That this transaction is NOT contingent upon Buyer's ability to obtain financing.

7. Due Diligence Materials. Within five (5) days of the execution of the Agreement, Seller will deliver to Buyer all Studies (defined below) and other books, records and documents relating to the Property that are not privileged or confidential and that are in Seller's possession or reasonable control (the "Due Diligence Materials").

8. Study Period. Seller agrees that for a period of _____ days from the date of the full execution of the Agreement (the "Study Period"), Buyer shall have the right to enter upon the Property for the purpose of performing, at Buyer's sole cost and expense, investigations of the Property as Buyer deems desirable, including, but not limited to, a title examination of the Property, surveys, soil tests, engineering studies, environmental studies and other physical investigations and inspections of the Property (collectively, "Studies"), provided that Buyer shall not perform soil borings or other invasive testing of the Property without Seller's prior written consent. Prior to any such entry, Buyer shall provide to Seller a certificate of insurance in favor of Seller in form and substance reasonably satisfactory to Seller. In conducting such Studies, Buyer agrees not to (i) disrupt Seller's ongoing activities on the Property, (ii) interrupt Seller's business activities, or (iii) interfere with the rights of any tenants under their leases at the Property. Buyer will indemnify and hold Seller harmless from and against any injury to persons or damage to property arising from its or its agents' entry on the Property and agrees to restore the Property to its condition prior to Buyer's entry thereon. In the event that Buyer is for any reason whatsoever dissatisfied, in its sole discretion, with the results of any of the Studies, then Buyer may terminate the Agreement by giving written notice to Seller prior to the expiration of the Study Period. Upon termination, the Agreement shall thereafter be null and void and of no further force and effect, except for the provisions that expressly survive termination of the Agreement, and Seller shall instruct the Escrow Agent to return the Deposit to Buyer.

9. <u>Closing.</u> Closing shall occur on a date mutually selected by Buyer and Seller to occur no more than _____ days after the expiration of the Study Period. At closing, Buyer shall pay to Seller the Purchase Price (less the Deposit and subject to adjustments and prorations described in the Agreement), in immediately available federal funds, by certified check or wire transfer.

10. <u>Closing Costs.</u> The Agreement shall provide for Seller and Buyer each to pay transfer and other recording taxes as is customary in the jurisdiction where the Property is located. Rent, taxes, and other similar items shall be adjusted to the Closing date.

11. <u>Exclusive Period.</u> In consideration of Buyer's efforts and expense in investigating the Property, Seller agrees that Seller shall not sell, offer to sell, or negotiate to sell the Property to any party other than Buyer until the date upon which this letter is terminated.

12. <u>Nonbinding.</u> It is understood that the proposal represented by this Letter of Intent is merely an expression of the major terms and conditions of a possible transaction and does not constitute an offer or an acceptance of an agreement. Either party shall have the right to terminate this letter at any time, in such party's sole discretion, by written notice to the other party. In the event of such termination, each party shall be responsible for its own costs and expenses and neither party shall have any obligation or liability to the other.

13. <u>Confidentiality.</u> The existence and terms of this Letter of Intent, all Due Diligence Materials, all Studies and the results thereof, and all discussions between the parties (and their respective employees, representatives and agents) with respect to the contemplated transaction will be and remain strictly confidential and will not be disclosed to any person or entity other than those employees, representatives and agents of the parties involved in the transaction who have a reasonable need to know, and other than as required by applicable law.

Please sign one (1) copy of this letter below and return it to us within fifteen (15) days from the date of this letter if the terms hereof are acceptable. This letter shall expire if not signed and returned within fifteen (15) days.

Sincerely,

_____

By: _____

AGREED to this _____ day of _____, ____.

_____

By: _____

# Appendix B

# Form of Contract of Sale

CONTRACT OF SALE BETWEEN

_____ AND _____

TABLE OF CONTENTS

### EXHIBITS

## CONTRACT OF SALE

CONTRACT OF SALE dated the _____ day of _____, 20\_\_, between _____, a [type of entity and state in which formed], having an office at _____ ("Seller"), and _____, a [type of entity and state in which formed], having an office at _____ ("Buyer").

### W I T N E S S E T H:

THAT the parties hereto, intending to be legally bound, hereby agree as follows:

1. <u>Definitions.</u>

In addition to the defined terms contained elsewhere in this Contract, the following terms shall have the following definitions:

"Appurtenances" shall have the meaning assigned to such term in Section 2.1(a) of this Contract.

"Buildings" shall mean the buildings situated on the Property.

"Business Day" shall mean any day other than a Saturday, Sunday, or any other day on which banking institutions in the State of _____ are authorized by law or executive action to close.

"Buyer" shall have the meaning assigned to such term in the Preamble of this Contract.

"Closing" shall have the meaning assigned to such term in Section 4.1 of this Contract.

"Closing Date" shall have the meaning assigned to such term in Section 4.1 of this Contract.

"Commitment" shall have the meaning assigned to such term in Section 3.5 of this Contract.

"Contract" shall mean this Contract of Sale, together with all Exhibits attached hereto, as it and they may be amended from time to time.

"Deed" shall have the meaning assigned to such term in Section 4.2(a) of this Contract.

"Down Payment" shall have the meaning assigned to such term in Section 2.2(a) of this Contract.

"Effective Date" shall mean the date on which the last party executes this Contract.

"Escrow Agent" shall mean the Title Company.

"Improvements" shall mean all buildings, fixtures, walls, fences, landscaping, and other structures and improvements situated on, affixed, or appurtenant to the Property.

"Land" shall have the meaning assigned to such term in Section 2.1(a) of this Contract.

"Leases" shall mean the Leases set forth on the Rent Roll.

"Lien" shall mean any lien, judgment, mortgage, deed of trust, charge, option, contractual restriction on transfer, security interest, tax lien, pledge, encumbrance, conditional sale or title retention arrangement, or any other claim against the Property (or any portion thereof), as the case may be, or any agreement to create or confer any of the foregoing, in each case whether arising by agreement or under any statute, law, governmental ordinance, rule, regulation, decree, order, or requirement of any governmental authority now or hereafter existing or otherwise.

"Other Property" shall mean all equipment, fixtures, machinery, and personalty owned by Seller and attached to, or specifically and exclusively used in connection with, the Property (and not owned by tenants under Leases), including without limitation, all contract rights, guarantees, and warranties of any nature, all architects', engineers', surveyors', zoning analysts', and other real estate professionals' plans, specifications, certifications, contracts, reports, data, or other technical descriptions, reports, or audits, all without warranty as to completeness or accuracy ("Contract Documents"), all governmental permits, licenses, certificates, and approvals in connection with the ownership of the Property ("Licenses"), all escrow accounts, deposits, instruments, documents of title, general intangibles, and business records pertaining to the Property, the lease files, and tenant correspondence files, and all of Seller's rights, claims, and causes of action, if any, to the extent they are assignable, under any warranties and/or guarantees of manufacturers, contractors, or installers, all rights against tenants and others relating to the Property or the operation or maintenance thereof (except as expressly provided otherwise herein), and any warranties from any previous owners of the Property (hereinafter collectively referred to as "Personal Property").

"Permitted Encumbrances" shall have the meaning assigned to such term in Section 3.2(a) of this Contract.

"Person" shall mean any natural person, partnership, corporation, association, and other form of business association or entity.

"Property" shall have the meaning assigned to such term in Section 2.1(a) of this Contract.

"Purchase Money Loan" shall have the meaning assigned to such term in Section 8.2(g) of this Contract.

"Purchase Price" shall have the meaning assigned to such term in Section 2.2 of this Contract.

"Rent Roll" shall mean the rent roll attached hereto as <u>Exhibit J.</u>

"Surveys" shall have the meaning assigned to such term in Section 3.4 of this Contract.

"Surviving Provisions" shall have the meaning assigned to such term in Section 2.3 of this Contract.

"Title Company" shall mean _____

_____.

"Transfer Documents" shall have the meaning assigned to such term in Section 4.2(a) of this Contract.

2. Purchase and Sale.

2.1   Contract to Buy and Sell. In consideration of the payment of the Purchase Price by Buyer to Seller and for other good and valuable consideration (including, but not limited to, the mutual covenants contained in this Contract) and subject to and in accordance with the terms and conditions of this Contract, Seller agrees to sell and convey to Buyer, and Buyer agrees to purchase from Seller and take title to that certain real property (consisting of approximately ____acres) commonly known as _____ _____, which is located in _____ _____ (the "Land"), as such Land is described on Exhibit A attached hereto, together with the Buildings and all other improvements located on the Land (the "Improvements"), all and singular the tenements, hereditaments, and privileges appurtenant thereto (collectively, the "Appurtenances"), the Other Property, and the Leases (the Land, the Improvements, the Appurtenances, the Other Property, and the Leases are hereinafter collectively referred to as the "Property").

2.2   Purchase Price. The purchase price for the Property (the "Purchase Price") is _____ ($_____), and shall be payable as follows:

(a)   Down Payment. A down payment in the amount of _____ _____ ($_____) (together will all interest earned thereon, the "Down Payment") shall be delivered to the Escrow Agent not later than two (2) Business Days after the Effective Date (but not prior to _____), by federal wire transfer of immediately available funds, to be held by the Escrow Agent in an interest-bearing account pursuant to the terms of an Escrow Contract among Seller, Buyer, and the Escrow Agent (the "Escrow Agreement") until 5:00 p.m. EST on the Due Diligence Expiration Date (as defined in Section 3.1(a) of this Contract), at which time the Down Payment shall become non-refundable provided that Buyer has not terminated this Contract as provided in Section 3.1(e) below. At Closing (as defined in Section 4.1 of this Contract), the Down Payment shall be credited against the Purchase Price.

(b)   Balance of Purchase Price. The balance of the Purchase Price (the "Balance"), subject to adjustment as provided in Article 5 of this Contract, shall be paid by Buyer on the Closing Date by federal wire transfer of immediately available funds to Title Company for the benefit of Seller.

(c)   [Buyer's Note and Mortgage. On the Closing Date, Buyer shall execute and deliver (i) a promissory note in the initial principal amount of _____ and 00/100 Dollars ($_____) by Buyer to the order of Seller, in the form attached to this Contract as Exhibit B-1 (the "Buyer's Note"); and (ii) a security instrument to secure Buyer's payment and performance obligations under the Buyer's Note and to encumber the Property with a ____ priority lien, in the form attached to this Contract as Exhibit B-2 (the "Buyer's Mortgage").]

2.3 Failure to Pay Down Payment. In the event that Buyer fails to fund the Down Payment not later than two (2) Business Days after the Effective Date for any reason whatsoever, this Contract shall immediately and automatically be null and void and of no further force and effect. Upon any termination of this Contract pursuant to this Section 2.3 or Section 3.1 of this Contract, no party shall have any further rights, duties, or obligations under this Contract, except for rights, duties, or obligations intended to survive the termination of this Contract (the "Surviving Provisions").

2.4 Interest for Down Payment. The Down Payment shall be deposited by the Escrow Agent in a federally insured (to the extent permitted by law) interest-bearing account and all interest earned on such account shall be added to the Down Payment and distributed to the party entitled to receive the Down Payment in accordance with the terms of this Contract.

2.5 Form of Escrow Provision for Down Payment.

[Note to drafter: If the parties and the Escrow Agent do not execute a separate Escrow Agreement, the Escrow Agent must sign the Contract to consent to this Section.]

(a) The Escrow Agent agrees to hold and disburse the Down Payment and all interest accruing thereon as provided by this Section 2.5. The Escrow Agent shall promptly (i) give Notice to Buyer and Seller of the receipt of the Down Payment by the Escrow Agent; (ii) deposit the Down Payment into an interest-bearing account at a federally insured financial institution in the State of _____; (iii) otherwise invest the Down Payment as provided from time to time in one or more Notices to the Escrow Agent executed by both Buyer and Seller; and (iv) release the principal amount of the Down Payment and interest thereon together to the party entitled to such principal as provided by Section 2.5(b). The Escrow Agent shall not be responsible for the rate of interest accruing on the Down Payment or for losses caused by the insolvency of the institution at which the Down Payment is on account if the Escrow Agent complies with this Section 2.5(a).

(b) The Escrow Agent shall not release or disburse any portion of the Down Payment, or any interest accrued thereon, to any person except as provided by (i) a settlement or closing statement executed by both Buyer and Seller for the Closing; (ii) one or more Notices to the Escrow Agent executed by both Buyer and Seller; or (iii) the order of a court exercising jurisdiction over the parties or the Down Payment. The Escrow Agent is further authorized to rely upon and comply with such settlement or closing statements, Notices, or orders without further notice to or consent by any third party, and the Escrow Agent shall not be obligated to inquire into the authenticity of, or authority for, signatures to any such settlement or closing statements, Notices, or orders. If the Escrow Agent has not received one or more of such settlement or closing statements, Notices, or orders providing for disposition of all portions of the Down Payment, and all interest accrued thereon, on or before _____ _____, then the Escrow Agent is hereby authorized to commence a suit in the nature of an interpleader in any court of competent jurisdiction and to tender the undisbursed amount of the Down Payment, and all undisbursed interest accrued thereon, into the custody of such court. Thereafter, the Escrow Agent shall have no further obligations or liabilities under this Contract or otherwise in connection with the Down Payment or any interest accrued thereon.

(c) In the event that this Contract is terminated under Section 3.1(b), 3.1(c), 4.3, 8.2(g), 9.1, 9.2, 10.2, or 10.3 of this Contract, the Down Payment shall be refunded to Buyer or Seller, as set forth in the applicable Section providing for such termination, by the Escrow Agent, without any further notice or authorization required (notwithstanding anything in the Escrow Agreement to the contrary), and this Contract shall be deemed terminated, whereupon neither party shall have any further liability to the other hereunder except for the Surviving Provisions.

(d) This Section 2.5 shall survive the expiration or termination of this Contract or the Closing.

(e) As consideration for performance by the Escrow Agent of its obligations under this Contract, the Escrow Agent shall be entitled to receive an escrow fee in the amount of _____ and 00/100 Dollars ($_____) (the "Escrow Fee") from Buyer and Seller. Buyer and Seller shall each pay to the Escrow Agent one-half (1/2) of the Escrow Fee promptly upon the release of the Down Payment to Buyer or Seller by the Escrow Agent as provided by Section 2.5(b) or, if the Escrow Agent commences a proceeding in the nature of an interpleader also as provided by Section 2.5(b), the Escrow Agent may deduct the Escrow Fee from the Down Payment before paying the Down Payment into the custody of the court.

(f) Buyer and Seller, jointly and severally, shall hold harmless and indemnify the Escrow Agent from and against all claims, costs, expenses, damages, and losses in connection with the performance by the Escrow Agent of its obligations under this Contract, except any such claims, costs, expenses, damages, and losses caused by the gross negligence or willful default of the Escrow Agent.

3. Title and Condition; Surveys; Buyer's Due Diligence Review.

3.1 Due Diligence Review/Rights Prior To and After Due Diligence Expiration Date.

(a) Due Diligence Review. From the Effective Date until 5:00 p.m. EST on that date which is _____ (___) days after the Effective Date (the "Due Diligence Expiration Date"), Buyer shall have the right, at its sole cost and expense, to inspect and review all characteristics and aspects of the Property, the Commitment, the Surveys, and the Leases, and to make inquiry of governmental agencies with regard to the Property (the "Due Diligence Review"). Within one (1) Business Day of the Effective Date, Seller shall provide Buyer with the most recent survey and title report or policy pertaining to the Property and shall make available to Buyer and its employees, representatives, counsel, and consultants access to all of its books, records, and files relating to the Property in Seller's possession or reasonable control (including, without limitation, all environmental reports generated by or on behalf of Buyer if and to the extent permitted by the preparers of such environmental reports) (collectively, the "Due Diligence Materials"). Seller agrees, to the extent reasonably feasible, to allow Buyer to make copies at Seller's office or at the property management office of such items as Buyer reasonably requests. Commencing on the Effective Date and continuing through the Closing Date or the earlier date on which this Contract terminates, Seller shall permit authorized representatives of Buyer to have access to the Property at mutually agreed upon reasonable times for purposes of satisfying Buyer with respect to the representations, warranties, and covenants of Seller set forth in this Contract and with respect to satisfaction of any diligence requirements of Buyer, provided that such access does not interfere in any material respect with the operation of the Property or the rights of the tenants in the Buildings. Buyer agrees that if Buyer chooses to obtain a new environmental study with respect to the Property, Buyer shall select and engage the provider of such environmental study promptly after the Effective Date and such environmental study shall be produced and reviewed as part of the Due Diligence Review. Notwithstanding the foregoing, Buyer shall not perform or cause to be performed, without Seller's prior written consent, any invasive or destructive sampling or testing of any media, including, but not limited to, water, soil, and all other media, which consent shall be in Seller's sole discretion. Seller reserves the right to have a representative present during any access to the Property by Buyer or its employees, agents, or consultants or during the performance of any testing (whether or not invasive) at the Property. Buyer shall make a commercially reasonable effort to coordinate its activities in connection with the Due Diligence Review with the activities of Seller and the business operations of the tenants at the Property. Buyer acknowledges that the Due Diligence Materials provided by Seller are made available to Buyer in their "AS IS, WHERE IS" condition "WITH ALL FAULTS." Seller has not verified the accuracy of any statements or information contained in the Due Diligence Materials or any method used to compile the Due Diligence Materials. Seller has not made and does not make any representation or warranty of any kind whatsoever, whether oral or written, express or implied, statutory, or otherwise with respect to the Due Diligence Materials, and in no event shall Buyer be entitled to rely on the accuracy or completeness of the Due

Diligence Materials without the express written permission of Seller or the applicable third party.

(b) <u>Termination Notice.</u> Buyer shall have the right, in its sole and absolute discretion, to terminate this Contract by delivering written notice of such decision (the "Termination Notice") to Seller and the Escrow Agent on or prior to 5:00 p.m. EST on the Due Diligence Expiration Date. Failure to deliver a Termination Notice on or prior to such deadline shall be deemed to constitute an election to go forward with this Contract.

(c) <u>Title and Survey Objections.</u> Buyer shall have until 5:00 p.m. EST on that date which is thirty (30) days after the Effective Date (the "Title and Survey Objection Date") to provide Seller with any objections Buyer has to any matters affecting title to the Property or to any matters set forth on any of the Surveys (as defined in Section 3.4) with respect to the Property. Buyer shall deliver written notice of any such title or Survey objections (the "Title and Survey Objection Notice") on or prior to the Title and Survey Objection Date to Seller. Seller shall, within five (5) days of its receipt of any such Title and Survey Objection Notice, deliver written notice to Buyer stating whether or not Seller will cure any of Buyer's title or survey objections. Seller's failure to deliver such a written notice within such time frame shall be deemed to be an election by Seller not to cure Buyer's title and survey objections. If Seller elects not to cure any of Buyer's title or survey objections, Buyer shall have the right to terminate this Contract by delivering a written notice so terminating this Contract to Seller and the Escrow Agent on or prior to 5:00 p.m. EST on the date that is ten (10) days after Buyer's receipt of Seller's response to the Title and Survey Objection Notice, or, if no such response was received, the date that is ten (10) days after the latest date by which such response was supposed to be received. If Buyer does not exercise such termination right, such unresolved title objection(s) shall be deemed to be Permitted Encumbrances (as defined in Section 3.2). Permitted Encumbrances shall not include (i) any liens, (ii) any violation of law recorded against the Property, or (iii) any exceptions, caused by Seller's voluntary acts after the Effective Date or first appearing of record after the Effective Date and not approved by Buyer hereunder, and Seller shall be required to remove each of the foregoing matters from title on or before the Closing Date hereunder. If Buyer fails to deliver a Title and Survey Objection Notice on or prior to the Title and Survey Objection Date in connection with the Property, Buyer shall be deemed to have waived its right to object to title matters and to any matters set forth on the Surveys for the Property and all matters relating to or affecting title or set forth on the Surveys for the Property shall be Permitted Encumbrances; provided, however, that Buyer shall have a three (3) Business Day period from Buyer's receipt of a title continuation report within which to notify Seller of any new title objections first disclosed thereby and the provisions of this subparagraph shall apply in respect of such new title defects.

(d) Waiver. Buyer's election to proceed to Closing, subject to and in accordance with this Contract, shall be an acknowledgment by Buyer that Buyer and Buyer's agents have had access to all documents and information relating to the Property as Buyer deemed necessary to complete the Due Diligence Review and make its own independent investment decision to acquire the Property; provided, however, that the foregoing shall not be in derogation of any other rights or remedies of Buyer under this Contract (including, without limitation, any other right to terminate expressly set forth in the Contract).

3.2    State of Title. Buyer shall take title to the Property subject to (i) the Leases; (ii) all standard utility easements; (iii) taxes, assessments, and governmental charges not yet due and payable or due and payable but not yet delinquent; (iv) applicable zoning regulations and ordinances provided the same do not prohibit or impair in any material respect the use of the Buildings as they are currently operated and constructed; and (vi) such other non-monetary items of record not objected to by Buyer in accordance with Section 3.1 of this Contract (collectively, the "Permitted Encumbrances").

3.3    Condition of Property. Except as otherwise set forth herein, and without limiting the provisions of Section 6.3 of this Contract, Seller makes no express or implied representations or warranties in connection with the Property. Buyer shall accept the Property on the Closing Date in its existing condition as of such date, "AS IS, WHERE IS" and "WITH ALL FAULTS." Buyer hereby acknowledges that it will make its own investigations. Buyer has been advised to investigate the condition and suitability of all aspects of the Property and all matters affecting the value or desirability of the Property, including, but not limited to, potential environmental hazards.

3.4    Surveys. Buyer may, at its sole cost and expense, procure ALTA surveys of the Property (the "Surveys").

3.5    Title Insurance. On the Closing Date, Seller shall convey to Buyer good and marketable fee simple title to the Property subject only to the Permitted Encumbrances, which title shall be insurable as such at regular rates by the Title Company, (a) with endorsements and affirmative insurance against mechanics' liens, (b) insuring against any violation of existing covenants, conditions, or restrictions, and insuring that future violation will not result in forfeiture of title, (c) confirming that there are no encroachments of improvements from adjoining land onto the Land, and (d) removing any exception for parties in possession other than tenants on the Rent Roll (the "Commitment").

3.6    Indemnification of Seller. Buyer shall be solely responsible for any and all damage or loss of any kind or nature whatsoever, whether to persons or to property, that may arise as a result of or otherwise because of the acts or omissions of Buyer or Buyer's employees, agents, or contractors in

connection with the Due Diligence Review, or Buyer or Buyer's employees, agents, or contractors entering upon the Property, and Buyer shall promptly and at Buyer's sole cost and expense restore the Property and repair any damage occasioned by such review and inspections to the condition the Property was in immediately prior to such review to the extent practicable. Buyer hereby agrees to indemnify, protect, defend (with counsel reasonably acceptable to Seller), save, and hold Seller harmless of and from all debts, duties, obligations, liabilities, suits, claims, demands, settlements, causes of action, damages, losses, fees, and expenses (including, without limitation, reasonable attorneys' fees and expenses and court costs) in any way relating to or that may arise out of or from a result of any act or omission of Buyer or Buyer's employees, agents, or contractors in connection with the Due Diligence Review or Buyer or Buyer's employees, agents, or contractors entering upon the Property or in exercising its rights under this Article 3. Prior to the time Buyer avails itself of the rights herein contained to enter upon the Property, Buyer shall deliver to Seller evidence that Buyer and Buyer's employees, agents, and contractors, or the particular party who intends to enter upon the Property, has in effect a fully paid policy of insurance that insures Buyer and Seller against any liability normally covered by a general public liability policy with limits of at least _____
Dollars ($_____) per occurrence of death of, or injury to, any one person or as otherwise reasonably requested by Seller. The policy or policies maintained, or caused to be maintained, pursuant to this Section 3.6 shall insure the contractual liability of Buyer covering the indemnities herein and shall (i) name Seller and, at Seller's request, Seller's lender, as an additional insured party, and (ii) contain a provision that the insurance provided thereunder shall be primary and noncontributing with any other insurance available to Seller. Buyer's obligations set forth in this Section 3.6 shall be a Surviving Provision.

3.7   Confidential Information. Except as required by court order or by operation of law, all matters reviewed or discovered by Buyer in the course of the Due Diligence Review and all other documents and materials furnished by or on behalf of Seller to Buyer pursuant to the transaction contemplated by this Contract shall be strictly confidential; provided, however, that Buyer shall have the right to provide such information to its attorneys, consultants, agents, advisors, members, partners, and prospective lenders (and each of their attorneys, consultants, agents, advisors, members, and partners) without the consent of Seller. Prior to Closing, Buyer shall not have any contact whatsoever with any form of media (including, but not limited to print, radio, television, or Internet) or other third parties (except for the United States Environmental Protection Agency, the _____
Department of Environmental Protection, City officials in the City where the Property is located, and other governmental authorities, provided Buyer advises Seller, in advance, of any such proposed contact) in connec-

tion with this transaction without Seller's prior written consent. The parties agree to provide each other with a copy for its review and reasonable approval of any announcement to be made regarding the transaction at Closing. If no Closing occurs hereunder (whether pursuant to the terms of Section 3.1 or any other provision of this Contract), Buyer's obligations under this Section 3.8 shall be Surviving Provisions.

3.8 Due Diligence Materials and Documents. Buyer agrees that, in the event this Contract is terminated or Closing is not completed for any reason, all Due Diligence Materials provided by Seller, and all copies thereof, will be returned to Seller promptly upon Seller's request. In addition, all tests, reports, analyses, compilations, and studies prepared by or for Buyer in connection with the transaction contemplated in this Contract will be delivered to Seller.

3.9 Tenant Estoppels. During the Due Diligence Review, Seller shall prepare tenant estoppel certificates in substantially the same form attached hereto as Exhibit C (each a "Tenant Estoppel" and collectively, the "Tenant Estoppels") addressed to each of the tenants listed in the Rent Roll. Seller shall deliver these Tenant Estoppels to these tenants and will request that these tenants complete and execute the Tenant Estoppels and return the executed Tenant Estoppels to Seller. Seller shall make diligent efforts to have these tenants execute and deliver the executed Tenant Estoppels to Seller prior to the Due Diligence Expiration Date and Seller shall promptly deliver copies of executed Tenant Estoppels to Buyer upon Seller's receipt of the same. It shall be a condition to Buyer's obligation to complete Closing that Seller deliver these Tenant Estoppels to the tenants, dated within thirty (30) days of Closing and in the form attached as Exhibit C hereto (or, if any tenant refuses to sign the requested form, an estoppel certificate in the form of the estoppel certificate that is required by the applicable Lease), without modification other than to a de minimis extent.

4. Closing.

4.1 Time and Place. Closing of the transaction contemplated by this Contract ("Closing") either shall be held at a location in the City of _____ _____, State of _____, selected by Buyer, or via escrow through the Escrow Agent, on or prior to _____ (the "Closing Date").

4.2 Settlement. At Closing:

(a) Transfer Documents. Seller shall convey and transfer to Buyer (i) good and marketable title to the Property, subject only to the Permitted Encumbrances, by executing, acknowledging, and delivering to Buyer a special warranty deed for the Property in substantially the form of the special warranty deed attached to this Contract as Exhibit D (the "Deed"); (ii) title to the Other Property, by executing and delivering to Buyer a bill of sale and assignment for such Other Property located at the Property in substantially the form of the bill of sale and assignment attached to this Contract as Exhibit E (the "Bill of Sale"); (iii) the Leases, by executing and delivering an assignment and assumption of leases agreement for the Property in substantially the form of the agreement that is attached to this Contract as Exhibit F (the "Lease Assignments"); and (iv) the Service Contracts (as hereinafter defined) listed on Exhibit G attached hereto, except to the extent such Service Contracts are to be terminated under Sections 6.1(b)(ii) and 7.1 of this Contract, by executing and delivering an assignment and assumption of service agreements for the Property (the "Service Contract Assignments") (the Deed, the Bill of Sale, the Lease Assignments and the Service Contract Assignments are hereinafter collectively referred to as the "Transfer Documents");

(b) FIRPTA Certificate. Seller shall deliver to Buyer a duly executed FIRPTA Certificate pursuant to Section 1445 of the Internal Revenue Code of 1986, as amended;

(c) Balance of Purchase Price. After crediting the Down Payment against the Purchase Price (if applicable), Buyer shall pay the remaining balance of the Purchase Price at Closing, net of any applicable Closing prorations and other credits, by delivering the remaining balance of the Purchase Price by federal wire transfer of immediately available funds to Seller;

(d) Certificates of Occupancy. Seller shall obtain and deliver new use and occupancy certificates (or the local equivalent) in the name of Buyer for the Property; and

(e) Other Closing Deliveries. Seller and Buyer shall also execute and/or deliver the following documents and items: (i) Seller shall deliver all original Leases, Service Contracts, books, and records relating to the Property, all warranties, building permits, plans and specifications for the Improvements and all tenant-occupied space within the Improvements, all keys to the Property, and copies of all other material documents, agreements, and correspondence and items relating to the ownership, operation, maintenance, or management of the Property, to the extent such items are in Seller's possession or reasonable control; (ii) Buyer and Seller shall execute and deliver a closing statement evidencing payment of the Purchase Price and reflecting all applicable prorations; (iii) Seller shall deliver a certificate executed by Seller confirming that all of Seller's representations and warranties set forth in this Contract are true and correct as of the Closing Date; (iv) Seller shall deliver an updated Rent Roll, which shall be certified by an officer of Seller as being true and correct as of the Closing Date and shall show all current rents, deposits, late fees, advance fees, expiration dates, rentals overdue for ten (10) days or more, tenant concessions, bonuses, and free rental amounts, and all other matters affecting tenants of the Property; (v) Buyer and Seller shall execute and deliver letters notifying the tenants of the change of ownership of the Property; (vi) Buyer and Seller shall deliver such resolutions, authorizations, consents, bylaws, or other corporate and/or partnership documents relating to Buyer and

Seller as may be required by the other or by the Title Company; (vii) Buyer and Seller shall deliver any other documents reasonably required by the other or by the Title Company to effectuate the transactions contemplated by this Contract; and (viii) Seller shall execute and deliver all appropriate _____ Realty Transfer Tax Affidavits.

4.3   <u>Liens and Encumbrances.</u> If at Closing there shall be any liens or encumbrances, other than the Permitted Encumbrances, that Seller has agreed to pay and discharge, Seller may use any portion of the balance of the Purchase Price payable at Closing to satisfy the same; provided, however, that Seller shall either (a) deliver to the Title Company at Closing instruments in recordable form and sufficient, in the reasonable judgment of the Title Company, to satisfy such liens and encumbrances of record, together with the cost of recording or filing said instruments, or (b) if Seller shall have made arrangements with the Title Company in advance of Closing, deposit with the Title Company such monies as may be acceptable to and required by it to insure the obtaining and recording of such satisfactions and the issuance of title insurance to Buyer either free of any such liens and encumbrances or with insurance insuring against enforcement of the same out of the Property; and provided, further, that if the aggregate amount of monies required to satisfy any judgment(s) of record against Seller shall equal or exceed the Purchase Price, Seller shall have the right to terminate this Contract by notice to Buyer. Upon such termination by Seller, this Contract shall terminate, the Down Payment shall be promptly refunded to Buyer by the Escrow Agent, and neither party shall have any further liability to the other hereunder other than under those provisions of this Contract that by their terms are intended to survive such termination. The existence of any such liens and encumbrances shall not be deemed objections to title if Seller shall comply with the foregoing requirements.

5.   <u>Apportionments and Allocation of Expenses.</u>

5.1   <u>Apportionments.</u> The following items shall be apportioned as of 11:59 p.m. EST on the day prior to the Closing Date (the "Adjustment Date"):

(a)   rents, including additional rent and rent escalations, common area maintenance charges, and other fixed charges payable under the Leases and received by Seller;

(b)   fuel, electric, water, and other utility costs;

(c)   municipal assessments and governmental license and permit fees;

(d)   real estate taxes and assessments other than special assessments, based on the rates and assessed valuation applicable in the fiscal year for which assessed;

(e)   water rates and sewer charges;

(f)   garbage and rubbish removal charges;

(g)   sewer taxes and rents; and

(h) payments made under any Service Contracts assigned to Buyer in accordance with this Contract, if any.

If any of the foregoing cannot be apportioned on the Closing Date because of the unavailability of the amounts which are to be apportioned, such items shall be apportioned on the basis of a good faith estimate by the parties and reconciled as soon as practicable after the Closing Date but, in any event, no later than sixty (60) days after the Closing Date. Seller shall prepare and circulate for review and approval before the Closing Date a year-to-date statement of additional rent and rent escalations, common area maintenance charges, and other fixed charges payable under the Leases and received by Seller.

5.2   Assessments. If on the Closing Date, the Property shall be or shall have been affected by any special or general assessment or assessments of real property taxes payable as a lump sum or which are or may become payable in installments of which the first installment is then a charge or Lien and has become payable, Seller shall pay or cause to be paid at Closing all unpaid installments of such assessments which relate to the period of time prior to the Closing Date and Buyer shall pay or shall thereafter cause to be paid all installments thereof which relate to the period of time after the Closing Date.

5.3   Insurance Policies. No insurance policies of Seller are to be transferred to Buyer, and no apportionment of premiums for any such policies shall be made.

5.4   Security Deposits. At Closing, Seller shall transfer to Buyer (or credit to Buyer against the Purchase Price) the amount of all unapplied security deposits under the Leases and shall cause any letters of credit to be transferred to Buyer.

5.5   Past Due Rents. If on the Closing Date, there are past due rents, additional rents, rent escalations, or common area maintenance charges or other fixed charges payable under the Leases, any amounts received by Buyer with respect to any such Leases after the Closing Date shall be applied, first, to all amounts then due and payable under the Leases, and second, to rents and other payments past due. Seller shall have the right to commence suits against tenants to recover rent arrearages (as well as any interest earned thereon or any late charges imposed thereon) for a period of twelve (12) months after the Closing Date and prosecute such suits to completion, provided that in no event shall Seller have the right to bring an unlawful detainer action or to terminate any tenant's lease.

5.6   Net Amount Owed. If a net amount is owed by Seller to Buyer pursuant to this Article 5, such amount shall be credited against the Purchase Price. If a net amount is owed by Buyer to Seller pursuant to this Article 5, such amount shall be credited to Seller against the Purchase Price or paid separately to Seller at Closing.

5.7 <u>Apportionment of Transfer Taxes and Other Costs.</u> [The cost of all real estate transfer taxes shall be paid fifty percent (50%) by Seller and fifty percent (50%) by Buyer.] Buyer shall be responsible for the cost of preparing the Deed. Seller shall be responsible for all other matters relating to the clearing of title which Seller elects or is obligated to cure and for the fees and expenses of Seller's attorneys. Buyer shall be responsible for the cost of premium for any policies of title insurance, any costs incurred by Buyer in preparing and performing the Due Diligence Review, the fees and expenses of Buyer's attorneys, and all recording charges due in connection with the Deed. All costs associated with the Closing shall be apportioned fifty percent (50%) percent to Buyer and fifty percent (50%) to Seller.

5.8 <u>Custom and Practice.</u> All other costs and expenses shall be apportioned in accordance with the custom and practice for transactions of the size and complexity contemplated by this Contract in the State where the Property is located.

5.9 <u>Survival of Obligations.</u> The obligations of the parties under this Article 5 shall be Surviving Provisions.

6. <u>Representations, Warranties, and Acknowledgments.</u>

6.1 <u>Seller's Representations and Warranties.</u> Seller represents and warrants to Buyer that:

(a) with regard to Seller:

(i) <u>Status and Authority of Seller.</u> Seller is a duly organized and validly existing _____ under the laws of the State of _____ that is in good standing and has all requisite power and authority to execute and deliver this Contract and the Transfer Documents and to perform its obligations under this Contract to consummate the transaction contemplated hereby;

(ii) <u>Action of Seller.</u> Seller has taken all necessary action to authorize the execution, delivery, and performance of this Contract, and upon the execution and delivery of any document to be delivered by Seller on or prior to the Closing Date, such document shall constitute the valid and binding obligation and agreement of Seller, enforceable against Seller in accordance with its terms, except as enforceability may be limited by bankruptcy, insolvency, reorganization, moratorium, or similar laws of general application affecting the rights and remedies of creditors;

(iii) <u>Litigation in Regard to Contract.</u> To Seller's knowledge there are no actions or proceedings pending or threatened which question the validity of this Contract, any action taken or to be taken by Seller hereunder, or the ability of Seller to consummate the transactions contemplated by this Contract, or otherwise affect Buyer's ability to own or operate the Property after Closing;

(iv) <u>Not a Foreign Person.</u> For purposes of Section 1445 of the United States Internal Revenue Code, as amended (the "Code"), Seller is not a foreign person (as such term is defined in the Code and applicable federal income tax regulations);

(v)   <u>No Violations of Contracts.</u> Neither the execution, delivery, or performance of this Contract by Seller, nor compliance with the terms and provisions hereof, will result in any breach of the terms, conditions, or provisions of, or conflict with or constitute a default under, or result in the creation of any Lien, charge, or encumbrance upon the Property pursuant to the terms of, any indenture, mortgage, deed of trust, note, evidence of indebtedness, or any other agreement or instrument by which Seller is bound; and

(vi)   <u>No Bankruptcy.</u> No petition in bankruptcy (voluntary or otherwise), assignment for the benefit of creditors, or petition seeking reorganization or arrangement or other action under federal or state bankruptcy laws has been filed or commenced or is pending or contemplated against Seller or the Property.

(b)   with regard to the Property:

(i)   <u>Defect Notices.</u> Seller has not received any notice from the holder of any mortgage presently encumbering the Property, from any insurance company which has issued a policy with respect to the Property, or from any board of fire underwriters or any other governmental agency or authority claiming any defects or deficiencies in the Property or suggesting or requesting the performance of any repairs, alterations, or other work to the Property, which have not been cured or repaired;

(ii)   <u>Service Contracts.</u> There are no management, leasing, service, equipment, supply, security, maintenance, construction, concession, or other agreements with respect to or affecting the Property, except for the agreements listed on <u>Exhibit G</u> to this Contract (collectively, the "Service Contracts"); Seller will deliver to Buyer true, correct, and complete copies of each of the Service Contracts (and any amendments, modifications, guarantees, warranties, bonds, and supplements thereto); neither Seller nor, to Seller's knowledge, the other party to any of the Service Contracts is in default thereunder and, to Seller's knowledge, no event or omission has occurred which, with the giving of notice or lapse of time, or both, would constitute a default or breach under any of the Service Contracts. Those Service Contracts listed on <u>Exhibit G</u> that Buyer has designated for termination in accordance with the provisions of Section 7.1 shall be terminated by Seller at or prior to Closing, and all sums due thereunder shall be paid in full by Seller at or prior to Closing;

(iii)   <u>Municipal Improvements.</u> To Seller's knowledge all street paving, curbing, sanitary sewers, storm sewers, and other municipal or governmental improvements which have been constructed or installed have been paid for and, to Seller's knowledge, will not hereafter be assessed, and all assessments heretofore made have been paid in full;

and there are no private contractual obligations relating to the installation of or connection to any sanitary sewers or storm sewers;

    (iv) <u>Violations of Law</u>. Seller has received no written notice relating to the Property of any violations of federal, state, or local laws, rules, regulations, orders, or other governmental requirements pertaining to zoning, subdivision, environmental, building, safety, and fire standards which have not been corrected, the zoning classification of the Property permits the uses currently being made thereof, and all such uses are being conducted in accordance with all applicable laws;

    (v) <u>Litigation Against the Property</u>. To Seller's knowledge there is no action, suit, or proceeding pending or threatened against or affecting Seller or the Property of any portion thereof, or any of the Leases or Service Contracts, or relating to or arising out of the ownership, management, or operation of the Property, in any court or before or by any federal, state, county, or municipal department, commission, board, bureau, or agency or other governmental instrumentality;

    (vi) <u>Utilities</u>. Water, sanitary sewer, storm sewer, drainage, electric, telephone, gas, and other public utility systems and lines serve the Property with capacity and in a manner adequate for the present use of the Property and are directly connected to the lines and other facilities of the respective public authorities or utility companies providing such services or accepting such discharge, either adjacent to the Property or through easements or rights of way appurtenant to and forming a part of the Property; and the water and sanitary sewer service described above is supplied by a public authority;

    (vii) <u>Condemnation</u>. Seller has not received any notice that any condemnation proceedings or other proceedings in the nature of eminent domain are currently pending in connection with the Property, and to Seller's knowledge no such proceedings are currently threatened;

    (viii) <u>Environmental Condition</u>. During Seller's ownership of the Property, no Hazardous Materials were deposited on the Property or onto neighboring properties by Seller or, to Seller's knowledge, any other party. For purposes of this Contract, the term "Hazardous Materials" means those elements and compounds which are designated as such in the Comprehensive Environmental Response, Compensation and Liability Act of 1980, as amended, all petroleum products and by-products, and any other hazardous substances as that term may be further defined in any and all applicable federal, state, and local laws. Seller has delivered to Buyer true, correct, and complete copies of all environmental reports in Seller's possession or reasonable control, which reports are listed on Exhibit H attached hereto;

    (ix) <u>Permits</u>. To Seller's knowledge, Seller has not failed to maintain or obtain any license or permit necessary for the operation of the

Property in the manner in which it is presently being operated. All warranties, guarantees, licenses, and permits held by Seller or otherwise benefiting the Property are listed on Exhibit I attached hereto;

(x) Tax Appeals. There are no pending tax appeals with respect to real property taxes or assessments against the Property; and

(xi) Insurance. Seller currently maintains, and shall maintain through the Closing Date, property and casualty insurance with respect to the Property in an amount not less than $_____, and Seller has no knowledge of any unrepaired casualty losses.

(c) with regard to the Leases:

(i) Full Force and Effect. Exhibit J attached hereto sets forth a true, correct, and complete schedule of all Leases and any amendments, modifications, supplements, and renewals thereto. The copies of the Leases delivered by Seller to Buyer are true, correct, and complete copies of the Leases and the same have not been further amended, modified, or supplemented; and no tenant thereunder has any right to extend or renew the term thereof except as expressly set forth in the Leases. Each of the Leases is in full force and effect, the tenant thereunder is in actual possession of the leased unit and open for business, and neither Seller nor, to Seller's knowledge, the tenant is in default under such Lease;

(ii) Claims of Tenants. No tenant has asserted any claim of which Seller has written notice that could adversely affect the right of Seller, as landlord under the Lease, to collect rent from such tenant, and no written notice of default or breach on the part of Seller, as landlord under any Lease, has been received from any tenant which has not been cured; and

(iii) Tenant Concessions. Except as set forth in the Leases, no tenant is entitled to any concession, allowance, rebate, or refund and no tenant has prepaid any rent or other charges for more than the current month.

The representations and warranties made in this Contract and in any other documents pertaining to the Closing (the "Closing Documents") by Seller shall be continuing and shall be deemed remade by Seller as of the Closing Date with the same force and effect as if made on, and as of, the Closing Date, and shall survive for one (1) year following the Closing Date.

6.2 Buyer's Representations and Warranties. Buyer represents and warrants to Seller that:

(a) Status and Authority of Buyer. Buyer is a duly organized and validly existing _____ under the laws of the State of _____ that is in good standing and has all requisite power and authority to executed and deliver this Contract and the Transfer Documents and to perform its obligations under this Contract to consummate the transaction contemplated hereby;

(b) <u>Action of Buyer.</u> Buyer has taken all necessary action to authorize the execution, delivery, and performance of this Contract, and upon the execution and delivery of any document to be delivered by Buyer on or prior to the Closing Date, such document shall constitute the valid and binding obligation and agreement of Buyer, enforceable against Buyer in accordance with its terms, except as enforceability may be limited by bankruptcy, insolvency, reorganization, moratorium, or similar laws of general application affecting the rights and remedies of creditors;

(c) <u>Authorizations and Consents.</u> Buyer has obtained all necessary authorizations and consents to enable it to execute and deliver this Contract, and as of the Closing Date, Buyer will have obtained all necessary authorizations and consents to enable it to consummate the transactions contemplated herein;

(d) <u>No Violation of Other Agreements.</u> The compliance with or fulfillment of the terms and conditions of this Contract will not conflict with, violate, or result in a breach of the terms, conditions, or provisions of, or constitute a default under, any of Buyer's organizational documents or any contract or agreement to which Buyer is a party or by which Buyer is otherwise bound;

(e) <u>Litigation.</u> There are no pending or, to the knowledge of Buyer, threatened actions or proceedings against Buyer that, if determined adversely to Buyer, would materially adversely affect Buyer's ability to perform its obligations under this Contract or that would enjoin or prevent the consummation of the Closing; and

(f) <u>Money Laundering and Patriot Act.</u> (i) Buyer is not named and is not acting, directly or indirectly, for or on behalf of any person, group, entity, or nation named by any Executive Order, including without limitation Executive Order 13224, or the United States Treasury Department as a terrorist, "Specially Designated National and Blocked Person," or other banned or blocked person, entity, nation, or transaction pursuant to any law, order, rule, or regulation that is enacted, enforced, or administered by the Office of Foreign Assets Control ("OFAC"); (ii) Buyer is not engaged in this transaction, directly or indirectly, for or on behalf of, or instigating or facilitating this transaction, directly or indirectly on behalf of, any such person, group, entity, or nation; and (iii) none of the proceeds used to consummate this transaction have been or will be derived from a "specified unlawful activity" as defined in, and Buyer is not otherwise in violation of, the Money Laundering Control Act of 1986, as amended, or any other applicable laws regarding money laundering activities. Furthermore, Buyer agrees to notify Seller immediately if Buyer was, is, or in the future becomes, a "senior foreign political figure" within the meaning of Section 312 of the USA PATRIOT Act of 2001, as amended or an immediate family member or close associate of a senior foreign political figure. Notwithstanding anything in this Contract to the contrary, Buyer understands that this Contract is a continuing transaction and that the foregoing representations, certifications, and warranties are ongoing and shall be and remain true and in force on the date hereof and throughout the term of the Contract and that any breach thereof shall be a default under the Contract (not subject to any notice or cure rights) giving rise to remedies by Seller, and Buyer hereby agrees to defend, indemnify, and hold harmless Seller from and against any and all claims, damages, losses, risks, liabilities, fines, penalties, forfeitures, and expenses (including without limitation costs and attorneys' fees) arising from or related to any breach of the foregoing representations, certifications, and warranties.

The representations and warranties made in this Contract and in the Closing Documents by Buyer shall be continuing and shall be deemed remade by Buyer as of the Closing Date with the same force and effect as if made on, and as of, the Closing Date and shall survive Closing.

6.3   Disclaimer; Buyer's Acknowledgments re: Condition of the Property; Acceptance of the Property. Buyer hereby acknowledges that prior to the Due Diligence Expiration Date, subject to the terms of this Contract, Buyer will have had the full and free opportunity to perform the Due Diligence Review and independently inspect and review all conditions of the Property including environmental conditions.

Buyer acknowledges and agrees that except as expressly set forth in this Contract or in the Closing Documents, Seller has not made, does not make, and specifically negates and disclaims any representations, warranties, promises, covenants, agreements, or guarantees of any kind or character whatsoever, whether express or implied, oral or written, past, present, or future, of, as to, concerning, or with respect to (a) the value, nature, quality, or condition of the Property, including, without limitation, the water, soil, and geology, (b) the income to be derived from the Property, (c) the suitability of the Property for any and all activities and uses which Buyer, Buyer's affiliates, or any tenant may conduct thereon, (d) the compliance of or by the Property or the operations at the Property with any laws, rules, ordinances, or regulations of any applicable governmental authority or body, (e) the habitability, merchantability, marketability, profitability, or fitness for a particular purpose of the Property, (f) the manner or quality of the construction or materials, if any, incorporated into the Property, (g) the manner, quality, and state of repair or lack of repair of the Property, (h) compliance with any environmental protection, pollution, or land use laws, rules, regulations, orders, or requirements, including the existence in or on the Property of Hazardous Materials, or (i) any other matter with respect to the Property. Additionally, except as expressly set forth in this Contract or in the Closing Documents, no person acting on behalf of Seller is authorized to make, and by execution hereof Buyer acknowledges that no person has made, any representation, agreement, statement, warranty, guarantee, or promise regarding the Property or the transaction contemplated herein; and no such representation, agreement, statement, warranty, guarantee, or promise, if any, made by any person acting on behalf of Seller shall be valid or binding upon Seller unless expressly set forth herein. Except as expressly set forth in this Contract or in the Closing Documents, Buyer further acknowledges and agrees that, having been given the opportunity to inspect the Property, Buyer and Buyer's affiliates shall rely solely on the Due Diligence Review and on their own independent investigation of the Property, subject to the terms of this Contract and the Closing Documents, and not on any information provided or to be provided by or on behalf of Seller, and agrees to accept the Property at the closing and waive all objections or claims against Seller (including, but not limited to, any right or claim of contribution or any claim purporting to arise out of Seller's own negligence) arising from or related to the Property or to any Hazardous Materials on the Property, other than with respect to claims against third parties. Buyer further acknowledges and agrees that any information provided or to be provided with respect to the Property was obtained from a variety of sources and that Seller has not made any independent investigation or verification of such information and makes no representations as to the accuracy, truthfulness, or completeness of such information except as expressly set forth in this Contract or in the Closing Documents. Except as expressly set forth in this Contract or in the Closing Documents, Seller is not liable or bound in any manner by any verbal or written statement, representation, or information pertaining to the Property, or the operation thereof, furnished by any real estate broker, contractor, agent, employee, servant, or other person. Buyer further acknowledges and agrees that, to the maximum extent permitted by law, the sale of the Property as provided for herein is made on an "AS IS, WHERE IS" condition and basis "WITH ALL FAULTS." It is understood and agreed that the Purchase Price has been determined through negotiation to reflect that the Property is being sold by Seller and purchased by Buyer in the foregoing condition.

7. Covenants.

In addition to the covenants contained in the other Sections of this Contract, the Seller hereby covenants with Buyer that, from the Effective Date until the Closing Date:

7.1 Approval of Contracts. Except as otherwise authorized by this Contract, Seller shall not enter into, modify, amend, or terminate the Leases or any other agreement with respect to the Property or grant any consent thereunder which would encumber or be binding upon Buyer from and after the Closing Date without in each instance obtaining the prior written consent of Buyer, which consent shall not be unreasonably withheld, conditioned, or delayed. On or prior to the Due Diligence Expiration Date, Buyer shall provide Seller with a list of Service Contracts which Buyer would like terminated prior to Closing and provided that Buyer delivers such written notice to Seller, Seller shall terminate all such Service Contracts prior to the Closing Date;

7.2    Operation of the Property. Seller shall continue to operate the Property as currently operated, in a good and businesslike fashion consistent with its past business practices, to cause the Property to be maintained in good working order and condition in a manner consistent with its past business practices, to keep current insurance policies in effect (or comparable replacements thereof), to not encumber the Property, and to provide Buyer with copies of any written violation notices or other written notices involving litigation, condemnation, environmental, zoning, or other land use regulation proceedings it receives;

7.3    Statements. Seller shall deliver to Buyer copies of any bills for real estate taxes and personal property taxes and copies of any notices pertaining to real estate taxes or assessments applicable to the Property that are received by Seller after the Effective Date, even if received after Closing. The obligations set forth in this Section 7.3 shall be Surviving Provisions; and

7.4    Estoppels. Seller shall cooperate with Buyer to attempt to obtain any estoppels requested by Buyer with respect to material agreements (other than the Leases) affecting the Property. Buyer shall request any such estoppels prior to the Due Diligence Expiration Date. The delivery of any requested estoppels (other than the Tenant Estoppels) shall not be a condition to Buyer's obligation to consummate Closing.

8.   Conditions to Obligations of Seller and Buyer.

8.1    Seller's Conditions. The obligations of Seller hereunder are subject to satisfaction of each of the following conditions as of the time of Closing:

(a)  Buyer shall have complied in all material respects with all of the terms, covenants, and conditions hereof to be complied with on the part of Buyer, including but not limited to the delivery to Seller of the Purchase Price payable hereunder, as adjusted as herein provided; and

(b)  All representations and warranties of Buyer in Section 6.2 of this Contract shall be true and correct at the time of Closing as if made at such time, provided, however, that such representations and warranties shall not survive Closing.

If Seller's Conditions listed above have not been satisfied to the sole satisfaction of Seller or waived in writing by Seller, and provided Seller is not in breach of this Contract, Seller shall be entitled to terminate this Contract and to pursue its remedies under Section 10.2 of this Contract.

8.2    Buyer's Conditions. The obligations of Buyer hereunder are subject to satisfaction of each of the following conditions as of the time of Closing:

(a)  Seller shall have complied in all material respects with all of the terms, covenants, and conditions hereof to be complied with on the part of Seller;

(b)  All representations and warranties of Seller in Section 6.1 of this Contract shall be true and correct at the time of Closing as if made at such time, provided, however, that such representations and warranties shall not survive Closing, except that those representations and warranties listed in Sections [6.1(b)(ii), 6.1(b)(iii), 6.1(b)(iv), 6.1(b)(v), 6.1(b)(vii), and 6.1(b)(viii), and in Section 6.1(c) (but only as to any Lease for which Seller is unable to obtain a Tenant Estoppel)] shall survive Closing for a period of six (6) months after Closing;

(c)  Buyer shall have received an owner's policy of title insurance for the Property, consistent with Sections 3.2 and 3.5 above;

(d)  The physical condition of the Property shall be substantially the same on the Closing Date as on the Effective Date, reasonable wear and tear excepted, and, as of the Closing Date, there shall be no litigation or administrative agency or other governmental proceeding of any kind whatsoever, pending or threatened, which after Closing would materially adversely affect the value of the Property or the ability of Buyer to operate the Property in the manner in which it is currently being operated;

(e)  There shall have been no material adverse change in the financial condition of any tenant during the period from the date of this Contract to the Closing Date;

(f)  Buyer shall have received the Tenant Estoppels required under Section 3.9 of this Contract; and

(g)  Buyer's obligation to consummate the Closing shall be conditioned upon receipt by Buyer, within _____ (\_\_) days after the date of this Contract, of a commitment by a third-party lender to make a loan to Buyer (a) in the minimum principal amount of _____ and 00/100 dollars ($_____); (b) for a minimum term of _____ _____ (\_\_) months; (c) at an annual rate of interest not to exceed _____ percent (\_\_\_%); and (d) to be secured by a first lien on the Property (a loan on such terms is called a "Purchase Money Loan"). Within _____ (\_\_) days after the date of this Contract, Buyer shall apply for a Purchase Money Loan, and shall thereafter diligently pursue obtaining a commitment for such Purchase Money Loan. If Buyer applies for and diligently pursues a commitment for the Purchase Money Loan, as provided by this Section 8.2(g), but does not receive such commitment within _____ (\_\_) days after the date of this Contract, Buyer may elect either to waive such condition and proceed to consummate the Closing or to terminate this Contract by giving Seller Notice thereof within _____ (\_\_) days after the date of this Contract. If Buyer does not give Seller such Notice within such time period, then Buyer shall be deemed to have waived Buyer's right to terminate this Contract as provided by this Section. If Buyer elects to terminate this Contract as provided by this Section, the Escrow Agent shall promptly thereafter return the Down Payment to Buyer and this Contract shall thereupon terminate and be of no further force or effect except as otherwise expressly provided by this Contract.

If Buyer's Conditions listed above have not been satisfied to the sole satisfaction of Buyer or waived in writing by Buyer, and provided Buyer is not in breach of this Contract, Buyer shall be entitled to terminate this Contract and pursue its remedies under Section 10.3 of this Contract.

9. Risk of Loss.

9.1   Casualty. If, between the Effective Date and the Closing Date, all or a portion of the Property is damaged or destroyed, Buyer shall, within ten (10) Business Days after receipt of notice of said damage or destruction, have the right either to terminate this Contract as to the entire Property, whereupon Seller shall promptly direct the Escrow Agent to return the Down Payment to Buyer, or to consummate the transaction contemplated hereby, in which event Seller's right to all insurance proceeds resulting from such damage or destruction shall be assigned in writing by Seller to Buyer at Closing and Seller shall have no further obligation to Buyer with regard to such damage or destruction.

9.2   Condemnation. If, between the Effective Date and the Closing Date, all or a portion of the Property shall be taken by reason of the exercise of the power of eminent domain (the "Taking Property"), Buyer shall, within ten (10) Business Days after receipt of notice of said taking, have the right either to terminate this Contract as to the entire Property, whereupon Seller shall promptly direct the Escrow Agent to return the Down Payment to Buyer, or to consummate the transaction contemplated hereby, in which event Seller's right to all compensation to which Seller may be entitled pursuant to the eminent domain law shall be assigned in writing by Seller to Buyer at Closing and Seller shall have no further obligation to Buyer with regard to such taking.

10. Remedies Upon Default.

10.1   Time of Essence. Time is of the essence with respect to all of the terms and conditions set forth in this Contract.

10.2   Seller's Remedies. If the Closing fails to occur as a result of a default by Buyer in the performance of its obligations under this Contract (a "Buyer Default"), Seller and Buyer agree that it would be impractical and extremely difficult to estimate the damages that Seller may suffer. Therefore, Seller and Buyer hereby agree that the reasonable estimate of the total net detriment that Seller would suffer in the event of a Buyer Default, and Seller's sole remedy (whether at law or in equity), shall be the right to receive from the Escrow Agent and retain the full amount of the Down Payment. The payment to Seller of the Down Payment as liquidated damages is not intended as a forfeiture or penalty within the meaning of applicable law and is intended to settle all issues and questions about the amount of damages suffered by Seller in the event of a Buyer Default. Upon the occurrence of any Buyer Default that remains uncured for _____ (__) Business Days after Seller gives Buyer Notice thereof, Buyer shall promptly execute and deliver written instructions directing the Escrow Agent to disburse the Down Payment to Seller as liquidated damages, and upon such disbursement this Contract shall terminate and be of no further force or effect except as otherwise expressly provided by this Contract.

10.3   Buyer's Remedies. If the Closing fails to occur as a result of a default by Seller in the performance of its obligations under this Contract (a "Seller Default"), Buyer may, as Buyer's sole remedy, either (i) terminate this Contract, upon giving Notice thereof to Seller, in which event Seller shall promptly execute and deliver written instructions directing the Escrow Agent to return the Down Payment to Buyer, and upon such disbursement this Contract shall terminate and be of no further force or effect except as otherwise expressly provided by this Contract[, and Seller also shall reimburse Buyer for its actual out-of-pocket expenses up to _____

_____ Dollars ($_____)], or (ii) commence a suit for specific performance of this Contract, provided such action is commenced within ninety (90) days following the Closing Date.

10.4   Attorneys' Fees. If any litigation is brought concerning this Contract or the Property, the party who prevails in the final judgment or order of court will be entitled to such party's reasonable attorneys' fees and direct costs and expenses in connection with the litigation.

10.5   Waiver of Tender. Formal tender of the balance of the Purchase Price by Buyer to Seller and of the Deed by Seller to Buyer is hereby waived by both Seller and Buyer.

11. Miscellaneous.

11.1   Broker. Each of Seller and Buyer represent and warrant to the other that no brokers were involved in connection with the transaction contemplated hereby. Seller further represents and warrants to Buyer that all brokerage fees incurred in connection with the Leases have been paid in full and that there will be no brokerage fees or commissions due in respect of any extension or renewal of any Lease. Each party hereby indemnifies and holds the other party harmless from and against any and all claims for any broker's commission or similar compensation that may be payable to any broker, finder, or other person or entity based solely upon such party's own acts. The provisions of this Section are Surviving Provisions.

11.2   Next Business Day. In the event that any date described herein for payment or performance of the provisions hereof falls on a Saturday, Sunday, or legal holiday, the time for such payment or performance shall be extended to the next Business Day.

11.3   Notices. Any notices or other communications between the parties hereto (each a "Notice," and collectively, "Notices") shall be in writing and shall be given (a) by hand, (b) by United States registered or certified mail, postage prepaid, return receipt requested, (c) by overnight courier service guaranteeing next Business Day delivery, or (d) via telecopier or facsimile transmission to the facsimile number listed below, addressed to the party for whom intended as follows:

(a) if to Seller:

_____

_____

_____

_____

_____

with a copy to be delivered to:

_____

_____

_____

_____

_____

(b) if to Buyer:

_____

_____

_____

_____

_____

with a copy to be delivered to:

_____

_____

_____

_____

_____

Either party may designate by Notice given to the other party a new address to which Notices hereunder shall thereafter be sent. All Notices hereunder shall be deemed to have been delivered (i) immediately upon actual receipt or refusal by the party to whom intended; (ii) three (3) Business Days after deposit thereof at any main or branch United States post office if sent in accordance with (b) above; (iii) one (1) Business Day after deposit thereof with an overnight courier service if sent in accordance with (c) above; (iv) immediately upon delivery by hand in accordance with (a) above; or (v) upon successful transmission of all pages on or before 7:00 P.M. local time of the recipient's facsimile machine or, if transmitted after such time or on a non-Business Day, then as of the next succeeding Business Day, if sent in accordance with (d) above.

 11.4 <u>Covenant Not to Record.</u> Buyer will not record this Contract or any memorandum thereof, and any such recording shall constitute a default by Buyer hereunder.

11.5 <u>Entire Contract; Merger.</u> All understandings and agreements, oral or written, heretofore had between the parties with respect to the subject matter hereof are merged in this Contract, which alone, with the attached Exhibits, fully and completely expresses their agreement. This Contract is entered into after full investigation, neither party relying upon any statement or representation not embodied in this Contract made by the other party. This Contract may not be terminated, modified, or amended, nor any provision hereof waived, in whole or in part, except by a writing signed by the party against whom enforcement of such termination, modification, amendment, or waiver is sought.

11.6 <u>Interpretation.</u> Whenever used in this Contract, the singular shall include the plural, the plural the singular, and the use of any gender shall be applicable to all genders. Any reference to a portion of this Contract surviving Closing is intended to mean that such portion will survive Closing, earlier termination of this Contract, or delivery of the Deed. Article and Section headings are inserted for convenience only and shall not form a part of the text of this Contract.

11.7 <u>Choice of Law; Binding Effect.</u> Enforcement of this Contract shall be governed by and construed in accordance with the laws of the State of

_____ .

11.8 <u>Counterparts/Facsimile.</u> This Contract may be executed in one or more counterparts, each of which shall be deemed an original, but all of which together shall constitute but one instrument. This Contract may be executed via facsimile followed by regular mail of the originals and shall be considered executed and binding upon receipt of the fax of the signature page of the last of the parties to sign this Contract.

11.9 <u>Waiver of Trial by Jury.</u> [Note to drafter: The law in some states may require a provision of this nature to be set forth in uppercase type.] To the extent permitted by law, each party hereby waives, irrevocably and unconditionally, trial by jury in any action brought on, under, or by virtue of or relating in any way to this Contract or any of the documents executed in connection herewith, the Property, or any claims, defenses, rights of set-off, or other actions pertaining hereto or to any of the foregoing.

11.10 <u>No Third Party Beneficiary.</u> The provisions of this Contract are not intended to benefit any person or entity not a party hereto.

11.11 <u>Severability.</u> If any provision of this Contract, or the application thereof to any person, entity, place, or circumstance, shall be held by a court of competent jurisdiction to be invalid, unenforceable, or void in any respect, the remainder of this Contract and such provisions as applied to other persons, entities, places, and circumstances shall remain in full force and effect.

11.12 <u>Time Is of the Essence.</u> The parties agree that time is of the essence.

IN WITNESS WHEREOF, the parties hereto have duly executed this Contract and caused their seals to be affixed hereto, so that this Contract constitutes a sealed instrument under _____ law, the day and year first above written.

SELLER:

_____

By:_____

Name:

Title:


BUYER:

_____

By:_____

Name:

Title:

CONSENT OF ESCROW AGENT: Escrow Agent hereby joins herein in order to be bound by Section 2.5 hereof.

ESCROW AGENT:

_____

By:_____

Name:

Title:

# Appendix C

## Form of Tenant Estoppel Certificate

_____

_____

_____

_____

and

_____

_____

_____

_____

Ladies and Gentlemen:

You have informed us of a pending sale of the project commonly known as _____ (the "Property").

For Ten Dollars ($10.00) and other good and sufficient consideration, receipt of which is hereby acknowledged, and for the purposes of providing information to _____ (together with its successors and assigns, "Lender"), and to _____ (together with its successors and assigns, "Buyer"), regarding the Property and the leased premises (the "Premises") in which the undersigned is a tenant under that certain lease agreement (the "Lease") dated _____ ___, _____, between _____ ("Tenant") and _____ _____ (such lessor and its successors and assigns are hereinafter referred to as "Landlord"), the undersigned Tenant does hereby certify and agree that:

1. The Lease, a true and correct copy of which (including all amendments and extensions) is attached hereto as <u>Exhibit A,</u> is in full force and effect, is valid and enforceable according to its terms against Tenant, and has not been modified, amended, supplemented, or changed in any respect, either orally or in writing, except as indicated in <u>Exhibit A.</u> The Premises contains approximately _____ rentable square feet.

2. a. <u>Term of Lease:</u> _____

      Date of Commencement: _____ _____, 19___

      Date of Expiration*: _____ _____, 20___

  *(to include any presently exercised option or renewal term)

 b. <u>Renewal Options:</u> _____

      Exercised: _____

      Not Exercised: _____

 c. <u>Current Monthly Rent: $</u>_____

 d. <u>Number of Square Feet in Premises:</u> _____

 e. <u>Current Share of Basic Operating Costs, Common Area Maintenance, Tax, and Insurance Contributions (as applicable):</u> Tenant pays its

proportionate share of annual operating expenses in excess of $_____
_____ per square foot of space in the Property. Tenant also currently pays annual electrical charges of $_____ per rentable square foot of space in the Premises.

    f. <u>Security Deposit</u>: $_____

    g. <u>Guarantor(s) (if any)</u>: _____

    h. <u>Parking Spaces</u>: _____

    3. Tenant has unconditionally accepted possession of the Premises, and all improvements, alterations, other work, and parking facilities to be performed or constructed by Landlord under the Lease have been completed as of the date hereof and unconditionally accepted by Tenant.

    4. All rent, charges or other payments due Landlord under the Lease have been paid as of the date of this certification, and there have been no prepayments of rent or other obligations.

    5. Neither Tenant nor, to the best of Tenant's knowledge, Landlord is in default under any terms of this Lease nor has any event occurred which, with the passage of time (after notice, if any required by the Lease), would become an event of default under the Lease. No event or condition has occurred which, with the passage of time (after notice, if any, required by the Lease), would give rise to any right or option of Tenant to terminate the Lease or discontinue the operation of business from the Premises.

    6. Tenant has no claims, counterclaims, defenses, or setoffs against Landlord arising from the Lease, nor is Tenant entitled to any concession, rebate, allowance, or free rent for any period after this certification. As of the date hereof, Tenant is not entitled to any partial or total abatement of rent or other amounts due under the Lease.

    7. As of the date hereof, there are no actions, whether voluntary or otherwise, which are pending or have been threatened against Tenant under any bankruptcy or insolvency laws of any State or the United States.

    8. Tenant is the actual occupant in possession and has not assigned, transferred, or sublet all or any part of the Premises, except for the following assignments, transfers, or subleases, if any: _____

    9. Tenant has never permitted, and will not permit, the generation, treatment, storage, or disposal of any hazardous substance as defined under federal, state, or local law on the Premises or the Property except for such substances of a type and only in a quantity normally used in connection with the occupancy or operation of buildings (such as nonflammable cleaning fluids and supplies normally used in the day-to-day operation of first-class offices), which substances are being held, stored, and used in strict compliance with federal, state, and local laws.

    10. Tenant's current address for notice under the Lease is _____
_____.

    11. This certification may not be changed, waived, or discharged orally, but only by an agreement in writing.

12. Tenant has no option or right of first refusal to purchase the Premises or the Property, or any portion thereof, or to terminate the Lease. Tenant has no interest in the Premises or the Property other than the leasehold interest provided in the Lease. Tenant has no knowledge of any prior sale, transfer, assignment, hypothecation, or pledge of the Property, the Premises, the Lease, or the rents payable thereunder.

13. This certification shall be binding upon, and shall inure to the benefit of, Buyer, Lender, Landlord, and Tenant, the respective successors and assigns of Buyer, Lender, Landlord, and Tenant, and all parties claiming through or under such persons or any such successor or assign, and Tenant acknowledges that Buyer is purchasing the Property in reliance on this certification.

IN WITNESS WHEREOF, the undersigned has caused this certificate to be executed as of the _____ day of _____, 20__.

_____

By: _____

Name: _____

Title: _____

**EXHIBIT A**
Lease

# Appendix D

# Form of FIRPTA Affidavit

FIRPTA AFFIDAVIT

(CORPORATE)

STATE OF            )
                   ) ss
COUNTY OF           )

Section 1445 of the Internal Revenue Code provides that a transferee (buyer) of a U.S. real property interest must withhold tax if the transferor (seller) is a foreign person. To inform the transferee (buyer) that the withholding of tax is not required upon disposition of a U.S. real property interest by _____ ("Seller"), the undersigned hereby certifies the following on behalf of Seller:

1. Seller is not a foreign corporation, foreign partnership, foreign trust, or foreign estate (as those terms are defined in the Internal Revenue Code and Income Tax regulations).
2. Seller's U.S. employer identification number is _____.
3. Seller's office address is: _____.

The undersigned understands that this certification may be disclosed to the Internal Revenue Service by the transferee and that any false statement made here could be punished by fine, imprisonment, or both.

Under penalties of perjury, I declare that I have examined this certification and, to the best of my knowledge and belief, it is true, correct, and complete, and I further declare that I have authority to sign this certification on behalf of Seller.

a _____

By: _____

Name: _____

Title:

SWORN TO AND SUBSCRIBED before me, the undersigned, a Notary Public for the jurisdiction aforesaid, on _____.

_____

Notary Public

My commission expires _____

# Appendix E

# Form of Due Diligence and Closing Checklist

**Note:** The particular provisions of a due diligence and closing checklist will vary widely, depending on the type and structure of the commercial real estate transaction; the type of property; the type and relationship of the parties; the terms of the contract of sale, the loan commitment, and the other transactional documents; the type of closing; and local real estate practice. Furthermore, the responsibilities of the parties and the role of the closing or escrow agent, who may be a title agent or lawyer, will vary according to local real estate practice. Accordingly, this Form is intended to be illustrative, and the practitioner should become familiar with the documents and with local practice before preparing a due diligence and closing checklist.

In some cases, the buyer and the seller may decide to share a common checklist that covers acquisition matters, and the buyer then will prepare a separate checklist that addresses loan issues. The parties may also decide to use separate checklists for due diligence and closing matters. The Form that follows is designed to be inclusive, covering both acquisition and loan issues, and including both due diligence and closing items, but is prepared from the perspective of the buyer/borrower. Note also that the Due Diligence Checklist arranges items in the sequence in which they appear in the Contract of Sale and the Loan Commitment, while some drafters prefer to group items on the basis of the party that is responsible for performing them.

## DUE DILIGENCE CHECKLIST

| SUBJECT | RESPONSIBLE PARTY | DATE | STATUS |
|---|---|---|---|
| **A. Acquisition Matters** | | | |
| • Execution of Contract of Sale | | | |
| • Confirmation of Buyer's delivery of down payment to Escrow Agent (Contract §§ 2.2(a), 2.5(a)) | | | |
| • Escrow Agent's deposit of down payment into interest-bearing account (Contract §§ 2.4, 2.5(a)) | | | |
| • Seller's provision of most recent title insurance policy to Buyer (Contract § 3.1(a)) | | | |

*(Continued)*

### DUE DILIGENCE CHECKLIST (*Continued*)

| SUBJECT | RESPONSIBLE PARTY | DATE | STATUS |
|---|---|---|---|
| • Buyer's obtaining of and review of an updated Title Commitment for the Property, including endorsements (Contract §§ 3.1(a), 3.5) | | | |
| • Seller's provision of most recent survey to Buyer (Contract § 3.1(a)) | | | |
| • Buyer's obtaining of an updated Survey (Contract §§ 3.1(a), 3.4) | | | |
| • Seller's provision to Buyer of true, correct, and complete copies of all Leases (Contract § 3.1(a)) | | | |
| • Seller's provision to Buyer of access to Seller's books and records (Contract § 3.1(a)) | | | |
| • Buyer's obtaining of a new environmental report (Contract § 3.1(a)) | | | |
| • Buyer's provision of Termination Notice to Seller by Due Diligence Expiration Date (Contract § 3.1(b)) | | | |
| • Buyer's provision of Title and Survey Objection Notice to Seller by Title and Survey Objection Date (Contract § 3.1(c)) | | | |
| • Seller's response to Title and Survey Objection Notice (Contract § 3.1(c)) | | | |
| • Buyer's notice of termination of Contract due to Seller's failure to cure title and survey matters (Contract § 3.1(c)) | | | |
| • Buyer's notice of objection to any matters disclosed in a title continuation report (Contract § 3.1(c)) | | | |

(*Continued*)

## DUE DILIGENCE CHECKLIST *(Continued)*

| SUBJECT | RESPONSIBLE PARTY | DATE | STATUS |
|---------|-------------------|------|--------|
| • Buyer's delivery to Seller, prior to Buyer's undertaking of due diligence review, of evidence that Buyer carries adequate insurance (Contract § 3.6) | | | |
| • Buyer's return to Seller of all due diligence documents, if Closing does not occur for any reason (Contract § 3.8) | | | |
| • Seller's preparation of Tenant Estoppels (Contract § 3.9) | | | |
| • Seller's delivery of Tenant Estoppels to tenants listed on Rent Roll (Contract § 3.9) | | | |
| • Seller's delivery of Tenant Estoppels to Buyer, after completion by tenants (Contract §§ 3.9, 8.2(f)) | | | |
| • Seller to cause all utility meters to be read (Contract § 5.1) | | | |
| • Apportionment of Transfer Taxes and Other Costs (Contract § 5.7) | | | |
| • Buyer to designate in writing Service Contracts to be terminated (Contract § 6.1(b)(ii)) | | | |
| • Seller to terminate those Service Contracts designated in writing by Buyer (Contract §§ 6.1(b)(ii), 7.1) | | | |
| • Buyer to confirm zoning compliance, including receipt of zoning letter from zoning authority, if available (Contract § 6.1(b)(iv)) | | | |

*(Continued)*

### DUE DILIGENCE CHECKLIST (*Continued*)

| SUBJECT | RESPONSIBLE PARTY | DATE | STATUS |
|---|---|---|---|
| • Buyer to receive copies of all approvals, including subdivision approvals, certificates of occupancy, zoning variances, special exceptions, and similar documents (Contract §§ 6.1(b)(iv), (ix)) | | | |
| • Buyer to investigate any code or other violations (Contract § 6.1(b)(iv)) | | | |
| • Buyer to receive copies of all prior reviews and approvals from architectural committees, if applicable (Contract § 6.1(b)(iv)) | | | |
| • Seller's delivery of all environmental reports to Buyer (Contract § 6.1(b)(viii)) | | | |
| • Buyer to investigate whether there are pending tax assessment proceedings (Contract § 6.1(b)(x)) | | | |
| • Buyer to investigate whether there are special assessments or other similar obligations to municipalities or government authorities (Contract § 6.1(b)(x)) | | | |
| • Buyer to confirm that Seller maintains adequate property and casualty insurance through the Closing Date (Contract § 6.1(b)(xi)) | | | |
| • Seller's delivery of tax bills to Buyer (Contract § 7.3) | | | |
| • Seller's delivery of non-Lease estoppels to Buyer (Contract § 7.4) | | | |
| • Buyer's application for Purchase Money Loan (Contract § 8.2(g)) | | | |

(*Continued*)

## DUE DILIGENCE CHECKLIST (*Continued*)

| SUBJECT | RESPONSIBLE PARTY | DATE | STATUS |
|---|---|---|---|
| • Buyer's notice of termination to Seller due to lack of receipt of commitment for Purchase Money Loan (Contract § 8.2(g)) | | | |
| **B. Loan Matters** | | | |
| • Borrower's delivery of Commitment Fee to Lender (Commitment § 9(a)) | | | |
| • Borrower's delivery of appraisal to Lender (Commitment § 10(a)) | | | |
| • Borrower's delivery of mortgagee's policy of title insurance to Lender (Commitment § 10(b)) | | | |
| • Borrower's delivery of survey to Lender (Commitment § 10(c)) | | | |
| • Borrower's delivery of environmental report to Lender (Commitment § 10(d)) | | | |
| • Borrower's delivery of all acquisition documents to Lender (Commitment § 10(e)) | | | |
| • Borrower's delivery of building plans and specifications to Lender (Commitment § 10(f)) | | | |
| • Borrower's delivery of an engineering report to Lender (Commitment § 10(f)) | | | |
| • Borrower's delivery of an architect's or engineer's certificate to Lender (Commitment § 10(g)) | | | |
| • Borrower's delivery of all insurance certificates to Lender (Commitment § 10(h)) | | | |
| • Borrower's delivery of a certified rent roll to Lender (Commitment § 10(i)) | | | |

(*Continued*)

## DUE DILIGENCE CHECKLIST (*Continued*)

| SUBJECT | RESPONSIBLE PARTY | DATE | STATUS |
|---|---|---|---|
| • Borrower's delivery of all leases to Lender (Commitment § 10(i)) | | | |
| • Borrower's delivery of an update to the certified rent roll to Lender (Commitment § 10(i)) | | | |
| • Borrower's delivery of all estoppel certificates to Lender (Commitment § 10(j)) | | | |
| • Borrower's delivery of the management agreement and all service contracts to the Lender (Commitment § 10(k)) | | | |
| • Borrower's delivery to Lender of evidence of all utility connections (Commitment § 10(l)) | | | |
| • Borrower's delivery of UCC searches to Lender (Commitment § 10(m)) | | | |
| • Borrower's delivery of other searches of public records to Lender (Commitment § 10(m)) | | | |
| • Borrower's delivery of evidence of its power to borrow to Lender (Commitment § 10(n)) | | | |
| • Borrower's delivery of certified copies of its formation documents and related materials to Lender (Commitment § 10(n)) | | | |
| • Borrower's delivery of all required financial statements to Lender (Commitment § 10(o)) | | | |
| • Borrower's delivery to Lender of all other documents required by Lender (Commitment § 10(v)) | | | |

(*Continued*)

## CLOSING CHECKLIST

| DOCUMENT/ITEM | RESPON-SIBLE PARTY | EXECUT-ING PARTIES | STATUS |
|---|---|---|---|
| **A. Purchase and Sale Documents** | | | |
| 1. Closing Documents | | | |
|   a. Contract of Sale | | | |
|   b. Assignment of Contract of Sale, if any | | | |
|   c. Deed (Contract § 4.2(a)(i)) | | | |
|   d. Bill of Sale (Contract § 4.2(a)(ii)) | | | |
|   e. Assignment of Leases by Seller and Assumption by Buyer (Contract § 4.2(a)(iii)) | | | |
|   f. FIRPTA Affidavit (Contract § 4.2(b)) | | | |
|   g. Seller's Representations Update Certificate (Contract § 4.2(e)(iii)) | | | |
|   h. Buyer's Representations Update Certificate, if required | | | |
| 2. Other Closing Deliveries | | | |
|   a. Delivery of balance of purchase price (Contract §§ 2.2(b), 4.2(c)) | | | |
|   b. Delivery of purchase money note and mortgage, if any (Contract § 2.2(c)) | | | |
|   c. Payoff from current lender, if any | | | |
|   d. Tenant Estoppel Certificates (Contract §§ 3.9, 8.2(f)) | | | |
|     (1) Required Tenants | | | |
|       i. | | | |
|       ii. | | | |
|     (2) Remaining Tenants | | | |

*(Continued)*

**CLOSING CHECKLIST (*Continued*)**

| DOCUMENT/ITEM | RESPON-SIBLE PARTY | EXECUT-ING PARTIES | STATUS |
|---|---|---|---|
| e. Delivery of Service Contract Assignments (Contract § 4.2(a)(iv)) | | | |
| f. Seller's delivery of new Certificates of Occupancy (Contract § 4.2(d)) | | | |
| g. Seller's delivery of documents and money adequate to satisfy liens (Contract § 4.3) | | | |
| h. Security deposits under the Leases (Contract § 5.4) | | | |
| i. Original Letters of Credit held by Seller as security deposits, if any (Contract § 5.4) | | | |
| **B. Title/Escrow Documents** | | | |
| 3. Buyer's Title Commitment (Contract §§ 3.1(a), 3.5) | | | |
| 4. Buyer's Pro Forma Title Policy, including endorsements (Contract §§ 3.5, 8.2(c)) | | | |
| 5. Seller's Affidavit (Contract § 4.2(e)(vii)) | | | |
| 6. Escrow Instructions (Contract § 2.5): | | | |
| a. Buyer | | | |
| b. Seller | | | |
| 7. Survey (Contract § 3.4) | | | |
| 8. Other documents/forms required by title company, if any (Contract § 4.2(e)(vii)) | | | |
| 9. Closing Statement (Contract § 4.2(e)(ii)) | | | |
| 10. Prorations/Adjustments/Taxes (Contract §§ 5.1–5.2) | | | |
| a. Rents | | | |

(*Continued*)

## CLOSING CHECKLIST (*Continued*)

| DOCUMENT/ITEM | RESPON-SIBLE PARTY | EXECUT-ING PARTIES | STATUS |
|---|---|---|---|
| b.  Payments and deposits made by Tenants for real estate taxes | | | |
| c.  Real property taxes | | | |
| d.  Utilities | | | |
| e.  Fuel | | | |
| f.  Charges, revenues, and deposits, if any, under Service Contracts not terminated prior to Closing | | | |
| g.  All customary items of revenue or expense, including all advance payments to occupy space or use facilities within the Buildings | | | |
| h.  Credits representing Leasing Costs | | | |
| 11.  Closing Costs/Expenses (Contract §§ 2.5(e), 3.1, 3.4, 5.7) | | | |
| a.  Escrow fees | | | |
| b.  Legal fees | | | |
| c.  Cost of updates to Survey | | | |
| d.  Cost of Title Commitment and any endorsements to Buyer's title insurance policy | | | |
| e.  Due diligence expenses and charges for any engineering reports or appraisals commissioned by Buyer | | | |
| f.  Special tax, impact fee, or assessment, if any | | | |
| g.  City and state charges to record documents in the Official Records | | | |

(*Continued*)

**CLOSING CHECKLIST (*Continued*)**

| DOCUMENT/ITEM | RESPON-SIBLE PARTY | EXECUT-ING PARTIES | STATUS |
|---|---|---|---|
| h.  Termination fees, if any, arising out of the termination of a Service Contract | | | |
| i.  State and local transfer taxes, including grantor's tax and grantee's tax | | | |
| j.  Leasing and brokerage costs | | | |
| **C.  Organizational Documents/Authority** | | | |
| 12.  Seller's Organizational Documents (Contract § 4.2(e)(vi)): | | | |
| a.  Certified Articles of Organization | | | |
| b.  Bylaws | | | |
| c.  Incumbency/Restrictions | | | |
| d.  Good Standing Certificate | | | |
| 13.  Buyer's Organizational Documents (Contract § 4.2(e)(vi)): | | | |
| a.  Certified Articles of Organization | | | |
| b.  Bylaws | | | |
| c.  Incumbency/Restrictions | | | |
| d.  Good Standing Certificate | | | |
| **D.  Other Deliveries** | | | |
| 14.  True and complete originals of all Leases (Contract § 4.2(e)(i)) | | | |
| 15.  Updated tenant list (Contract § 4.2(e)(iv)) | | | |
| 16.  Letters to existing Tenants notifying them of sale (Contract § 4.2(e)(v)) | | | |
| 17.  Letters to Service Contractors notifying them of sale (Contract § 4.2(e)(vi)) | | | |

(*Continued*)

## CLOSING CHECKLIST (*Continued*)

| DOCUMENT/ITEM | RESPON-SIBLE PARTY | EXECUT-ING PARTIES | STATUS |
|---|---|---|---|
| 18. Keys (Contract § 4.2(e)(i)) | | | |
| 19. Operating manuals; warranties and guarantees; building plans; permits; real estate tax bills; current water, sewer, and utility bills; Service Contracts (to the extent assumed); and copies of operating statements (Contract § 4.2(e)(i)) | | | |
| **E. Loan Requirements** | | | |
| 20. Appraisal (Commitment § 10(a)) | | | |
| 21. Environmental Report (Commitment § 10(d)) | | | |
| 22. All acquisition documents to Lender (Commitment § 10(e)) | | | |
| 23. Plans and specifications (Commitment § 10(f)) | | | |
| 24. Report addressing physical condition of property (Commitment § 10(g)) | | | |
| 25. All required insurance certificates (Commitment § 10(h)) | | | |
| 26. Copies of Leases, including all amendments and exhibits (Commitment § 10(i)) | | | |
| 27. Certified Rent Roll (Commitment § 10(i)) | | | |
| 28. Tenant Estoppels (Commitment § 10(j)) | | | |
| 29. Management agreement and all service contracts (Commitment § 10(k)) | | | |
| 30. Evidence of all utility connections (Commitment § 10(l)) | | | |
| 31. UCC Searches (Commitment § 10(m)) | | | |

(*Continued*)

## CLOSING CHECKLIST (*Continued*)

| DOCUMENT/ITEM | RESPON-SIBLE PARTY | EXECUT-ING PARTIES | STATUS |
|---|---|---|---|
| 32. Other searches of public records; background and credit reports (Commitment § 10(m)) | | | |
| 33. Evidence of Borrower's power to borrow (Commitment § 10(n)) | | | |
| 34. Certified copies of Borrower's formation documents and related materials (Commitment § 10(n)) | | | |
| 35. All required financial statements of Borrower and Guarantors (Commitment § 10(o)) | | | |
| 36. Borrower's Certificate (Commitment § 10(p)) | | | |
| 37. Legal Opinion (Commitment § 10(q)) | | | |
| 38. Inventory of Personal Property (Commitment § 10(r)) | | | |
| 39. Evidence demonstrating that Borrower is in compliance with money laundering, anti-terrorism, and other similar laws (Commitment § 10(s)) | | | |
| 40. Written notice of proposed Closing Date (Commitment § 10(t)) | | | |
| 41. All other documents required by Lender (Commitment § 10(v)) | | | |
| 42. Borrower's delivery to Lender of its initial escrow deposit of taxes and insurance (Commitment § 8(c)(iv)) | | | |
| 43. Borrower's payment to Lender of all of Lender's closing costs and expenses (Commitment § 15) | | | |
| 44. Zoning report/zoning opinion, if required | | | |

(*Continued*)

### CLOSING CHECKLIST (*Continued*)

| DOCUMENT/ITEM | RESPON-SIBLE PARTY | EXECUT-ING PARTIES | STATUS |
|---|---|---|---|
| 45. Subordination, nondisturbance, and attornment agreements, if required | | | |
| 46. Agreement assigning and sub-ordinating management fees, if required | | | |
| 47. Current tax bills, if required | | | |
| 48. Taxpayer Identification Number Certificate | | | |
| 49. Closing Statement | | | |
| 50. Closing Agenda | | | |
| **F. Loan Documents** | | | |
| 51. Loan Agreement | | | |
| 52. Promissory Note (Commitment § 8(a)) | | | |
| 53. Mortgage/Deed of Trust (Com-mitment §§ 2, 8(a)(i)) | | | |
| 54. Security Agreement and Fixture Filing (Commitment § 8(a)(i)) | | | |
| 55. UCC Financing Statements (Com-mitment § 8(a)(i)) | | | |
| 56. Assignment of Leases and Rents (Commitment § 8(a)(ii)) | | | |
| 57. Guarantee (Commitment § 8(a)(iii) | | | |
| 58. Environmental Indemnity Agree-ment (Commitment § 8(a)(iv)) | | | |
| 59. Other security documents required by Lender (Commitment § 8(a)(iv)) | | | |
| **G. Lender's Title Requirements** | | | |
| 60. Title Commitment, with under-lying documents (Commitment § 10(b)) | | | |

(*Continued*)

### CLOSING CHECKLIST (*Continued*)

| DOCUMENT/ITEM | RESPON-SIBLE PARTY | EXECUT-ING PARTIES | STATUS |
|---|---|---|---|
| 61. Policy of Title Insurance (Commitment § 10(b)) | | | |
| 62. Survey (Commitment § 10(c)) | | | |
| 63. Required Endorsements | | | |
| **H. Borrower's Requirements** | | | |
| 64. Lender's Delivery of Principal Amount to Borrower (Commitment § 14) | | | |

# Appendix F

## Checklist of Title Endorsements

**Note:** The buyer's lawyer should remember that some states limit the availability of title endorsements, that not every title company offers all of these endorsements, that insurers charge an additional fee for some of these endorsements, and that some endorsements have different names in different states. The buyer's lawyer should discuss title endorsements with the title company representative when first placing the order for title insurance.

Access Endorsement: Insures against loss or damage sustained by the insured if the land does not have actual vehicular and pedestrian access to and from an adjacent public street.

Condominium Endorsement: Insures that the overall premises constitutes a valid condominium regime and protects the policyholder from any failure of title arising out of the exercise of a right of first refusal by the condominium board.

Contiguity Endorsement: Protects against loss or damage sustained of failure of the parcels that make up the land to be contiguous.

Environmental Protection Lien Endorsement: Protects against any loss or damage arising from the insured mortgagee not having priority over any environmental protection lien filed in accordance with state law.

Fairway Endorsement: Preserves policy coverage upon the recharacterization of a partnership or a limited liability company as a corporation.

Mezzanine Financing Endorsement: Provides that (i) there will be no denial of coverage as the result of the transfer of any membership interests in owner to the mezzanine lender; and (ii) the title insurer waives its right of subrogation and indemnity against any of the insured owner's equity owners until the mezzanine loan is paid in full.

Non-Imputation Endorsement: Prohibits the use of the defense of "knowledge imputed by law" and is commonly requested when the proposed insured entity owner does not want any knowledge of the transaction "imputed" or transferred to the proposed owner by other parties connected to the entity owner, such as outgoing members, partners, managers, or officers of the entity owner.

Residential Mortgage Endorsement: Protects against any loss caused by any encroachment of the building on the premises onto any easement or right of way as well as any violation of any covenant or restriction excepted in the policy.

<u>Restrictions, Encroachments, Minerals Endorsement:</u> Insures against loss or damage sustained by reason of the existence of any of the following: (i) violations on the land of any enforceable covenants, conditions or restrictions; and (ii) encroachments of improvements on the land onto adjoining land, including forced removal of any such encroachment, or any encroachments onto the land of improvements located on adjoining lands.

<u>Same-as-Survey Endorsement:</u> Insures against loss by reason of any violations, variations, encroachments, or adverse circumstances that would have been disclosed by an accurate survey.

<u>Street Assessments Endorsement:</u> Insures the lender against loss or damage sustained by reason of assessments for street improvements gaining priority over the lien of the insured mortgage.

<u>Tax Parcel Endorsement:</u> Insures against loss or damage sustained by the insured by reason of the land not being assessed for real estate tax purposes under the correct tax identification number.

<u>Zoning Endorsement:</u> States the zoning classification of the subject property and the permitted uses of the property and insures against loss or damage arising from a court order prohibiting the use of the land or requiring removal or alteration of the improvements on the land.

# Appendix G

# Lease Review Summary Form

LEASE REVIEW SUMMARY

1. Lease:
   a. Title of document (including amendments, modifications, and sup-
      plements): _____

      _____ (Page___)

   b. Date(s) of execution: _____ (Page___)

   c. Commencement date: _____ (Page___)

2. Landlord:
   a. Name: _____

      _____ (Page___)

   b. Type of entity: _____

      _____ (Page___)

   c. Notice address:_____

      _____ (Page___)

3. Tenant:
   a. Name (and trade name, if different): _____

      _____ (Page___)

   b. Type of entity: _____

      _____ (Page___)

   c. Notice address: _____

      _____ (Page___)

4. Premises:
   a. Address and store number, if any: _____

      _____ (Page___)

   b. Square footage (specify gross/leased/leaseable/usable/
      other): _____

      _____ (Page___)

5. Permitted Use(s):_____ (Page ___)

6. Primary Lease Term:

    a. _____ yrs. _____mos.        (Page ___)

    b. Commencement date: _____(Page ___)

    c. Expiration date: _____ (Page ___)

    d. Lease year: _____ (Page ___)

7. Rental (Primary Term Only):

    a. Free rent period: _____ (Page ___)

    b. Base rent: _____(Page ___)

    c. Common area maintenance, HVAC, and operating costs:

        (1) Contribution payable: _____ (Page ___)
        Based on gross/leased/leaseable/usable/other (specify) square
        footage of:

        _____ (Page___)

        (2) Cost stop: _____ (Page ___)

        (3) Adjustments to tenant contribution based on actual costs/CPI/
            other (specify):

        _____

        _____ (Page___)

        (4) "Gross up" clause: ____yes ____no    (Page ___)

        (5) Unusual exceptions to common area expenses:

        _____ (Page___)

    d. Real estate taxes and other impositions:
        (1) Full pro rata: ___yes ____no      (Page ___)
        Based on gross/leased/leaseable/usable/other (specify) square
        footage of:

        _____ (Page___)

        (2) Increase over base year if not full prorata:
        ____yes ____no      (Page ___)

        (3) Capped: _____ (Page ___)

    e. Any special provisions or exceptions:
        (1) Rental based on lease of personal property:

        _____ (Page___)

        (2) Other: _____ (Page ___)

f. Percentage rent:
(1) \_\_\_\_% of gross sales or receipts/net income/gross or net amount above a base or floor (specify breakpoint):

_____ (Page\_\_\_)

(2) When due: _____ (Page \_\_\_)

(3) Carrybacks or carryforwards: _____

_____ (Page\_\_\_)

(4) Percentage rent lease year: _____(Page \_\_\_)

(5) Any specific deductions or exclusions: _____

_____ (Page\_\_\_)

(6) Tenant contribution to common area expenses offset against Percentage Rent: \_\_\_\_yes \_\_\_\_no     (Page \_\_\_)

(7) Other offsets against percentage rent: _____

_____ (Page\_\_\_)

g. Adjustments to minimum or percentage rent:
(1) Any reductions or increases during option periods: _____

_____ (Page\_\_\_)

(2) CPI or other similar index increases (specify): _____

_____ (Page\_\_\_)

h. Merchants' association and/or advertising contributions:
(1) Membership required: \_\_\_\_yes \_\_\_\_no     (Page \_\_\_)

(2) Membership dues: _____ (Page \_\_\_)

8. Options to Renew:
a. Number and term of each:_____

_____ (Page\_\_\_)

b. Notice to be given before: _____

_____ (Page\_\_\_)

c. Rental Increases: _____

_____ (Page\_\_\_)

9. Security Deposit/Prepaid Rent:
a. Amount and form: _____     (Page \_\_\_)

b. Interest accrues to Tenant: \_\_\_\_yes \_\_\_\_no     (Page \_\_\_)

10. Alterations and Additions:
    a. Initial buildout:
        (1) Who performs:    \_\_\_\_L    \_\_\_T          (Page \_\_)
        (2) Who pays:        \_\_\_L    \_\_\_T          (Page \_\_)
        (3) Cost cap: _____(Page \_\_)
        (4) Other restrictions/requirements: _____

        _____ (Page\_\_)

    b. Additional work:
        (1) Who performs:    \_\_\_\_L    \_\_\_T          (Page \_\_)
        (2) Who pays:        \_\_\_L    \_\_\_T          (Page \_\_)
        (3) Approval by Landlord: _____

        _____ (Page\_\_)

        (4) Other restrictions/requirements: _____

        _____ (Page\_\_)

11. Maintenance Responsibilities:
    a. Exterior:             \_\_\_\_L    \_\_\_T          (Page \_\_)
    b. Roof:                 \_\_\_\_L    \_\_\_T          (Page \_\_)
    c. Parking:            \_\_\_\_L    \_\_\_T          (Page \_\_)
    d. Interior:             \_\_\_\_L    \_\_\_T          (Page \_\_)
    e. Plumbing:          \_\_\_\_L    \_\_\_T          (Page \_\_)
    f. Electrical:          \_\_\_\_L    \_\_\_T          (Page \_\_)
    g. HVAC:               \_\_\_\_L    \_\_\_T          (Page \_\_)
    h. Other (specify):     \_\_\_\_L    \_\_\_T

        _____ (Page\_\_)

12. Provision of Service:
    a. Utilities:             \_\_\_\_L    \_\_\_T          (Page \_\_)
    b. Janitorial/cleaning:    \_\_\_\_L    \_\_\_T          (Page \_\_)
    c. Trash removal:       \_\_\_\_L    \_\_\_T          (Page \_\_)
    d. Elevator:            \_\_\_\_L    \_\_\_T          (Page \_\_)
    e. Parking:             \_\_\_\_L    \_\_\_T          (Page \_\_)
    f. Other (specify):      \_\_\_\_L    \_\_\_T

        _____ (Page\_\_)

13. Operations:
    a. Restrictions: _____

        _____ (Page\_\_)

    b. Exclusives: _____

        _____ (Page\_\_)

c.  Radius clause: _____

_____ (Page___)

d.  Continuous operations clause: _____

_____ (Page___)

(1)  Hours of operation: _____(Page ___)

(2)  Days of operation: _____(Page ___)

e.  Kiosks allowed: ____yes ____no                    (Page ___)

14. Assignment and Subletting:
   a.  Landlord's written approval required:
       ____yes ____no                                (Page ___)

   If yes, standard is absolute discretion/reasonable approval/related
   or preapproved entity/other (specify):

   _____ (Page___)

   b.  Landlord has right to cancel lease if notified of proposed assign-
       ment or sublease:
       ____yes ____no                                (Page ___)

   c.  Excess rent payable to Landlord: ____yes ____no   (Page ___)

15. Subordination, Nondisturbance, and Attornment:
   a.  All present or future mortgages: ____yes ____no   (Page ___)

       If no, explain: _____

   _____ (Page___)

   b.  Execution of estoppel certificates required:
       ____yes ____no                                (Page ___)

       If no, explain: _____

   _____ (Page___)

   c.  Tenant agrees to attorn to Landlord's successor in interest:
       ____yes ____no                                (Page ___)

16. Casualty and Condemnation:
   a.  Right of cancellation: _____

   _____ (Page___)

   b.  Obligation to rebuild: _____

   _____ (Page___)

17. Insurance, Liability:

a. Landlord insurance responsibility and amounts:
   (1) Fire: _____ (Page ___)
   (2) Common area liability: _____ (Page ___)
   (3) Property damage: _____ (Page ___)
   (4) Personal injury: _____ (Page ___)
   (5) Other (specify): _____ (Page ___)
   (6) Certificates to Tenant (specify times and special provisions):

   _____ (Page___)

   (7) Waiver of subrogation:
   ____yes    ____no                                (Page ___)

b. Tenant insurance responsibility and amounts:
   (1) Fire:_____(Page ___)
   (2) Property damage: _____ (Page ___)
   (3) Personal injury: _____ (Page ___)
   (4) Business interruption: _____ (Page ___)
   (5) Other (specify): _____ (Page ___)
   (6) Certificates to Landlord (specify times and special provisions):

   _____ (Page___)

   (7) Waiver of subrogation:
   ____yes    ____no                                (Page ___)

c. Landlord liability limited to interest in property:
   ____yes    ____no                                (Page ___)

18. Default:
   a. Notice required for payment defaults:
      ____yes    ____no                             (Page ___)

   b. Grace or cure periods:_____

   _____ (Page___)

   c. Default interest or late charge: _____

   _____ (Page___)

   d. Notice to any third party required (specify): _____

   _____ (Page___)

   e. Any nonstandard provisions: _____

   _____ (Page___)

19. Right of First Refusal or First Offer:
   a. List: _____

      _____ (Page___)

   b. Rental:_____

      _____ (Page___)

20. Guaranty:
   a. By whom: _____ (Page ___)

   b. Cap on amount: _____ (Page ___)

   c. Duration: _____ (Page ___)

21. Leasehold Mortgages (list):

   _____

   _____ (Page___)

22. Brokerage Fees:
   a. Primary lease term:

      (1) Payable by: ____L ____T (Page ___)

      (2) Payable to: _____

      _____ (Page___)

      (3) Amount:_____(Page ___)
   b. Renewal term(s):

      (1) Payable by: ____L ____T (Page ___)

      (2) Payable to: _____

      _____ (Page___)

      (3) Amount:_____(Page ___)

23. Unusual Landlord Obligations (list):

   _____

   _____ (Page___)

24. Special Cancellation Provisions (list):

   _____

   _____ (Page___)

25. Other (list):

   _____

   _____ (Page___)

# Appendix H

# Form of Subordination, Nondisturbance, and Attornment Agreement

**Note:** This document should be executed in recordable form in accordance with the requirements of the jurisdiction in which the Property is located, with appropriate notary blocks attached and completed, in case the parties decide to record it either in connection with the closing or prior to a foreclosure.

SUBORDINATION, NONDISTURBANCE, AND ATTORNMENT
AGREEMENT

THIS SUBORDINATION, NONDISTURBANCE, AND ATTORN-MENT AGREEMENT ("this Agreement") is made this _____ day of _____, 20__ (the "Effective Date"), by and between _____, a _____, whose address is _____ (together with its successors and assigns, the "Mortgagee"), as mortgagee, and _____ _____, a _____, whose address is _____ (together with its successors and assigns, the "Tenant"), as tenant.

### Introduction

A. _____, a _____, whose address is _____ (together with its successors and assigns, the "Landlord"), owns the land described in Exhibit A to this Agreement (such land, together with all improvements thereon, and all easements, rights, and ways appurtenant thereto or in anywise belonging and all of Landlord's right, title, and interest in all public ways adjoining the same is collectively called the "Property"). The improvements on such land are commonly known as _____ _____.

B. Mortgagee has made a loan to Landlord in the original principal amount of _____ Dollars ($_____) (the "Loan").

C. To secure the Loan, Landlord has encumbered the Property by entering into that certain _____ dated _____, 20__, in favor of Mortgagee (as amended, increased, renewed, extended, spread, consolidated, severed, restated, or otherwise changed from time to time, the "Mortgage") [to be] recorded [on _____, 20__, at liber _____, folio ___] in the land records of _____ County, _____ (the "Land Records").

D. Landlord, as lessor, and Tenant, as lessee, entered into the _____ dated as of _____ (together with all amendments, modifications, and supplements thereto, the "Lease"), for the demise of [a portion of] the Property to Tenant (the "Premises"). The Premises are commonly known as [Suite] _____.

[E. A memorandum of the Lease [is to be recorded in the Land Records prior to the recording of this Agreement.] [was recorded on _____, 20__, [at liber ____, folio ___] in the Land Records.]]

F. Mortgagee and Tenant desire to agree upon the relative priorities of their interests in the Property and their rights and obligations if certain events occur.

G. Landlord, as borrower of the Loan and lessor under the Lease, joins in executing and delivering this Agreement solely to give its consent and agreement to this Agreement.

NOW THEREFORE, in consideration of the premises, and for other good and valuable consideration, the receipt and adequacy of which are acknowledged by the parties, Mortgagee and Tenant agree as follows:

## Agreement

1. Definitions.

For purposes of this Agreement, the following terms shall have the meanings set forth in this Section 1:

1.1 Construction-Related Obligation. A "Construction-Related Obligation" means any obligation of Landlord under the Lease to make, pay for, or reimburse Tenant for any alterations, demolition, or other improvements or work at the Property, including the Premises. "Construction-Related Obligations" shall not include: (a) reconstruction or repair following fire, casualty, or condemnation; or (b) day-to-day maintenance and repairs.

1.2 Event of Foreclosure. An "Event of Foreclosure" means: (a) foreclosure under the Mortgage; (b) any other exercise by Mortgagee of rights and remedies (whether under the Mortgage or under applicable law, including bankruptcy law) as holder of the Loan or of the Mortgage, as a result of which any party other than Landlord succeeds Landlord as owner of the Property; or (c) delivery by Landlord to Mortgagee (or Mortgagee's designee or nominee) of a deed or other conveyance of Landlord's interest in the Property in lieu of foreclosure or any exercise of Mortgagee's rights and remedies.

1.3 Former Landlord. A "Former Landlord" means any party that was landlord under the Lease prior to an Event of Foreclosure.

1.4 Offset Right. An "Offset Right" means any right or alleged right of Tenant to any offset, defense (other than one arising from actual payment and performance, which payment and performance would bind a Successor Landlord as provided by this Agreement), claim, counterclaim, reduction, deduction, or abatement against Tenant's payment of Rent or performance of Tenant's other obligations under the Lease, arising (whether under the Lease or applicable law) from Landlord's breach or default under the Lease.

1.5 <u>Rent.</u> The "Rent" means any fixed rent, base rent, additional rent, or other payments due from Tenant under the Lease.

1.6 <u>Successor Landlord.</u> A "Successor Landlord" means any party that becomes owner of the Property as the result of an Event of Foreclosure. "Successor Landlord" shall not mean any successor or assignee of Landlord that becomes the owner of the Property other than as the result of an Event of Foreclosure.

1.7 <u>Termination Right.</u> A "Termination Right" means any right of Tenant to cancel or terminate the Lease or to claim a partial or total eviction arising (whether under the Lease or under applicable law) from Landlord's breach or default under the Lease.

2. <u>Subordination.</u>

The Lease shall be, and shall at all times remain, subject and subordinate to the Mortgage, the lien imposed by the Mortgage, all advances made under the Mortgage, and any modifications, amendments, or extensions of the Mortgage.

3. <u>Nondisturbance, Recognition, and Attornment.</u>

3.1 <u>No Exercise of Lease Remedies Against Tenant.</u> So long as the Tenant is not in default beyond any applicable notice and cure periods under the Lease (an "Event of Default"), Mortgagee shall not name or join Tenant as a defendant in any exercise of Mortgagee's rights and remedies upon a default under the Mortgage unless applicable law requires Tenant to be made a party thereto as a condition to proceeding against Landlord or prosecuting such rights and remedies. If applicable law does so require, Mortgagee may join Tenant as defendant in such action only for such purpose and not to terminate the Lease or otherwise adversely affect Tenant's rights under the Lease or this Agreement in such action.

3.2 <u>Nondisturbance and Attornment.</u> If the Lease has not been terminated as a result of an Event of Default by Tenant, then, upon the occurrence of an Event of Foreclosure:

(a) the Successor Landlord shall not terminate or disturb Tenant's possession of the Premises under the Lease, except in accordance with the terms of the Lease and this Agreement;

(b) the Successor Landlord shall be bound to Tenant under all the terms and conditions of the Lease, except as otherwise provided by this Agreement;

(c) Tenant shall recognize and attorn to the Successor Landlord as Tenant's direct lessor under the Lease as modified by this Agreement; and

(d) the Lease shall continue in full force and effect as a direct lease, in accordance with its terms, except as otherwise provided by this Agreement, between the Successor Landlord and Tenant.

3.3 Further Documentation. The provisions of this Section 3 shall be effective and self-operative without any need for the Successor Landlord or Tenant to execute any further documents. Tenant and the Successor Landlord shall, however, confirm the provisions of this Agreement in writing upon request by either of them.

4. Protection of Successor Landlord.

The Successor Landlord shall not be liable for or bound by any of the following matters:

4.1 Claims Against Successor Landlord. Any Offset Right that Tenant may have against any Former Landlord relating to any event or occurrence before the date of an Event of Foreclosure, including any claim for damages of any kind whatsoever as the result of any breach by a Former Landlord that occurred before the date of such Event of Foreclosure. The foregoing shall not limit either (a) Tenant's right to exercise against a Successor Landlord any Offset Right available to Tenant because of events occurring or continuing after the date of the Event of Foreclosure; or (b) the Successor Landlord's obligation to correct any conditions that existed as of the date of the Event of Foreclosure and which violate the Successor Landlord's obligations as landlord under the Lease.

4.2 Prepayments. Any payment of Rent that Tenant may have made to a Former Landlord more than thirty (30) days in advance.

4.3 Payment; Security Deposit. Any obligation (a) to pay Tenant any sum that any Former Landlord owed to Tenant; or (b) with respect to any security deposited with a Former Landlord, unless such security was actually delivered to the Successor Landlord. [This paragraph is not intended to apply to a Successor Landlord's obligation to make any payment that constitutes a "Construction-Related Obligation."]

4.4 Modification, Amendment or Waiver. Any modification or amendment of the Lease, or any waiver of any terms of the Lease, made without Mortgagee's written consent.

4.5 Surrender or Other Termination. Any consensual or negotiated surrender, cancellation, or termination of the Lease, in whole or in part, agreed upon between Landlord and Tenant, unless effected unilaterally by Tenant pursuant to the express terms of the Lease.

5. Exculpation of Successor Landlord.

Upon the occurrence of any Event of Foreclosure, the Lease shall be deemed to have been automatically amended to provide that the Successor Landlord's obligations and liability under the Lease shall never extend beyond the Successor Landlord's interest (or the interest of its successors or assigns), if any, in the Property from time to time, including insurance and condemnation proceeds, the Successor Landlord's interest in the Lease, and the proceeds from any sale or other disposition of the Property by the Successor Landlord (collectively, the "Successor Landlord's Interest"). Tenant shall look exclusively to the Successor Landlord's Interest (or that of its successors and assigns) for payment or discharge of any obligations of the Successor Landlord under the Lease as modified by this Agreement. If Tenant obtains any money judgment against the Successor Landlord with respect to the Lease or the relationship between the Successor Landlord and Tenant, then Tenant shall look solely to the Successor Landlord's Interest (or that of its successors or assigns) to collect such judgment. Tenant shall not collect or attempt to collect any such judgment out of any other assets of the Successor Landlord.

6. Mortgagee's Right to Cure.

6.1 Notice to Mortgagee. Before exercising any Termination Right or Offset Right, Tenant shall provide Mortgagee with notice of the breach or default by Landlord or the Successor Landlord under the Lease giving rise to such Termination Right or Offset Right (the "Mortgagee's Default Notice") and, thereafter, the opportunity to cure such breach or default as provided by this Section 6.

6.2 Mortgagee's Cure Period. After Mortgagee receives a Mortgagee's Default Notice, Mortgagee shall have a period of thirty (30) days beyond the time available to Landlord or the Successor Landlord under the Lease in which to cure the breach or default by Landlord or the Successor Landlord. Mortgagee shall have no obligation to cure (and shall have no liability or obligation for not curing) any breach or default by Landlord or the Successor Landlord, except to the extent that Mortgagee agrees to undertake such cure in writing.

6.3 Extended Cure Period. In addition, in the event the cure of any breach or default by Landlord or the Successor Landlord under the Lease requires possession and control of the Property, provided that Mortgagee delivers written notice to Tenant within thirty (30) days after receipt of the Mortgagee's Default Notice that it intends to exercise reasonable efforts to cure or cause to be cured by a receiver such breach or default within the period permitted by this Section 6.3, Mortgagee's cure period shall continue for such additional time as Mortgagee may reasonably require either to (a) obtain possession and control of the Property and thereafter cure the breach or default with reasonable diligence and continuity; or to (b) obtain the appointment of a receiver and give such receiver a reasonable period of time in which to cure the breach or default.

7. Miscellaneous.

7.1 Notices. All notices or other communications required or permitted under this Agreement shall be in writing and given by certified mail (return receipt requested) or by nationally recognized overnight courier service that regularly maintains records of items delivered. Each party's address is as set forth in the opening paragraph of this Agreement, subject to change by notice given as provided by this Section 7.1. Notices shall be effective the next business day after being sent by overnight courier service, and five (5) business days after being sent by certified mail (return receipt requested).

7.2 Due Authorization.

(a) Mortgagee has full authority to enter into this Agreement, and has duly authorized the execution and delivery of this Agreement by all actions required by Mortgagee's organizational documents.

(b) Tenant has full authority to enter into this Agreement, and has duly authorized the execution and delivery of this Agreement by all actions required by Tenant's organizational documents.

7.3 Successors and Assigns. This Agreement shall bind and benefit the parties, their successors and assigns, any Successor Landlord, and its successors and assigns. If Mortgagee assigns the Mortgage, then upon delivery to Tenant of written notice thereof accompanied by the assignee's written assumption of all obligations under this Agreement, all liability of the assignor shall terminate.

7.4 Entire Agreement. This Agreement constitutes the entire agreement between Mortgagee and Tenant regarding the subordination of the Lease to the Mortgage and the rights and obligations of Tenant and Mortgagee as to the subject matter of this Agreement.

7.5 Interaction with Lease and with Mortgage. If any terms of this Agreement conflict with any terms of the Lease, then the terms of this Agreement shall govern. This Agreement supersedes, and upon execution and delivery shall constitute full compliance with, any provisions in the Lease that provide for subordination of the Lease to, or for delivery of nondisturbance agreements by the holder of, the Mortgage. Mortgagee confirms that Mortgagee has consented to Landlord's entering into the Lease.

7.6 Mortgagee's Rights and Obligations. Except as expressly provided in this Agreement, Mortgagee shall have no obligations to Tenant with respect to the Lease.

7.7 Amendments. This Agreement may be amended, discharged, or terminated, or any of its provisions waived, only by a written instrument executed by the party to be bound, provided that this Agreement shall automatically terminate upon expiration or other termination of the Lease, or Landlord's repayment of the entire indebtedness under the Loan.

7.8 Counterparts. This Agreement may be executed in any number of counterparts, each of which shall be deemed an original and all of which together shall constitute one and the same instrument.

7.9 Governing Law. This Agreement shall be governed by the laws of the [State] [Commonwealth] of _____, excluding any _____ choice of law principles.

IN WITNESS WHEREOF, the parties have duly executed this Agreement under seal on the Effective Date.

<pre>
                        _____, a

WITNESS:                _____, Mortgagee

_____         By: _____ (SEAL)

                        Its: _____


                        _____, a

WITNESS:                _____, Tenant

_____         By: _____ (SEAL)

                        Its:  _____
</pre>

### Consent of Landlord

Landlord, as landlord under the Lease and borrower under the Mortgage, consents and agrees to this Agreement. Landlord is not a party to this Agreement, and joins in executing and delivering this Agreement solely to give its consent and agreement hereto.

<pre>
                        _____, a

WITNESS:                _____, Landlord

_____         By: _____ (SEAL)

                        Its: _____
</pre>

[Add notary block in the form required by the state in which the document will be recorded.]

### EXHIBIT A
### Description of Property

# Appendix I

# Form of Loan Commitment

**Note:** The particular provisions of loan commitments will vary widely, depending on the lender's underwriting practices, the type of loan (such as land development, construction, permanent, conduit, or refinance), the type of collateral (such as raw land or improved land), and local real estate practice. The following form attempts to include only common provisions that appear in most permanent loan commitments to fund the acquisition of improved property, and certain alternative provisions are shown in brackets. Accordingly, the practitioner should consider the use of other forms in this book to supplement it and should become familiar with the lender's underwriting practices, the type of loan, the type of collateral, and local real estate practice before preparing a loan commitment. The practitioner also should be aware that, instead of a loan commitment, some lenders use a loan application format in which similar terms and conditions appear in an application document from the borrower to the lender and which the lender will approve in writing when it is acceptable. In either event, the lender's lawyer customarily prepares the document at the borrower's expense. This form is in the format of a loan commitment.

[On Lender's Letterhead]
[Borrower's name and address]
Re: $_____ Loan to _____
Dear _____:
     We are pleased to advise you that _____, a
_____ ("Lender"), has approved your request for a mortgage loan on the following terms and conditions (the "Loan"):
1. <u>Borrower.</u>
     The borrower of the Loan shall be _____, a
_____ ("Borrower"). The direct and indirect ownership and control of Borrower shall be subject to the approval of Lender. [Borrower shall be and, at all times during the term of the Loan, remain a single-purpose entity that does not engage in any business other than owning and operating the Property (defined in Section 2) and that does not acquire or own material assets other than the Property and incidental personal property. Borrower shall create or amend its organizational documents as Lender may require to conform such documents to the provisions of this Section 1.] Borrower may not assign or transfer this Commitment.
2. <u>Collateral.</u>
     The Loan shall be secured by a first-priority lien or security interest in:
     (a) Borrower's fee simple estate in that tract of land containing approximately _____ acres and more particularly described in <u>Exhibit A</u> to this Commitment (the "Land"), on which exists the __-story building

containing approximately _____ square feet of space, commonly known as
_____, _____, _____ (the "Build-
ing") (the Land and the Building together are called the "Property"); and

(b) All fixtures and personal property owned by Borrower and used
in connection with the Property (the "Personal Property").

3.  Principal Amount.

The principal amount of the Loan shall be _____
Dollars ($_____) (the "Principal Amount").

4.  Interest Rate.

The Principal Amount shall bear interest at the annual rate of ___ percent (____%) (the "Agreed Rate"), payable as set forth in Section 6, unless
and until a default shall occur under the Loan Documents (defined in Section 8(a)) and continue beyond any applicable notice and cure periods
described in the Loan Documents (an "Event of Default"). If an Event of
Default occurs, the Principal Amount shall bear interest from the date of
the default at an annual rate (the "Default Rate") which is the greater of
(a) _____ percent (____%); or (b) _____ percent (___%) plus the prime
rate announced by _____, or its succes-
sors, from time to time, with each change thereof automatically effecting
a change in the Default Rate, until such Event of Default is cured. Interest,
whether at the Agreed Rate or at the Default Rate, shall be calculated on the
basis of twelve (12) 30-day months, with any partial month calculated on
the basis of a 360-day year.

5.  Maturity.

The Principal Amount and all accrued interest thereon, if not sooner
paid, shall be due and payable on the first day of the _____
(_____) full calendar month following the Closing Date (defined in Section
14(a)) (the "Maturity Date").

6.  Payments.

(a) Borrower shall pay to Lender _____ (___)
equal installments of interest and principal, in amounts necessary to fully
amortize the Principal Amount over _____ (___)
months, from the Closing Date through the Maturity Date, monthly in
arrears, commencing on the first day of the calendar month next succeeding the Closing Date (with a prorated payment of interest only for any initial partial month).

(b) Lender shall apply any amounts received on account of the Loan
(i) first, [to the Prepayment Premium (defined in Section 7), if any; (ii) second,] to any unpaid costs, expenses, or other charges due to Lender as
provided by the Loan Documents; (iii) third, to any unpaid Late Charges
(defined in Section 8(c)(viii)); (iv) fourth, to any accrued and unpaid interest on the Principal Amount; and (v) fifth, to the Principal Amount then
outstanding, in reverse order of maturity, and the amount of the monthly
installments as provided in Section 6(a), except for the final unpaid install-

ment thereof, shall not be decreased by reason of any partial payment or prepayment of the Principal Amount.

7. Prepayment.

[Borrower may prepay the Principal Amount in whole or in part at any time before the Maturity Date without premium or penalty.]

[Before the _____ (_th) anniversary of the Closing Date, Borrower shall not have the right or privilege to make, and Lender shall not be obligated to accept, a prepayment of all or any part of the Principal Amount unless Borrower shall pay to Lender, together with any prepayment of all or any part of the Principal Amount, a prepayment premium (the "Prepayment Premium") equal to the greater of (a) ___ percent (_%) of the Principal Amount then outstanding which Borrower is prepaying, or (b) the mortgage yield maintenance fee calculated as set forth in Exhibit B to this Commitment. Borrower shall give _____ (_) days' prior written notice to Lender of its intent to prepay all or any part of the Principal Amount. If a foreclosure of the Loan occurs, the court shall include the Prepayment Premium in the amount found to be due to Lender in the decree or order of foreclosure. There shall be no Prepayment Premium due if the Loan is prepaid in whole or in part because of a taking of the Property or a casualty at the Property.]

8. Loan Documents.

(a) The Loan shall be evidenced by a promissory note to the order of Lender, in a form acceptable to Lender (the "Note"), and secured by:

(i) A mortgage, deed of trust, or other appropriate lien document, security agreement, and financing statement (the "Mortgage"), and any UCC financing statements incidental thereto, in favor of Lender, or trustees for the benefit of Lender, conveying and mortgaging, and granting and perfecting a first-priority lien and security interest in, the Property, the Personal Property, and all proceeds resulting therefrom;

(ii) A collateral assignment and security agreement and UCC financing statements incidental thereto, executed by Borrower in favor of Lender, assigning for collateral purposes, and granting and perfecting a security interest in, all leases and use and occupancy agreements and tenancies, all rents and revenues therefrom, and all guaranties given in connection therewith, and the Personal Property;

(iii) A guarantee of payment and performance of Borrower's obligations in connection with the Loan (the "Guarantee") by _____ _____, _____, and _____ (collectively, "Guarantors"). The Guarantee shall provide that Guarantors shall be unconditionally liable thereunder, jointly and severally; and

(iv) Such other documents and instruments as Lender reasonably may request as security for the Loan, including an environmental indemnity agreement (the "Environmental Indemnity") to be executed by Borrower and Guarantors.

The Note, the Mortgage, the Guarantee, the Environmental Indemnity, and the other documents identified above are collectively referred to as the "Loan Documents."

(b) All Loan Documents shall be (i) satisfactory to Lender in form, substance, scope, and content, consistent with the terms and conditions of this Commitment; (ii) prepared by Lender's counsel; and (iii) delivered to Borrower for its review.

(c) In addition to the provisions of this Commitment, the Loan Documents shall contain such terms, conditions, and provisions as Lender and its counsel may reasonably require in order to close the Loan, including but not limited to, the provisions that:

(i)        No mortgage lien or other lien, inferior, subordinate, or superior to the lien and security interests of the Loan Documents, shall voluntarily or involuntarily be created, permitted, or filed against the Property, without Lender's approval, except for general real estate taxes and assessments which are a lien on the Property and not yet due and payable;

(ii)        Until the Loan has been repaid in full, Borrower shall not cause or permit, without the prior written approval of Lender, the sale, conveyance, master leasing, assignment, transferring, encumbrance, or disposition of (A) all or any portion of the Property; or (B) directly or indirectly, the control or management of Borrower by _____, or the transfer of any direct or indirect ownership interests in Borrower;

(iii)        Borrower shall waive, to the extent permitted by law, all rights of redemption, equitable and statutory, in the Property;

(iv)        Borrower shall deposit with Lender monthly an amount equal to one-twelfth (1/12) of the annual estimated general real estate taxes and assessments and hazard and liability insurance premiums for the Property, which deposits shall [not] accrue interest for the benefit of Borrower;

(v)        Unless Lender otherwise elects, all present and future leases of the Property shall be (A) subject and subordinate to the Loan Documents, provided that Lender shall agree not to disturb any present (i.e., as of the Closing Date) tenant in the exercise of its rights under its lease upon foreclosure of the Mortgage, or sale or deed in lieu of such foreclosure; and (B) collaterally assigned to Lender;

(vi)        Borrower shall submit to Lender all proposed leases of the Property prior to Borrower's execution thereof, for Lender's review and approval, and shall not enter into any such leases without the prior written approval of Lender. Thereafter, Borrower shall not cause or permit any change, supplement, or waiver of any term, condition, or provision of any lease approved by Lender, or the termination, cancellation, or surrender thereof, except on the express terms and conditions of such lease;

(vii)        Borrower shall not cause or permit any Hazardous Materials to be present at the Property, except in compliance with all applicable federal, state, and local laws and regulations. For purposes of this Commitment, "Hazardous Materials" means any chemicals, pollutants, contaminants, wastes, toxic substances, or petroleum products defined in, governed under, or regulated pursuant to any applicable federal, state, or local laws or regulations relating to pollution, the protection of human health, or the environment; and

(viii) Borrower shall not be given notice of or be permitted any grace period to correct any monetary default under the Loan Documents. If Borrower fails to make any payment on the date when due, Lender shall have the right to charge Borrower a late payment charge equal to ____ percent (_%) of such late payment (the "Late Charge"). In addition, interest shall accrue on the Principal Amount at the Default Rate from the date due until received by the Lender. The Loan Documents shall provide for written notices of nonmonetary defaults to Borrower during the term of the Loan and _____ (__) days to cure the corresponding defaults, except for defaults relating to:

(A) A material breach of Borrower's representations and warranties;

(B) Institution of bankruptcy or other proceedings relating to insolvency of Borrower or any principal of Borrower;

(C) Dissolution of Borrower or any principal thereof;

(D) Prohibited transfers of the Property or the management or control of Borrower, or the creation of additional encumbrances on the Property;

(E) Failure to pay taxes or insurance premiums when due, subject to the right to contest such taxes, provided Lender receives a bond therefor or other security acceptable to Lender;

(F) Failure to pay a final judgment as required; and

(G) Engagement in any business unrelated to the Property; which defaults shall have no grace period and require no notice to cure.

(d) [All of the Loan Documents shall provide that neither Borrower nor any direct or indirect owner of an interest in Borrower shall have personal liability for payment of the principal of or interest on the Loan, and that in the event of any default, Lender's sole recourse shall be against the Property and any other collateral securing the Loan and under the Guarantee; provided, however, that Borrower and such direct and indirect owners shall remain personally liable as otherwise provided by the Loan Documents or applicable law for the following: (A) as provided by the Guarantee, with respect to the Guarantors; (B) Borrower's failure to pay real estate taxes or assessments against the Property, to the extent proceeds are available; (C) Borrower's failure to insure the Property as required by the Loan Documents; (D) rent or other income from the Property received after a default under the Loan Documents and which is not applied to the Loan or to the expenses of operating or maintaining the Property; (E) conversion, diversion, misapplication, or misappropriation of security deposits, reserve accounts, insurance proceeds, or condemnation awards in connection with the Property; (F) waste; (G) amounts due under the Environmental Indemnity; and

(H) fraud or intentional misrepresentation in connection with the transactions contemplated by this Commitment or any of the Loan Documents.]

9.  Commitment Fee; Acceptance of Commitment.

(a) In consideration of the issuance of this Commitment, Borrower shall, upon and as a condition of its acceptance of this Commitment, pay to Lender, in immediately available funds, a nonrefundable fee in the amount of _____ dollars ($_____) (the "Commitment Fee"), which Commitment Fee shall have been earned by Lender upon the acceptance by Borrower of this Commitment.

(b) If, within _____ (__) days after the date of this Commitment, this Commitment is not accepted in writing by Borrower as herein provided or Lender has not received the Commitment Fee, then this Commitment and the obligations of Lender hereunder, without notice to Borrower, shall expire and be of no further force or effect. This Commitment shall be effective or enforceable against Lender only upon receipt by Lender of written acceptance by Borrower and the Commitment Fee as herein provided.

10. Conditions Precedent to Closing of the Loan.

As conditions precedent to the closing of the Loan, Borrower, at its expense and not fewer than _____ (__) days before the Closing Date (unless a different time period is otherwise specified herein), shall deliver or cause to be delivered to Lender, for Lender's review and approval, the following items in form, substance, scope, and content satisfactory to Lender:

(a) An appraisal (i) prepared by an MAI appraiser who is engaged and compensated by Borrower and approved by Lender, (ii) made in conformity with the Code of Professional Ethics and Standards of Professional Practices of the American Institute of Real Estate Appraisers, and (iii) stating the market value of the Property to be at least $_____ as of a date not more than _____ (__) days before the Closing Date;

(b) Within ___ (__) days after the Closing Date, an ALTA 2006 form of mortgagee's policy of title insurance (i) in an amount equal to the Principal Amount; (ii) issued by a title insurance company satisfactory to Lender; (iii) insuring the Mortgage as a valid first-priority lien on the Property, subject only to such exceptions to title as Lender may approve; and (iv) insuring that the Property has access to public rights of way. The title policy shall include such endorsements as Lender reasonably may require. Borrower shall furnish or cause to be furnished to Lender a commitment for such title policy, together with complete and legible copies of each and all documents therein shown of record affecting title to the Property;

(c) An "as-built" survey of the Property, dated not more than _____ (__) days before the Closing Date and prepared by a licensed surveyor in accordance with ALTA/ACSM standards, showing each of the matters set forth as special exceptions in the title policy (by reference to book and page), the boundaries of the Property (through the use of course bearings and distances), and the location of any improvements in relation thereto and all dimensions thereof, and all easements, set-back lines, rights of way, and encroachments. The survey will be certified to Lender and the title insurer issuing the commitment and policy described in Section 10(b) and comply with all requirements set forth in Exhibit C to this Commitment;

(d) A report, dated not more than _____ (__) days before the Closing Date and prepared by a qualified consultant or expert engaged and compensated by Borrower and approved by Lender, which evaluates (i) whether any Hazardous Materials are present in soil or water at or adjacent to the Property, (ii) whether the Property has ever been used as a repository for Solid and Hazardous Waste as defined in 42 U.S.C. § 9601, and (iii) whether the operations at the Property will comply with all applicable environmental laws. Such evaluations will be based upon a physical inspection of the Property and a historical review of the previous and current uses of the Property. If such review indicates that Hazardous Materials may exist in the soil or the buildings at the Property, then the applicable consultant or expert shall have the right, upon reasonable notice, to enter and investigate the Property and to take such samples as may be necessary to perform soil, water, or other analyses;

(e) All documents relating to the purchase of the Property by Borrower;

(f) Complete plans and specifications used for the construction of the Building (the "Plans"), together with an engineering report, dated not more than _____ (__) days before the Closing Date, from an engineering firm engaged by Lender and compensated by Borrower, evaluating the Plans (including a review of the Plans and a complete mechanical, electrical, and structural components analysis thereof and ongoing reports during any construction based on physical inspections showing that construction of the Building has been completed substantially in accordance with the Plans);

(g) An architect's or engineer's certificate in favor of Lender, dated not more than _____ (__) days before the Closing Date, or, if such certificate cannot be obtained by Borrower's best efforts, other evidence showing that (i) the Building and all other improvements existing on the Property have been constructed substantially in accordance with the Plans and comply with all applicable zoning, land use, building, fire, life safety protection, and, if applicable, seismic safety laws, statutes, codes, and regulations; and (ii) all permits necessary for occupancy and use of the Property have been issued;

(h) Certificates of insurance issued by such companies with such limits and coverages as Lender may require or approve, including without limitation (i) "all risk" fire and extended coverage insurance covering the Property for the full replacement cost thereof with a waiver of subrogation, if available, and replacement cost agreed amount endorsements, with Lender named as loss payee; (ii) public liability and property damage insurance having at least a $_____ single limit coverage, with Lender named as additional insured; (iii) flood insurance, if the Property is located in a flood hazard area; and (iv) rent loss insurance equal to not less than twelve (12) months' rental interruption coverage;

(i)  A rent roll certified by Borrower as being true, correct, and complete, and complete and legible copies of all leases and occupancy agreements affecting the Property. Borrower shall update such certified rent roll to the Closing Date;

(j)  An estoppel certificate, in the form of <u>Exhibit D</u> to this Commitment, from each tenant of the Property;

(k) The current management agreement for the Property, together with all service contracts for the Property;

(l)  Evidence that the Property is served by adequate storm sewer, sanitary sewer, telephone, gas, electric, and water service;

(m) Central and local UCC searches showing the security interests in the Personal Property in favor of Lender to be valid and clear of all claims, security interests, and encumbrances, and such bankruptcy, judgment, federal and state tax lien, building code violation, and other searches of public records as Lender may require with respect to the Property, Borrower, or any other persons having any interest in Borrower or the Property;

(n) Evidence of Borrower's qualification, power, and authority to borrow the Principal Amount and to execute and deliver this Commitment, the Loan Documents, and all other documents in connection with the Loan, together with certified copies of the formation documents of Borrower and formation documents of all direct and indirect owners of interests in Borrower;

(o) The current financial statements of Borrower, all direct and indirect owners of interests in Borrower, and the Guarantors, each prepared and certified in such manner as Lender may require;

(p) On the Closing Date, the Certificate of an officer of Borrower, certifying that the representations and warranties of Borrower set forth in this Commitment are true and correct as of the Closing Date;

(q) On the Closing Date, opinions of counsel for Borrower indicating that the Loan Documents are valid and binding and enforceable according to their terms, subject only to the principles of equity and bankruptcy and to such other limitations, qualifications, and assumptions by Borrower's counsel as Lender deems reasonable under the circumstances, and covering such other matters with respect to the Loan Documents, Borrower, the Property, and the transaction hereby contemplated as may reasonably be required by Lender;

(r)  An inventory showing the location of all Personal Property (and, if applicable, the make, model, and serial number thereof) certified by Borrower as being true, complete, and correct and certifying that the items specified on such inventory are owned by Borrower free and clear of conditional sales contracts and other liens, encumbrances, or security interests;

(s) Evidence satisfactory to Lender demonstrating that Borrower is in compliance with all applicable laws pertaining to money laundering, all anti-terrorism laws, and all other similar laws;

(t) Written notice to Lender of the proposed Closing Date;

(u) On the Closing Date, originals of all of the Loan Documents duly executed by Borrower and the Guarantors, as applicable; and

(v) Such other documents, data, and papers with respect to the Property, Borrower, or the Loan as Lender may reasonably require in accordance with its then customary lending practices.

11. <u>Representations and Warranties.</u>

Borrower, by its acceptance of this Commitment, represents and warrants to and covenants with Lender that:

(a) Borrower is a _____, duly organized and in good standing under the laws of the State of _____, and authorized to do business in the jurisdiction where the Property is located;

(b) This Commitment constitutes the legal, valid, and binding obligation of Borrower enforceable in accordance with its terms, Borrower has full power and authority to enter into and perform the terms and conditions of this Commitment, Borrower has obtained all necessary approvals and consents to the borrowing of the Loan as contemplated by this Commitment, and the person executing this Commitment for Borrower is fully and duly empowered and authorized so to act;

(c) The compliance with or fulfillment of the terms and conditions of this Commitment will not conflict with, violate, constitute a default under, or result in a breach of the terms, conditions, or provisions of any of Borrower's organizational documents or any contract or agreement to which Borrower is a party or by which Borrower is otherwise bound;

(d) There are no pending or, to the knowledge of Borrower, threatened actions or proceedings against Borrower that, if determined adversely to Borrower, would materially adversely affect Borrower's ability to perform its obligations under this Commitment or that would enjoin or prevent the consummation of the Closing;

(e) There are no brokerage commissions payable in connection with the transactions contemplated by this Commitment to any party claiming through Borrower or arising out of the actions of Borrower;

(f) To the knowledge of Borrower, there are no Hazardous Materials present at the Property;

(g) None of the representations of Borrower in this Commitment, or in any other document or paper delivered or made to Lender or any agent, employee, or director thereof by or on behalf of Borrower in connection with the transactions contemplated by this Commitment, contain any untrue statement of a material fact or omit to state a material fact necessary in order to make any representation contained herein or therein not misleading in light of the circumstances in which such representation is made; and

(h) The representations set forth in this Section 11 shall be true and correct as of the date of acceptance of this Commitment by Borrower and as of the Closing Date and shall survive the closing of the Loan and the execution and delivery of the Loan Documents.

12. Indemnifications.

(a) Borrower shall indemnify and hold Lender harmless against and from any and all claims and demands for brokerage commissions or finders' fees, and attorneys' fees and court costs associated therewith, asserted against Lender in connection with the Loan and based upon any conduct of Borrower.

(b) The relationship between Lender and Borrower shall be only that of creditor-debtor. No relationship of agency, partnership, or joint- or co-venture shall be created by or inferred from this Commitment or the Loan Documents. Borrower shall indemnify, save, defend, and hold Lender harmless against and from any and all claims and demands asserted against Lender as being the agent, partner, or joint- or co-venturer of Borrower, and attorneys' fees, expenses, and court costs associated therewith.

13. Events of Default.

Upon the occurrence or existence of any of the following events on or before the Closing Date, Lender may terminate this Commitment and all of Lender's obligations hereunder without liability:

(a) If Borrower or any of the direct or indirect owners of interests in Borrower (i) makes a general assignment for the benefit of creditors; (ii) admits in writing the inability to pay debts as they become due; (iii) files a petition for bankruptcy; (iv) is adjudicated a bankrupt or insolvent; (v) files a petition seeking any reorganization, arrangement, composition, readjustment, liquidation, dissolution, receivership, or similar relief under any present or future statute, law, or regulation; (vi) files an answer admitting or not contesting the material allegations of a petition against it in any such proceeding; (vii) seeks or consents to or acquiesces in the appointment of any trustee, receiver, or liquidator for Borrower or any of its properties; or (viii) discontinues or suspends its business as a going concern;

(b) If any involuntary proceeding against Borrower or any of the direct or indirect owners of interests in Borrower seeking any reorganization, bankruptcy, arrangement, composition, readjustment, liquidation, dissolution, receivership, or similar relief under any present or future statute, law, or regulation is not dismissed by the earlier of (i) ninety (90) days after the commencement thereof; or (ii) the Closing Date;

(c) If there is any unrepaired damage to or destruction of the Building or any other improvements on the Property or any part thereof materially impairing the use of the Property, unless provision for such repair or restoration has been made to Lender's satisfaction;

(d) If any portion of the Property is taken by condemnation or eminent domain or is subject to pending proceedings therefor so as to cause or threaten (i) any loss of parking spaces, (ii) the Property to become a non-conforming use, or (iii) any adverse effect upon access from the Property to public streets;

(e) If any material adverse change occurs in the condition (financial or otherwise) or business of Borrower, any of its subsidiaries, or any other legal entity whose condition, financial or otherwise, was a material consideration by Lender in the issuing of this Commitment, including but not limited to any of the Guarantors (Lender, in its sole discretion, shall determine materiality);

(f) If there is any attachment, seizure, levy upon, or taking of possession by any receiver, custodian, or assignee for the benefit of creditors of any part of the property of Borrower;

(g) If there is any assignment or attempted assignment, voluntary or by operation of law, of this Commitment without Lender's prior written approval;

(h) If any representation, warranty, covenant, or statement made by Borrower in this Commitment shall be breached or violated, or proves to be false, misleading, or inaccurate in any material respect; or

(i) If there is any other uncured default by Borrower in its obligations under this Commitment.

14. <u>Closing.</u>

(a) On the date on which all of the terms and conditions set forth in this Commitment are satisfied in full (the "Closing Date"), Lender shall disburse the Principal Amount to Borrower, for the sole purpose of purchasing the Property. Borrower shall diligently prosecute the satisfaction of all terms, conditions, and provisions contained in this Commitment so that the Closing Date shall occur on or before _____.

(b) Lender shall make no disbursement of the Principal Amount if (i) Borrower is in default under this Commitment or any of the Loan Documents or an event shall have occurred that, but for the giving of notice or passage of time, would constitute a default under this Commitment or any of the Loan Documents; or (ii) each of the conditions set forth in Section 10 has not been satisfied or waived in writing by Lender.

(c) If, without the fault of Lender, the Closing Date has not occurred on or before _____ then, at the option of Lender, this Commitment and Lender's obligations hereunder, without notice to Borrower, shall terminate and be of no further force or effect.

15. <u>Costs and Expenses.</u>

Regardless of whether the closing of the Loan is consummated or the Principal Amount disbursed to Borrower, Borrower shall pay on or before the Closing Date all costs, fees, and expenses of Lender in connection with the negotiation and origination of the Loan, including but not limited to all survey costs, title charges and premiums, escrow expenses, filing fees, recordation and transfer taxes, certification costs, attorneys' fees, fees of engineers, brokers, appraisers, environmental consultants, and Lender's inspecting engineer, and all other costs and expenses incidental to the transactions contemplated by this Commitment, and shall be responsible for the payment and performance of all of the terms and conditions hereof. The costs and expenses of Lender contemplated by this Section 15 shall be in addition to and exclusive of the Commitment Fee.

16. Miscellaneous.

(a) This Commitment, together with the Exhibits attached hereto, is the entire agreement between the parties with respect to the Loan, and all prior statements, discussions, negotiations, and agreements, oral or written, are superseded by this Commitment and merged herein. The terms, conditions, representations, and warranties contained in this Commitment shall survive the closing of the Loan and shall not be merged in the Loan Documents. If any of the terms and conditions of the Loan Documents conflict with or are inconsistent with the terms and conditions of this Commitment, the terms and conditions of the Loan Documents shall prevail.

(b) If any provision of this Commitment shall be adjudged to be unenforceable, this Commitment shall, at Lender's election, be deemed to be automatically reformed to the extent possible to render this Commitment enforceable and, in any event, the invalidity or unenforceability of any provision of this Commitment shall not affect or impair the validity or enforceability of the remaining provisions of this Commitment.

(c) Section headings herein are for convenience only and do not bear on the construction or interpretation of the content of this Commitment.

(d) Time is of the essence of this Commitment.

(e) No change, amendment, modification, waiver, cancellation, or discharge of this Commitment or any term or provision hereof shall be valid or binding unless such change, amendment, modification, waiver, cancellation, or discharge is in writing and signed by Lender.

(f) All notices, demands, elections, deliveries, approvals, and other communications between the parties required or desired to be given in connection with this Agreement (each, a "Notice"), to be effective under this Commitment, shall be in writing and shall be deemed to be given and received (i) when delivered personally; (ii) one (1) business day after deposit with a national overnight courier service (such as FedEx); or (iii) three (3) business days after deposit with the United States Postal Service as certified mail, return receipt requested; in any event with all charges or postage prepaid, and addressed as follows:

If to Lender,

_____

_____

_____

_____

with a copy to

_____

_____

_____

_____

And if to Borrower,

_____

_____

_____

_____

with a copy to

_____

_____

_____

_____

Either party may from time to time designate another address for the receipt of future Notices by a Notice given as provided in this Section 16(f) to the other party at the address set forth in, or as last provided by such other party in accordance with, this Section 16(f).

(g) The terms, covenants, and conditions of this Commitment shall be binding upon and inure to the benefit of Lender and Borrower and their respective successors and permitted assigns.

(h) This Commitment may be executed in two or more counterparts, each of which shall be deemed an original and all of which, taken together, shall constitute and be deemed to be one and the same instrument.

(i) This Commitment shall be governed by the laws of the [State] [Commonwealth] of _____, excluding any _____ choice of law principles, and the Loan Documents shall be governed by and construed under the laws of the State in which the Property is located.

If the foregoing is acceptable to you, please acknowledge your acceptance of and agreement with the terms, conditions, and provisions of this Commitment by executing the enclosed copy of this Commitment where provided and returning the executed copy to the undersigned, together with the Commitment Fee. Any form of acceptance by Borrower of this Commitment other than on the terms, conditions, and provisions set forth herein, including without limitation, a conditional, modified, or limited acceptance, shall be a counteroffer to Lender to be accepted or rejected by Lender in its sole and absolute subjective discretion.

Very truly yours,

_____, Lender

By: _____

Its: _____

We hereby accept and agree to the terms, conditions, and provisions of this Commitment this _____ day of _____, _____.

_____,

a _____, Borrower

By: _____,

Its: _____

## EXHIBIT A
### Legal Description of the Land

## EXHIBIT B
### Method of Calculating Mortgage Yield Maintenance Fee

## EXHIBIT C
### Survey Requirements

## EXHIBIT D
### Estoppel Certificate

# Appendix J

# Form of Promissory Note

**Note:** The particular provisions of promissory notes will vary widely depending on the terms of the loan commitment, such as whether the note will bear a fixed or floating rate of interest; whether principal is to be amortized and, if so, the term of such amortization as distinguished from the term of the loan; whether further advances will be made; whether and when prepayment is permitted; and whether the repayment obligations are with recourse to the borrower. The following form attempts to include only typical provisions that would appear in a simple secured promissory note for a loan such as the one described in Appendix I, Form of Loan Commitment, and certain alternative provisions are shown in brackets. Accordingly, the practitioner should consider the use of provisions that are included in other forms in this book to supplement this form and should become familiar with the terms of the loan commitment before preparing a promissory note.

## PROMISSORY NOTE

$_____                                          Date _____

1. FOR VALUE RECEIVED, _____,
a _____, as maker, with its principal place of business at
_____ ("Borrower"), hereby promises to pay to the order of
_____, having an address of _____, or
its assigns ("Lender"), on or before the Maturity Date (hereinafter defined),
the principal sum of _____ Dollars
($_____) (the "Principal Amount"), and to pay interest on the Principal
Amount from the date of this Note to maturity at the annual rate of ___ percent (____%) (the "Agreed Rate"), payable as set forth in Section 4, unless
and until an Event of Default (defined in Section 4(e)) occurs. If an Event
of Default occurs, the Principal Amount shall bear interest from the date
of the Event of Default at an annual rate (the "Default Rate") which is the
greater of (a) _____ percent (____%); or (b) ____ percent (____%) plus
the prime rate announced by _____, or
its successors, from time to time, with each change thereof automatically
effecting a change in the Default Rate, until such Event of Default is cured.
Interest, whether at the Agreed Rate or at the Default Rate, shall be calculated on the basis of twelve (12) 30-day months, with any partial month
calculated on the basis of a 360-day year.

2. This Promissory Note (the "Note") evidences the obligation to make
repayment of a loan (the "Loan") made by Lender to Borrower. This Note
is secured in part as provided by the Mortgage, dated this date by Borrower
to Lender and recorded in the land records of _____ County,

_____ (together with all supplements and amendments thereto or extensions thereof, the "Mortgage"). Reference is hereby made to the Mortgage and the other documents executed to evidence or secure the Loan (this Note, the Mortgage, and such other documents, together with any amendments, modifications, and supplements thereto, are collectively called the "Loan Documents") for a description of the property thereby mortgaged, granted, or assigned, the nature and extent of the security for this Note, the rights of Lender and Borrower with respect to such security and otherwise, and the terms upon which this Note is delivered.

3. Capitalized terms used but not defined in this Note shall have the meanings given to them in the Mortgage.

4. The Principal Amount, accrued interest thereon, and the Late Charges (defined in Section 5), if any, shall be payable at the office of Lender located at the address set forth in paragraph 1 of this Note or such other address as may be provided by Lender in writing from time to time (the "Payment Address"), in immediately available funds, in the following manner:

(a) Beginning on the first day of _____, 20__, and continuing on the first day of each month to and including _____ 1, 20__, Borrower shall pay to Lender monthly installments of the Principal Amount and interest at the Agreed Rate each in the amount of _____ Dollars ($_____), in arrears (with a prorated payment of interest only at the Agreed Rate for any initial partial month); and

(b) The Principal Amount, all accrued interest thereon, and any Late Charges, if not sooner paid, shall be due and payable on _____ 1, 20__ (the "Maturity Date").

(c) Lender shall apply any amounts received on account of the Loan (i) first, [to the Prepayment Premium (defined in Section 4(d)), if any; (ii) second,] to any unpaid costs, expenses, or other charges due to Lender as provided by the Loan Documents; (iii) third, to any unpaid Late Charges; (iv) fourth, to any accrued and unpaid interest on the Principal Amount; and (v) fifth, to the Principal Amount then outstanding, in reverse order of maturity, and the amount of the monthly installments as provided in Section 4(a), except for the final unpaid installment thereof, shall not be decreased by reason of any partial payment or prepayment of the Principal Amount.

[(d)  Borrower may prepay the Principal Amount in whole or in part at any time before the Maturity Date without premium or penalty.]

[(d)  Before the _____ (_th) anniversary of the date of this Note, Borrower shall not have the right or privilege to make, and Lender shall not be obligated to accept, a prepayment of all or any part of the Principal Amount unless Borrower shall pay to Lender, together with any prepayment of all or any part of the Principal Amount, a prepayment premium (the "Prepayment Premium") equal to the greater of (a) ___ percent (__%) of the Principal Amount then outstanding which Borrower is prepaying, or

(b) the mortgage yield maintenance fee calculated as set forth in <u>Exhibit A</u> to this Note. Borrower shall give _____ (__) days' prior written notice to Lender of its intent to prepay all or any part of the Principal Amount.]

(e) Upon the occurrence of a default by Borrower under this Note, the Mortgage, or any of the other Loan Documents, that continues beyond the expiration of any applicable cure period or grace period hereunder or thereunder (an "Event of Default"), Lender shall have the right to accelerate the Maturity Date and declare the Principal Amount, all accrued and unpaid interest thereon, and any Late Charges to be immediately due and payable.

5. Borrower shall not be given notice of or be permitted any grace period to correct any failure to make any payment of principal or interest. If Borrower fails to make any payment on the date when due, Lender shall have the right to charge Borrower a late payment charge equal to ____ percent (_%) of such late payment (the "Late Charge"). In addition, interest shall accrue on the Principal Amount at the Default Rate from the date due until received at the Payment Address.

[6. Borrower does hereby authorize any clerk of any court of record or any attorney, upon the occurrence of an Event of Default, to enter in any court of competent jurisdiction in the [State] of _____ or any other State or Territory of the United States judgment by confession against Borrower and in favor of Lender for the Principal Amount, together with all accrued and unpaid interest thereon, the Late Charges, and actual attorneys' fees not to exceed ___ percent (_%) thereof and court costs, without stay of execution or right of appeal and expressly waiving the benefit of all exemption laws and all irregularity or error in entering such judgment or the execution thereon. No single exercise of the foregoing power to confess judgment shall be deemed to exhaust the power, whether or not any such exercise shall be held by any court to be invalid, voidable, or void, but the power shall continue undiminished, and it may be exercised from time to time as often as Lender shall elect, until such time as Lender shall have received payment in full of all indebtedness of Borrower to Lender.]

[7. Neither Borrower nor any direct or indirect owner of an interest in Borrower shall have personal liability for payment of the Principal Amount, interest thereon, Late Charges, or any other costs, expenses, or other charges due to Lender as provided by the Loan Documents and, in the event of any default, Lender's sole recourse shall be against the Property and any other collateral securing the Loan and under the Guarantee; provided, however, that Borrower and such direct and indirect owners shall remain personally liable as otherwise provided by the Loan Documents or applicable law for the following: (a) as provided by the Guarantee, with respect to the Guarantors; (b) Borrower's failure to pay real estate taxes or assessments against the Property, to the extent that funds are available; (c) Borrower's failure to insure the Property as required by the Loan Documents; (d) rent or other income from the Property received after a default under the Loan Documents and which is not applied as provided by the Loan Documents or to the expenses of operating or maintaining the Property; (e) conversion, diversion, misapplication, or misappropriation of security deposits, reserve accounts, insurance proceeds, or condemnation awards in connection with the Property; (f) waste; (g) amounts due under the Environmental Indemnity (as defined in the Mortgage); and (h) fraud or intentional misrepresentation in connection with the transactions contemplated by any of the Loan Documents.]

8. Should any indebtedness represented by this Note be collected at law or in equity, or in bankruptcy or other proceeding, or if Lender engages attorneys for collection on this Note after a default hereunder, under the Mortgage, or under any of the other Loan Documents, Borrower agrees to pay, in addition to the Principal Amount, Late Charges, and interest due and payable hereon, all actual costs of collecting or attempting to collect such indebtedness, including actual attorneys' fees and expenses (including those incurred in connection with any appeal).

[9. Upon the occurrence of an Event of Default, Lender shall have the right, in addition to all other remedies provided by this Note, the Mortgage, and the other Loan Documents, at law and in equity, to set off or recoup any or all amounts due under this Note or any other obligation of Borrower to Lender against any and all accounts, credits, money, securities, or other property on deposit with, held by, or in the possession of Lender to the credit of or for the account of Borrower, without prior notice to or consent by Borrower.]

10. Borrower expressly waives presentment, protest, notice of protest, demand, intention to accelerate the maturity of this Note, dishonor and nonpayment of this Note, and all other notices of any kind except as expressly provided hereunder or in the Mortgage or the other Loan Documents, and expressly agrees that this Note, or any payment hereunder, may be extended from time to time without in any way affecting the liability of Borrower and endorsers or guarantors hereof. All payments due under this Note, the Mortgage, or the other Loan Documents are payable without relief from any valuation or appraisement laws.

11. [Note to drafter: The law in some states may require a provision of this nature to be set forth in uppercase type.] Borrower hereby waives trial by jury in any action or proceeding to which Borrower and Lender may be parties arising out of or in any way pertaining to this Note, the Mortgage, or the other Loan Documents. This waiver constitutes a waiver of trial by jury of all claims against all parties to such actions or proceedings, including claims against parties who are not parties to this Note, the Mortgage, or the other Loan Documents.

12. If any provision (or any part of any provision) contained in this Note shall for any reason be held to be invalid, illegal, or unenforceable in any respect, such invalidity, illegality, or unenforceability shall not affect any

other provision (or remaining part of the affected provision) of this Note, but this Note shall be construed as if such invalid, illegal, or unenforceable provision (or part thereof) had never been contained herein, but only to the extent it is invalid, illegal, or unenforceable.

13. No provision of this Note shall require the payment or permit the collection of interest in excess of the maximum permitted by law. If any such excess interest is so provided for, or adjudicated to be so provided for, in this Note, Borrower shall not be obligated to pay such interest in excess of the amount permitted by law, the right to demand the payment of any such excess shall be and is hereby waived, and this provision shall control over any other provision of this Note.

14. All notices, demands, and other communications between Borrower and Lender required or desired to be given in connection with this Note, to be effective hereunder, shall be given as provided by the Mortgage.

15. This Note, the Mortgage, and the other Loan Documents collectively contain the entire agreement of Borrower and Lender with respect to the matters set forth herein and therein, and all prior statements, discussions, negotiations, and agreements, oral or written, are superseded by this Note, the Mortgage, and the other Loan Documents and merged herein or therein.

16. The relationship between Lender and Borrower shall be only that of creditor and debtor. No relationship of agency, partnership, or joint- or co-venture shall be created by or inferred from this Note, the Mortgage, or the other Loan Documents. Borrower shall indemnify, save, defend, and hold Lender harmless from and against any and all claims and demands asserted against Lender as being the agent, partner, or joint- or co-venturer of Borrower, and attorneys' fees, expenses, and court costs associated therewith.

17. Time is of the essence of this Note.

18. This Note shall be governed by the laws of the [State] [Commonwealth] of _____, excluding any _____ choice of law principles.

19. Borrower represents and warrants that all of the proceeds received by Borrower in connection with this Note shall be used for business or commercial purposes, and Borrower stipulates that the Loan shall be construed for all purposes as a commercial loan and that it is being made for purposes other than personal, family, or household purposes.

IN WITNESS WHEREOF, Borrower has caused this Promissory Note to be duly executed and delivered under seal as of the date first above written.

_____, a

_____, Borrower

By: _____ (SEAL)

Its: _____

WITNESS:

_____

EXHIBIT A
Method of Calculating Mortgage Yield Maintenance Fee

# Appendix K

## Form of Mortgage

**Note:** Mortgages and deeds of trust are highly state-specific instruments. This Form of Mortgage is intended to be illustrative, but the drafter must be sure to use a document that complies with the law of the state in which the mortgaged property is located. This is particularly important with respect to the remedies available under the mortgage, which can vary dramatically from state to state.

In loan transactions in which the loan is secured by both a lien on the borrower's real property and a UCC security interest in the borrower's personal property, it is common practice in some states to combine the mortgage and the security agreement into one instrument. This Form of Mortgage serves both of those roles. However, the Form of Security Agreement that appears in Appendix M can serve as a free-standing security agreement. Note as well that this Form of Mortgage contemplates a separate Assignment of Leases and Rents (such as the Form that appears in Appendix L) and a separate environmental indemnity agreement.

In many cases, the parties to a mortgage will simultaneously execute a loan agreement, particularly if the loan is a construction loan. If the loan is a pure acquisition loan, however, the parties are less likely to execute a separate loan agreement. The Form of Mortgage that follows is intended to serve as an acquisition mortgage. Consequently, it assumes that the parties will not concurrently execute a loan agreement.

**PREPARED BY AND
UPON RECORDATION
RETURN TO:**

_____

_____

_____

MORTGAGE, ASSIGNMENT OF RENTS,
SECURITY AGREEMENT, AND FIXTURE FILING

THIS MORTGAGE, ASSIGNMENT OF RENTS, SECURITY AGREE-
MENT, AND FIXTURE FILING (this "Mortgage") is made as of this \_\_\_\_
day of _____, 20\_\_, by _____, a _____, hav-
ing an address at _____, as grantor ("Borrower"), to _____
\_\_\_\_, a _____, having an address at _____,
as beneficiary ("Lender").

WITNESSETH:

WHEREAS, this Mortgage is given to secure a loan (the "Loan") in
the principal sum of _____ evidenced by that certain
Promissory Note dated the date hereof made by Borrower to Lender (such
Note, together with all extensions, renewals, replacements, restatements,
or modifications thereof being hereinafter referred to as the "Note"). The
sums due under the Note and this Mortgage are referred to collectively
herein as the "Indebtedness";

WHEREAS, Borrower desires to secure the payment of the Indebtedness and the performance of all of its obligations under the Note and the
other Loan Documents (as hereinafter defined); and

WHEREAS, payment, fulfillment, and performance by Borrower of
its obligations under the Loan Documents are secured hereby, and each and
every term and provision of the Note, including the rights, remedies, obligations, covenants, conditions, agreements, indemnities, representations,
and warranties of the parties therein, are hereby incorporated by reference
herein as though set forth in full and shall be considered a part of this Mortgage (the Note, this Mortgage, and that certain Assignment of Leases and
Rents of even date herewith made by Borrower in favor of Lender [the
"Assignment of Leases"], together with all other documents evidencing or
securing the Indebtedness or delivered in connection with the making of
the Loan and executed by Borrower, any guarantor and/or any principal of
Borrower, are referred to collectively as the "Loan Documents").

NOW THEREFORE, in consideration of the making of the Loan by
Lender and the covenants, agreements, representations, and warranties set
forth in this Mortgage:

# ARTICLE I
# GRANTS OF SECURITY

1.1 <u>Property Mortgaged.</u> Borrower does hereby irrevocably mortgage, grant, pledge, and assign to Lender and its successors and assigns the following property, rights, interests, and estates now owned, or hereafter acquired by Borrower (collectively, the "<u>Property</u>"):

a. <u>Land.</u> The real property described in <u>Exhibit A</u> attached hereto and made a part hereof (the "<u>Land</u>");

b. <u>Additional Land.</u> All additional lands, estates, and development rights hereafter acquired by Borrower for use in connection with the Land and the development of the Land and all additional lands and estates therein which may, from time to time, by supplemental mortgage or otherwise, be expressly made subject to the lien of this Mortgage;

c. <u>Improvements.</u> The buildings, structures, fixtures, additions, enlargements, extensions, modifications, repairs, replacements, and improvements now or hereafter erected or located on the Land (collectively, the "<u>Improvements</u>");

d. <u>Easements.</u> All easements, rights-of-way or use, rights, strips and gores of land, streets, ways, alleys, passages, sewer rights, water, water courses, water rights and powers, air rights and development rights, and all estates, rights, titles, interests, privileges, liberties, servitudes, tenements, hereditaments, and appurtenances of any nature whatsoever, in any way now or hereafter belonging, relating, or pertaining to the Land and the Improvements, and the reversion and reversions, remainder and remainders, and all land lying in the bed of any street, road, or avenue, opened or proposed, in front of or adjoining the Land, to the center line thereof, and all the estates, rights, titles, interests, dower and rights of dower, curtesy and rights of curtesy, property, possession, claim, and demand whatsoever, both at law and in equity, of Borrower of, in, and to the Land and the Improvements and every part and parcel thereof, with the appurtenances thereto;

e. <u>Equipment.</u> All "equipment," as such term is defined in Article 9 of the Uniform Commercial Code (as hereinafter defined), now owned or hereafter acquired by Borrower which is used at or in connection with the Improvements or the Land or is located thereon or therein (including, but not limited to, all machinery, equipment, furnishings, and electronic data-processing and other office equipment now owned or hereafter acquired by Borrower and any and all additions, substitutions, and replacements of any of the foregoing), together with all attachments, components, parts, equipment, and accessories installed thereon or affixed thereto (collectively, the "<u>Equipment</u>"). Notwithstanding the foregoing, Equipment shall not include any property belonging to tenants under leases or covered by equipment leases except to the extent that Borrower shall have any right or interest therein;

f.   <u>Fixtures.</u> All Equipment now owned or hereafter acquired by Borrower which is so related to the Land and Improvements that it is deemed fixtures or real property under the law of the particular state in which the Equipment is located, including, without limitation, all building or construction materials intended for construction, reconstruction, alteration, or repair of or installation on the Property, construction equipment, appliances, machinery, plant equipment, fittings, apparatuses, fixtures, and other items now or hereafter attached to, installed in, or used in connection with any of the Improvements or the Land, temporarily or permanently, including, but not limited to, engines, devices for the operation of pumps, pipes, plumbing, cleaning, call, and sprinkler systems, fire extinguishing apparatuses and equipment, heating, ventilating, plumbing, laundry, incinerating, electrical, air conditioning, and air cooling equipment and systems, gas and electric machinery, appurtenances and equipment, pollution control equipment, security systems, disposals, dishwashers, refrigerators and ranges, recreational equipment and facilities of all kinds, and water, gas, electrical, storm and sanitary sewer facilities, utility lines and equipment (whether owned individually or jointly with others, and, if owned jointly, to the extent of Borrower's interest therein), and all other utilities whether or not situated in easements, all water tanks, water supply, water power sites, fuel stations, fuel tanks, fuel supply, and all other structures, together with all accessions, appurtenances, additions, replacements, betterments, and substitutions for any of the foregoing and the proceeds thereof (collectively, the "<u>Fixtures</u>"). Notwithstanding the foregoing, "Fixtures" shall not include any property which is covered by equipment leases or which tenants are entitled to remove pursuant to leases except to the extent that Borrower shall have any right or interest therein;

g.   <u>Personal Property.</u> All furniture, furnishings, objects of art, machinery, goods, tools, supplies, appliances, general intangibles, contract rights, accounts, accounts receivable, franchises, licenses, certificates and permits, inventory, and articles of personal property and accessions thereof and renewals and replacements thereof and substitutions therefor, if any, whether tangible or intangible (other than Fixtures), which are now or hereafter owned by Borrower and which are located within or about the Land and the Improvements, together with all accessories, replacements, and substitutions thereto or therefor and the proceeds thereof (collectively, the "<u>Personal Property</u>"), and the right, title, and interest of Borrower in and to any of the Personal Property which may be subject to any security interests, as defined in the Uniform Commercial Code, as adopted and enacted by the state or states where any of the Property is located (the "<u>Uniform Commercial Code</u>"), and all proceeds and products of the above;

h.   <u>Leases and Rents.</u> All leases, subleases, sub-subleases, lettings, licenses, concessions, or other agreements (whether written or oral) pursuant to which any person is granted a possessory interest in, or right to use or occupy, all or any portion of the Land and the Improvements, and every modification, amendment, or other agreement relating to or entered into in connection with such leases, subleases, sub-subleases, and other agreements, and every guarantee of the performance and observance of the covenants, conditions, and agreements to be performed and observed by the other party thereto, heretofore or hereafter entered into, whether before or after the filing by or against Borrower of any petition for relief under the Bankruptcy Code, and all proceeds from the sale or other disposition of any of the above (collectively, the "Leases"), and all right, title, and interest of Borrower, its successors and assigns therein and thereunder, including, without limitation, cash or securities deposited thereunder to secure the performance by the lessees of their obligations thereunder, and all rents, additional rents, revenues, issues, and profits (including all oil and gas or other mineral royalties and bonuses), license, lease, sublease, sub-sublease, and concession fees, and rentals and proceeds, if any, from business interruption or other loss of income insurance from the Land and the Improvements, whether paid or accruing before or after the filing by or against Borrower of any petition for relief under the Bankruptcy Code, and the right to receive and apply any of the above to the payment of the Indebtedness (collectively, the "Rents");

   i.   Condemnation Awards. All awards or payments, including interest thereon, which may heretofore and hereafter be made with respect to the Property, whether from the exercise of the right of eminent domain (including, but not limited to, any transfer made in lieu of or in anticipation of the exercise of the right), or for a change of grade, or for any other injury to or decrease in the value of the Property;

   j.   Insurance Proceeds. All proceeds in respect of the Property under any insurance policies covering the Property, including, without limitation, the right to receive and apply the proceeds of any insurance, judgments, or settlements made in lieu thereof for damage to the Property;

   k.   Tax Certiorari. All refunds, rebates, or credits in connection with reduction in real estate taxes and assessments charged against the Property as a result of tax certiorari or any applications or proceedings for reduction;

   l.   Rights. The right, in the name and on behalf of Borrower, to appear in and defend any action or proceeding brought with respect to the Property and to commence any action or proceeding to protect the interest of Lender in the Property;

   m.   Agreements. All agreements, contracts, certificates, instruments, franchises, permits, licenses, plans, specifications, and other documents, now or hereafter entered into, and all rights therein and thereto, respecting or pertaining to the use, occupation, construction, management, or operation of the Land and any part thereof and any Improvements and any part thereof or respecting any business or activity conducted on the Land and any part thereof and all right, title and interest of Borrower therein and thereunder;

n. Trademarks. All tradenames, trademarks, servicemarks, logos, copyrights, goodwill, books and records, and all other general intangibles relating to or used in connection with the operation of the Property;

o. Accounts. All reserves, escrows, and deposit accounts maintained by Borrower with respect to the Property, including, without limitation, all accounts established or maintained pursuant to the Loan Documents, together with all deposits or wire transfers made to such accounts and all cash, checks, drafts, certificates, securities, investment property, financial assets, instruments, and other property held therein from time to time, and all proceeds, products, distributions or dividends, or substitutions thereon and thereof;

p. Proceeds. All proceeds of any of the foregoing, including, without limitation, proceeds of insurance and condemnation awards, whether cash, liquidation or other claims, or otherwise; and

q. Other Rights. Any and all other rights of Borrower in and to the items set forth in Subsections (a) through (p) above.

AND without limiting any of the other provisions of this Mortgage, to the extent permitted by applicable law, Borrower expressly grants to Lender, as secured party, a security interest in the portion of the Property which is or may be subject to the provisions of the Uniform Commercial Code which are applicable to secured transactions; it being understood and agreed that the Improvements and Fixtures are part and parcel of the Land (the Land, the Improvements, and the Fixtures collectively referred to as the "Real Property"), appropriated to the use thereof and, whether affixed or annexed to the Real Property or not, shall for the purposes of this Mortgage be deemed conclusively to be real estate and conveyed hereby.

1.2    Assignment of Rents. Borrower hereby absolutely and unconditionally assigns to Lender all of Borrower's right, title, and interest in and to all current and future Leases and Rents; it being intended by Borrower that this assignment constitutes a present, absolute assignment and not an assignment for additional security only. Nevertheless, subject to the terms of the Assignment of Leases and Section 7.2(h) of this Mortgage, Lender grants to Borrower a revocable license to collect, receive, use, and enjoy the Rents. Borrower shall hold the Rents, or a portion thereof sufficient to discharge all current sums due on the Indebtedness, for use in the payment of such sums.

If any conflict or inconsistency exists between the assignment of Rents in this Mortgage and the assignment of Rents in the Assignment of Leases, the terms of the Assignment of Leases shall control.

1.3    Security Agreement. This Mortgage is both a real property mortgage and a "security agreement" within the meaning of the Uniform Commercial Code. The Property includes both real and personal property, and all other rights and interests, whether tangible or intangible in nature, of Borrower in the Property. By executing and delivering this Mortgage, Borrower hereby grants to Lender, as security for the Obligations (as hereinafter defined), a security interest in the Fixtures, the Equipment, the Personal Property, and other property constituting the Property to the full extent that the Fixtures, the Equipment, the Personal Property, and such other property may be subject to the Uniform Commercial Code (said portion of the Property so subject to the Uniform Commercial Code being called the "Collateral"). If any Event of Default (as hereinafter defined) shall occur and be continuing, Lender, in addition to any other rights and remedies which it may have, shall have and may exercise immediately and without demand, any and all rights and remedies granted to a secured party upon default under the Uniform Commercial Code, including, without limiting the generality of the foregoing, the right to take possession of the Collateral or any part thereof and to take such other measures as Lender may deem necessary for the care, protection, and preservation of the Collateral. Upon request or demand of Lender after the occurrence and during the continuance of an Event of Default, Borrower shall, at its expense, assemble the Collateral and make it available to Lender at a convenient place (at the Land if tangible property) reasonably acceptable to Lender. Borrower shall pay to Lender on demand any and all expenses, including reasonable legal expenses and attorneys' fees, incurred or paid by Lender in protecting its interest in the Collateral and in enforcing its rights hereunder with respect to the Collateral after the occurrence and during the continuance of an Event of Default. Any notice of sale, disposition, or other intended action by Lender with respect to the Collateral sent to Borrower in accordance with the provisions hereof at least ten (10) business days prior to such action shall, except as otherwise provided by applicable law, constitute reasonable notice to Borrower. The proceeds of any disposition of the Collateral, or any part thereof, may, except as otherwise required by applicable law, be applied by Lender to the payment of the Indebtedness in such priority and proportions as Lender in its discretion shall deem proper. The principal place of business of Borrower (debtor) is as set forth on page one hereof and the address of Lender (secured party) is as set forth on page one hereof.

1.4    Fixture Filing. Certain of the Property is or will become "fixtures" (as that term is defined in the Uniform Commercial Code) on the Land, and this Mortgage, upon being filed for record in the real estate records of the city or county wherein such fixtures are situated, shall operate also as a financing statement, naming Borrower as the debtor and Lender as the secured party, in accordance with the applicable provisions of the Uniform Commercial Code, upon such of the Property that is or may become fixtures.

1.5    Pledges of Monies Held. Borrower hereby pledges to Lender any and all monies now or hereafter held by Lender or on behalf of Lender in connection with the Loan.

## CONDITIONS TO GRANT

TO HAVE AND TO HOLD the above granted and described Property unto and to the use and benefit of Lender and its successors and assigns forever, to secure payment to Lender of the Obligations at the time and in the manner provided in the Note and this Mortgage;

PROVIDED, HOWEVER, these presents are upon the express condition that, if Borrower shall well and truly pay to Lender the Indebtedness at the time and in the manner provided in the Note and this Mortgage, shall well and truly perform the Other Obligations as set forth in this Mortgage, and shall well and truly abide by and comply with each and every covenant and condition set forth herein and in the Loan Documents, these presents shall cease, terminate, and be void; provided, however, that Borrower's obligation to indemnify and hold harmless Lender pursuant to the provisions hereof shall survive any such payment or release.

## ARTICLE II
## INDEBTEDNESS AND OBLIGATIONS SECURED

2.1    Indebtedness. This Mortgage and the grants, assignments, and transfers made in Article I are given for the purpose of securing the Indebtedness, including, but not limited to, the obligations of Borrower to pay to Lender the principal and interest owing pursuant to the terms and conditions of the Note.

2.2    Other Obligations. This Mortgage and the grants, assignments, and transfers made in Article I are also given for the purpose of securing the following (the "Other Obligations"):

a.  the performance of all other obligations of Borrower contained herein;

b.  the performance of each obligation of Borrower contained in any other Loan Document; and

c.  the performance of each obligation of Borrower contained in any renewal, extension, amendment, modification, consolidation, change of, or substitution or replacement for all or any part of the Note or any other Loan Document.

2.3    Indebtedness and Other Obligations. Borrower's obligations for the payment of the Indebtedness and the performance of the Other Obligations may sometimes be referred to collectively herein as the "Obligations."

## ARTICLE III
## BORROWER'S COVENANTS, REPRESENTATIONS, AND WARRANTIES

Borrower covenants, represents, warrants, and agrees that:

3.1    Payment of Indebtedness. Borrower will pay the Indebtedness at the time and in the manner provided in the Note and this Mortgage.

3.2   <u>Incorporation by Reference.</u> Borrower shall observe and perform each and every term, covenant, condition, provision, and agreement to be observed or performed by Borrower pursuant to any other Loan Document and any amendments, modifications, or changes thereto. All the terms, covenants, conditions, provisions, and agreements contained in the Loan Documents are hereby made a part of this Mortgage to the same extent and with the same force as if fully set forth herein.

3.3.   <u>Insurance.</u> Borrower shall obtain and maintain, or cause to be maintained, in full force and effect at all times insurance with respect to Borrower and the Property issued by such companies with such limits and coverages as Lender may require or approve, including without limitation (i) "all risk" fire and extended coverage insurance covering the Property for the full replacement cost thereof with a waiver of subrogation, if available, and replacement cost agreed amount endorsements, with Lender named as loss payee; (ii) public liability and property damage insurance having at least a $_____ single limit coverage, with Lender named as additional insured; (iii) flood insurance, if the Property is located in a flood hazard area; and (iv) rent loss insurance equal to not less than twelve (12) months' rental interruption coverage.

3.4   <u>Maintenance of Property.</u> Borrower shall cause the Property to be maintained in a good and safe condition and repair. Borrower shall promptly repair, replace, or rebuild any part of the Property which may be destroyed by any casualty, or become damaged, worn, or dilapidated, or which may be affected by any condemnation, and shall complete and pay for any structure at any time in the process of construction or repair on the Land.

3.5   <u>Waste.</u> Borrower shall not commit or suffer any waste of the Property or make any change in the use of the Property, except as provided for in the Loan Documents, which will in any way materially increase the risk of fire or other hazard arising out of the operation of the Property, or take any action that might invalidate or allow the cancellation of any insurance policy, or do or permit to be done thereon anything that may in any way materially impair the value of the Property or the security of this Mortgage. Borrower will not, without the prior written consent of Lender, permit any drilling or exploration for or extraction, removal, or production of any minerals from the surface or the subsurface of the Land, regardless of the depth thereof or the method of mining or extraction thereof.

3.6   <u>Payment for Labor and Materials.</u> Borrower will promptly pay when due all bills and costs for labor, materials, and specifically fabricated materials (the "<u>Labor and Material Costs</u>") incurred in connection with the Property and not permit to exist beyond the due date thereof in respect of the Property or any part thereof any lien or security interest, even though inferior to the liens and the security interests hereof, and in any event not permit to be created or exist in respect of the Property or any part thereof any other or additional lien or security interest other than the liens or security interests hereof except for liens expressly permitted by the Note, this Mortgage, or any of the other Loan Documents.

3.7    Labor and Material Costs. After prior written notice to Lender, Borrower, at its own expense, may withhold payment of Labor and Material Costs and contest by appropriate legal proceeding, promptly initiated and conducted in good faith and with due diligence, the amount or validity or application in whole or in part of any of the Labor and Material Costs, provided that (i) no Event of Default has occurred and is continuing under the Note, this Mortgage, or any of the other Loan Documents; (ii) such proceeding shall suspend the collection of the Labor and Material Costs from Borrower and from the Property or Borrower shall have paid all of the Labor and Material Costs under protest; (iii) neither the Property nor any part thereof or interest therein will be in danger of being sold, forfeited, terminated, canceled, or lost; and (iv) Borrower shall have furnished the security as may be required in the proceeding, or as may be reasonably requested by Lender to insure the payment of any contested Labor and Material Costs, together with all interest and penalties thereon.

3.8    Anti-Money Laundering Laws; USA Patriot Act. (i) Borrower is not named and is not acting, directly or indirectly, for or on behalf of any person, group, entity, or nation named by any Executive Order, including without limitation Executive Order 13224, or the United States Treasury Department as a terrorist, "Specially Designated National and Blocked Person," or other banned or blocked person, entity, nation, or transaction pursuant to any law, order, rule, or regulation that is enacted, enforced, or administered by the Office of Foreign Assets Control ("OFAC"); (ii) Borrower is not engaged in this transaction, directly or indirectly, for or on behalf of, or instigating or facilitating this transaction, directly or indirectly on behalf of, any such person, group, entity, or nation; and (iii) none of the proceeds used to consummate this transaction have been or will be derived from a "specified unlawful activity" as defined in, and Borrower is not otherwise in violation of, the Money Laundering Control Act of 1986, as amended, or any other applicable laws regarding money laundering activities. Furthermore, Borrower agrees to notify Lender immediately if Borrower was, is, or in the future becomes, a "senior foreign political figure" within the meaning of Section 312 of the USA PATRIOT Act of 2001, as amended or an immediate family member or close associate of a senior foreign political figure. Notwithstanding anything in this Mortgage to the contrary, Borrower understands that this Mortgage is a continuing transaction and that the foregoing representations, certifications, and warranties are ongoing and shall be and remain true and in force on the date hereof and throughout the term of the Mortgage and that any breach thereof shall be a default under the Mortgage (not subject to any notice or cure rights) giving rise to remedies by Lender, and Borrower hereby agrees to defend, indemnify, and hold harmless Lender from and against any and all claims, damages, losses, risks, liabilities, fines, penalties, forfeitures, and expenses (including without limitation costs and attorneys' fees) arising from or related to any breach of the foregoing representations, certifications, and warranties.

3.9   Warranty of Title. Borrower warrants that Borrower has good title to the Property and has the right to mortgage, give, grant, bargain, sell, alien, enfeoff, convey, confirm, pledge, hypothecate, assign, transfer, and set over the same and that Borrower possesses an unencumbered estate in the Property free and clear of all liens whatsoever except for any easements and restrictions listed in a schedule of exceptions to coverage in any title insurance policy issued to Lender contemporaneously with the execution and recordation of this Mortgage and insuring Lender's interest in the Property.

3.10   Payment of Taxes, Etc. Borrower shall pay all taxes, assessments, water rates, and sewer rents now or hereafter levied or assessed or imposed against the Property or any part thereof (the "Taxes") and all ground rents, maintenance charges, other impositions, and other charges, including, without limitation, vault charges and license fees for the use of vaults, chutes, and similar areas adjoining the Property, now or hereafter levied or assessed or imposed against the Property or any part thereof (the "Other Charges") as the same become due and payable. Borrower will deliver to Lender receipts for payment or other evidence reasonably satisfactory to Lender that the Taxes and Other Charges have been so paid or are not then delinquent no later than thirty (30) days prior to the date on which the Taxes and/or Other Charges would otherwise be delinquent if not paid.

After prior notice to Lender, Borrower, at its own expense, may contest by appropriate legal proceeding, promptly initiated and conducted in good faith and with due diligence, the amount or validity or application of any Taxes or Other Charges, provided that (i) no Event of Default has occurred and is continuing, (ii) such proceeding shall suspend the collection of the Taxes or Other Charges, (iii) such proceeding shall be permitted under and be conducted in accordance with the provisions of any other instrument to which Borrower is subject and shall not constitute a default thereunder, (iv) no part of or interest in the Property will be in danger of being sold, forfeited, terminated, canceled, or lost, (v) Borrower shall have furnished such security as may be required in the proceeding, or as may be reasonably requested by Lender, to insure the payment of any such Taxes or Other Charges, together with all interest and penalties thereon, and (vi) Borrower shall promptly upon final determination thereof pay the amount of such Taxes or Other Charges, together with all costs, interest, and penalties. Lender may pay over any such security or part thereof held by Lender to the claimant entitled thereto at any time when, in the judgment of Lender, the entitlement of such claimant is established.

3.11   Compliance with Applicable Laws and Regulations. All of the Improvements and the use of the Property comply with, and shall remain in compliance with, in all material respects, all applicable statutes, rules, regulations, and private covenants now or hereafter relating to the ownership, construction, use, or operation of the Property, including all applicable statutes, rules, and regulations pertaining to requirements for equal opportunity, anti-discrimination, fair housing, environmental protection, zoning, and land use. The Improvements comply with, and shall remain in compliance with, in all material respects, applicable health, fire, and building codes. There is no evidence of any illegal activities relating to controlled substances on the Property. All certifications, permits, licenses, and approvals, including, without limitation, certificates of completion and occupancy permits required for the legal use, occupancy, and operation of the Property as a _____ have been obtained and are in full force and effect for space that is leased and occupied. All of the Improvements comply with all material requirements of any applicable zoning and subdivision laws and ordinances.

3.12    Use of the Property. Unless required by applicable law or consented to in writing by Lender, Borrower shall not allow changes in the use for which all or any part of the Property is being used at the time this Mortgage was executed.

ARTICLE IV
OBLIGATIONS AND RELIANCE

4.1    Relationship of Borrower and Lender. The relationship between Borrower and Lender is solely that of debtor and creditor, and Lender has no fiduciary or other special relationship with Borrower, and no term or condition of any of the Note, this Mortgage, and the other Loan Documents shall be construed so as to deem the relationship between Borrower and Lender to be other than that of debtor and creditor.

4.2    No Reliance on Lender. The general partners, members, principals, and (if Borrower is a trust) beneficial owners of Borrower are experienced in the ownership and operation of properties similar to the Property, and Borrower and Lender are relying solely upon such parties' expertise and business plan in connection with the ownership and operation of the Property. Borrower is not relying on Lender's expertise, business acumen, or advice in connection with the Property.

4.3    No Lender Obligations. Notwithstanding the provisions of Subsections 1.1(h), (m), and (n) or Section 1.2, Lender is not undertaking the performance of (i) any obligations under the Leases; or (ii) any obligations with respect to such agreements, contracts, certificates, instruments, franchises, permits, trademarks, licenses, and other documents.

By accepting or approving anything required to be observed, performed, or fulfilled or to be given to Lender pursuant to this Mortgage, the Note, or the other Loan Documents, including, without limitation, any officer's certificate, balance sheet, statement of profit and loss or other financial statement, survey, appraisal, or insurance policy, Lender shall not be deemed to have warranted, consented to, or affirmed the sufficiency, legality, or effectiveness of same, and such acceptance or approval thereof shall not constitute any warranty or affirmation with respect thereto by Lender.

4.4    Reliance. Borrower recognizes and acknowledges that in accepting the Loan Documents, Lender is expressly and primarily relying on the truth and accuracy of the warranties and representations set forth in the Loan Documents without any obligation to investigate the Property and notwithstanding any investigation of the Property by Lender, that such reliance existed on the part of Lender prior to the date hereof, that the warranties and representations are a material inducement to Lender in making the Loan, and that Lender would not be willing to make the Loan and accept this Mortgage in the absence of the warranties and representations as set forth in the Loan Documents.

ARTICLE V
FURTHER ASSURANCES

5.1    Recording of Mortgage, Etc. Borrower, forthwith upon the execution and delivery of this Mortgage, and thereafter, from time to time, will cause this Mortgage and any of the other Loan Documents creating a lien or security interest or evidencing the lien hereof upon the Property, and each instrument of further assurance, to be filed, registered, or recorded in such manner and in such places as may be reasonably required by any present or future law in order to publish notice of and fully to protect and perfect the lien or security interest hereof upon, and the interest of Lender in, the Property. Borrower will pay all taxes, filing, registration, or recording fees, and expenses incident to the preparation, execution, acknowledgment, and/or recording of the Note, this Mortgage, the other Loan Documents, any note, deed of trust, or mortgage supplemental hereto, any security instrument with respect to the Property and any instrument of further assurance, and any modification or amendment of the foregoing documents, and all federal, state, county, and municipal taxes, duties, imposts, assessments, and charges arising out of or in connection with the execution and delivery of this Mortgage, any deed of trust or mortgage supplemental hereto, any security instrument with respect to the Property, or any instrument of further assurance, and any modification or amendment of the foregoing documents, except where prohibited by law so to do.

5.2    Further Acts, Etc. Borrower will, at the cost of Borrower, and without expense to Lender, do, execute, acknowledge, and deliver all and every such further acts, deeds, conveyances, deeds of trust, assignments, notices of assignments, transfers, and assurances as Lender shall, from time to time, reasonably require, for the better assuring, conveying, assigning, transferring, and confirming unto Lender the property and rights hereby deeded, granted, bargained, sold, conveyed, confirmed, pledged, assigned, warranted, and transferred, or intended now or hereafter so to be, or which Borrower may be, or may hereafter become, bound to convey or assign to Lender, or for carrying out the intention or facilitating the performance of the terms of this Mortgage or for filing, registering, or recording this Mortgage, or for complying with all applicable legal requirements. Borrower, on demand, will execute and deliver, and in the event it shall fail so to execute and deliver, hereby authorizes Lender to execute in the name of Borrower, or without the signature of Borrower to the extent Lender may lawfully do so, one or more financing statements (including, without limitation, initial financing statements and amendments thereto and continuation statements), with or without the signature of Borrower as authorized by applicable law, to evidence more effectively the security interest of Lender in the Property. Borrower also ratifies its authorization for Lender to have filed any like initial financing statements, amendments thereto, and continuation statements, if filed prior to the date of this Mortgage. Borrower grants to Lender an irrevocable power of attorney coupled with an interest for the purpose of exercising and perfecting upon an Event of Default any and all rights and remedies available to Lender at law and in equity, including without limitation such rights and remedies available to Lender pursuant to this Section 5.2. To the extent not prohibited by applicable law, Borrower hereby ratifies all acts Lender has lawfully done in the past or shall lawfully do or cause to be done in the future by virtue of such power of attorney.

5.3   Changes in Tax, Indebtedness, Credit, and Documentary Stamp Laws. If any law is enacted or adopted or amended after the date of this Mortgage which imposes a tax, either directly or indirectly, on the Indebtedness or Lender's interest in the Property (other than income taxes), Borrower will pay the tax, with interest and penalties thereon, if any. If Lender is advised by counsel chosen by it that the payment of tax by Borrower would be unlawful or taxable to Lender or unenforceable or provide the basis for a defense of usury, then Lender shall have the option by written notice of not less than two hundred seventy (270) days to declare the Indebtedness immediately due and payable.

If at any time the United States of America, any State thereof, or any subdivision of any such State shall require revenue or other stamps to be affixed to the Note, this Mortgage, or any of the other Loan Documents or impose any other tax or charge on the same, Borrower will pay for the same, with interest and penalties thereon, if any.

5.4   Splitting and Sale of Note and Mortgage. At the sole election of Lender, this Mortgage and the Note shall, at any time until the same shall be fully paid and satisfied, be split or divided into two or more notes and two or more security instruments, each of which shall cover all or a portion of the Property to be more particularly described therein. To that end, Borrower, upon written request of Lender, shall execute, acknowledge, and deliver, or cause to be executed, acknowledged, and delivered by the then owner of the Property, to Lender and/or its designee or designees substitute notes and security instruments in such principal amounts, aggregating not more than the then unpaid principal amount of the Note, and containing terms, provisions, and clauses similar to those contained herein and in the Note, and such other documents and instruments as may be required by Lender. The Note or a partial interest in the Note (together with this Mortgage and the other Loan Documents) may be sold one or more times without prior notice to Borrower.

5.5   Replacement Documents. Upon receipt of an affidavit of an officer of Lender and an indemnity from Lender reasonably acceptable to Borrower as to the loss, theft, destruction, or mutilation of the Note or any other Loan Document which is not of public record, and, in the case of any such mutilation, upon surrender and cancellation of such Note or other Loan Document, Borrower will issue, in lieu thereof, a replacement Note or other Loan Document, dated the date of such lost, stolen, destroyed, or mutilated Note or other Loan Document, in the same principal amount thereof and otherwise of like tenor.

ARTICLE VI
DUE ON SALE/ENCUMBRANCE

6.1   Lender Reliance. Borrower acknowledges that Lender has examined and relied on the experience of Borrower and its general partners, members, principals, and (if Borrower is a trust) beneficial owners in owning and operating properties such as the Property in agreeing to make the Loan, and will continue to rely on Borrower's ownership of the Property as a means of maintaining the value of the Property as security for repayment of the Indebtedness and the performance of the Other Obligations. Borrower acknowledges that Lender has a valid interest in maintaining the value of the Property so as to ensure that, should Borrower default in the repayment of the Indebtedness or the performance of the Other Obligations, Lender can recover the Indebtedness by a sale of the Property.

6.2   Transfer Defined. As used in this Article VI and in Article VII, "Transfer" shall mean any voluntary or involuntary sale, conveyance, alienation, hypothecation, mortgage, lease, grant, bargain, encumbrance, pledge, assignment, transfer, or other disposition of: (a) all or any part of the Property or any estate or interest therein including, but not limited to, (i) an installment sales agreement wherein Borrower agrees to sell the Property or any part thereof for a price to be paid in installments, (ii) an agreement by Borrower leasing all or a substantial part of the Property for other than actual occupancy by a space tenant thereunder and its affiliates, or

(iii) a sale, assignment, or other transfer of, or the grant of a security interest in, Borrower's right, title, and interest in and to any Leases or any Rents; or (b) any ownership interest in (i) Borrower or (ii) any corporation, partnership, limited liability company, trust, or other entity owning, directly or indirectly, any interest in Borrower.

6.3    No Transfer. Borrower shall not permit or suffer any Transfer to occur unless Lender shall consent thereto in writing.

6.4    Lender's Rights. Lender shall not be required to demonstrate any actual impairment of its security or any increased risk of default hereunder in order to declare the Indebtedness immediately due and payable upon a Transfer without Lender's consent in violation of the terms and provisions of this Mortgage. This provision shall apply to every Transfer, other than any Transfer permitted pursuant to this Mortgage, regardless of whether voluntary or not, or whether or not Lender has consented to any previous Transfer.

## ARTICLE VII
### EVENTS OF DEFAULT AND RIGHTS AND REMEDIES UPON AN EVENT OF DEFAULT

7.1    Events of Default. The occurrence of any one or more of the following shall constitute an event of default under this Mortgage (each an "Event of Default"):

(a)    if any payment or deposit due under the Note, this Mortgage, or any other Loan Document is not paid when due;

(b)    subject to Borrower's right to contest as provided herein, if any of the Taxes or Other Charges are not paid when the same are due and payable;

(c)    if the insurance policies required under Section 3.3 are not kept in full force and effect, or if such policies are not delivered to Lender within ten (10) days following request;

(d)    if Borrower permits or suffers any Transfer (as defined in Section 6.2) without Lender's prior written consent;

(e)    if any representation or warranty of Borrower made herein or in any other Loan Document or in any certificate, report, financial statement, or other instrument or document furnished to Lender shall have been knowingly false or misleading in any material respect when made;

(f)    if Borrower shall make an assignment for the benefit of creditors or if Borrower shall generally not be paying its debts as they become due;

(g)    if a receiver, liquidator, or trustee of Borrower shall be appointed or if Borrower shall be adjudicated a bankrupt or insolvent, or if any petition for bankruptcy, reorganization, or arrangement pursuant to federal bankruptcy law, or any similar federal or state law, shall be filed by or against, consented to, or acquiesced in by, Borrower or if any proceeding for the dissolution or liquidation of Borrower shall be instituted; however, if such appointment, adjudication, petition, or proceeding was involuntary and not consented to by Borrower, upon the same not being discharged, stayed or dismissed within ninety (90) days;

(h)    if Borrower shall be in default under any other deed of trust or security agreement covering any part of the Property whether it be superior or junior in lien to this Mortgage;

(i)    subject to Borrower's right to contest as provided herein, if the Property becomes subject to any mechanic's, materialman's or other lien and such lien is not removed of record within thirty (30) days of the filing or recording of such lien (except a lien for local real estate taxes and assessments not then due and payable);

(j)    if Borrower fails to cure properly any violations of laws or ordinances affecting the Property within thirty (30) days after Borrower first receives notice of any such violations;

(k)    except as permitted in this Mortgage, the alteration, improvement, demolition, or removal of any of the Improvements without the prior consent of Lender;

(l)    if Borrower shall continue to be in default under any term, covenant, or provision of the Note or any of the other Loan Documents, beyond applicable cure periods contained in those documents;

(m)    if Borrower fails to cure a default under any other term, covenant, or provision of this Mortgage within thirty (30) days after Borrower first receives notice of any such default; provided, however, if such default is reasonably susceptible of cure, but not within such thirty (30) day period, then Borrower may be permitted up to an additional ninety (90) days to cure such default provided that Borrower diligently and continuously pursues such cure; or

(n)    if Borrower ceases to operate the Property or any material portion thereof continuously as a _____ for any reason whatsoever (other than temporary cessation in connection with any condemnation, casualty, repair, or renovation thereof undertaken in accordance with the terms of this Mortgage or with the consent of Lender).

7.2    Remedies. Upon the occurrence and during the continuance of any Event of Default, Borrower agrees that Lender may take such action, without notice or demand, as it deems advisable to protect and enforce its rights against Borrower and in and to the Property, including, but not limited to, the following actions, each of which may be pursued concurrently or otherwise, at such time and in such order as Lender may determine, in its sole discretion, without impairing or otherwise affecting the other rights and remedies of Lender:

(a) declare the entire unpaid Indebtedness to be immediately due and payable;

(b) institute proceedings, judicial or otherwise, for the complete foreclosure of this Mortgage under any applicable provision of law, in which case the Property or any interest therein may be sold for cash or upon credit in one or more parcels or in several interests or portions and in any order or manner;

(c) with or without entry, to the extent permitted and pursuant to the procedures provided by applicable law, institute proceedings for the partial foreclosure of this Mortgage for the portion of the Indebtedness then due and payable, subject to the continuing lien and security interest of this Mortgage for the balance of the Indebtedness not then due, unimpaired and without loss of priority;

(d) sell for cash or upon credit the Property or any part thereof and all estate, claim, demand, right, title, and interest of Borrower therein and rights of redemption thereof, pursuant to power of sale or otherwise, at one or more sales, as an entirety or in parcels, at such time and place, upon such terms, and after such notice thereof, as may be required or permitted by law, and, without limiting the foregoing:

(i) In connection with any sale or sales hereunder, Lender shall be entitled to elect to treat any of the Property which consists of a right in action or which is property that can be severed from the Real Property covered hereby or any Improvements without causing structural damage thereto as if the same were personal property, and dispose of the same in accordance with applicable law, separate and apart from the sale of Real Property. Where the Property consists of Real Property, Personal Property, Equipment, or Fixtures, whether or not such Personal Property or Equipment is located on or within the Real Property, Lender shall be entitled to elect to exercise its rights and remedies against any or all of the Real Property, Personal Property, Equipment, and Fixtures in such order and manner as is now or hereafter permitted by applicable law;

(ii) Lender shall be entitled to elect to proceed against any or all of the Real Property, Personal Property, Equipment, and Fixtures in any manner permitted under applicable law, and if Lender so elects pursuant to applicable law, the power of sale herein granted shall be exercisable with respect to all or any of the Real Property, Personal Property, Equipment, and Fixtures covered hereby, as designated by Lender, and Lender is hereby authorized and empowered to conduct any such sale of any Real Property, Personal Property, Equipment, and Fixtures in accordance with the procedures applicable to Real Property;

(iii) Should Lender elect to sell any portion of the Property which is Real Property, or which is Personal Property, Equipment, or Fixtures that the Lender has elected under applicable law to sell together with Real Property in accordance with the laws governing a sale of Real Property, Lender shall give such notice of Event of Default, if any, and election to sell as may then be required by law. Thereafter, upon the expiration of such time and the giving of such notice of sale as may then be required by law, and without the necessity of any demand on Borrower, Lender, at the time and place specified in the notice of sale, shall sell such Property or part thereof at public auction to the highest bidder for cash in lawful money of the United States. Lender may from time to time postpone any sale hereunder by public announcement thereof at the time and place noticed therefor; and

(iv) If the Property consists of several lots, parcels, or items of property, Lender shall, subject to applicable law, (A) designate the order in which such lots, parcels, or items shall be offered for sale or sold, or (B) elect to sell such lots, parcels, or items through a single sale, or through two or more successive sales, or in any other manner Lender designates. Any Person, including Borrower or Lender, may purchase at any sale hereunder. Should Lender desire that more than one sale or other disposition of the Property be conducted, Lender shall, subject to applicable law, cause such sales or dispositions to be conducted simultaneously, or successively, on the same day, or at such different days or times and in such order as Lender may designate, and no such sale shall terminate or otherwise affect the lien of this Mortgage on any part of the Property not sold until all the Indebtedness has been paid in full. In the event Lender elects to dispose of the Property through more than one sale, except as otherwise provided by applicable law, Borrower agrees to pay the costs and expenses of each such sale and of any judicial proceedings wherein such sale may be made;

(e) institute an action, suit, or proceeding in equity for the specific performance of any covenant, condition, or agreement contained in this Mortgage, the Note, or the other Loan Documents;

(f) recover judgment on the Note either before, during, or after any proceedings for the enforcement of this Mortgage or the other Loan Documents;

(g) apply for the appointment of a receiver, trustee, liquidator, or conservator of the Property, without notice and without regard for the adequacy of the security for the Indebtedness and without regard for the solvency of Borrower, any guarantor, any indemnitor with respect to the Loan, or any person liable for the payment of the Indebtedness;

(h) revoke the license granted to Borrower under Section 1.2 hereof, and Lender may upon written notice enter into or upon the Property, either personally or by its agents, nominees, or attorneys, and dispossess Borrower and its agents and servants therefrom, without liability for trespass, damages, or otherwise, and exclude Borrower and its agents or servants wholly therefrom, and take possession of all books, records, and accounts relating thereto, and Borrower agrees to surrender possession of the Property and of such books, records, and accounts to Lender upon demand, and thereupon Lender may (i) use, operate, manage, control, insure, maintain, repair, restore, and otherwise deal with all and every part of the Property and conduct the business thereat, (ii) complete any construction on the Property in such manner and form as Lender deems advisable, (iii) make alterations, additions, renewals, replacements, and improvements to or on the Property, (iv) exercise all rights and powers of Borrower with respect to the Property, whether in the name of Borrower or otherwise, including, without limitation, the right to make, cancel, enforce, or modify Leases, obtain and evict tenants, and demand, sue for, collect, and receive all Rents of the Property and every part thereof, (v) require Borrower to pay monthly in advance to Lender, or any receiver appointed to collect the Rents, the fair and reasonable rental value for the use and occupation of such part of the Property as may be occupied by Borrower, (vi) require Borrower to vacate and surrender possession of the Property to Lender or to such receiver and, in default thereof, Borrower may be evicted by summary proceedings or otherwise, and (vii) apply the receipts from the Property to the payment of the Indebtedness, in such order, priority, and proportions as Lender shall deem appropriate in its sole discretion, after deducting therefrom all expenses (including reasonable attorneys' fees) incurred in connection with the aforesaid operations and all amounts necessary to pay any taxes, other applicable charges, insurance, and other expenses in connection with the Property, as well as just and reasonable compensation for the services of Lender and its counsel, agents, and employees;

(i)   exercise any and all rights and remedies granted to a secured party upon default under the Uniform Commercial Code, including, without limiting the generality of the foregoing: (i) the right to take possession of the Fixtures, the Equipment, and the Personal Property, or any part thereof, and to take such other measures as Lender may deem necessary for the care, protection, and preservation of the Fixtures, the Equipment, and the Personal Property, and (ii) request Borrower at its expense to assemble the Fixtures, the Equipment, and the Personal Property and make them available to Lender at a convenient place acceptable to Lender. Any notice of sale, disposition, or other intended action by Lender with respect to the Fixtures, the Equipment, and/or the Personal Property sent to Borrower in accordance with the provisions hereof at least five (5) business days prior to such action, shall constitute commercially reasonable notice to Borrower;

(j)   apply any sums then deposited or held in escrow or otherwise by or on behalf of Lender in accordance with the terms of this Mortgage or any other Loan Document to the payment of the following items in any order in its uncontrolled discretion:

> (i)   taxes and other applicable charges,
> (ii)  insurance premiums,
> (iii) interest on the unpaid principal balance of the Note,
> (iv)  amortization of the unpaid principal balance of the Note, and
> (v)   all other sums payable pursuant to the Note, this Mortgage, and the other Loan Documents, including without limitation advances made by Lender pursuant to the terms of this Mortgage; or

(k)  pursue such other remedies as Lender may have under applicable law.

In the event of a sale, by foreclosure, power of sale, or otherwise, of less than all of the Property, this Mortgage shall continue as a lien and security interest on the remaining portion of the Property unimpaired and without loss of priority.

7.3   Application of Proceeds. The purchase money, proceeds, and avails of any disposition of the Property, or any part thereof, or any other sums collected by Lender pursuant to the Note, this Mortgage, or the other Loan Documents, may be applied by Lender to the payment of the Indebtedness in such order of priority and proportions as Lender in its discretion shall deem proper, to the extent consistent with law.

7.4   Right to Cure Defaults. Upon the occurrence and during the continuance of any Event of Default, Lender may remedy such Event of Default in such manner and to such extent as Lender may deem necessary to protect the security hereof, but without any obligation to do so and without notice to or demand on Borrower, and without releasing Borrower from any obligation hereunder. Lender is authorized to enter upon the Property for such purposes, or appear in, defend, or bring any action or proceeding to protect its interest in the Property or to foreclose this Mortgage or collect the Indebtedness, and the cost and expense thereof (including reasonable attorneys' fees to the extent permitted by law), with interest as provided in this Section 7.4, shall constitute a portion of the Indebtedness and shall be due and payable to Lender upon demand. All such costs and expenses incurred by Lender in remedying such Event of Default, or in appearing in, defending, or bringing any such action or proceeding, shall bear interest at the rate of __% (the "Default Rate") for the period after notice from Lender that such cost or expense was incurred to the date of payment to Lender. All such costs and expenses incurred by Lender together with interest thereon calculated at the Default Rate shall be deemed to constitute a portion of the Indebtedness and be secured by this Mortgage and the other Loan Documents and shall be immediately due and payable upon demand by Lender therefor.

7.5   Actions and Proceedings. Lender has the right to appear in and defend any action or proceeding brought with respect to the Property and to bring any action or proceeding, in the name and on behalf of Borrower, which Lender, in its discretion, decides should be brought to protect its interest in the Property.

7.6   Recovery of Sums Required to Be Paid. Lender shall have the right from time to time to take action to recover any sum or sums which constitute a part of the Indebtedness as the same become due, without regard to whether or not the balance of the Indebtedness shall be due, and without prejudice to the right of Lender thereafter to bring an action of foreclosure, or any other action, for a default or defaults by Borrower existing at the time such earlier action was commenced.

7.7   Examination of Books and Records. At reasonable times and upon reasonable notice, Lender and its agents, accountants, and attorneys shall have the right to examine the records, books, and other papers of Borrower which reflect upon its financial condition, at the Property or at any office regularly maintained by Borrower where the books and records are located. Lender and its agents shall have the right to make copies and extracts from the foregoing records and other papers. In addition, at reasonable times and upon reasonable notice, Lender and its agents, accountants, and attorneys shall have the right to examine and audit the books and records of Borrower pertaining to the income, expenses, and operation of the Property during reasonable business hours at any office of Borrower where the books and records are located. This <u>Section 7.7</u> shall apply throughout the term of the Note and without regard to whether an Event of Default has occurred or is continuing.

7.8 <u>Other Rights, Etc.</u> (a) The failure of Lender to insist upon strict performance of any term hereof shall not be deemed to be a waiver of any term of this Mortgage. Borrower shall not be relieved of Borrower's obligations hereunder by reason of (i) the failure of Lender to comply with any request of Borrower or any guarantor or indemnitor with respect to the Loan to take any action to foreclose this Mortgage or otherwise enforce any of the provisions hereof or of the Note or the other Loan Documents, (ii) the release, regardless of consideration, of the whole or any part of the Property, or of any person liable for the Indebtedness or any portion thereof, or (iii) any agreement or stipulation by Lender extending the time of payment or otherwise modifying or supplementing the terms of the Note, this Mortgage, or the other Loan Documents.

(b) It is agreed that the risk of loss or damage to the Property is on Borrower, and Lender shall have no liability whatsoever for decline in value of the Property, for failure to maintain any policies of insurance, or for failure to determine whether insurance in force is adequate as to the amount of risks insured. Possession by Lender shall not be deemed an election of judicial relief, if any such possession is requested or obtained, with respect to any Property or collateral not in Lender's possession.

(c) Upon an Event of Default, Lender may resort for the payment of the Indebtedness to any other security held by Lender in such order and manner as Lender, in its discretion, may elect. Upon an Event of Default, Lender may take action to recover the Indebtedness, or any portion thereof, or to enforce any covenant hereof without prejudice to the right of Lender thereafter to foreclose this Mortgage. The rights of Lender under this Mortgage shall be separate, distinct, and cumulative, and none shall be given effect to the exclusion of the others. No act of Lender shall be construed as an election to proceed under any one provision herein to the exclusion of any other provision. Lender shall not be limited exclusively to the rights and remedies herein stated but shall be entitled to every right and remedy now or hereafter afforded at law or in equity.

7.9    <u>Right to Release Any Portion of the Property.</u> Lender may release any portion of the Property for such consideration as Lender may require without, as to the remainder of the Property, in any way impairing or affecting the lien or priority of this Mortgage, or improving the position of any subordinate lienholder with respect thereto, except to the extent that the obligations hereunder shall have been reduced by the actual monetary consideration, if any, received by Lender for such release, and may accept by assignment, pledge, or otherwise any other property in place thereof as Lender may require without being accountable for so doing to any other lienholder. This Mortgage shall continue as a lien and security interest in the remaining portion of the Property.

7.10   <u>Recourse and Choice of Remedies.</u> Neither Borrower nor any direct or indirect owner of an interest in Borrower shall have personal liability for payment of the Indebtedness or the Other Obligations, or any other charges due to Lender as provided by any of the Loan Documents, and, in the event of any Event of Default, Lender's sole recourse shall be against the Property and under the Guarantee (as hereinafter defined); provided, however, that Borrower and such direct and indirect owners shall remain personally liable as otherwise provided by the Loan Documents or applicable law for the following: (a) as provided by the guarantee of even date herewith given by _____ (the "<u>Guarantors</u>") in favor of Lender (the "<u>Guarantee</u>"), with respect to the Guarantors, (b) Borrower's failure to pay real estate taxes or assessments against the Property, to the extent that funds are available, (c) Borrower's failure to insure the Property as required by the Loan Documents, (d) rent or other income from the Property received after a default under the Loan Documents and which is not applied as provided by the Loan Documents or to the expenses of operating or maintaining the Property, (e) conversion, diversion, misapplication, or misappropriation of security deposits, reserve accounts, insurance proceeds, or condemnation awards in connection with the Property, (f) waste, (g) amounts due under the environmental indemnity of even date herewith given by _____ in favor of Lender (the "<u>Environmental Indemnity</u>"), and (h) fraud or intentional misrepresentation in connection with the transactions contemplated by any of the Loan Documents.

7.11   <u>Right of Entry.</u> Upon reasonable notice to Borrower, Lender and its agents shall have the right to enter and inspect the Property at all reasonable times.

ARTICLE VIII
INDEMNIFICATION

8.1    <u>General Indemnification.</u> Borrower shall, at its sole cost and expense, protect, defend, indemnify, release, and hold harmless the

Indemnified Parties from and against any and all claims, suits, liabilities (including, without limitation, strict liabilities), actions, proceedings, obligations, debts, damages, losses, reasonable costs, expenses, fines, penalties, charges, fees, judgments, awards, amounts paid in settlement, and punitive damages, of whatever kind or nature (including but not limited to reasonable attorneys' fees and other costs of defense) (collectively, the "Losses") imposed upon or incurred by or asserted against any Indemnified Parties and directly or indirectly arising out of or in any way relating to any one or more of the following: (a) ownership of this Mortgage, the Property, or any interest therein, or receipt of any Rents; (b) any amendment to, or restructuring of, the Indebtedness, the Note, this Mortgage, or any of the other Loan Documents; (c) any and all lawful actions that may be taken by Lender in connection with the enforcement of the provisions of this Mortgage, the Note, or any of the other Loan Documents, whether or not suit is filed in connection with same, or in connection with Borrower, any guarantor or indemnitor, and/or any partner, joint venturer, or shareholder thereof becoming a party to a voluntary or involuntary federal or state bankruptcy, insolvency, or similar proceeding; (d) any accident, injury to or death of persons, or loss of or damage to property occurring in, on, or about the Property or any part thereof or on the adjoining sidewalks, curbs, adjacent property, or adjacent parking areas, streets, or ways; (e) any use, nonuse, or condition in, on, or about the Property or any part thereof or on the adjoining sidewalks, curbs, adjacent property, or adjacent parking areas, streets, or ways; (f) any failure on the part of Borrower to perform or be in compliance with any of the terms of this Mortgage; (g) performance of any labor or services or the furnishing of any materials or other property in respect of the Property or any part thereof; (h) the failure of any person to file timely with the Internal Revenue Service an accurate Form 1099-B, Statement for Recipients of Proceeds from Real Estate, Broker, and Barter Exchange Transactions, which may be required in connection with this Mortgage, or to supply a copy thereof in a timely fashion to the recipient of the proceeds of the transaction in connection with which this Mortgage is made; (i) any failure of the Property to be in compliance with any applicable legal requirements; (j) the enforcement by any Indemnified Party of the provisions of this Article VIII; (k) any and all claims and demands whatsoever which may be asserted against Lender by reason of any alleged obligations or undertakings on its part to perform or discharge any of the terms, covenants, or agreements contained in any Lease; (l) the payment of any commission, charge, or brokerage fee to anyone claiming through Borrower which may be payable in connection with the funding of the Loan; or (m) any material misrepresentation made by Borrower in this Mortgage or any other Loan Document; provided, however, Borrower shall not indemnify any Indemnified Party from any loss or expense arising from such Indemnified Party's willful misconduct, illegal acts, fraud, or gross negligence.

Any amounts payable to Lender by reason of the application of this Section 8.1 shall become due and payable upon five (5) business days' written notice and shall bear interest at the Default Rate from the date of such notice from Lender until paid. "Indemnified Parties" means Lender and any Person who is or will have been involved in the origination of the Loan, any Person who is or will have been involved in the servicing of the Loan secured hereby, any Person in whose name the encumbrance created by this Mortgage is or will have been recorded, persons and entities who may hold or acquire or will have held a full or partial interest in the Loan secured hereby (including, but not limited to, investors or prospective investors in the Loan, as well as custodians, trustees, and other fiduciaries who hold or have held a full or partial interest in the Loan secured hereby for the benefit of third parties), as well as the respective directors, officers, shareholders, partners, employees, agents, servants, representatives, contractors, subcontractors, affiliates, subsidiaries, participants, successors, and assigns of any and all of the foregoing (including but not limited to any other person who holds or acquires or will have held a participation or other full or partial interest in the Loan, whether during the term of the Loan or as a part of or following a foreclosure of the Loan, and including, but not limited to, any successors by merger, consolidation, or acquisition of all or a substantial portion of Lender's assets and business).

8.2 Mortgage and/or Intangible Tax. Borrower shall, at its sole cost and expense, protect, defend, indemnify, release, and hold harmless the Indemnified Parties from and against any and all Losses imposed upon or incurred by or asserted against any Indemnified Parties and directly or indirectly arising out of or in any way relating to any tax on the making and/or recording of this Mortgage, the Note, or any of the other Loan Documents, but excluding any income, franchise, or other similar taxes.

8.3 Duty to Defend; Attorneys' Fees and Other Fees and Expenses. If any of the Indemnified Parties claims indemnification hereunder, such Indemnified Party shall promptly notify Borrower of the nature and basis of the claim or legal or administrative proceeding giving rise to such claim or indemnification. After notice by the Indemnified Party, Borrower shall defend such Indemnified Party (if requested by any Indemnified Party, in the name of the Indemnified Party) by attorneys and other professionals reasonably approved by the Indemnified Party and shall have the right to negotiate and enter into and/or consent to any settlement, subject to the prior approval of the Indemnified Party (which approval shall not be unreasonably withheld), provided that (i) such approval shall not be required in connection with any settlement which includes any unconditional release of the Indemnified Party and all related actions for all liability for which the Indemnified Party is seeking indemnification, and (ii) there is no admission of wrongdoing on the part of the Indemnified Party. If Borrower has assumed the defense of any action brought against the Indemnified Parties, then the Indemnified Parties shall not settle such action without the consent of Borrower. Notwithstanding the foregoing, the Indemnified Parties may engage their own attorneys and other professionals to defend or assist them in the event the defense as conducted by Borrower is not proceeding or being conducted in a satisfactory manner or that a conflict of interest exists between any of the parties represented by Borrower's counsel in such action or proceeding; provided, <u>however</u>, (i) that so long as no Event of Default exists, the Indemnified Parties shall provide Borrower with ten (10) business days' prior written notice of any such engagement pursuant to this Section (unless the Indemnified Parties determine, in their sole discretion, that their interest may be adversely affected prior to the expiration of such notice period, in which case, the Indemnified Parties may take immediate action and send written notice to Borrower thereafter), and (ii) the Indemnified Parties shall not enter into any settlement of such a proceeding without the consent of Borrower, which consent shall not be unreasonably withheld, conditioned, or delayed. Borrower shall not be liable for the expenses of more than one such separate counsel unless an Indemnified Party shall have reasonably concluded that there may be legal defenses available to it that are different from or additional to those available to another Indemnified Party. Upon demand, Borrower shall pay or, in the sole and absolute discretion of the Indemnified Parties, reimburse, the Indemnified Parties for the payment of reasonable fees and disbursements of attorneys, engineers, environmental consultants, laboratories, and other professionals in connection therewith.

## ARTICLE IX
## WAIVERS

9.1    <u>Waiver of Counterclaim.</u> To the extent permitted by applicable law, Borrower hereby waives the right to assert a counterclaim, other than a mandatory or compulsory counterclaim, in any action or proceeding brought against it by Lender arising out of or in any way connected with this Mortgage, the Note, any of the other Loan Documents, or the Obligations.

9.2    <u>Marshalling and Other Matters.</u> To the extent permitted by applicable law, Borrower hereby waives the benefit of all appraisement, valuation, stay, extension, reinstatement, and redemption laws now or hereafter in force and all rights of marshalling in the event of any sale hereunder of the Property or any part thereof or any interest therein. Further, Borrower hereby expressly waives any and all rights of redemption from sale under any order or decree of foreclosure of this Mortgage on behalf of Borrower, and on behalf of each and every person acquiring any interest in or title to the Property subsequent to the date of this Mortgage, and on behalf of all other persons, to the extent permitted by applicable law.

9.3    <u>Waiver of Notice.</u> To the extent permitted by applicable law, Borrower shall not be entitled to any notices of any nature whatsoever from

Lender except with respect to matters for which this Mortgage or the Loan Documents specifically and expressly provide for the giving of notice by Lender to Borrower and except with respect to matters for which Lender is required by applicable law to give notice, and Borrower hereby expressly waives the right to receive any notice from Lender with respect to any matter for which this Mortgage does not specifically and expressly provide for the giving of notice by Lender to Borrower.

9.4    Waiver of Statute of Limitations. To the extent permitted by applicable law, Borrower hereby expressly waives and releases, to the fullest extent permitted by law, the pleading of any statute of limitations as a defense to payment of the Indebtedness or performance of its Other Obligations.

9.5    Survival. The indemnifications made pursuant to Article VIII herein shall in no way be impaired by any satisfaction, release, or other termination of this Mortgage, any assignment or other transfer of all or any portion of this Mortgage or Lender's interest in the Property (but, in such case, shall benefit both the Indemnified Parties and any assignee or transferee), any exercise of Lender's rights and remedies pursuant hereto, including but not limited to foreclosure or acceptance of a deed or assignment in lieu of foreclosure, any exercise of any rights and remedies pursuant to the Note or any of the other Loan Documents, any transfer of all or any portion of the Property (whether by Borrower or by Lender following foreclosure or acceptance of a deed or assignment in lieu of foreclosure or at any other time), any amendment to this Mortgage, the Note, or the other Loan Documents, and any act or omission that might otherwise be construed as a release or discharge of Borrower from the obligations pursuant hereto.

ARTICLE X
NOTICES

All notices, demands, elections, deliveries, approvals, and other communications between the parties required or desired to be given in connection with this Mortgage (each, a "Notice"), to be effective under this Mortgage, shall be in writing and shall be deemed to be given and received (i) when delivered personally; (ii) one (1) business day after deposit with a national overnight courier service (such as FedEx); or (iii) three (3) business days after deposit with the United States Postal Service as certified mail, return receipt requested; in any event with all charges or postage prepaid, and addressed as follows:

If to Lender,

_____
_____
_____
_____
_____

with a copy to

_____

_____

_____

_____

And if to Borrower,

_____

_____

_____

_____

with a copy to

_____

_____

_____

_____

Either party may from time to time designate another address for the receipt of future Notices by a Notice given as provided in this Article X to the other party at the address set forth in, or as last provided by such other party in accordance with, this Article X.

## ARTICLE XI
## APPLICABLE LAW

11.1   <u>Governing Law.</u> This Mortgage was negotiated in the State of _____, and made by Borrower and accepted by Lender in the State of _____, and the proceeds of the Note secured hereby were disbursed from the State of _____, which State the parties agree has a substantial relationship to the parties and to the underlying transaction embodied hereby, and in all respects, including, without limiting the generality of the foregoing, matters of construction, validity and performance, this Mortgage and the obligations arising hereunder shall be governed by, and construed in accordance with, the laws of the State of _____ to contracts made and performed in such State (without regard to principles of conflict of laws) and any applicable law of the United States of America, except that at all times the provisions for the creation, perfection, priority, and enforcement of the liens and security interests created pursuant hereto and pursuant to the other Loan Documents with respect to the Property shall be governed by and construed according to the law of the State in which the Property and Fixtures are located.

Any legal suit, action, or proceeding against Lender or Borrower arising out of or relating to this Mortgage may at Lender's option be instituted in any federal or state court in the city of _____, county of

_____, and Borrower and Lender each waives any objections which it may now or hereafter have based on venue and/or forum non conveniens of any such suit, action, or proceeding, and Borrower and Lender each hereby irrevocably submits to the jurisdiction of any such court in any suit, action, or proceeding.

11.2 <u>Usury Laws.</u> Notwithstanding anything to the contrary, (a) all agreements and communications between Borrower and Lender are hereby and shall automatically be limited so that, after taking into account all amounts deemed interest, the interest contracted for, charged, or received by Lender shall never exceed the maximum lawful rate or amount, (b) in calculating whether any interest exceeds the lawful maximum, all such interest shall be amortized, prorated, allocated, and spread over the full amount and term of all principal indebtedness of Borrower to Lender, and (c) if through any contingency or event, Lender receives or is deemed to receive interest in excess of the lawful maximum, any such excess shall be deemed to have been applied toward payment of the principal of any and all then outstanding indebtedness of Borrower to Lender, or if there is no such indebtedness, shall immediately be returned to Borrower.

11.3 <u>Provisions Subject to Applicable Law.</u> All rights, powers, and remedies provided in this Mortgage may be exercised only to the extent that the exercise thereof does not violate any applicable provisions of law and are intended to be limited to the extent necessary so that they will not render this Mortgage invalid, unenforceable, or not entitled to be recorded, registered, or filed under the provisions of any applicable law. If any term of this Mortgage or any application thereof shall be invalid or unenforceable, the remainder of this Mortgage and any other application of the term shall not be affected thereby.

11.4 <u>Waiver of Jury Trial.</u> [Note to drafter: The law in some states may require a provision of this nature to be set forth in uppercase type.] Borrower hereby agrees not to elect a trial by jury of any issue triable of right by jury and waives any right to trial by jury fully to the extent that any such right shall now or hereafter exist with regard to the Note, this Mortgage, or the other Loan Documents, or any claim, counterclaim, or other action arising in connection therewith. This waiver of right to trial by jury is given knowingly and voluntarily by Borrower, and is intended to encompass individually each instance and each issue as to which the right to a trial by jury would otherwise accrue. Lender is hereby authorized to file a copy of this paragraph in any proceeding as conclusive evidence of this waiver by Borrower.

### ARTICLE XII
### MISCELLANEOUS PROVISIONS

12.1 <u>No Oral Change.</u> This Mortgage, and any provisions hereof, may not be modified, amended, waived, extended, changed, discharged, or terminated orally or by any act or failure to act on the part of Borrower or Lender, but only by an agreement in writing signed by the party against whom enforcement of any modification, amendment, waiver, extension, change, discharge, or termination is sought.

12.2   Successors and Assigns. This Mortgage shall be binding upon and inure to the benefit of Borrower and Lender and their respective successors and assigns forever.

12.3   Unenforceable Provisions. If any term, covenant, or condition of the Note or this Mortgage is held to be invalid, illegal, or unenforceable in any respect, the Note and this Mortgage shall be construed without such provision.

12.4   Headings, Etc. The headings and captions of various Sections of this Mortgage are for convenience of reference only and are not to be construed as defining or limiting, in any way, the scope or intent of the provisions hereof.

12.5   Number and Gender. Whenever the context may require, any pronouns used herein shall include the corresponding masculine, feminine, or neuter forms, and the singular form of nouns and pronouns shall include the plural and vice versa.

12.6   Entire Agreement. The Note, this Mortgage, and the other Loan Documents constitute the entire understanding and agreement between Borrower and Lender with respect to the transactions arising in connection with the Indebtedness and supersede all prior written or oral understandings and agreements between Borrower and Lender with respect thereto. Borrower hereby acknowledges that, except as incorporated in writing in the Note, this Mortgage, and the other Loan Documents, there are not, and were not, and no persons are or were authorized by Lender to make, any representations, understandings, stipulations, agreements, or promises, oral or written, with respect to the transaction which is the subject of the Note, this Mortgage, and the other Loan Documents.

12.7   Limitation on Lender's Responsibility. No provision of this Mortgage shall operate to place any obligation or liability for the control, care, management, or repair of the Property upon Lender, nor shall it operate to make Lender responsible or liable for any waste committed on the Property by the tenants or any other person, or for any dangerous or defective condition of the Property, or for any negligence in the management, upkeep, repair, or control of the Property resulting in loss or injury or death to any tenant, licensee, employee, or stranger. Nothing herein contained shall be construed as constituting Lender a "mortgagee in possession."

12.8   Joint and Several. If more than one person has executed this Mortgage as "Borrower," the representations, covenants, warranties, and obligations of all such Persons hereunder shall be joint and several.

## ARTICLE XIII
## STATE-SPECIFIC PROVISIONS

[The drafter should be sure that all appropriate state-specific provisions are included or modified here.]

13.1 <u>Principles of Construction.</u> In the event of any inconsistencies between the terms and conditions of this <u>Article XIV</u> and the other terms and conditions of this Mortgage, the terms and conditions of this <u>Article XIV</u> shall control and be binding.

13.2 <u>Fixture Filing Provision.</u> Upon recording of this Mortgage in the real property records, this Mortgage shall be effective as a financing statement filed as a fixture filing. In addition, a carbon, photographic, or other reproduction of this Mortgage and/or any financing statement relating thereto shall be sufficient for filing and/or recording as a financing statement. The filing of any other financing statement relating to any personal property rights or interests described herein shall not be construed to diminish any right or priority hereunder.

13.3 <u>Lender's Remedies.</u> Lender shall have all of the remedies provided under _____ law.

13.4 <u>Lien Law Trust Fund.</u> Borrower will, in compliance with the Lien Law of the State of _____, receive the advances secured hereby and will hold the right to receive such advances as a trust fund to be applied first for the purpose of paying the cost of improvements before using any part of the total of the same for any other purpose.

13.5 <u>Mortgage Tax Statement.</u> Borrower represents that this Mortgage does not encumber real property principally improved or to be improved by one or more structures containing in the aggregate not more than six residential dwelling units, each having their own separate cooking facilities.

13.6 <u>Rights and Remedies.</u> Borrower specifically consents and agrees that Lender may exercise rights and remedies hereunder and under the other Loan Documents separately or concurrently and in any order that Lender may deem appropriate.

13.7 <u>Power of Sale.</u> If an Event of Default exists and is continuing, Lender may, at Lender's election, either with or without entry or taking possession of the Property as provided herein or otherwise, personally or by its agents or attorneys, and without prejudice to the right to bring an action for foreclosure of this Mortgage, sell the Property or any part thereof pursuant to any procedures provided by applicable law, including, without limitation, the procedures set forth in the _____ Real Property Actions and Proceedings Law (and any amendments or substitute statutes in regard thereto), and all estate, right, title, interest, claim, and demand therein, and right of redemption thereof, at one or more sales as an entity or in parcels, and at such time and place upon such terms and after such notice thereof as may be required or permitted by applicable law.

IN WITNESS WHEREOF, THIS MORTGAGE has been executed by Borrower as of the day and year first above written.

_____ , a
_____ , Borrower
By: _____ (SEAL)
Its: _____

[Add notary block in the form required by the state in which the Mortgage will be recorded.]

EXHIBIT A
Description of Property

# Appendix L

# Form of Assignment of Leases and Rents

## ASSIGNMENT OF LEASES AND RENTS

THIS ASSIGNMENT OF LEASES AND RENTS (this "Assignment") is made this _____ day of _____, 20_, by and between _____ _____, a _____ having an address at _____ _____, as assignor ("Assignor"), and _____, a _____ _____ having an address at _____ _____, as assignee ("Assignee").

### Introduction

Assignee has made a loan to Assignor (the "Loan"), as evidenced by the Promissory Note dated this date by Assignor in the principal amount of _____ Dollars ($_____) (together with any modifications, amendments, replacements, substitutions, extensions, or renewals thereof, the "Note").

The Note shall be secured in part by a Mortgage dated this date by Assignor to Assignee, granting a first-priority lien on the land described in Exhibit A to this Assignment and all improvements situated thereon (such land and improvements are collectively called the "Property"), which Mortgage is intended to be recorded immediately prior to this Assignment among the land records of _____ County, _____ (together with any modifications, amendments, or supplements thereto, the "Mortgage").

As a condition precedent to making the Loan, Assignee has required that Assignor further secure the payment and performance of all the obligations of Assignor in connection with the Loan by entering into this Assignment.

### Agreement

In consideration of the foregoing and to induce Assignee to make the Loan to Assignor, Assignor hereby covenants, warrants, represents, and agrees with Assignee as follows:

1. Defined Terms.

The capitalized terms used but not defined in this Assignment shall have the meanings given to them in the Mortgage.

2. Assignment.

Assignor hereby absolutely and presently grants, transfers, and assigns to Assignee, its successors, and assigns, all of the right, title, interest, and estate of Assignor in and to (a)(i) all leases, subleases, licenses, concessions, use agreements, occupancy agreements, or tenancies, whether or not specifically listed in this Assignment and whether or not executed or in effect on the date hereof or subsequent hereto, and relating to or affecting the Property; (ii) any modifications, amendments, renewals, supplements, and extensions thereto; (iii) all credits, deposits (security, escrow, or otherwise), and advance payments made or given thereunder; and (iv) any guarantees of the tenants', licensees', concessionaires', users', or occupants' obligations thereunder (items (i) through (iv) are collectively referred to as the "Leases"); and (b) all rents, issues, profits, fees, income, and revenues from the Leases, including, without limitation, claims for the recovery of damages to the Property by proceeds of any insurance policy or otherwise, claims for damages resulting from acts of insolvency or bankruptcy, lump sum payments, or the cancellation or termination of any Lease, awards payable by reason of condemnation action or the exercise of any right of first refusal or option to purchase, and the proceeds of any rental insurance carried by Assignor on the Property (collectively, the "Rents").

3. Security.

This Assignment is for the purpose of securing (a) payment of the indebtedness evidenced by the Note; (b) payment of all other sums with interest thereon becoming due and payable to Assignee under the provisions of this Assignment or under the provisions of any other document evidencing or securing the Loan (this Assignment, the Note, the Mortgage, and such other documents evidencing or securing the Loan, together with any amendments, modifications, and supplements thereto, are collectively called the "Loan Documents"); and (c) performance and fulfillment of each and every term, covenant, and condition set forth in the Loan Documents.

4. Performance of Leases.

With respect to each of the Leases, Assignor (a) shall faithfully abide by, perform, and fulfill each and every term, covenant, and condition of the Leases to be performed or fulfilled by Assignor; (b) at the sole cost and expense of Assignor, shall enforce or secure the performance of each and every material term, covenant, and condition of the Leases to be performed or fulfilled by Assignor; (c) shall not modify, extend, or in any way alter any material term, covenant, or condition of any of the Leases, without the prior written consent of Assignee; and (d) shall not accept payment of Rents more than one (1) month in advance as payable under any of the Leases, or waive, excuse, condone, or in any manner release or discharge any tenants, licensees, concessionaires, users, and occupants of any part of the Property (including, but not limited to, all parties claiming an interest under any of the Leases) (collectively, the "Tenants") of or from the terms, covenants, or conditions to be performed or fulfilled by such party, including the obligation to pay any Rents in the manner and at the place and time specified therein.

5. Defense of Actions.

Assignor, at Assignor's sole cost and expense, shall appear in and defend any action or proceeding arising out of or in any manner connected with any of the Leases or the obligations, duties, or liabilities of Assignor or of any of the Tenants, and shall pay all costs and expenses of Assignee, including actual attorneys' fees and expenses, in any such action or proceeding to which Assignee may be a party.

6. Protection of Security.

Upon the occurrence of a default under any of the Loan Documents and upon Assignor's failure to cure such default within any applicable cure period or grace period (an "Event of Default"), at Assignee's option, and without releasing Assignor from any obligation under this Assignment or the other Loan Documents, Assignee may make or do such acts in such manner and to such extent as Assignee may deem necessary to protect the security of this Assignment, including specifically, without limiting its general powers, appearing in and defending any action or proceeding purporting to affect the security hereof or the rights, privileges, or powers of Assignee, and also performing and discharging each and every term, covenant, and condition of Assignor set forth in any of the Leases, and, in exercising any such powers, may pay the costs and expenses thereof, employ counsel, and incur and pay attorneys' fees and expenses.

7. Payment of Expenses.

Assignor shall immediately reimburse Assignee upon demand all sums expended by Assignee under the authority of this Assignment, together with interest thereon at the Default Rate set forth in the Note.

8. Absolute Assignment; Rights of Assignor Before Event of Default.

This Assignment is intended to be and shall constitute an unconditional, absolute, and present assignment by Assignor to Assignee of all of Assignor's right, title, and interest in and to the Leases and Rents (subject to the terms and conditions hereof), and not an assignment in the nature of a pledge of such Leases and Rents or the mere grant of a security interest therein. Notwithstanding that this Assignment is effective immediately, so long as there shall exist no Event of Default, Assignor shall have the privilege under a revocable license to collect as they become due, but not prior to accrual, all Rents from the Property, and to receive and hold the same. Assignor shall receive and hold such Rents in trust as a fund to be applied to the payment of real estate taxes, insurance, maintenance, repair, and Lease obligations with respect to the Property, and to the payment of interest, principal, and other sums becoming due under the Note, before retaining or disbursing any part of the Rents for any other purpose.

9. Rights of Assignee Upon Event of Default.

(a) Upon or at any time after the occurrence of an Event of Default, Assignee may do any or all of the following: (i) revoke Assignor's license to collect, retain, use, and enjoy the Rents and to exercise any other rights of Assignor under the Leases, as provided by Section 8; (ii) declare all sums secured by this Assignment immediately due and payable and, at its option, without notice and without regard to the adequacy of security for the indebtedness hereby secured, either in person or by agent, with or without bringing any action or proceeding, or by a receiver to be appointed by a court, enter upon, take possession of, manage, and operate the Property or any part thereof; (iii) make, cancel, enforce, or modify any of the Leases; (iv) obtain and evict Tenants, and fix or modify any of the Rents; and (v) perform any acts which Assignee deems proper to protect the security of this Assignment, and either with or without taking possession of the Property, in its own name sue for or otherwise collect and receive the Rents, including those past due and unpaid, and apply the Rents, less costs and expenses of operation and collection, including just and reasonable compensation for all its employees and other agents (including, but not limited to, attorneys' fees and expenses and management and rental commissions), to any indebtedness secured by this Assignment. The exercise of any or all such rights by Assignee as provided by this Section 9(a) shall not cure or waive any Event of Default or waive, modify, or affect notice of default under the Loan Documents, or invalidate any act done pursuant to such notice, and Assignee may continue to exercise any or all of such rights until such Event of Default has been cured. Assignee may exercise its rights and privileges under this Assignment whenever any Event of Default has occurred.

(b) If Assignee receives any Rents as provided by this Assignment, Assignee shall apply such amounts on account of the Loan in the order provided by the Note.

(c) Assignee shall not be obligated to maintain or repair the Property but shall be entitled to do so upon the occurrence of an Event of Default, to the extent Assignee determines it to be necessary or appropriate, in its discretion. Such maintenance or repair may include, without limitation, the purchase of furniture, equipment, and other personal property used in connection with the Property, and the costs thereof including all taxes imposed thereon or therefor shall be part of the costs and expenses of operation. Assignee shall not be obligated to perform or fulfill, nor does it hereby undertake to perform or fulfill, any term, condition, or covenant under the Leases, or under or by reason of this Assignment.

(d) Assignee may act upon any notice, request, consent, demand, statement, note, or other paper or document believed by it to be genuine and to have been signed by the party or parties purporting to sign the same. Assignee shall not be liable for any error of judgment, or for any act done or step taken or omitted, or for any mistake of law or fact, or for anything which it may do or refrain from doing in good faith. Assignee shall not have any accountability under this Assignment except for its own willful default or gross negligence.

(e) Any default by Assignor in the performance of any term, covenant, or condition of this Assignment and not cured within any applicable cure period provided in this Assignment shall constitute and be deemed to be an Event of Default under the Loan Documents, entitling Assignee to every and all rights, privileges, and remedies set forth therein.

(f) Assignor, on its own behalf and that of any successors or assigns, hereby authorizes and directs all Tenants to pay Rents directly to Assignee, and to treat Assignee as the other party under the applicable Lease, with all of the rights, powers, and privileges granted by Assignor to Assignee under this Assignment or by such Tenant to Assignor under the applicable Lease, after receiving written instructions to do so from Assignee, notwithstanding any instructions to the contrary from Assignor. Assignor, on its own behalf and that of any successors or assigns, hereby further authorizes all Tenants to recognize the claims and demands of Assignee under this Assignment without investigating (i) the reason for any action taken by Assignee or the validity or the amount of indebtedness owing to Assignee; (ii) the existence of any Event of Default; or (iii) the application to be made by Assignee of any sums to be paid to Assignee. The sole signature of Assignee shall be sufficient for the exercise of any rights under this Assignment and the sole receipt of Assignee for any sums received shall be a full discharge and release therefor to any Tenant. Checks for all or any part of the Rents payable to Assignee under this Assignment shall be drawn to the exclusive order of Assignee.

(g) The rights, powers, privileges, and discretions specifically granted to Assignee by this Assignment are not in limitation of but in addition to those to which Assignee is entitled under any present or future general or local law relating to such assignments in the [State] [Commonwealth] of _____. The rights, powers, privileges, and discretions (hereinafter collectively called the "rights") to which Assignee may be entitled shall inure to the benefit of its successors and assigns. All the rights of Assignee are cumulative and not alternative and may be enforced successively or concurrently. Failure of Assignee to exercise any of its rights shall not impair any of its rights nor be deemed a waiver of such rights. No waiver of any of Assignee's rights shall be deemed to apply to any other such rights. No waiver by Assignee shall be effective unless in writing and signed by Assignee.

(h) Upon an Event of Default, Assignee, and not Assignor, shall be deemed to be the creditor of each Tenant in respect of any assignment for the benefit of creditors, bankruptcy, reorganization, insolvency, dissolution, or receivership proceedings affecting such tenant.

10. <u>Indemnity.</u>

Assignor shall indemnify and hold Assignee harmless against and from (a) any and all costs, expenses, liability, loss, or damage which Assignee incurs under any of the Leases or under or by reason of this Assignment; and (b) any and all claims and demands whatsoever which may be asserted against Assignee by reason of any alleged obligations or undertaking on its part to perform or discharge any of the terms, covenants, or conditions contained in any of the Leases. Should Assignee incur any such liability, loss, or damage under any of the Leases or under or by reason of this Assignment, or in the defense of any such claims or demands, the amount thereof, including costs, expenses, and reasonable attorneys' fees, shall be secured by this Assignment, and Assignor shall reimburse Assignee therefor immediately upon demand, with interest at the Default Rate set forth in the Note. Upon the failure of Assignor so to reimburse Assignee, Assignee may declare all sums secured by this Assignment to be immediately due and payable.

11.     Subsequent Leases.

Until the indebtedness secured by this Assignment shall have been paid in full, Assignor shall make, execute, and deliver to Assignee, upon demand, any and all instruments that may be necessary to assign to Assignee all subsequent Leases affecting all or any part of the Property, upon the same or substantially the same terms and conditions as are set forth in this Assignment, to the extent that such assignment is not already effected by this Assignment.

12.     Termination.

Upon the payment in full of all indebtedness secured by this Assignment and the termination of the Mortgage of record, this Assignment shall terminate and become void and of no further effect. The affidavit of Assignee or any officer of Assignee showing any part of such indebtedness to remain unpaid shall be and constitute conclusive evidence, as to any third party, of the validity, effectiveness, and continuing force of this Assignment. Any such third party may and is hereby authorized to rely on such affidavit.

13.     Assignor's Representations.

Assignor hereby represents that (a) Assignor has not accepted Rent under any Lease more than thirty (30) days in advance of its accrual, and payment thereof has not otherwise been forgiven, discounted, or compromised; (b) Assignor has not done anything which might prevent Assignee from, or limit Assignee in, acting under any of the provisions of this Assignment; (c) to Assignor's knowledge, it has not breached any term, covenant, or condition, of any of the Leases; (d) to Assignor's knowledge, no Tenant has a right of deduction, counterclaim, recoupment, or set-off under any of the Leases; (e) all of the Leases are subject and subordinate to the Loan Documents; (f) Assignor is the sole owner of the entire lessor's interest in the Leases and the Rents thereunder and such interest is free and clear of all liens and encumbrances; (g) no other assignment of any interest in any of the Leases or Rents is in effect; (h) the Leases submitted to Assignee are true and complete copies of all of the Leases now existing and there have been no material written or oral modifications thereto; (i) Assignor has not received any funds or deposits from any tenant except as expressly provided for in a Lease; (j) no Tenant has a right of first refusal or right of first offer or any similar right to purchase the Property; and (k) to the best of Assignor's knowledge, no Tenant has used or placed on the Property any hazardous materials in violation of any environmental laws.

14.     Notices.

All notices, elections, deliveries, and other communications between the parties required or desired to be given in connection with this Assignment, to be effective hereunder, shall be given as provided by the Mortgage.

15.     Miscellaneous.

(a) This Assignment shall not be amended or modified in any manner except by a document in writing executed by Assignee.

[(b) Assignor hereby waives trial by jury in any action or proceeding to which Assignor and Assignee or any holder of the Leases may be parties, arising out of or in connection with this Agreement or any of the Leases. This waiver constitutes a waiver of trial by jury of all claims against all parties to such actions or proceedings, including claims against parties who are not parties to this Assignment.]

(c) This Assignment, together with the other Loan Documents, is the entire agreement between the parties with respect to the matters set forth herein and therein, and all prior statements, discussions, negotiations, and agreements, oral or written, are superseded by this Assignment and the other Loan Documents and merged herein and therein.

(d) Time is of the essence of this Assignment.

(e) This Assignment shall be governed by the laws of the [State] [Commonwealth] of _____, excluding any _____ choice of law principles.

(f)  Assignor shall, from time to time, without charge and within five (5) business days after request by Assignee in writing, execute, acknowledge, and deliver, and request each Tenant to execute, acknowledge, and deliver, to Assignee a written statement in form and substance reasonably satisfactory to Assignee, certifying to certain matters relating to the Leases.

[(g) Neither Assignor nor any direct or indirect owner of an interest in Assignor shall have personal liability for payment of the principal amount, interest thereon, late charges, or any other costs, expenses, or other charges due to Assignee as provided by the Loan Documents and, in the event of any default, Assignee's sole recourse shall be against the Property and any other collateral securing the Loan and under the Guarantee; provided, however, that Assignor and such direct and indirect owners shall remain personally liable as otherwise provided by the Loan Documents or applicable law for the following: (i) as provided by the Guarantee, with respect to the Guarantors; (ii) Assignor's failure to pay real estate taxes or assessments against the Property, to the extent that funds are available; (iii) Assignor's failure to insure the Property as required by the Loan Documents; (iv) rent or other income from the Property received after a default under the Loan Documents and which is not applied as provided by the Loan Documents or to the expenses of operating or maintaining the Property; (v) conversion, diversion, misapplication, or misappropriation of security deposits, reserve accounts, insurance proceeds, or condemnation awards in connection with the Property; (vi) waste; (vii) amounts due under the Environmental Indemnity (as defined in the Loan Commitment); and (viii) fraud or intentional misrepresentation in connection with the transactions contemplated by the Commitment or any of the Loan Documents.]

IN WITNESS WHEREOF, Assignor has duly executed and delivered this Assignment of Leases and Rents under seal on the date first written above.

_____ , a
_____ , Borrower

By: _____ (SEAL)

Its: _____

[Add notary block in the form required by the state in which the Assignment of Leases and Rents will be recorded.]

EXHIBIT A
Description of Property

# Appendix M

# Form of Security Agreement

**Note:** In loan transactions in which the loan is secured by both a lien on the borrower's real property and a UCC security interest in the borrower's personal property, it is common practice in many states to combine the mortgage and the security agreement into one instrument. The Form of Mortgage in this book serves both of those roles. However, the form that follows is designed solely as a security agreement.

SECURITY AGREEMENT

THIS SECURITY AGREEMENT (this "Agreement") is made this ___ day of _____, 20__, by _____, a _____ _____ having an address at _____, as debtor ("Borrower"), in favor of _____, a _____ _____ having an address at _____, as secured party ("Lender").

### Introduction

Lender has made a loan to Borrower (the "Loan"), as evidenced by the Promissory Note dated this date by Borrower in the principal amount of _____ Dollars ($_____) (together with any modifications, amendments, replacements, substitutions, extensions, or renewals thereof, the "Note").

The Note shall be secured in part by a Mortgage dated this date by Borrower to Lender, granting a first-priority lien on the land described in <u>Exhibit A</u> to this Assignment and all improvements situated thereon (such land and improvements are collectively called the "Property"), which Mortgage is intended to be recorded among the land records of _____ County, _____ (together with any modifications, amendments, or supplements thereto, the "Mortgage").

As a condition precedent to making the Loan, Lender has required that Borrower further secure the payment and performance of all the obligations of Borrower in connection with the Loan by entering into this Agreement.

### Agreement

In consideration of the foregoing and to induce Lender to make the Loan to Borrower, Borrower hereby covenants, warrants, represents, and agrees with Lender as follows:

1. <u>Defined Terms.</u>

The capitalized terms used but not defined in this Agreement shall have the meanings given to them in the Mortgage.

2. Security.

As security for (a) the payment of the indebtedness evidenced by the Note; (b) the payment of all other sums with interest thereon becoming due and payable to Lender under the provisions of this Assignment or under the provisions of any other document evidencing or securing the Loan (this Agreement, the Note, the Mortgage, and such other documents evidencing or securing the Loan, together with any amendments, modifications, and supplements thereto, are collectively called the "Loan Documents"); and (c) the performance and fulfillment of each and every term, covenant, and condition set forth in the Loan Documents, Borrower hereby grants to Lender a security interest in all of Borrower's now owned and hereafter acquired personal property used in connection with the Property, including but not limited to (a) all of Borrower's now owned and hereafter acquired equipment, and all replacements and substitutions therefor and thereof, and all accessions thereto (the "Equipment"); (b) all of Borrower's now owned and hereafter acquired inventory, and all products, replacements, and substitutions therefor and thereof, and all accessions thereto (the "Inventory"); (c) all of Borrower's now owned and hereafter acquired general intangibles, including without limitation, all licenses, permits, things in action, contractual rights, goodwill, literary rights, rights to performance, copyrights, trademark, and patents (the "General Intangibles"); (d) all of Borrower's now owned and hereafter acquired rights to payment for goods sold or leased or for services rendered (the "Accounts"); (e) all of Borrower's now owned and hereafter acquired chattel paper (the "Chattel Paper"); and (f) all of Borrower's now owned and hereafter acquired instruments, notes, items of payment, negotiable documents, and documents of title (the "Instruments"); together with all cash and noncash proceeds (including insurance proceeds) of the Equipment, Inventory, General Intangibles, Accounts, Chattel Paper, and Instruments (the "Proceeds") (such Equipment, Inventory, General Intangibles, Accounts, Chattel Paper, Instruments, and Proceeds are collectively referred to as the "Collateral"). Lender shall have all of the rights and remedies of a secured party under the Uniform Commercial Code of the state where the Collateral is located.

3. Borrower's Representations.

Borrower hereby represents to Lender that:

(a) Borrower is a _____, duly organized and in good standing under the laws of the State of _____, and authorized to do business in the State of _____;

(b) This Agreement constitutes the legal, valid, and binding obligation of Borrower enforceable in accordance with its terms, Borrower has full power and authority to grant a security interest in the Collateral and to enter into and perform the terms and conditions of this Agreement, Borrower has obtained all necessary approvals and consents to the granting of a security interest in the Collateral as contemplated by this Agreement, and the person executing this Agreement for Borrower is fully and duly empowered and authorized so to act;

(c) The compliance with or fulfillment of the terms and conditions of this Agreement will not conflict with, violate, constitute a default under, or result in a breach of the terms, conditions, or provisions of any of Borrower's organizational documents or any contract or agreement to which Borrower is a party or by which Borrower is otherwise bound;

(d) Borrower is the legal and beneficial owner and holder of all of the Collateral absolutely free and clear of any lien, security interest, pledge, option, or other charge or encumbrance other than the security interests of Lender under this Agreement. No Uniform Commercial Code Financing Statement that names Borrower as a debtor, other than those which name Lender as the secured party, has been filed in any place, and Borrower has not signed any financing statement or any security agreement authorizing any other secured party thereunder to file any such financing statement;

(e) To the knowledge of Borrower, Borrower is not in breach of any law or regulation, or the order of any court or federal, state, municipal, or other governmental authority, in connection with the Collateral;

(f) Borrower is not (i) a party to any action, suit, or proceeding at law or in equity, or by or before any governmental instrumentality or agency, (ii) aware of any facts, allegations, claims, or circumstances that may result in Borrower becoming a party to any action, suit, or proceeding at law or in equity, or by or before any governmental instrumentality or agency, (iii) engaged in any settlement negotiations relating to any claim or allegation, or (iv) a judgment debtor;

(g) Borrower, at Borrower's sole cost and expense, will defend Lender's title or interest in and to the Collateral against any and all attachments, liens, claims, encumbrances, security interests, or other impediments of any nature, however arising, of all persons whomsoever;

(h) Borrower, at Borrower's sole cost and expense, shall appear in and defend any action or proceeding arising under, growing out of, or in any manner connected with the Collateral, and pay all costs and expenses of Lender, including attorneys' fees, in any such action or proceeding in which Lender may appear; and

(i) The address for Borrower on the first page of this Agreement is Borrower's [sole place of business] [chief executive office].

4. Covenants of Borrower.

Borrower covenants and agrees as follows:

(a) Borrower shall maintain Borrower's [sole place of business] [chief executive office] in the State of _____. Borrower shall not change the location of Borrower's [sole place of business] [chief executive office] without Lender's prior written consent;

(b) Borrower shall keep all tangible items of the Collateral and all books and records relating to all of the Collateral in the State of _____ ;

(c) Borrower shall not sell, assign, transfer an interest in, or otherwise dispose of or further encumber its right, title, and interest in and to the Collateral without the prior written consent of Lender; provided, however, that Borrower shall be permitted to sell Inventory in the ordinary course of Borrower's business for fair consideration in cash or on account at normal and customary trade terms;

(d) Borrower shall pay all taxes and fees relating to the ownership of the Collateral, shall keep and maintain the Equipment and the Inventory in good condition, and shall provide all maintenance and service and make all repairs necessary for such purpose. If any parts or accessories forming part of the Equipment or the Inventory become worn out, lost, destroyed, damaged beyond repair, or otherwise permanently rendered unfit for use, Borrower, at its sole cost and expense, shall within a reasonable time replace such parts or accessories, or cause the same to be replaced, by replacement parts or accessories which are free and clear of all liens, encumbrances, or rights of others and have a value and utility at least equal to the parts or accessories replaced. All Equipment, Inventory, accessories, parts, and replacements which are added to or become attached to the Equipment or Inventory shall immediately be deemed incorporated in the Equipment or Inventory, as the case may be, and subject to the security interest granted by Borrower in this Agreement. Lender shall have the right to inspect the Equipment and the Inventory and all maintenance records relating thereto at all reasonable times;

(e) Borrower shall maintain the Collateral free from all claims, liens, encumbrances, and legal processes and shall notify Lender within ___ (_) days after receipt of notice of any lien, attachment, or judicial proceeding affecting the Collateral in whole or in part;

(f) Borrower, at its sole cost and expense, shall obtain and maintain all-risk insurance covering the Equipment and Inventory for the full replacement value thereof. The insurance shall be by insurers and in form and substance satisfactory to Lender. All insurance for loss or damage shall provide that losses, if any, shall be payable to Lender. Borrower shall pay the premiums for all such insurance and deliver to Lender the policies of insurance or duplicates thereof, or other evidence satisfactory to Lender of such insurance coverage. Each insurer shall agree, by endorsement upon the policy or policies issued by it, or by independent instrument furnished to Lender, that (i) it will give Lender thirty (30) days' prior written notice of the effective date of any material alteration or cancellation of such policy; and (ii) the coverage of Lender shall not be terminated, reduced, or affected in any manner regardless of any breach or violation by Borrower of any warranties, declarations, or conditions of such insurance policy or policies. The proceeds of such insurance payable as a result of loss of or damage to the Equipment or Inventory shall be applied, at Lender's option, toward (i) the replacement, restoration, or repair of the Equipment or Inventory which may be lost, stolen, destroyed, or damaged; or (ii) payment of the Loan, in the order provided by the Note. Borrower irrevocably appoints Lender as Borrower's attorney-in-fact to make claim for, receive payment of, and execute and endorse all documents, checks, or drafts received in payment for loss or damage under any of such insurance policies;

(g) Borrower shall promptly execute and deliver any Uniform Commercial Code Financing Statement or other document reasonably required, or procure any document reasonably required (including Uniform Commercial Code Financing Statement releases, as necessary), and pay all costs to file or record such documents, including but not limited to any documentary or stamp tax or filing or recording fee, to perfect and maintain the perfection and the priority of the security interest granted under this Agreement. If any part of the Collateral is of a type as to which it is necessary or desirable for Lender to take possession of such part of the Collateral in order to perfect, or maintain the priority of, Lender's security interest, then upon Lender's request, Borrower shall deliver such part of the Collateral to Lender; and

(h) Borrower, upon request of Lender, shall make available to Lender or its designees, for inspection and copying, all of Borrower's records in connection with the Collateral.

5. <u>Account Covenants.</u>

(a) Borrower shall deliver to Lender within _____ (__) days after the end of each calendar month a listing and aging report for the Accounts, in form and substance reasonably satisfactory to Lender, together with such other information and financial reports as Lender may request in Lender's reasonable discretion from time to time.

(b) Upon the request of Lender, Borrower shall deposit, or cause to be deposited, all checks, drafts, cash, and other remittances in payment of, or on account of payment of, any and all Accounts (all of the foregoing herein collectively referred to as "items of payment") to an account (the "Collateral Account") designated by Lender at a bank or other financial institution designated by Lender. Lender shall not be responsible for the solvency of any such bank or other financial institution or the management and administration of the Collateral Account. Lender shall have the sole right to access and make withdrawals from the Collateral Account. Borrower shall deposit such items of payment for credit to the Collateral Account within one (1) banking day after the receipt thereof and in precisely the form received, except for the endorsement of Borrower where necessary to permit the collection of such items of payment, which endorsement Borrower hereby agrees to make. Pending such deposit, Borrower will not commingle any such items of payment with any of its other funds or property, but will hold them separate and apart. Lender shall be entitled to apply the funds in the

Collateral Account against Borrower's obligations secured by this Agreement from time to time.

6. Additional Rights of Lender and Duties of Borrower.

(a) In addition to all other rights which Lender may have under this Agreement or under the other Loan Documents, at law, in equity, or otherwise, upon the occurrence of a default under this Agreement or any of the other Loan Documents and upon Borrower's failure to cure such default within any applicable cure period or grace period (an "Event of Default"), Lender shall have the rights set forth in this Section 6(a). Borrower hereby irrevocably appoints Lender as Borrower's attorney-in-fact, with power of substitution, to do each of the following in the name of Borrower or in the name of Lender or otherwise, for the use and benefit of Lender, but at the sole cost and expense of Borrower, and without notice to Borrower, upon the occurrence of an Event of Default:

(i)    Notify the account debtors obligated on any Accounts to make payments thereon directly to Lender, and take control of the cash and noncash proceeds of any Collateral;

(ii)   Compromise, extend, or renew any of the Collateral or deal with the same as Lender may deem advisable;

(iii)  Release, make exchanges in or substitutions to, or surrender all or an y part of the Collateral;

(iv)   Remove from Borrower's place(s) of business all books, records, ledger sheets, correspondence, invoices, and documents relating to or evidencing any of the Collateral, without cost or expense to Lender, and make such use of Borrower's place(s) of business as may be reasonably necessary to administer, control, and collect the Collateral;

(v)    Repair, alter, or supply goods, if any, necessary to fulfill in whole or in part the purchase order of any account debtor;

(vi)   Demand, collect, receipt for, and give renewals, extensions, discharges, and releases of any of the Collateral;

(vii)  Institute and prosecute legal and equitable proceedings to enforce collection of, or realize upon, any of the Collateral;

(viii) Settle, renew, extend, compromise, compound, exchange, or adjust claims with respect to any of the Collateral or any legal proceedings brought with respect thereto;

(ix)   Endorse the name of Borrower upon any items or payment relating to the Collateral or upon any proof of claim in bankruptcy against an account debtor; and

(x)    Receive and open all mail addressed to Borrower and notify the postal authorities to change the address for the delivery of mail to Borrower to such address as Lender may designate.

(b) Borrower shall:

(i) Make no material change to the terms of any Account, Chattel Paper, or Instrument without the prior written permission of Lender;

(ii) On demand, make available in form acceptable to Lender proof of the sale or lease of goods or satisfactory performance of services which gave rise to the Accounts; and

(iii)When requested, regularly advise Lender of any delay in delivery or performance, or claims made, in regard to any Collateral.

7. <u>Remedies.</u>

(a) Upon the occurrence of an Event of Default, Lender may exercise any one or more of its remedies under common or statutory law, including but not limited to the Uniform Commercial Code of the jurisdiction in which the Collateral is located, and at any time thereafter may do any one or more of the following, all of which are hereby authorized by Borrower:

(i) Exercise Lender's rights of enforcement under common or statutory law and in addition to those rights, at Lender's sole discretion, require Borrower (at Borrower's sole cost and expense) to forward promptly any or all of the Equipment and Inventory to Lender at such location as shall be reasonably required by Lender, or, without breach of the peace, enter upon the premises where any such Equipment or Inventory is located and take immediate possession of and remove the Equipment or Inventory by summary proceedings or otherwise, all without liability from Lender to Borrower for or by reason of such entry or taking of possession, whether for the restoration of damage to property caused by such taking or otherwise;

(ii) Sell or otherwise dispose of the Collateral at a commercially reasonable public or private sale or otherwise at such price as Lender may deem best, for cash, credit, or otherwise, with the right of Lender to purchase and to apply the proceeds: first, to the settlement of all liens or claims on the Collateral prior to the security interest of Lender; second, to the payment of all expenses connected with the taking and selling of the Collateral; and third, to the payment of all indebtedness of Borrower to Lender under this Agreement and the other Loan Documents; and, in case of any deficiency, Lender may collect such deficiency from Borrower; or

(iii)Exercise any other right or remedy which may be available to Lender under this Agreement, the other Loan Documents, or applicable law, or proceed by appropriate court action to enforce the terms hereof or to recover damages for the breach hereof or to rescind this Agreement in whole or in part.

(b) In addition, Borrower shall be liable for any and all unpaid additional sums due under this Agreement or under the other Loan Documents, before, after, or during the exercise of any of the foregoing remedies, and for all legal fees and other costs and expenses incurred by reason of any Event of Default or the exercise of Lender's remedies with respect thereto. No remedy referred to in this Section 7 is intended to be exclusive, but each shall be cumulative, and shall be in addition to any other remedy referred to in this Agreement or in any of the other Loan Documents, or otherwise available at law or in equity. To the extent permitted by applicable law, Borrower hereby waives any notice or other mandatory requirements of law, now or hereafter in effect, which might require Lender to sell or use any part of the Collateral in mitigation of Lender's damages; provided, however, that Borrower does not waive any requirement of law that Lender act in a commercially reasonable manner. Borrower hereby waives any and all existing or future claims to any offset against the sums due under this Agreement or under the other Loan Documents, and agrees to make the payments of such sums regardless of any offset or claim which may be asserted by Borrower or on its behalf in connection with this Agreement or the other Loan Documents. The failure of Lender to exercise, or any delay by Lender in the exercise of, the rights granted under this Agreement upon the occurrence of an Event of Default shall not constitute a waiver of any such right upon the continuation or recurrence of any such Event of Default. Lender may take or release other security, may release any party primarily or secondarily liable for the Loan, may grant extensions, renewals, or indulgences with respect to the Loan, and may apply any other security held by it with respect to the Loan to the satisfaction of the Loan without prejudice to any of Lender's rights under this Agreement.

8. Notices.

(a) All notices, elections, deliveries, and other communications between the parties required or desired to be given in connection with this Agreement, to be effective hereunder, shall be given as provided by the Mortgage.

(b) Borrower agrees that five (5) days' prior notice of the time and place of any public sale of the Collateral, or of the time after which a private sale of the Collateral will be made, is commercially reasonable notice.

9. Further Assurances.

Borrower will promptly and duly execute and deliver to Lender such further documents and assurances and take such further action as Lender may from time to time reasonably request in order to carry out the intent and purpose of this Agreement and to establish and protect the rights and remedies created or intended to be created in favor of Lender under this Agreement.

10. Successors and Assigns.

This Agreement shall inure to the benefit of Lender and its successors and assigns, and shall be binding upon the [successors] [heirs, personal representatives,] and permitted assigns of Borrower. This Agreement may not be assigned by Borrower without the prior written consent of Lender.

11. Miscellaneous.

[(a) Neither Borrower nor any direct or indirect owner of an interest in Borrower shall have personal liability for payment of the Principal Amount, interest thereon, Late Charges, or any other costs, expenses, or other charges due to Lender as provided by the Loan Documents and, in the event of any default, Lender's sole recourse shall be against the Property and any other collateral securing the Loan and under the Guarantee; provided, however, that Borrower and such direct and indirect owners shall remain personally liable as otherwise provided by the Loan Documents or applicable law for the following: (i) as provided by the Guarantee, with respect to the Guarantors; (ii) Borrower's failure to pay real estate taxes or assessments against the Property, to the extent that funds are available; (iii) Borrower's failure to insure the Property as required by the Loan Documents; (iv) rent or other income from the Property received after a default under the Loan Documents and which is not applied as provided by the Loan Documents or to the expenses of operating or maintaining the Property; (v) conversion, diversion, misapplication, or misappropriation of security deposits, reserve accounts, insurance proceeds, or condemnation awards in connection with the Property; (vi) waste; (vii) amounts due under the Environmental Indemnity (as defined in the Loan Commitment); and (viii) fraud or intentional misrepresentation in connection with the transactions contemplated by the Commitment or any of the Loan Documents.]

(b) This Agreement shall not be amended or modified in any manner except by a document in writing executed by Lender.

[(c) Borrower hereby waives trial by jury in any action or proceeding to which Borrower and Lender or any holder of the Collateral may be parties, arising out of or in connection with this Agreement or the Collateral. This waiver constitutes a waiver of trial by jury of all claims against all parties to such actions or proceedings, including claims against parties who are not parties to this Agreement.]

(d) This Agreement, together with the other Loan Documents, is the entire agreement between the parties with respect to the matters set forth herein and therein, and all prior statements, discussions, negotiations, and agreements, oral or written, are superseded by this Agreement and the other Loan Documents and merged herein and therein.

(e) Time is of the essence of this Agreement.

(f) This Agreement shall be governed by the laws of the [State] [Commonwealth] of _____, excluding any _____ choice of law principles, regardless of the location of the Collateral.

IN WITNESS WHEREOF, Borrower has duly executed and delivered this Security Agreement under seal on the date first written above.

_____, a

_____, Borrower

By: _____ (SEAL)

Its: _____

WITNESS:

_____

EXHIBIT A
Description of Property

# Appendix N

## Form of Loan Guarantee

GUARANTEE

THIS GUARANTEE, made on _____, 20___, by _____ _____, a _____ having an address at _____ ("Guarantor"), for the benefit of _____, a _____ having an address at _____ ("Lender"),

WITNESSES THAT:

WHEREAS, _____, a _____ ("Borrower") is indebted to Lender for a loan (the "Loan") in the principal sum of $_____, evidenced by a Promissory Note of even date herewith from Borrower to Lender (the "Note"), and secured by, *inter alia*, a Mortgage of even date herewith and intended to be recorded among the Land Records of _____ County, _____, from Borrower to Lender (the "Mortgage") covering, *inter alia*, all of that real property in the said County which is described therein (which real property, and all other real or personal property or rights or interests therein now or at any time hereafter securing the Loan, are referred to herein collectively as the "Property");

WHEREAS, to induce Lender to make the Loan, Guarantor has agreed to guarantee to Lender and its successors and assigns as holder of the Note, by Guarantor's execution and delivery of this Guarantee, Borrower's full and timely performance of its obligations under the Note, the Mortgage, and each other document signed by Borrower in connection with the Loan (which documents, together with this Guarantee and all amendments and supplements to any of those documents now or hereafter made, are referred to collectively herein as the "Loan Documents"), on the terms and subject to the limitations set forth herein; and

WHEREAS, in making the Loan, Lender is relying on Guarantor's said agreement, as set forth in this Guarantee.

NOW, THEREFORE, IN CONSIDERATION of Lender's agreement to make the Loan, and for other good and valuable consideration, the receipt and adequacy of which Guarantor hereby acknowledges, the parties hereto hereby agree as follows:

Section 1.     Guarantee.

1.1.     Guarantor hereby unconditionally and irrevocably guarantees to Lender the due and punctual:

1.1.1.     Payment in full (and not merely the collectibility) of (a) the principal sum of the Loan and all interest accruing thereon, in each case when due and payable, whether on any installment payment date or at the stated or accelerated maturity of any or all of the Loan, and each other sum at any time becoming due and payable under the Note, the Mortgage, and the other Loan Documents, all in accordance therewith; and (b) all loss, damages, or costs incurred by Lender and arising out of any default by Borrower under the Note or the other Loan Documents, regardless of whether the loss, damages, or costs are expressly provided for therein, or are then otherwise allowable by law; and

1.1.2.    Performance (and not merely the enforceability) of all of Borrower's other obligations under the Note and the other Loan Documents.

1.2.    If Borrower fails duly and punctually to pay any of the principal sum, any interest accruing thereon, any other such sum or charge, or any such loss, damages, or costs, Guarantor shall forthwith pay them, with interest thereon from the date on which Borrower's payment thereof became due, at the Default Rate (as defined in the Note).

Section 2.    Certain Lender Rights. Lender may, in the exercise of its sole and absolute discretion, without (a) providing notice to, or obtaining the consent of, Guarantor, or (b) releasing or affecting Guarantor's obligations and liabilities hereunder, from time to time:

2.1.    Waive compliance with or any default occurring under, or grant any other indulgence with respect to, the Note or any other Loan Document;

2.2.    Modify or supplement the Note or any other Loan Document;

2.3.    Grant any extension or renewal of or with respect to the Note, the Mortgage, or any other Loan Document, and/or effect any release, compromise, or settlement in connection therewith;

2.4.    Advance any sum if Lender deems it necessary or advisable to perform any term of, or satisfy any condition in, the Note or any other Loan Document, if Borrower is then in default thereunder;

2.5.    Assign or otherwise transfer the Note, the Mortgage, and any other Loan Document or any interest of Lender therein;

2.6.    Deal in all respects with Borrower as if this Guarantee were not in effect; and

2.7.    Agree to the substitution, sale, transfer, exchange, release, or other disposition of any or all of the Property or any Loan Document.

Section 3.    Guarantor Liability.

3.1.    Guarantor's liability under this Guarantee (a) shall be primary, direct, and immediate; (b) shall not be conditioned or contingent on Lender's pursuit of any remedy which it has against Borrower or any other Person (as hereinafter defined) under the Note, the Mortgage, or any other Loan Document, pursuant thereto or at law or in equity; and (c) shall be unconditional, irrespective of the genuineness, validity, regularity, or enforceability of the Note, the Mortgage, or the other Loan Documents, or the adequacy of any consideration or security given therefor or in connection therewith, or any other circumstance which might otherwise constitute a legal or equitable discharge of a surety or guarantor under applicable law. Guarantor hereby waives all defenses at law or in equity otherwise available to it due to any of those circumstances.

3.2. Without limiting the generality of the forgoing terms of this Section, Lender shall not be required (a) to make any demand of Borrower or any other Person, or (b) otherwise to pursue or exhaust its remedies against Borrower or any other Person, or against any or all of the Property (including any other property by which the Loan may hereafter in any manner be secured), before, simultaneously with, or after enforcing any of Lender's rights and remedies hereunder against Guarantor. Any one or more successive and/or concurrent actions may be brought hereon against Guarantor, either as part of any action brought against Borrower, or in one or more separate actions, as often as Lender deems advisable in the exercise of its sole and absolute discretion. Guarantor hereby waives diligence, presentment, protest, notice of dishonor, demand for payment, extension of time for payment, notice of acceptance of this Guarantee, nonpayment at maturity, and indulgences and notice of every kind, and consents to all forbearances and extensions of the time for payment under the Note or performance under the Loan Documents, all changes in the terms of the Loan Documents hereafter made, and all substitutions, exchanges, or releases of all or any part of the collateral therefor. The parties hereto intend that Guarantor remain liable hereunder until the entire principal of the Loan and all interest and other sums due or to become due under the Loan Documents are fully paid and Borrower's other obligations under the Loan Documents are fully performed, notwithstanding any act, omission, or other event which may otherwise operate as a legal or equitable discharge of Guarantor.

3.3. Guarantor's liability under this Guarantee shall continue after any assignment or transfer by Borrower or Lender of any of their rights under the Note or any other Loan Document, or in the Property.

Section 4. <u>Waivers.</u> Guarantor hereby expressly waives (a) presentment and demand for payment of any of the principal sum of the Loan or any interest thereon or other sum payable under the Loan Documents, and protest of any nonpayment thereof; (b) notice of acceptance of this Guarantee and of presentment, demand, and protest; (c) notice of any default hereunder or under any of the other Loan Documents, and of any indulgence with respect thereto; (d) demand for observance or performance, and enforcement, of any term of this Guarantee or any other Loan Document; and (e) all other notices and demands otherwise required by law to be given or made. Guarantor agrees that if this Guarantee is enforced by suit or otherwise, or if Lender exercises any right or remedy under any Loan Document upon any default by Borrower or Guarantor thereunder, Guarantor shall reimburse Lender on demand for all reasonable attorneys' fees and other costs which it incurs in connection therewith.

Section 5.    <u>Bankruptcy or Insolvency.</u>

5.1.    Anything in this Guarantee or the other Loan Documents to the contrary notwithstanding, Lender may, in the exercise of its sole and absolute discretion, as to Guarantor, accelerate the debt evidenced and secured by the Loan Documents, if:

5.1.1.    Guarantor (a) applies for or consents to the appointment of a receiver, trustee, or liquidator of Guarantor or of all or a substantial part of its assets; (b) files a voluntary petition in bankruptcy, or admits in writing its inability to pay its debts as they come due; (c) makes an assignment for the benefit of creditors; (d) files a petition or an answer seeking a reorganization or an arrangement with creditors or seeking to take advantage of any insolvency law; (e) performs any other act of bankruptcy; or (f) files an answer admitting the material allegations of a petition filed against Guarantor in any bankruptcy, reorganization, or insolvency proceeding; or

5.1.2.    (a) An order, judgment or decree is entered by any court of competent jurisdiction adjudicating Guarantor a bankrupt or an insolvent, or approving a petition seeking a reorganization, or appointing a receiver, trustee, or liquidator of Guarantor or of all or a substantial part of its assets; or (b) there otherwise commences, as to Guarantor or any of its assets, any proceeding under any bankruptcy, reorganization, arrangement, insolvency, readjustment, receivership, or like law or statute, and if in either case the order, judgment, decree, or proceeding continues unstayed for any period of 60 consecutive days or continues in effect for any period of 10 consecutive days after any stay thereof expires.

5.2.    Nothing in this Section shall impair any right which Lender may have under the Note or the other Loan Documents to accelerate the debt on the occurrence of any default or other event provided therein and entitling Lender to accelerate the debt, whether or not relating to Guarantor.

5.3.    If payment of any sum paid by or for the account of Borrower or Guarantor under the Loan Documents is at any time rescinded or must otherwise be restored or returned by Lender on the insolvency, bankruptcy, dissolution, liquidation, or reorganization of Borrower or Guarantor, or on or as a result of the appointment of a receiver, intervenor or conservator of, or trustee or similar officer for Borrower or Guarantor or any of its assets, or otherwise, then as to all or so much of the payment as is rescinded, restored, or returned, this Guarantee shall continue to be effective or be reinstated, as the case may be, as though the payment had not been paid. Nothing herein shall be construed to require Guarantor to pay any amounts previously collected by Lender which are not so rescinded, restored, or returned by Lender.

Section 6.    <u>Limits on Certain Guarantor Rights.</u>

6.1.    If Guarantor advances or at this time has advanced any sum to Borrower, or if Borrower in any other manner is or becomes indebted to Guarantor, that sum and debt shall be subordinate in all respects to all amounts then or thereafter due and owing to Lender under the Note or any other Loan Document.

6.2.   Anything in this Guarantee, the other Loan Documents, or applicable law to the contrary notwithstanding, Guarantor shall have no right of subrogation in or to any of Lender's rights under this Guarantee or the Note or any of the other Loan Documents unless and until any and all amounts now or hereafter owed to Lender under the Note and the other Loan Documents (including the entire principal of the Loan and any and all interest accruing thereon, regardless of whether, at the time in question, any one or more installments thereof are not yet due and payable under the Note) are paid in full.

Section 7 .   Guarantor Financial Statements. Guarantor shall, if requested to do so by Lender, deliver to Lender, by not later than the first day of _____ in each calendar year while this Guarantee is in effect, an annual financial statement for Guarantor prepared [and certified by an independent certified public accountant] as of the last day of the immediately preceding calendar year, in reasonable form and detail, show-ing Guarantor's assets, liabilities, and net worth, and certified to Lender in writing by Guarantor as being true and correct.

Section 8.   Effect of Guarantee. Guarantor hereby represents and warrants to Lender that (a) Guarantor (i) has a financial interest in Bor-rower, (ii) has examined or has had an opportunity to examine the Note, the Mortgage, and each other Loan Document, and (iii) has full power, authority, and legal right to sign, seal, acknowledge, and deliver this Guarantee; (b) this Guarantee is Guarantor's binding legal obligation; and (c) the making of the Loan to Borrower confers a good and valuable benefit on Guarantor.

Section 9.   Notices. Any notice, demand, consent, approval, request, or other communication or document to be given hereunder (a "Notice") to a party hereto shall be (a) in writing and (b) deemed to have been given (i) on the third business day after being sent as certified or registered mail in the United States mail, postage prepaid, return receipt requested, or (ii) on the next business day after being deposited with a reputable over-night courier service (with instructions to deliver it on that next business day), or (iii) on being sent by facsimile or another means of immediate elec-tronic communication, in each case to the party's address party set forth above or any other address in the United States of America which it des-ignates from time to time by Notice to each other party hereto, or (iv) if the party's receipt is acknowledged in writing, on its hand or other actual delivery to the party.

Section 10.   General.

10.1.   Effect. This Guarantee (a) shall become effective on and only on its execution and delivery by each party hereto, and (b) with _____ and the other Loan Documents, represents the complete understanding, and supersedes all prior written or oral negotiations, representations, guaranties, warranties, promises, statements, or agreements, between or among them as to its subject matter. No determination by any court, governmental body, or otherwise that any term hereof is invalid or unenforceable in any instance shall affect the validity or enforceability of (a) any other term hereof, or (b) the term in any circumstance not controlled by the determination. Each term shall be valid and enforceable to the fullest extent allowed by, and be construed if possible to be consistent with, applicable law. No party hereto shall be deemed to have waived exercise of any right hereunder unless the waiver is made expressly and in writing. A Person's delay or omission in exercising a right shall not be deemed a waiver of its future exercise. No waiver made in any instance of exercise of a right shall be deemed a waiver as to any other instance or right.

10.2.   Amendment. This Guarantee may be amended by and only by a document signed and delivered by each party hereto.

10.3.   Governing Law. This Guarantee shall be given effect and construed under the law of _____ (ignoring its conflicts of laws principles). Any action or proceeding arising hereunder shall be brought in the courts of _____, but if under the Constitution, laws, or treaties of the United States of America it must be brought in a United States District Court, it shall be brought in the United States District Court for the District of _____ or any successor federal court having original jurisdiction.

10.4.   Construction. As used herein, (a) "Person" means a natural person, trustee, corporation, partnership, limited liability company, or other legal entity; "Lender" means the Person so named above and each other subsequent holder of the Note; "include," "includes," and "including" mean "including but not limited to," unless expressly stated to the contrary; and (b) all references made (i) in the neuter, masculine, or feminine gender shall be deemed made in all genders; (ii) in the singular or plural number shall also be deemed made in the plural or singular number; (iii) to Guarantor, Lender, or Borrower shall be deemed made to each Person so named above and its heirs, personal representatives, successors, and assigns; and (iv) to any Section, subsection, paragraph, or subparagraph shall, unless therein expressly indicated to the contrary, be deemed made to that part of this Guarantee. The headings of those parts are provided only for convenience of reference and shall not be considered in construing their contents. Any writing or plat referred to herein as being attached hereto as an exhibit or otherwise designated herein as an exhibit hereto is hereby made a part hereof. This Guarantee may be signed in counterparts, each of which shall be deemed an original and all of which, taken together, shall constitute one and the same document.

10.5.   Assignment. This Guarantee shall bind and benefit the parties hereto and their heirs, personal representatives, successors, and assigns hereunder.

10.6.   Time of Essence. Time shall be of the essence of this Guarantee, but if the last day for a Person to exercise a right or perform a duty hereunder is a Saturday, Sunday, or statutory holiday, it shall have until the next day other than such a day to do so.

10.7.   Documentary Stamp or Other Tax. If the State of _____ _____, the said County, or any other governmental entity having jurisdiction over the Property or the Mortgage at any time hereafter levies any documentary stamp tax, recordation tax, or other, similar tax on the Mortgage, any other Loan Document, or any or all of the debt or obligations secured thereby, Guarantor shall promptly pay the tax, and shall defend, indemnify, and hold harmless Lender against and from all liability, claim of liability, or expense arising out of any failure by Guarantor to do so.

10.8.   Jury Trial Waiver. [Note to drafter: The law in some states may require a provision of this nature to be set forth in uppercase type.] Each party hereto waives any right which it may otherwise have to a trial by jury in connection with any suit or proceeding at law or in equity brought by any party hereto or which otherwise relates to this Guarantee, as a result of a default or otherwise.

IN WITNESS WHEREOF, Guarantor has signed and sealed this Guarantee or caused it to be signed and sealed on its behalf by its authorized representatives on the date first above written.

WITNESS or ATTEST:

_____          _____[(SEAL)]
                                    Guarantor

# Appendix O

## Form of Certificate of Secretary, with Attached Resolutions

**Note**: The following form of officer's certificate is for a corporation. The forms of certificates for partnerships and limited liability entities are substantially parallel. The resolutions attached as Exhibit C, in the form of a unanimous written consent of directors, authorize the corporation to purchase the property and to borrow the proceeds of the loan.

CERTIFICATE OF SECRETARY

I, the undersigned Secretary of _____, a corporation organized and existing under the laws of the [State] [Commonwealth] of _____ (the "Borrower"), do hereby certify to _____, a _____, its successors, endorsees, and assigns (collectively, the "Lender") that:

1. I am the duly qualified, elected, and acting Secretary of Borrower, a corporation duly organized and existing and in good standing under the laws of the [State] [Commonwealth] of _____, and that as such Secretary I have custody of and am familiar with the corporate records of Borrower;

2. Attached to this Certificate as Exhibit A is a true, correct, and complete copy of the Articles of Incorporation of Borrower as filed with _____ (the "_____") on _____, 20__, together with all amendments thereto adopted through the date of this Certificate. The Articles of Incorporation, and any amendments thereto attached as part of Exhibit A, have been duly filed with the _____ and are in full force and effect as of the date of this Certificate;

3. Attached to this Certificate as Exhibit B is a true, correct, and complete copy of the By-Laws of Borrower, as amended to the date hereof, and such By-Laws were in full force and effect on the date of the Unanimous Written Consent of Directors referred to in paragraph 4 below and remain in full force and effect as of the date of this Certificate;

4. Attached to this Certificate as Exhibit C is a true, correct, and complete copy of the Unanimous Written Consent of Directors of Borrower, which Unanimous Written Consent of Directors and the resolutions set forth therein have not been revoked, modified, amended, or rescinded and are in full force and effect as of the date of this Certificate; and

5. The persons whose names, titles, and signatures appear on the Incumbency and Signature Schedule of Borrower attached to this Certificate as Exhibit D are duly qualified, elected, and acting officers of Bor-

rower and hold the offices set forth opposite their respective names in such Incumbency and Signature Schedule as of the date of this Certificate, and the signatures therein appearing opposite their respective names are the genuine signatures of such officers.

IN WITNESS WHEREOF, I have hereunto set my hand this ____ day of _____, 20__.

_____

Secretary

## EXHIBIT A
Articles of Incorporation

## EXHIBIT B
By-Laws

## EXHIBIT C
Unanimous Written Consent of Directors

## UNANIMOUS WRITTEN CONSENT
Board of Directors

_____

As of _____, 20__

THE UNDERSIGNED, being all of the directors of _____ _____, a corporation organized and existing under the laws of the [State] [Commonwealth] of _____ (the "Corporation"), hereby waive the calling or holding of a meeting of directors, consent to the following actions, and direct that this Unanimous Written Consent be filed with the minutes of proceedings of the Corporation:

RESOLVED: That the [Title of Officer] of the Corporation be, and hereby is, authorized to execute and deliver, on behalf of the Corporation, (i) the Contract of Sale dated _____, 20__, by and between _____ _____ (the "Seller"), as seller, and the Corporation, as buyer, a copy of which is attached hereto (the "Contract"), for the Seller to sell to the Corporation the real and personal property described in the Contract (the "Property") for the purchase price of _____ _____ Dollars ($_____) and on the terms and conditions of the Contract, and (ii) all documents required to convey the Property to the Corporation as provided by the Contract (collectively, the "Transfer Documents"); and that the [Title of Officer] is hereby authorized in such officer's discretion to approve any changes in the form, substance, and content of the Transfer Documents as may be necessary or desirable in order to purchase the Property, his execution and delivery of the Transfer Documents, as the case may be, to be conclusive evidence of such approval; and

FURTHER RESOLVED: That the [Title of Officer] of the Corporation be, and hereby is, authorized to execute and deliver, on behalf of the Corporation, (i) the loan commitment letter dated _____, 20__, from _____ (the "Lender"), a copy of which is attached hereto (the "Commitment"), for the Lender to extend a loan to the Corporation in the maximum principal amount of _____ _____ Dollars ($_____) (the "Loan"), and (ii) all documents required by the Lender to evidence or secure the Loan as provided by the Commitment (collectively, the "Loan Documents"); and that the [Title of Officer] is hereby authorized in such officer's discretion to approve any changes in the form, substance, and content of the Loan Documents as may be necessary or desirable in order to obtain the Loan, his execution and delivery of the Loan Documents, as the case may be, to be conclusive evidence of such approval; and

[FURTHER RESOLVED: That the execution and delivery of the Contract and the Commitment prior to this date by the [Title of Officer] of the Corporation, on behalf of the Corporation, is hereby ratified; and]

FURTHER RESOLVED: That the [Title of Officer] of the Corporation be, and hereby is, authorized and directed to execute and deliver to the Lender, on behalf of the Corporation, all other instruments, documents, agreements, and certificates in addition to the Commitment and the Loan Documents as may be now or hereafter required by the Lender to evidence or secure the Loan as provided by the Commitment and the Loan Documents, all such instruments, documents, agreements, and certificates to contain such terms, covenants, and conditions as may be approved by the [Title of Officer] of the Corporation, his execution and delivery thereof on behalf of the Corporation to be conclusive evidence of his approval; and

FURTHER RESOLVED: That the [Title of Officer] of the Corporation, or any other officer or employee of the Corporation specifically designated in writing to the Lender by the [Title of Officer] of the Corporation, be, and each of them hereby is, authorized to do such further acts and things as may be necessary or advisable, in his, her, or their judgment, on behalf of the Corporation, to carry out the terms of the Loan Documents and the purpose of these Resolutions; and

FURTHER RESOLVED: That the [Title of Officer] of the Corporation, or any other officer or employee of the Corporation specifically designated in writing to the Lender by the [Title of Officer] of the Corporation, be, and each of them hereby is, authorized to specify to the Lender, on behalf of the Corporation, orally, by telephone, or in writing, the amount or amounts of advances or disbursements of the Loan to be made under the Loan Documents and to do such further acts and things as may be necessary or advisable, in his, her, or their judgment, to carry out the terms of the Loan Documents and the purpose of these Resolutions; and

FURTHER RESOLVED: That, to induce the Lender to rely thereon, the Secretary of the Corporation be, and the Secretary hereby is, authorized and empowered to certify to the Lender, on behalf of the Corporation, a copy of these Resolutions and the specimen signature of the [Title of Officer] of the Corporation or any other officer of the Corporation executing the Transfer Documents or the Loan Documents on behalf of the Corporation, and that the Lender may consider such officers to continue in office and these Resolutions to remain in full force and effect until written notice to the contrary shall be received by the Lender from the Board of Directors of the Corporation.

_____, Director

_____, Director

_____, Director

## EXHIBIT D
### Incumbency and Signature Schedule

| Name | Office | Signature |
| --- | --- | --- |
|  |  |  |
|  |  |  |
|  |  |  |

# Appendix P

# Form of Bill of Sale

**Note:** Bills of sale may be "blanket," covering all personal property at a particular location, or itemized, covering specifically listed items. Tangible personal property is sometimes sold together in the same bill of sale with intangible personal property, such as contract rights, warranties, licenses, permits, or accounts receivable. The following form is a combination "blanket" and itemized bill of sale, for tangible personal property only, and is prepared on the assumption that any intangible personal property to be sold in the transaction will be covered by a separate assignment document. The practitioner also should be aware that local law may hold that certain warranties are implied in the sale of personal property.

BILL OF SALE

FOR VALUE RECEIVED, _____, a _____ (the "Seller"), hereby grants, sells, assigns, transfers, conveys, and delivers to _____, a _____ _____ (the "Buyer"), [with covenants of [general] [special] warranty] [without warranty or recourse], all of Seller's right, title, and interest in and to the following (collectively, the "Personalty"):

All tangible personal property and fixtures, including but not limited to the items listed in Exhibit A attached to this Bill of Sale, located at or upon the premises commonly known as _____ _____ and as further described in Exhibit B attached to this Bill of Sale.

TO HAVE AND TO HOLD the Personalty unto Buyer and Buyer's successors and assigns forever.

IN WITNESS WHEREOF, Seller has duly executed and delivered this Bill of Sale under seal on this ____ day of _____, 20__.

WITNESS:                          _____,

_____          a _____, Seller
                                 By: _____ (SEAL)
                                 Its: _____

EXHIBIT A
Included Personal Property

EXHIBIT B
Description of Real Property

# Appendix Q

# Form of Post-Closing Agreement

**Note:** Post-closing agreements may cover a variety of matters, usually relating to obligations of the seller that have not been, or could not be, performed before the closing, such as maintenance or repairs to the property, environmental remediation, cure of title defects, removal of seller's personal property from the property, or registering the transfer of certain personal property. The performance of the seller's obligations under the post-closing agreement may be by the seller or by the buyer, and may or may not be secured by an escrow of purchase money funds. The following form contemplates that purchase money funds will be escrowed and attempts to create a flexible framework that should accommodate almost any post-closing agreement of the parties. Certain alternative provisions are shown in brackets. However, the practitioner should carefully consider making any modifications to the form that may be necessary to reflect the agreement of the parties accurately.

POST-CLOSING AGREEMENT

THIS POST-CLOSING AGREEMENT ("this Agreement") is made this \_\_\_\_ day of _____, 20\_\_, by and among _____, a _____ (the "Buyer"), as buyer, _____, a _____ (the "Seller"), as seller, and _____, a _____ _____ (the "Escrow Agent"), as escrow agent.

Introduction

Buyer, as buyer, and Seller, as seller, have entered into the Contract of Sale dated _____ \_\_, 20\_\_ (the "Contract of Sale"), which provides for the purchase and sale of the real property described in Exhibit A to the Contract of Sale (the "Property").

The Contract of Sale provides that Buyer's obligation to consummate the Closing is conditioned upon the satisfaction of certain conditions, including but not limited to the performance by Seller of the matters described in <u>Exhibit A</u> to this Agreement (the "Seller's Post-Closing Obligations"). As of this date, such conditions have not been satisfied, but in lieu of such satisfaction the parties have agreed to consummate the Closing and to enter into this Agreement.

The Escrow Agent has agreed to serve as the escrow agent for the Escrowed Funds (defined in Section 4(b)) in consideration of the fee payable as provided by Section 4(e) of this Agreement.

Agreement

NOW, THEREFORE, in consideration of the foregoing and other good and valuable consideration, the receipt and sufficiency of which are hereby acknowledged, the parties agree as follows:

1. Defined Terms.

Capitalized terms used but not defined in this Agreement are used as defined in the Contract of Sale.

2. Seller's Post-Closing Obligations.

(a) [Seller] [Buyer] shall perform all of Seller's Post-Closing Obligations (i) on or before _____ __, 20__ (the "Post-Closing Completion Date"); (ii) in compliance with all applicable governmental laws, regulations, codes, and requirements; and (iii) to the extent that Seller's Post-Closing Obligations pertain to improvements, repairs, or maintenance to the Property or any improvements thereon, in a workmanlike manner, using practices and materials customary in the trade. [Before Seller commences performing any of Seller's Post-Closing Obligations at the Property, Seller shall provide to Buyer, in writing, Seller's choice of contractors and consultants to perform such Seller's Post-Closing Obligations, together with any plans and specifications therefor, and such contractors, consultants, plans, and specifications shall be subject to Buyer's approval, such approval not to be unreasonably withheld or delayed.] On or before the Post-Closing Completion Date, [Seller] [Buyer] shall promptly give [Buyer] [Seller] true and complete copies of all bills, statements, or invoices for the Post-Closing Costs. [Seller shall not be obligated to expend more than the amount of the Escrowed Funds in performing Seller's Post-Closing Obligations, and Buyer shall not be obligated to reimburse Seller for expenditures of any amounts in excess of the Escrowed Funds.]

(b) Upon completion of Seller's Post-Closing Obligations as provided by Section 2(a), Buyer and Seller shall promptly deliver to the Escrow Agent a Notice (as defined in Section 5), executed by both Buyer and Seller, instructing the Escrow Agent [to release the Escrowed Funds to Seller.] [(i) to disburse to Buyer an amount of the Escrowed Funds not to exceed the actual costs and expenses, including attorneys' and consultants' fees and disbursements, incurred by or on behalf of Buyer to perform Seller's Post-Closing Obligations (collectively, the "Post-Closing Costs"); and (ii) to release any balance of the Escrowed Funds to Seller.] Neither Buyer nor Seller shall be obligated to execute or deliver the Notice to the Escrow Agent as provided by this Section 2(b) if such party has not received true and complete copies of all bills, statements, or invoices for the Post-Closing Costs in the aggregate amount thereof.

[3. Seller's Right of Entry.

(a) From the date of this Agreement through the Post-Closing Completion Date, Seller and its contractors, employees, and agents shall have the right, subject to the rights of tenants under Leases, to enter upon the

Property, solely for the purpose of performing Seller's Post-Closing Obligations, with reasonable advance notice to Buyer and, if required by Buyer, accompanied by a representative of Buyer. Seller, in the exercise of such right of entry, shall use all reasonable efforts not to damage the Property or to interfere unreasonably with Buyer's or Buyer's tenants' operation thereof.

(b) Seller shall indemnify and hold Buyer harmless against and from all costs, claims, damages, or liability of any kind resulting from all acts or omissions of Seller or its contractors, employees, or agents arising out of or relating to the exercise of the right of entry set forth in Section 3(a). The provisions of this Section 3(b) shall survive the expiration or termination of this Agreement.]

4. Escrowed Funds.

(a) Seller and Buyer hereby appoint the Escrow Agent as escrow agent under this Agreement, and the Escrow Agent hereby accepts such appointment on the terms and conditions of this Agreement.

(b) The Escrow Agent hereby acknowledges receipt of proceeds of the sale of the Property in the amount of _____ Dollars ($_____) ([together with all interest and other income accruing thereon,] the "Escrowed Funds"), which Escrowed Funds are to be held and disbursed as provided by Section 4(c). [All interest or income accruing on the principal amount of the Escrowed Funds shall be a part of the Escrowed Funds for all purposes of this Agreement.]

(c) The Escrow Agent shall promptly deposit and maintain the Escrowed Funds in [an interest-bearing] [a non-interest-bearing], federally insured account, to which [officers of the Escrow Agent are the sole signatories] [the Escrow Agent is the sole signatory], at a financial institution located in the [State] [Commonwealth] of _____. The Escrow Agent shall not release or disburse any portion of the Escrowed Funds, or any interest accrued thereon, to any person except as provided by (i) one or more Notices executed jointly on behalf of Buyer and Seller; or (ii) the order of a court exercising jurisdiction over the parties or the Escrowed Funds. The Escrow Agent shall not be obligated to inquire into the authenticity of, or authority for, signatures to any such Notice. If the Escrow Agent has not received one or more of such Notices providing for disposition of all portions of the Escrowed Funds on or before the Post-Closing Completion Date, then the Escrow Agent is hereby authorized to commence a suit in the nature of an interpleader in any court of competent jurisdiction and to tender the undisbursed amount of the Escrowed Funds into the custody of such court. Thereafter, the Escrow Agent shall have no further obligations or liabilities under this Agreement or otherwise in connection with the Escrowed Funds.

(d) Buyer and Seller, jointly and severally, shall indemnify and hold the Escrow Agent harmless from and against all claims, costs, expenses, damages, and losses in connection with the performance by the Escrow Agent of its obligations under this Agreement, except any such claims, costs, expenses, damages, or losses caused by the gross negligence or willful default of the Escrow Agent. The provisions of this Section 4(d) shall survive the expiration or termination of this Agreement.

(e) As consideration for performance by the Escrow Agent of its obligations under this Agreement, the Escrow Agent shall be entitled to receive an escrow fee in the amount of _____ Dollars ($_____) (the "Escrow Fee") from Buyer and Seller. Buyer and Seller shall each pay to the Escrow Agent one-half (1/2) of the Escrow Fee promptly upon the first release of the Escrowed Funds to Buyer or Seller by the Escrow Agent as provided by Section 4(c); provided, however, that if the Escrow Agent commences a proceeding in the nature of an interpleader as provided by Section 4(c) before the Escrow Agent has been paid, the Escrow Agent is hereby authorized to deduct the Escrow Fee from the Escrowed Funds before paying the Escrowed Funds into the custody of the court.

(f) The Escrow Agent may resign and be discharged from its duties under this Agreement at any time by giving Notice of such resignation to Seller and Buyer, specifying a date at least _____ (__) after the date of the Notice when such resignation shall take effect. Upon receipt of such Notice, Buyer and Seller shall appoint a successor Escrow Agent on or before the effective date of the resignation of the predecessor Escrow Agent. Such successor Escrow Agent shall become the Escrow Agent on the terms and conditions of this Agreement upon the resignation date specified in the Notice from the resigning Escrow Agent; provided, however, that the resigning Escrow Agent shall continue to serve until its successor accepts the appointment as Escrow Agent by giving Notice of such acceptance to Seller, Buyer, and the resigning Escrow Agent.

(g) Seller and Buyer shall jointly have the right at any time and without cause to discharge the Escrow Agent and appoint a substitute Escrow Agent by giving Notice thereof to the Escrow Agent then acting, specifying a date when such discharge and appointment shall take effect. Such substitute Escrow Agent shall become the Escrow Agent on the terms and conditions of this Agreement upon the appointment date specified in such Notice; provided, however, that the discharged Escrow Agent shall continue to serve until its substitute accepts the appointment as Escrow Agent by giving Notice of such acceptance to Seller, Buyer, and the discharged Escrow Agent.

5. <u>Notices.</u>

All notices, demands, elections, deliveries, instructions to the Escrow Agent, and other communications among the parties required or desired to be given in connection with this Agreement (each, a "Notice"), to be effective under this Agreement, shall be in writing and shall be deemed to be given and received (i) when delivered personally; (ii) one business day after deposit with a national overnight courier service (e.g., FedEx); or (iii) three (3) business days after deposit with the United States Postal Service as certified mail, return receipt requested; in any event with all charges or postage prepaid and addressed as follows:

If to Buyer,

_____

_____

_____

_____

with a copy to

_____

_____

_____

_____

If to Seller,

_____

_____

_____

_____

with a copy to

_____

_____

_____

_____

And if to the Escrow Agent,

_____

_____

_____

_____.

Any party may from time to time designate another address for the receipt of future Notices by a Notice given as provided in this Section 5 to the other parties at the addresses set forth in, or as last provided by such other parties in accordance with, this Section 5.

6. Termination of Agreement.

Except as otherwise expressly provided, this Agreement shall terminate upon (a) the full performance of all of Seller's Post-Closing Obligations; and (b) the disposition of all of the Escrowed Funds as provided by Section 4(c).

7. Miscellaneous.

(a) This Agreement, together with the Exhibits attached hereto, is the entire agreement among the parties with respect to the matters set forth herein, and all prior statements, discussions, negotiations, and agreements, oral or written, are superseded by this Agreement and merged herein. This Agreement shall survive the Closing.

(b) This Agreement is binding upon and shall inure to the benefit of the parties and their respective [successors and assigns] [heirs and personal representatives].

(c) If either Seller or Buyer prevails against the other in any judicial proceeding in connection with the enforcement of this Agreement or the disposition of the Escrowed Funds, the prevailing party shall be entitled to recover its actual attorneys' fees and court costs in such proceeding from the other party.

(d) This Agreement may be executed in two or more counterparts and all counterparts shall collectively constitute a single agreement. This Agreement shall become effective only upon execution and delivery by all parties.

(e) Time shall be of the essence of this Agreement.

(f) This Agreement shall be governed by the laws of the [State] [Commonwealth] of _____, excluding any _____ choice of law principles.

IN WITNESS WHEREOF, the parties have duly executed this Post-Closing Agreement under seal on the date first written above.

WITNESS:
_____ , a
_____ , Buyer
_____ By: _____ (SEAL)
Its: _____

WITNESS:
_____ , a
_____ , Seller
_____ By: _____ (SEAL)
Its: _____

WITNESS:
_____ , a
_____ , Escrow Agent
_____ By: _____ (SEAL)
Its: _____

EXHIBIT A
Seller's Post-Closing Obligations

[Describe in detail, attaching any applicable plans and specifications]

# Appendix R

# Form of Closing Instruction Letter from Buyer

**Note:** When the parties are unable to conduct a table closing, the timing and logistics of consummating a closing between widely separated parties often preclude the negotiation and execution of a joint escrow agreement to govern funding and the execution, delivery, and recording of closing documents. In these situations, it is a customary practice for each party or its counsel to issue a separate closing instruction letter to a common closing or escrow agent, who then countersigns the letters to form separate escrow agreements. The closing instruction letters from the buyer, the seller, and the lender will each address a different set of issues. Obviously, the escrow agent must be careful to confirm that the separate sets of instructions are not contradictory and that the contemplated logistics of funding and of execution, delivery, and recording of documents will work. The following form is for a closing instruction letter from the buyer's lawyer, for the purchase of property financed in part by a loan such as the one described in Appendix I, Form of Loan Commitment.

[Letterhead of Sender]

[Date]

[Means of Delivery]
[Escrow Agent Name]
[Escrow Agent Address]
Attention: _____

Re: [Address of Property]

Dear [Escrow Agent Name]:

    This firm represents _____, a _____ (the "Buyer"), the buyer of the above-referenced property (the "Property") under the Contract of Sale dated _____, 20__ (the "Contract of Sale"), by and between Buyer and _____, a _____ (the "Seller"). Buyer and Seller have scheduled the consummation of the transactions contemplated by the Contract of Sale (the "Closing") for _____, 20__. _____, a _____ (the "Escrow Agent"), as agent for _____ (the "Title Company"), has issued Commitment No. _____ (the "Title Commitment") for owner's and lender's title insurance for the Property. In connection therewith, the Escrow Agent has been engaged by Buyer to assist with the Closing, including the holding of documents in escrow, the filing and recording of documents, and the disbursement of funds. This letter constitutes the instructions to the Escrow Agent as escrow agent on behalf of Buyer with respect to the Closing.

_____, a _____ (the "Lender"), has issued its commitment letter dated _____, 20__, to Buyer, to fund up to _____ Dollars ($_____) of the cost of purchasing the Property (the "Loan Funding"). The Lender will deliver separate instructions to the Escrow Agent with respect to the Closing and the Loan Funding.

Buyer is prepared to deliver the following documents duly executed on behalf of Buyer (collectively, the "Buyer's Documents") and funds to the Escrow Agent in escrow:

(1) [List titles of all documents required to be delivered by Buyer under the Contract of Sale] [indicate number of originals of each];

(2) [List titles of all documents required to be delivered by Buyer under the Loan Commitment] [indicate number of originals of each];

(3) [Form HUD-1 Settlement Statement or other closing statement showing the sources and disbursements of all funds in connection with the Closing] (the "Closing Statement") [indicate number of originals]; and

(4) The amount shown on the Closing Statement to be funded by Buyer (the "Buyer's Funding").

With respect to the Closing, Buyer hereby instructs the Escrow Agent as follows:

1. Buyer will deliver the Buyer's Documents by separate transmittal and the Buyer's Funding by federal wire transfer, as provided by the instructions attached as <u>Exhibit A</u> to this letter, to the Escrow Agent upon the occurrence of all of the following:

(a) The Escrow Agent shall have delivered to me the enclosed copy of this letter, without any modifications, additions, or deletions, duly executed on behalf of the Escrow Agent where indicated below; [and

(b) The Title Company shall have delivered to me an original insured closing service letter in a form acceptable to Buyer, duly executed on behalf of such insurer;]

2. Upon receipt, the Escrow Agent shall hold the Buyer's Documents and the Buyer's Funding in escrow, pending the satisfaction of the terms and conditions set forth in Paragraph 3 below. The Escrow Agent shall not release the Buyer's Documents or the Buyer's Funding to any other person or party until such terms and conditions have been satisfied, and the Escrow Agent shall not make or permit any changes, additions, or deletions to the Buyer's Documents without my prior consent. However, the Escrow Agent may permit the examination and execution of the Buyer's Documents by Seller or Seller's counsel, provided that the Buyer's Documents do not leave the custody and control of the Escrow Agent;

3. The Escrow Agent may release the Buyer's Documents and the Buyer's Funding from escrow only upon the occurrence of all of the following:

(a) The Escrow Agent shall have delivered to me, by facsimile at (___) ___-____, a counterpart of the Closing Statement, without any modifications, additions, or deletions, duly executed on behalf of Seller; and

(b) The Escrow Agent shall have confirmed to me in writing that: (i) all conditions in the Title Commitment that must be satisfied prior to the issuance to Buyer of an owner's title insurance policy in the form attached as Exhibit B to this letter (the "Title Policy") have been satisfied; (ii) the Escrow Agent has received the Buyer's Funding and the Loan Funding in its escrow account, and the Escrow Agent has received sufficient funds to make all disbursements shown on the Closing Statement; (iii) the Escrow Agent has in its custody and control the following documents duly executed on behalf of Seller (collectively, the "Seller's Documents"):

(1) The deed conveying the Property from Seller to Buyer, in the form attached as Exhibit C to this letter (the "Deed");

[(2) The Bill of Sale conveying certain personal property from Seller to Buyer, in the form attached as Exhibit D to this letter (the "Bill of Sale");]

(3) [List titles of all other documents required to be delivered by Seller under the Contract of Sale] [indicate number of originals of each]; and

(4) The Closing Statement [indicate number of originals]; and

(iv) all originals of the Buyer's Documents and the Seller's Documents have been duly executed, witnessed, and acknowledged on behalf of the parties thereto where provided, and the appropriate exhibits have been attached to all such originals; provided, however, that the Escrow Agent is not obligated to inquire into or confirm the authorization for or authenticity of any signatures on behalf of any party;

4. Upon the satisfaction of the conditions and release of the Buyer's Documents and the Buyer's Funding as provided by Paragraph 3 above, the Escrow Agent shall, promptly and in the following order:

(a) First, make all disbursements as shown on the Closing Statement;

(b) Second, record the Deed among the appropriate public records of _____ County, _____;

(c) Third, deliver to me, by overnight courier, the following executed documents:

(i) the Deed [one date-stamped copy];

[(ii) the Bill of Sale [indicate number of originals]];

(iii) the Closing Statement [indicate number of originals]; and

(iv) [List all other Seller's Documents] [indicate for each the number and whether originals or copies]; and

(d) Fourth, deliver the Title Policy to me on or before _____ __, 20__; and

5. If at any time during the course of satisfying the terms and conditions of this letter the Escrow Agent is unable to satisfy any such term or

condition, the Escrow Agent shall contact me immediately and await my further instructions. If the Escrow Agent is unable to satisfy all of the terms or conditions of this letter on or before _____, 20__, the Escrow Agent shall immediately thereafter return all of the Buyer's Documents and the Buyer's Funding to Buyer.

Please acknowledge the Escrow Agent's acceptance, as escrow agent for Buyer, of the instructions set forth in this letter by countersigning and returning to me the enclosed copy of this letter.

Very truly yours,

[Name of Sender]

Attachments

We hereby accept and agree to be bound by the foregoing instructions.

_____,

a _____,
Escrow Agent
By: _____
Its: _____
Date: _____, 20__

EXHIBIT A
Wiring Instructions for Escrow Agent

EXHIBIT B
Form of Owner's Title Insurance Policy

EXHIBIT C
Form of Deed

[EXHIBIT D
Form of Bill of Sale]

# About the Authors

**Gregory M. Stein** is the Woolf, McClane, Bright, Allen & Carpenter Distinguished Professor of Law at the University of Tennessee College of Law, where he teaches property, real estate finance, real estate development, and land use courses. He regularly contributes law review articles and continuing legal education chapters in these areas, and he speaks frequently on these topics. He is a Fellow of the American College of Real Estate Lawyers. Prior to joining the faculty of the University of Tennessee, Stein practiced commercial real estate law with Paul, Weiss, Rifkind, Wharton & Garrison in New York. He is a graduate of Harvard College and Columbia Law School.

**Morton P. Fisher, Jr.,** is a partner in the Baltimore office of Ballard Spahr Andrews & Ingersoll, LLP. He has been involved in a variety of real estate transactions, representing developers, lending institutions, commercial tenants, and other parties. He lectures and writes regularly on real estate topics and is a former president of the American College of Real Estate Lawyers, a former chair of the American Bar Association Section of Real Property, Trust and Estate Law, and a member of the American Law Institute. Fisher is a graduate of Dartmouth College and Yale Law School.

**Marjorie P. Fisher** is a Senior Associate in the real estate group in the Washington, DC, office of the Pillsbury law firm. She represents lenders, owners, and developers of real estate in a variety of complex real estate transactions, including portfolio acquisitions and sales, forward sales, dispositions, loans, joint ventures, office and retail leases, and ground leases. Her work covers a broad spectrum of commercial properties, including hospitality, office, retail, and technology. She is a graduate of Wesleyan College and UCLA Law School.

# Index